9/11 and the Wars in Afghanistan and Iraq

9/11 and the Wars in Afghanistan and Iraq

A CHRONOLOGY AND REFERENCE GUIDE

Tom Lansford

 ABC-CLIO

Santa Barbara, California • Denver, Colorado • Oxford, England

Library of Congress Cataloging-in-Publication Data

Lansford, Tom.
    9/11 and the wars in Afghanistan and Iraq : a chronology and reference guide / Tom Lansford.
        p. cm.
    Includes bibliographical references and index.
    ISBN 978–1–59884–419–1 (hardback : acid-free paper) — ISBN 978–1–59884–420–7 (ebook)
1. September 11 Terrorist Attacks, 2001. 2. Terrorism—United States. 3. Afghan War, 2001– 4.
Iraq War, 2003– 5. United States—Foreign relations—2001– I. Title. II. Title: Nine-Eleven and the wars in Afghanistan and Iraq.
HV6432.7.L375   2011
973.931—dc23   2011022896

ISBN: 978–1–59884–419–1
EISBN: 978–1–59884–420–7

16 15 14 13 12   1 2 3 4 5

This book is also available on the World Wide Web as an eBook.
Visit www.abc-clio.com for details.

ABC-CLIO, LLC
130 Cremona Drive, P.O. Box 1911
Santa Barbara, California 93116-1911

This book is printed on acid-free paper ∞

Manufactured in the United States of America

For the victims of the September 11, 2001, terrorist attacks and their families

Contents

Preface

The September 11, 2001, attacks on the United States were the deadliest and costliest terrorist strikes in history. Although the nation had suffered the devastating consequences of terrorist attacks in the past, 9/11 forever undermined the sense of domestic security and invulnerability that had characterized the United States since the 1962 Cuban Missile Crisis during the height of the Cold War. After that September day in 2001, Americans became increasingly willing to exchange civil liberties and individual freedoms in exchange for promises of greater personal security and protection from future attacks.

In response to the 9/11 attacks, the administration of Republican President George W. Bush undertook dramatic steps in both foreign and domestic policy. The United States invaded Afghanistan in October 2001 and defeated the Taliban regime. The Bush administration concurrently launched an international effort to suppress terrorism, naming the effort the "global war on terror." In addition to increasing intelligence and law enforcement cooperation with nations around the globe, the United States also provided military assistance and aid, and even deployed troops in areas of Asia, Africa, and South America. In one of the most controversial components of the war on terror, in 2003 the United States led a coalition of nations in a preemptive war against the Iraqi regime of Saddam Hussein. The war followed a period of intense diplomatic wrangling in which the Bush administration and its allies accused the Saddam regime of developing weapons of mass destruction and supporting terrorism. Although the United States and its allies quickly overthrew the Saddam government, a bloody insurgency spread throughout Iraq. The insurgency lasted more than five years and killed more U.S. troops than the initial invasion. Meanwhile, remnants of the Taliban regrouped in border areas of Pakistan and launched a rebellion against the pro-Western government of Afghan President Hamid Karzai. The ongoing fighting in Afghanistan and Iraq overshadowed other successes in the war on terror. In addition, the international standing of the United States was eroded by the failure to uncover weapons of mass destruction in Iraq and the United States' inability to defeat the insurgencies in Afghanistan and Iraq.

The war on terror also changed the politics and culture of the United States. The U.S. government undertook the largest reorganization since World War II, when the Department of Homeland Security was created from existing agencies and bureaus in 2002. In addition, new laws and regulations forever altered the way Americans traveled, attended public events, and even opened a checking account. Although the nation rallied together after the 9/11 attacks, divisions emerged over the war in Iraq and the conduct of the war on terror. Opposition to the Iraq War in the United States and other countries grew dramatically, especially after 2005. Bush's domestic popularity declined substantially. and the president's political party lost control of Congress in 2006. Two years later, Barack Obama, who opposed the Iraq War, was elected the nation's first African American president. The war on terror and the conflicts in Afghanistan and Iraq dominated Obama's foreign policy. One chapter of the war on terror closed when U.S. special operations forces killed al Qaeda leader Osama bin Laden on May 2, 2011, at a safe haven in Pakistan.

The 9/11 attacks did not occur in isolation, but were the culmination of decades-old trends in international terrorism. This book analyzes the causes and impact of the 9/11 terrorist attacks on the United States and on the global community. The following chapters trace the rise and maturation of contemporary global terrorism from the 1970s through the 1990s and the efforts of the United States to develop effective domestic and international counterterrorism tactics and strategies. The work also explores the complex relationship between events in the Middle East and Southwest Asia and the rise of international terrorism. Particular attention is devoted to the causes of modern terrorism and the development of transnational terrorist groups such as al Qaeda, as well as the social, cultural, and economic impact of the 9/11 strikes. Furthermore, the book examines the interconnectedness between the global war on terror and U.S. domestic politics, including the development of new laws such as the USA PATRIOT Act and the economic, political, cultural, and social reactions to the attacks.

This project would not have been possible without the help and generous support of numerous people. I would like to particularly acknowledge the assistance of Matthew Williams, Brad Irvin, and Felix Rodriguez in researching and reviewing the manuscript. My sincere thanks go to Jack Covarrubias for assistance in preparing the work. I also wish to thank Pat Carlin for his patience and his suggestions for the manuscript. Finally, as always, my love and thanks go to the girls in my life, Gina, Ella, and Kate.

Abbreviations

ACLU	American Civil Liberties Union
ANSWER	Act Now to Stop War and End Racism
ANZUS	Australia, New Zealand, United States Treaty
ATF	Alcohol, Tobacco and Firearms Bureau
AWACS	Airborne Warning and Control System
BBC	British Broadcasting Corporation
CIA	Central Intelligence Agency
CIS	Commonwealth of Independent States
CNN	Cable News Network
CPA	Coalition Provisional Authority
DHS	Department of Homeland Security
DNI	Director of National Intelligence
EU	European Union
FAA	Federal Aviation Administration
FBI	Federal Bureau of Investigation
FEMA	Federal Emergency Management Agency
FISA	Foreign Intelligence Service Act
IAEA	International Atomic Energy Agency
ICE	Immigration and Customs Enforcement
IED	Improvised Explosive Device
IRA	Irish Republican Army
G-8	Group of Eight Most Industrialized Countries
GDP	Gross Domestic Product
GOP	Grand Old Party (the Republican Party)
GPS	Global Positioning System
ISAF	International Security Assistance Force
ISG	Iraq Survey Group
NATO	North Atlantic Treaty Organization
NSA	National Security Agency

NSC	National Security Council
OAS	Organization of American States
PDD	Presidential Decision Directive
PLO	Palestine Liberation Organization
PRT	Provincial Reconstruction Teams
RICO	Racketeer Influenced and Corrupt Organization
TSA	Transportation Safety Administration
UAE	United Arab Emirates
UK	United Kingdom
UN	United Nations
UNMOVIC	United Nations, Monitoring, Verification and Inspection Commission
UNSCOM	United Nations Special Commission
USA PATRIOT ACT	Uniting and Strengthening America by Providing Appropriate Tools Required to Intercept and Obstruct Terrorism Act 2001
SAS	Special Air Service
WMD	Weapons of Mass Destruction
WTC	World Trade Center

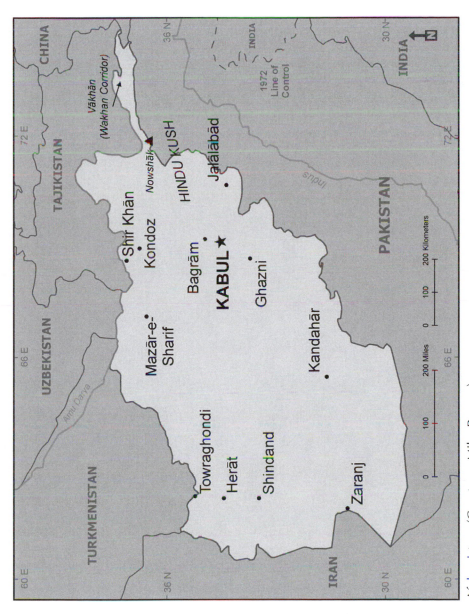

Afghanistan. (Courtesy: Mike Pappas)

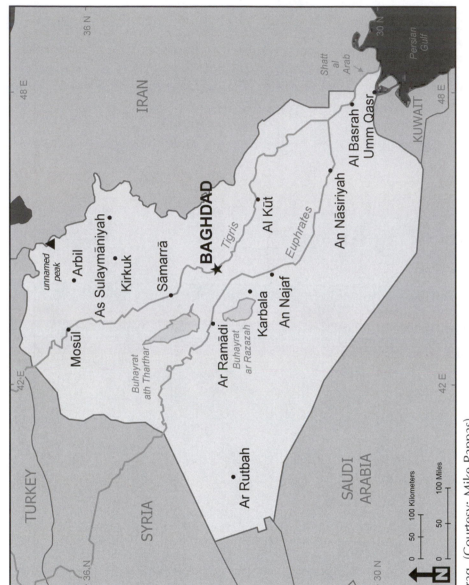

Iraq. (Courtesy: Mike Pappas)

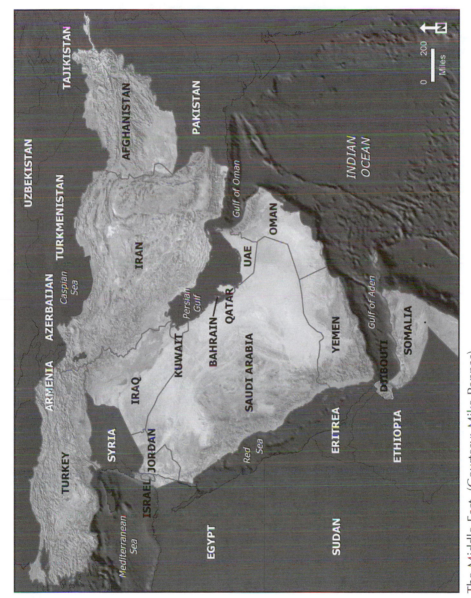

The Middle East. (Courtesy: Mike Pappas)

1

Overview: The Rise of Osama bin Laden and Global Terrorism

The September 11, 2001, terrorist attacks were the culmination of a long, violent campaign waged by fundamentalist, extremist Islamic groups. These terrorist groups targeted the United States for a variety of reasons. U.S. society, with its high degree of individual freedom and expression, was perceived as antithetical to the religious and cultural values of the extremists. In addition, since 1948, the United States had been a staunch ally of Israel, a country that terrorist groups sought to destroy in order to establish a Palestinian state. Following the Iranian Revolution in 1979, tensions between the United States and Iran, including U.S. support for Iraq during the Iran-Iraq War, led Tehran to back a variety of anti-American and anti-Western terrorist groups. Meanwhile, the United States supported a number of regimes in the Middle East, including Saudi Arabia, Kuwait, and the United Emirates, that were labeled as corrupt and un-Islamic by the terrorists. U.S. planners were also slow to recognize the danger of terrorism, even after al Qaeda, a new global terrorist network, was formed. Despite attacks through the 1980s and 1990s, terrorism was initially not perceived as a significant security threat to the United States. As global terrorist organizations grew in power, size, and scope, the United States was sluggish in its response to the growing threat, allowing anti-American groups to organize financial, recruitment, and training networks. Concurrently, U.S. attention in the Persian Gulf in the late 1980s and through the 1990s was mainly focused on Iraq, with which the United States fought the 1991 Gulf War. The United States spent the 1990s endeavoring to force the Iraqi regime of Saddam Hussein to comply with United Nations (UN) sanctions to eliminate its stockpile of chemical and biological weapons.

Origins of Global Terrorism

The Roots of Contemporary Terrorism

Terrorism is the deliberate use of violence against civilians and nonmilitary targets in an effort achieve a political goal through fear and intimidation. Terrorism in one form or another has existed throughout history. However, a new age of terrorism began in the late 1960s and early 1970s. Groups such as the Irish Republic Army (IRA) in Northern Ireland or the Red Brigade in Italy began to increasingly rely on external monetary and logistical support to conduct terrorist campaigns. In some cases, external funds were provided by other governments as part of efforts to destabilize countries or undermine regimes. For instance, the Soviet Union supplied monies for several terrorist groups in Western Europe, including the Red Brigade. In other cases, donations came from individuals and groups. Many Irish Americans secretly gave money to the IRA. This dramatically increased the amount of funding available to terrorist groups and made it more difficult for governments to track the flow of funds to illicit groups.

Meanwhile, in the 1967 Six-Day War, Israel achieved a dramatic military victory and captured the West Bank from Jordan, the Golan Heights from Syria, and the Gaza Strip and Sinai Peninsula from Egypt. Groups such as the Palestinian Liberation Organization (PLO) sought the restoration of these areas and the creation of an independent state of Palestine. Unable to defeat Israel in a series of wars in the Middle East, some anti-Israeli Palestinian groups and their supporters turned to terrorism. They sought to pressure the Israeli government into agreeing to concessions in order to avoid further violence.

Most scholars and terrorism experts trace the modern age of terrorism to an incident on July 22, 1968, when a Palestinian terrorist group hijacked an Israeli airliner. The hijacking ended peacefully, but it ushered in an era when terrorist groups increasingly sought to gain publicity and notoriety in order to spread their message.[1] Then on September 5, 1972, Palestinian terrorists from the Black September group took 11 Israeli hostages during the Olympic Games in Munich, Germany. The hostages and a German police officer were killed in the incident. The brutal attack led the United States and other governments to increase counterterrorism efforts, including installing metal detectors and X-ray machines at airports and creating watch-lists to reduce the chance that passengers were known terrorists.

In 1973, Israel was attacked by a coalition of Arab states in the Yom Kippur War (Ramadan War). The conflict ended in a military stalemate. It accelerated efforts to find a peaceful solution to the conflict between Israel and the Palestinians. These efforts culminated on September 17, 1979, when Israel and Egypt signed the Camp David Accords. Sponsored by the United States, the accords were a breakthrough in Middle East peace and normalized relations between the two nations. The agreements also committed the United States to annual subsidies for Egypt and Israel to support the peace process. Some Muslims expressed a sense of betrayal toward Egypt. Egyptian President Anwar Sadat, who signed the Accords, was assassinated on October 6, 1981, by the Egyptian branch of Islamic Jihad.

U.S. support for Israel during the Yom Kippur War also provoked increasing anger among Arabs and Muslims. The resentment toward the United States exploded in 1979 at the end of the Iranian Revolution, which overthrew the pro-Western Shah and installed a fundamentalist Shiite Islamic government. Iranian students and radicals stormed the U.S. Embassy in Tehran and took 66 Americans hostage. Fifty-three hostages remained in captivity from November 4, 1979, until January 20, 1981. The incident ushered in a period of deep tension between the United States and Iran, which began to provide financial support, weapons, and training to a range of anti-Israeli and anti-Western terrorist groups, including Hezbollah and Islamic Jihad. Terrorism also expanded because of the impact of three bloody and long-lasting conflicts in the Islamic world: the Soviet occupation of Afghanistan (1979–1989), the Iran-Iraq War (1980–1988), and the Lebanese Civil War (1975–1990).

The Invasion of Afghanistan

While the United States was preoccupied with the Middle East, America's Cold War enemy, the Soviet Union, sought to expand its power and influence in Southwest Asia. On April 28, the leader of Afghanistan's communist party, Nur Muhammad Taraki, seized power in a military coup with Soviet support. During the coup, Afghan President Mohammad Daoud Khan was assassinated. On December 5, Taraki signed a treaty with the Kremlin that permitted the deployment of Soviet troops in the country at the request of the Afghan government. Meanwhile, Soviet military advisors entered Afghanistan.

A new power struggle in Afghanistan resulted in the assassination of President Taraki on September 14, 1979. Taraki had begun to make overtures to Western countries in an attempt to decrease the nation's growing ties to the Soviet Union. Taraki was replaced by Hafizullah Amin. The new president proved to be unpopular and weak. On December 24, the Soviet Union invaded and quickly conquered Afghanistan. The United States and other Western powers, along with Pakistan, condemned the invasion. In an address to the nation following the invasion, President Jimmy Carter declared that "we must recognize the strategic importance of Afghanistan to stability and peace. A Soviet-occupied Afghanistan threatens both Iran and Pakistan and is a steppingstone to possible control over much of the world's oil supplies."[2] In response, the United States and its allies boycotted the 1980 Olympics in Moscow and implemented a variety of economic sanctions against the Soviets.

The United States and the Middle Eastern states also provided substantial military and economic assistance to anti-Soviet Islamic fighters known as the

Mujahedeen. Muslims from around the world joined the Mujahedeen who fought a bloody guerilla war against Soviet forces that had superior weapons and technology. Between 1979 and 1991, the United States and its allies provided the Mujahedeen over $7 billion in weapons and ammunition, including state-of-the-art anti-aircraft missiles. Afghanistan became one of the most heavily armed countries in the world. More than 400,000 rifles and shoulder-fired machine guns were imported by the Mujahedeen, and more than 10 million landmines were placed throughout the nation, making Afghanistan the most mined country in the world.

Unable to suppress the Mujahedeen insurgency, and after intense domestic and international pressure, the Soviets agreed to withdraw through the 1988 Geneva Accords. The accords allowed both the United States and the Soviet Union to continue to supply weapons to groups in Afghanistan. By the time the negotiations were complete, more than 50 percent of Afghanistan's villages and towns, as well as 40 percent of its farmlands, were destroyed by fighting, along with 25 percent of the country's roads. After the accords were finalized, the United Nations initiated a program to demine the country.

The Soviets completed their withdrawal from Afghanistan on February 15, 1989. During the bloody occupation, approximately 15,000 Soviet troops were killed, along with more than 1.5 million Afghan rebels and civilians. A civil war erupted between former Mujahedeen groups in the country after the Soviets withdrew.

Approximately 80,000 Mujahedeen fought against the Soviets at the peak of the conflict. Many were trained in Pakistan with support from the U.S. Central Intelligence Agency (CIA). Some Mujahedeen saw the conflict as a holy war or jihad between the Islamic world and the atheistic Soviet Union. Many fighters became increasingly radicalized. After fighting in Afghanistan, large numbers of the Mujahedeen returned to their native countries. Some joined terrorist groups or antigovernment insurgencies using military skills they acquired as Mujahedeen. The former Mujahedeen, including figures such as Osama bin Laden, often emerged as leaders of extremist groups in the Muslim world.

Iran-Iraq War

Iraqi dictator Saddam Hussein grew alarmed at Iran's support for Shiite groups in his country and invaded Iran on September 22, 1980. The two countries fought a lengthy and bloody war that lasted until 1988. The United States, France, and other European countries supported Iraq, which was perceived as a counterweight to the growing radicalism of the Iranian regime. Iraq received military and financial aid. Western backing for Iraq was one of the reasons that Iran supported anti-Western terrorist groups such as Hezbollah and Islamic Jihad.

Although Iraq launched its invasion without warning, Iranian forces quickly halted the Iraqi advance and drove the invading force back. Iraq, which had an extensive program for weapons of mass destruction (WMDs), began to use chemical weapons against the Iranians. On June 7, 1981, Israel carried out a preemptive air strike that destroyed a nuclear plant outside of Baghdad. The facility was part of an Iraqi WMD program to develop nuclear weapons.

In March 1988, Iraqi security forces used mustard gas and tabun, both chemical weapons, to suppress Kurds in the northern areas of the country. Approximately 4,000 were killed by the WMDs in a campaign that lasted until 1989 (more than 50,000 Kurds were killed by all means during the offensive). The attacks followed a more limited use of chemical weapons against Kurdish civilians the previous year. In April, Iraq utilized chemical weapons against Iranian forces during an offensive to retake the Fao Peninsula in southern Iraq.

After eight years of combat, the United Nations was able to facilitate ceasefire negotiations that ended the Iraq-Iraq War on August 20, 1988. The war resulted in a stalemate with neither side making any significant gains. The conflict killed more than 1 million Iranians and Iraqis and saddled Iraq with more than $75 billion in foreign debt.

The Lebanese Civil War

Meanwhile, Lebanon had been in the midst of a civil war between Christians and Muslims since 1975. In 1976, Syria sent troops into Lebanon under the pretext of restoring order, but they took unofficial control over large areas of the north and east of the country. Some Palestinian Muslims took control over most of the south of Lebanon and used bases in these areas to launch attacks against Israel. In 1982, Israel invaded Lebanon in an effort to defeat the anti-Israeli PLO and to counteract the growing influence of Syria. Anti-Israeli groups such as the Palestinian Hamas, Lebanese Hezbollah, and Lebanese Islamic Jihad emerged after the invasion to resist the Israelis. They used terrorism to publicize their agendas, attract funds from wealthy opponents of Israel, and develop political and social networks that sometimes rivaled the scope of existing governments. Hezbollah and Hamas both received considerable aid from Iran. For instance, Iran sent soldiers to Lebanon to help found Hezbollah and train its fighters.[3] Iran sought to export the values of its revolution and create other fundamentalist Shiite regimes in the Middle East.

In an effort to prevent the conflict from spreading and to foster a negotiated settlement, the United Nations deployed an international peacekeeping force to southern Lebanon. The force became a target for Islamic militants who perceived that the civil war weakened the Lebanese government and reinforced their growing power and influence in the country. On April 18, 1983, Hezbollah conducted one of the first major suicide bombings. Hezbollah suicide bombers drove an explosive-laden truck into the U.S. Embassy in Beirut, Lebanon, killing 63 people, including 17 Americans. Suicide bombings subsequently became increasingly common as a form of terrorist attack in the Middle East.

The United States and other countries initially increased the size of their peace-keeping forces in Lebanon in order to demonstrate their commitment to a peaceful settlement. Then, on October 23, 1983, suicide bombers attacked the military barracks in Beirut that housed the peacekeepers. The attacks killed 241 American and 58 French servicemen. The terrorist group Islamic Jihad claimed responsibility. On December 12, 1983, five people were killed and 62 injured in suicide attacks by Islamic Jihad on the U.S. and French embassies in Kuwait City. International troops withdrew from Lebanon in February and March 1984. However, that did not stop terrorist attacks on Western targets. Instead, the leaders of many terrorist groups believed the incidents demonstrated that Western governments would not accept casualties and would withdraw their forces, rather than face domestic discontent over the human or financial costs of overseas military operations. Consequently, some groups increased action against the United States and the West. Meanwhile, Israel maintained troops in Lebanon until 2000.

Tensions between the Israelis and Palestinians resulted in the First Intifada, a popular uprising against Israeli rule in the West Bank and Gaza that began on December 19, 1987. The intifada included nonviolent resistance, as well as increased terrorist acts. During the rebellion, approximately 1,500 Palestinians were killed, along with 164 Israelis. The uprising ended in 1993.

Anti-American Terrorism

Libya

Throughout the 1980s, the United States was frequently targeted by Islamic terrorists. For instance, on June 13, 1985, terrorists backed by Hezbollah and Islamic Jihad hijacked Transworld Airlines (TWA) Flight 847. U.S. Navy diver Robert Stethem was murdered by the hijackers. Then, on April 5, 1986, a popular nightclub was bombed in Berlin, Germany, by terrorists supported by Libya. The attack killed three U.S. soldiers and a female civilian, and wounded 230 others. Evidence linked the Libyan regime of Muammar Gaddafi to the bombing, and U.S. President Ronald W. Reagan ordered a series of naval strikes and airstrikes against Libya in response. The U.S. retaliation prompted additional Libyan-backed terrorist strikes.

On December 21, 1987, a bomb destroyed Pan-American Flight 103 midair over Lockerbie, Scotland, killing all 259 passengers and crew, and 11 people on the ground. U.S. and foreign intelligence services discovered evidence linking Libya to the bombing. A range of economic and diplomatic sanctions were enacted against Libya. Eventually, Abdelbaset Ali Mohmed al-Megrahi, a Libyan, was tried and found guilty of the bombing by a Scottish court in 2001, and the Libyan government accepted formal responsibility for the attack in 2003.

Lebanese Hostage Crisis and Iran

Even after U.S. troops withdrew from Lebanon in 1984, Americans continued to be targeted by Hezbollah and other extremists. From 1984 through 1991,

Hezbollah and Islamic Jihad routinely kidnapped Westerners in Lebanon. In some cases the hostages were ransomed by their governments, but more often the terrorist groups kept their victims in an effort to force political concessions by the United States and other governments. In some instances, the victims were killed. Lt. Col. William F. Buckley, a U.S. intelligence officer, was kidnapped in 1984 and tortured to death. In 1985, President Reagan's senior national security advisors concocted an elaborate scheme to free the hostages and provide weapons to anti-communist insurgents in Nicaragua (which was forbidden by U.S. law at the time). In what became known as the Iran-Contra Scandal, the United States sold missiles to Iran for use in its war with Iraq. In exchange, Iran paid for the missiles and put pressure on Hezbollah and Islamic Jihad to release hostages. The funds from the missile sales were used to purchase arms and supplies for the contras.

Instead of ending the crisis, the Iran-Contra Scandal encouraged new rounds of hostage taking in Lebanon. It was not until 1991, when the United States pressured Israel into releasing 51 prisoners with ties to Hezbollah and other extremist groups, that the remaining hostages were freed. Some Americans, including Joseph Cicippio, Allman Steen, and Jesse Turner, had been held hostage for more than five years. On December 4, 1991, American Terry Anderson, the longest held captive, was freed after being held more than seven years.

The Persian Gulf War and Iraq

Invasion of Kuwait

Crippled by a massive debt from its eight-year war with Iran, the Iraqi regime of Saddam Hussein sought to keep oil prices high in the late 1980s and early 1990s, since fossil fuels were Iraq's main export. However, other states in the Persian Gulf, including Kuwait, continued to flood the market with inexpensive petroleum. This infuriated the Iraqi dictator. Saddam's advisors were also convinced that the Kuwaitis were illegally tapping into Iraqi oil deposits. They further publicly contended that Kuwait was historically part of Iraq. Saddam decided to invade Kuwait in order to take control of the country's oil production.

On August 2, 1990, more than 120,000 Iraqi troops invaded and quickly overran Kuwait. The invasion brought international condemnation against the Saddam Hussein regime. The U.S. administration of President George H. W. Bush asserted that Iraqi control of Kuwait presented a clear danger to U.S. economic interests and began to force an international effort to dislodge Saddam. A series of UN Security Council resolutions ordered Iraq to withdraw and authorized the use of military force if the regime did not. Bush assembled a diplomatic and military coalition of 34 nations opposed to the invasion, including Arab states such as Saudi Arabia, Egypt, and Syria. The forces were deployed to states in the Persian Gulf, including Saudi Arabia, in an operation known as Desert Shield. By November, more than 230,000 American troops were in Saudi Arabia to protect the kingdom from any potential Iraqi strike. Eventually, more than 530,000 U.S. troops were dispatched to the region. The presence of non-Muslim troops in Saudi Arabia, home to some of the holiest sites in Islam, angered Islamic fundamentalists, including bin Laden.

Operation Desert Storm

On January 16, 1991, Operation Desert Storm (the liberation of Kuwait) began with massive U.S.-led coalition airstrikes and cruise missile attacks against Iraqi positions. Addressing the nation on that evening, Bush answered critics who asked why the coalition attacked when it did instead of waiting and trying to negotiate a peaceful settlement. Bush declared, "Some may ask: Why act now? Why not wait? The answer is clear: The world could wait no longer. Sanctions, though having some effect, showed no signs of accomplishing their objective. Sanctions were tried for well over 5 months, and we and our allies concluded that sanctions alone would not force Saddam from Kuwait."[4]

In an effort to undermine coalition air superiority, the Iraqis set fire to thousands of oil rigs. The Iraqis also released more than a million gallons of oil into the Persian Gulf to prevent an amphibious landing. On February 24, coalition ground forces crossed into Kuwait and quickly defeated the Iraqis. The Iraqis fired short-range rockets, known as "Scud" missiles, at coalition bases and at Israel in an unsuccessful effort to escalate the conflict. Under U.S. pressure, Israel did not intervene in the war.

Coalition forces drove to within 150 miles of Baghdad, but retreated under orders from the United States, after Bush declared a ceasefire on February 27. On March 3, the conflict ended when the Iraqis accepted the terms of the U.S. armistice. During the fighting, 345 coalition soldiers were killed, and more than 1,000 wounded. Estimates of Iraqi dead were between 10,000 and 20,000 dead and 70,000 wounded. The conflict cost the allies approximately $76 billion, of which the Persian Gulf states led by Saudi Arabia paid $36 billion, while Germany and Japan, which were constitutionally forbidden from deploying troops overseas at the time, paid another $16 billion.

Under the terms of the ceasefire and UN resolutions, the Iraqis agreed to UN inspections designed to dismantle the country's WMD programs through Security Council Resolution 687. Passed on April 3, 1991, the resolution required Iraq to immediately disclose all of its WMDs and WMD programs. The country then had to disarm or destroy those WMDs under UN supervision. In addition, Iraq was ordered to allow UN inspectors access to various sites as part of an ongoing verification program. Finally, Iraq was forbidden from possessing missiles with a range of more than 150 kilometers (93.2 miles), such as the Scud missiles used during the Persian Gulf War. The UN resolution was in response to the past use of chemical weapons by Iraq on both its domestic population and during the war with Iran, and the country's well-publicized efforts to acquire WMDs. In order to oversee the inspections, the United Nations created the UN Special Commission (UNSCOM) to work with the International Atomic Energy Agency (IAEA). On April 18, Iraq provided a list of chemical weapons and facilities, as well as an inventory of missiles that exceeded the maximum range. UNSCOM was critical of the initial report, and Iraq issued a second, more comprehensive report in May. The first UNSCOM inspection took place on June 9. UNSCOM personnel later seized nuclear equipment and documentation on the country's illicit nuclear program from the Iraqis.

Through Security Council Resolution 688 in April 1991, the United Nations established no-fly zones over northern and southern Iraq to protect Kurds and Iraqi Shiites who had been targeted by the Saddam regime. Iraq was not allowed to fly airplanes or helicopters in these regions. Eventually the Kurdish areas of the north became semiautonomous with a high degree of self-government.

The Persian Gulf War and the Media

The Persian Gulf War dramatically altered media coverage. Cable news stations, such as the Cable News Network (CNN), were able to provide around-the-clock coverage of the conflict and beam satellite images of the fighting around the world. CNN eventually broadcast to more than 210 countries and had a worldwide audience of more than 1.5 billion at its peak. The new format meant that news could be reported as it was happening. Coverage of the war accelerated the loss of market share by the news programs of the traditional broadcasting stations in the United States, including ABC, CBS, and NBC. Critics charged that the news was increasingly reported without appropriate analysis or context. Meanwhile, the U.S. military developed a system whereby journalists participated in pools to receive information and briefings. The system was highly criticized for the high degree of control the military attempted to place on the flow of information.

The dominance of CNN and traditional international broadcasters such as the British Broadcasting Corporation (BBC) led to the creation of Al Jazeera, an Arabic- and English-language, satellite news service based in Qatar. Al Jazeera was created in 1996 with a $150 million grant from the emir of Qatar. The service provided news from a Muslim perspective and quickly became highly popular among Arabs. Meanwhile, also in 1996, News Corporation created Fox News, a conservative U.S.-based cable news service. Fox News quickly drew viewers from established news networks in the United States such as CNN.

Cheat and Retreat

Through the 1990s, U.S. officials accused the Saddam regime of engaging in a strategy of "cheat and retreat"—Iraq would violate or attempt to violate the terms of the ceasefire or UN resolutions. If caught, it would comply briefly, before testing the ability of the coalition to enforce the mandates.

UNSCOM teams met with repeated difficulties during inspections in Iraq, including being denied access to facilities, personnel, and documentation. Iraq also attempted to block aerial inspections by UNSCOM. Meanwhile, in March 1992, Iraq issued a new report that disclosed the prior existence of additional chemical weapons and ballistic missiles, but asserted that both the WMDs and the missiles had been destroyed outside of UNSCOM. The United Nations declared this a violation of Resolution 687, but no action was taken. Throughout the next several years, Iraq continued to obstruct UNSCOM, prompting repeated military strikes by the United States, France, and the United Kingdom on behalf of the UN. In July 1992, UNSCOM began the large-scale destruction of Iraq's known chemical weapons. This included mustard gas and the nerve agent tabun.

William J. Clinton was elected U.S. president in 1992, and he continued the main points of his predecessor's Iraq policy. Under Clinton, the United States endeavored to contain the Saddam regime through economic and military sanctions and rigorous enforcement of the no-fly zones. At the beginning of 1993, before Clinton entered office, U.S. and allied air units bombed military installations in Iraq after the country deployed missiles and troops in areas where the weapons and soldiers were prohibited by UN resolutions. On January 19, Iraq withdrew the forces. On April 14, Iraqi intelligence agents tried unsuccessfully to assassinate former U.S. President Bush. Clinton ordered air strikes against Iraqi military targets in response.

On April 14, 1995, the UN Security Council created the "Oil for Food" program through Resolution 986, which allowed Iraq limited oil exports in order to purchase food and medicine under UN supervision. Critics of the program charged that Saddam used profits from the program to purchase military equipment and enrich himself and his supporters, instead of acquiring humanitarian supplies for his people (a charge later proven to be true).

In August 1995, two of Saddam's sons-in-law defected to Jordan, where they revealed evidence that Iraq had initiated a new program to develop nuclear weapons. The two were invited back to Iraq and promised clemency by Saddam. However, when they returned in February 1996, both were killed. In November, Jordanian officials intercepted and confiscated a large shipment of missile parts bound for Iraq that violated UN restrictions, reaffirming U.S. charges that Iraq was continuing to violate UN resolutions.

UNSCOM destroyed the Al-Hakam biological warfare site in Iraq in May 1996 after it discovered that Iraq had an extensive biological weapons program and had produced a variety of weaponized bacteria, including botulism and anthrax, as well as the toxic protein ricin, all of which could be dispersed in warheads.

UNSCOM completed the destruction of Iraq's known stockpile of chemical weapons and equipment and materials used to make WMDs in October 1997. That same month, Iraq called for U.S. members of UNSCOM to be withdrawn and that the United Nations cease aerial inspections. The United Nations rejected the Iraqi demand and ordered Iraq to increase its compliance with UNSCOM, especially in the areas of biological weapons and missiles. As tensions rose, most UNSCOM personnel were withdrawn at the beginning of November, but returned at the end of the month. Inspectors continued to complain that Iraqi officials were not cooperating fully. In light of Iraqi noncooperation with UNSCOM, the UN Security Council adopted Resolution 1137, condemning Iraq's actions and calling on the Saddam regime to fully comply with past UN requirements.

The continuing cheat-and-retreat strategy of the Iraqi regime frustrated British and American officials who sought to develop international support for even stronger measures against Iraq. However, few Muslim nations were willing to endorse stronger measures. Saddam had emerged as a hero to many in the Middle East. He was perceived as one of the few leaders who was able and willing to stand up to the United States and the West. Saddam encouraged this sentiment in a variety of ways, including providing an increasing amount of financial support to various Arab groups. Saddam also began to offer a $10,000 bounty to the families of suicide bombers who died in attacks against Israel. In addition, nations such as France and Russia had begun to trade with Iraq under the Oil for Food program and had developed lucrative oil exploration deals with Iraq that would take effect if economic sanctions stopped. Not only were these countries unwilling to support stronger sanctions, but they also wanted the existing UN measures reduced.

The End of Inspections

The Clinton administration began to argue publicly for the overthrow of the Saddam regime following the 1997 incident. On October 21, 1998, Clinton signed into law the Iraq Liberation Act. The legislation catalogued Iraq's violations of international law and UN resolutions and committed the United States to support regime change in Iraq and provide aid for anti-Saddam groups. U.S. intelligence agencies began to provide covert financial assistance to insurgent groups in Iraq.

Also in October 1998, UN weapons inspectors reported that Iraq continued to possess stockpiles of the nerve agent VX. The following month, Iraq ceased cooperation with the inspections. Increasing tensions between UNSCOM and the Iraqi government forced the evacuation of the remaining inspectors. In December, to punish Iraq, the United States and the United Kingdom launched aerial and cruise missile attacks in a campaign dubbed Operation Desert Fox. The strikes targeted military installations and suspected WMD sites. Concerns were raised within the Clinton administration that Iraq might sell or distribute chemical or biological weapons to terrorist groups. As a precaution against a potential WMD attack, the United States began to require that military personnel be vaccinated against anthrax as the result of intelligence that Iraq and other countries had programs to use the disease as a biological weapon.

On December 17, 1999, the United Nations created, through Security Council Resolution 1284, the UN Monitoring, Verification and Inspection Commission (UNMOVIC). UNMOVIC superseded UNSCOM and was tasked to oversee investigations and inspections of Iraq's WMD program. A major difference between the two organizations was that UNMOVIC's inspectors were UN employees whereas UNSCOM's personnel had been foreign nationals assigned to the body. This elicited complaints from the Iraqi government that U.S. and UK inspectors were unfairly critical of the regime. Nonetheless, UNMOVIC inspectors remained barred from entering Iraq by the Saddam regime until 2002.

Al Qaeda

Sometime in late 1987 or early 1988, Osama bin Laden, a Saudi-born Mujahedeen, formed a new fundamentalist group, al Qaeda (meaning "the base" or "the foundation" in Arabic). The leadership of al Qaeda consisted of former Mujahedeen and figures such as Egyptian-born Ayman al-Zawahiri, who had considerable experience as a terrorist. Bin Laden and his lieutenants wanted to create a new brand of terrorist group. Al Qaeda was created to serve as a coordinating body for Islamic terrorist groups all over the globe. The organization would raise funds, and provide training, weapons, and other logistical support, for attacks throughout the world. Bin Laden believed this would allow al Qaeda to spread Islamic revolution across the globe. It would also permit al Qaeda to coordinate widespread campaigns against selected targets.

Al Qaeda initially concentrated its efforts on the Afghan civil war, where fundamentalist Islamic groups battled local warlords, secular groups, and rival Muslim factions. In the early 1990s, al Qaeda also supported separatist Muslim groups in Chechnya fighting the Russians, in Kosovo battling the Serbs, and in Kashmir fighting the Indians. Bin Laden, who came from a wealthy Saudi family and was a multimillionaire, created an elaborate financial system to funnel money from donors and supporters to groups and operations. In 1991, al Qaeda moved much of its operations from Afghanistan to Sudan. Once in Sudan, al Qaeda established new training bases and opened legitimate businesses, including construction companies and import/export firms, in an effort to expand its financial resources.

Jihad against the United States

The withdrawal of the Soviet Union from Afghanistan was seen by bin Laden and his colleagues as a major victory. The Soviet Union was one of two global superpowers along with the United States. In 1991, at the end of the Cold War, the Soviet Union broke into a number of smaller countries, including Russia. Bin Laden believed that the demise of the Soviet Union was a result of the country's defeat in Afghanistan.

The 1991 Persian Gulf War infuriated bin Laden and the al Qaeda leadership. They opposed the deployment of U.S. and coalition forces to Saudi Arabia, arguing that non-Muslim troops should not be permitted in the Islamic holy land. In addition, bin Laden saw the Gulf War as a modern crusade that pitted Christians against Muslims. He particularly denounced the Muslim states that joined the U.S.-led coalition. Through the remainder of the 1990s, al Qaeda would undertake ever-widening operations in the Persian Gulf in countries that were allies of the United States.

By the end of the Persian Gulf War, bin Laden was committed to a holy war against the United States. He believed that since al Qaeda had defeated one superpower, the Soviet Union, it could beat the remaining one, the United States. Bin Laden and his aides were also convinced that the United States would be easier to defeat. There was a sense that Americans would not accept casualties, based on previous experiences in Lebanon. Bin Laden also believed that the strengths that the United States possessed, its advanced technology and strong economy, could be used against the country.

Bin Laden supported a plan to attack the World Trade Center (WTC) in New York City. On February 26, 1993, al Qaeda–affiliated terrorists detonated a bomb in a rental van in the basement parking lot of the WTC, in an effort to collapse Tower 1 of the WTC's twin towers in the hope that the falling building would also destroy its sister tower. The terrorists packed more than 1,300 pounds of explosives into the vehicle, which also contained poisonous sodium cyanide tablets (the terrorists wanted the explosion to disperse the cyanide to sicken or kill people). The attack killed six and wounded over 1,000, and it destroyed five floors of the parking garage, but it did relatively minor structural damage to the building. The cyanide was burned during the explosion and therefore did not affect anyone. More than 50,000 people had to be evacuated from the buildings. Militant Sheik Umar Abd al-Rahman, Ramzi Yousef, and nine others with links to al Qaeda were subsequently tried and convicted for their role in the attack.

Somalia

In 1991, an al Qaeda team traveled to Somalia, where they trained Muslim fighters and attempted to form a terrorist network. At the time, Somalia was in the midst of a devastating civil war. In December 1990, a UN-sponsored peacekeeping force was deployed to Somalia in an effort to restore peace and provide humanitarian assistance to the population after interclan conflict and civil war destroyed the country's infrastructure and left thousands dead or starving.

By 1993, UN forces were attempting to end the clan warfare. On October 3–4, 1993, a U.S. operation to capture warlords led to a running battle in the streets of Mogadishu, the capital of Somalia. The fighting left 18 U.S. soldiers dead, along with some 2,000 Somali fighters and civilians. Graphic images of the bodies of the

U.S. dead being dragged through the streets undermined domestic support in the United States and prompted President Clinton to withdraw American forces from Somalia. The incident reinforced the perception among anti-U.S. radicals that the American people were unwilling to tolerate military casualties and would force the government to withdraw from overseas missions if U.S. service personnel were killed.

Al Qaeda's Global Reach

In April 1994, Saudi Arabia revoked bin Laden's citizenship and froze his financial assets because of the al Qaeda leader's links to terrorism. Nonetheless, bin Laden still had access to a personal fortune worth an estimated $300 million. In addition, al Qaeda continued to receive funding and backing from supporters throughout the Persian Gulf and Middle East, including Saudi Arabia. Estimates showed that al Qaeda received about $10–20 million per month in donations and funding, more than enough to fund an ever-expanding series of attacks against the United States and Western targets.

In January 1995, al Qaeda plotter Ramzi Yousef attempted to launch a terrorism campaign. Yousef plotted an assassination attempt against Pope John Paul II and a complicated plan to destroy 12 U.S. airliners in flight during a 48-hour period. Filipino police uncovered the plot, which prevented most of the strikes, but one bomb exploded on an airplane, killing one. The failed plot was part of al Qaeda's strategy of undertaking ever more spectacular acts of terrorism. Yousef was captured the following month in Pakistan during a joint U.S.-Pakistani operation. He was extradited to the United States and convicted of his role in both the 1993 WTC bombing and the 1995 plot. Meanwhile, on November 13, seven people were killed when Islamic terrorists linked to al Qaeda detonated a car bomb at a military training facility in Riyadh, Saudi Arabia.

In May 1996, Bin Laden was expelled from Sudan under pressure from the United States because of his ties to terrorism. He returned to Afghanistan and established new bases and training facilities. On June 25, al Qaeda–linked terrorists detonated a truck bomb at a U.S. military housing complex, the Khobar Towers, outside of Riyadh, Saudi Arabia. The attack killed 20, including 19 Americans, and wounded more than 370.

The Taliban

When bin Laden returned to Afghanistan, he quickly allied himself with the Taliban. The Taliban were a Sunni political-religious organization, formed in Afghanistan in 1994 under former Mujahedeen leader Mullah Mohammad Omar. The group was composed of mainly ethnic Pashtuns and sought to impose a conservative version of sharia, or Islamic law, throughout Afghanistan. The Taliban won a series of military victories throughout 1994 against other Afghan factions. The organization drew recruits from Pakistan and other Muslim states, and had more than 3,000 foreign fighters serving in its ranks by 1995.

Al Qaeda fighters fought alongside the Taliban, and by September 1996, they conquered Kabul, the country's capital, while Afghanistan's president, Burhanuddin Rabbani, fled into exile. By the end of the year, the Taliban had effective control over about two-thirds of Afghanistan. By 2000, the group controlled 90 percent of the country. The Taliban's success was made possible by internal conflict among their enemy forces. In addition, many Afghans initially welcomed the Taliban because they provided stability and order.

Only Pakistan, Saudi Arabia, and the United Arab Emirates recognized the Taliban as the legitimate rulers of the country. Most foreign governments, including the United States, continued to recognize Rabbani as the legitimate leader of the nation. They also provided support for the anti-Taliban Northern Alliance, led by Ahmad Shah Massoud. The Northern Alliance drew its support mainly from ethnic Tajiks and Uzbeks, minority groups opposed to the Pashtun-dominated Taliban.

Concerned over the possibility that al Qaeda and other groups would acquire some of the advanced weaponry left in Afghanistan from the Soviet occupation, in 1996, the CIA initiated a secret $55 million program to purchase anti-aircraft missiles and other weapons from Afghans. Meanwhile, commercial aircraft stopped flying over Afghanistan for fear of being attacked by terrorist groups with anti-aircraft weaponry.

Once the Taliban took power, they worked with al Qaeda to implement a strict version of Islamic law. Music, television, and the internet were forbidden, as were many public celebrations, including wedding parties. There were limitations on what books could be owned, and kite flying, a very popular pastime, was banned. Men were required to grow their beards and wear Islamic garb. Women were not allowed to work, go to school (all schools for girls were closed), or travel in public transportation. Women were also forbidden from wearing makeup of any kind and had to wear a burqa (a head-to-toe garment that completely covered the body, except for the eyes) in public. Women could not leave their home without permission from their husband or other male family members, nor speak to any males if they were not related. Homosexuality was banned, and non-Muslims had to wear badges identifying themselves. Punishment for many of the social restrictions was severe. For instance, women caught with painted fingers or toes had those fingers or toes cut off. The new laws and restrictions drew international condemnation from human rights bodies and women's groups.

After initially suppressing the production of poppies (used to make opium and heroin), the Taliban began to support cultivation. By 1999, poppy production had doubled in Afghanistan, which reemerged as the world's leading supplier of heroin and opium. The Taliban controlled an estimated 90 percent of the country's drug trade. The regime used funds from the drug trade to support terrorist groups and Islamic fundamentalists, as well as purchase weaponry. For instance, the Taliban trained and supplied weapons to Chechen rebels fighting for independence from Russia.

The Embassy Bombings and the USS *Cole*

In February 1998, bin Laden distributed a fatwa, or religious decree, against the United States. The document asserted that it was the duty of all Muslims to kill Americans and their allies because of the presence of U.S. troops in Saudi Arabia. Most Muslim religious leaders dismissed the fatwa.

On August 7, 1998, al Qaeda carried out its largest terrorist attack to date. Al Qaeda terrorists carried out simultaneous truck bombings at the U.S. embassies in Nairobi, Kenya, and Dar-es-Salaam, Tanzania. The bombings killed 224 and injured more than 4,000. They demonstrated the growing global reach of the terrorist group and highlighted its efforts to undertake ever-larger and more deadly terrorist attacks. In retaliation, on August 20, the United States launched a series of ineffectual air strikes against suspected al Qaeda bases in Afghanistan and Sudan. In announcing the attacks, President Clinton addressed the American people and endeavored to explain his decision to retaliate and who were the targets of the U.S. strikes: "Our target was terror. Our mission was clear—to strike at the network of radical groups affiliated with and funded by Osama bin Laden, perhaps the preeminent organizer and financier of international terrorism in the world today. The groups associated with him come from diverse places, but share a hatred for democracy, a fanatical glorification of violence, and a horrible distortion of their religion to justify the murder of innocents."[5]

The U.S. attacks caused few casualties and did little to disrupt al Qaeda's network of bases. In Sudan, the Al Shifa pharmaceutical plant was targeted because U.S. intelligence suspected it was involved in the production of chemical weapons, but evidence after the raid proved this assumption to be incorrect. The inability of the United States to effectively damage al Qaeda encouraged bin Laden and his aides to plot additional attacks.

The United States increased security funding for its embassies by 50 percent over the next two years, and in November 1998, the Clinton administration offered a $5 million reward for information that led to the capture or death of bin Laden.

In January 1999, the United States issued a comprehensive indictment of bin Laden and other senior al Qaeda leaders for their roles in the 1998 Embassy Bombings and other terrorist attacks. The Clinton administration endeavored unsuccessfully to negotiate bin Laden's surrender with the Taliban. In July, Clinton imposed economic sanctions on the Taliban because of their refusal to turn over bin Laden for prosecution. The United States, the United Kingdom, and Russia convinced the UN Security Council to adopt Resolution 1267 in October, which identified al Qaeda and the Taliban as terrorist organizations. The measure also placed sanctions on both groups in an effort to limit funding and arms sales to the organizations and called on the Taliban to turn over bin Laden for prosecution. The Taliban and al Qaeda rejected the demands.

U.S. and foreign law enforcement and intelligence agencies foiled an al Qaeda attack in December 1999. Known as the Millennium Plot, Ahmed Ressam was tasked to undertake a bomb attack against the Los Angeles International Airport. Other terrorists planned strikes on tourist sites in Jordan that were expected to be filled with foreign Christian visitors for the Christmas holidays.

However, Jordanian officials apprehended 28 suspected attackers and passed intelligence to U.S. officials. Ressam was arrested by immigration officials as he endeavored to cross into the United States from Canada in a car filled with explosives and bomb-making materials. The failure of the attacks embarrassed bin Laden, who had sought a series of major attacks that would rival the 1998 Embassy Bombings. Consequently, the al Qaeda leader authorized another attack. Al Qaeda terrorists planned to drive an explosive-laden boat into the U.S. Navy destroyer, the *Sullivans*. On January 3, 2000, while the terrorists were preparing for the attack, their overloaded craft sank.

Al Qaeda launched a second suicide boat strike on October 12, 2000. Terrorists drove a boat filled with 600–700 pounds of explosives into the side of the USS *Cole*, in the Yemeni port of Aden. The attack killed 17, injured 39, and left a 40-foot hole in the side of the vessel. The *Cole* did not sink. It was repaired and returned to active service 14 months later. The Clinton administration warned the Taliban that it would attack Afghanistan if concrete evidence emerged that bin Laden and al Qaeda were responsible for the *Cole* attack. However, Clinton decided to defer any action to the next administration since the United States was on the eve of a presidential election. U.S. Defense Department officials noted that the Navy needed to do a better job of protecting ships in foreign harbors and be aware that U.S. vessels always face dangers overseas. Admiral Vern Clark noted that the Navy "must do a better job of both training and equipping our ships to operate within reasonable risk, and that means risk will never go away completely. . . . We must do this especially when our ships are called upon to operate in high-threat areas." [6]

Yemeni authorities subsequently arrested more than 100 for their involvement in the attack. Fifteen were convicted and given lengthy prison sentences, while two of the ringleaders were executed. Following the attack, the UN Security Council adopted Resolution 1333 in December, which placed additional sanctions on the Taliban in response to its failure to turn over bin Laden for prosecution. Among other restrictions, the measure forbade Taliban leaders from traveling outside of Afghanistan and placed an arms embargo on the regime.

By September 2001, the United States estimated that al Qaeda had operatives in more than 60 countries and had formed links with a variety of other terrorist groups in Asia, Africa, and the Middle East. Al Qaeda had become the world's most dangerous terrorist group.

Conclusion

By the end of the 20th century, the United States had been engaged in a 20-year struggle against international terrorism. The hijackings and kidnappings of the 1970s had given way to suicide attacks using massive car or truck bombs capable of causing tremendous loss of life and damage to property. Terrorists had struck American targets in Africa, Asia, Europe, and the Middle East as well as within the United States. By 2000, al Qaeda, under the leadership of bin Laden, had emerged as the main terrorist enemy of the United States, and it was a ruthless and dedicated foe. From its base in Afghanistan, al Qaeda carried out a series of escalating attacks against the United States and its allies inspired by bin Laden's fatwa that called for holy war against the United States and the West. In response, the United States had undertaken limited military action against al Qaeda and had used international organizations such as the United Nations to impose sanctions and other diplomatic punishments against the organization and its Taliban allies with little to no effect. Meanwhile, the United States had fought a war against Iraq, and then spent a decade attempting to contain the Saddam regime and force Iraqi compliance with a series of UN resolutions. Nonetheless, the United States of 2000 was in many ways less secure than it had been in 1990. Al Qaeda's global network had grown in size and capability, while Iraq had forced UN inspectors out of the country and Saddam appeared more firmly in power than he had at the end of the 1991 Gulf War.

Notes

1. Robert P. Watson, "The Politics and History of Terror," in *America's War on Terror*, 2nd ed. Tom Lansford, Robert P. Watson, and Jack Covarrubias (Aldershot: Ashgate, 2009), 2.

2. James E. Carter, "Speech on Afghanistan," January 4, 1980.

3. James M. Poland, *Understanding Terrorism: Groups, Strategies, and Responses*, 3rd ed. (Upper Saddle River, NJ: Prentice Hall, 2010), 81.

4. George H. W. Bush, "Address to the Nation Announcing Allied Military Action in the Persian Gulf," January 16, 1991.

5. Bill Clinton, "Address to the Nation," August 20, 1998, reprinted by PBS, *Newshour.*

6. Gerry J. Gilmore, "Cohen Absolves USS *Cole* Skipper, Crew," Armed Forces Press Service, January 22, 2001.

2

The 9/11 Attacks

By 2000, al Qaeda was in the midst of planning a range of attacks against the United States. Bin Laden and other al Qaeda leaders were infuriated that their succession of attacks through the 1990s and the 2000 USS *Cole* bombing had made little impact on U.S. policy. U.S. troops were still stationed in the Middle East, the United States continued to support Israel diplomatically and with both financial and military assistance, and American culture seemed to be making even deeper inroads into the Muslim world. Bin Laden desperately sought a major attack on the United States that would strike at the heart of American capitalism. He was particularly intrigued by a plot masterminded by Khalid Sheikh Mohammad, the uncle of 1993 WTC plotter Ramzi Yousef. Mohammad developed a plan to fly hijacked aircraft into the WTC and other U.S. targets. Bin Laden approved the scheme in 1999, setting in motion the most devastating terrorist attack in world history.

The 9/11 Plot

The idea of using airplanes as weapons was not new. During World War II, Japanese pilots, known as Kamikazes, had undertaken suicide missions by crashing their aircraft into U.S. and allied vessels. On September 12, 1994, Frank Eugene Corder crashed a small, stolen, single-engine airplane into the south lawn of the White House (Corder was not apparently trying to crash into the White House, but land the plane on the grass). The incident prompted changes in aerial security in Washington, D.C., and led several U.S. security and law enforcement agencies to launch studies on the possibility of suicide attacks by aircraft. Meanwhile, several terrorist groups had developed plans in the 1990s to hijack airliners and use them as missiles against Western targets, but none had actually been able to carry out their plots. For instance, in December 1994, French law enforcement officials discovered and disrupted an attempt by Algerian Islamic extremists to fly a hijacked plane into the Eiffel Tower in Paris.

Sometime in September 1999, bin Laden approved Khalid Sheikh Mohammad's plan to use hijacked airliners to attack multiple targets in the United States. Mohammad oversaw the logistics of the planning, while bin Laden and his senior aides selected the terrorists who would ultimately carry out the attack. The al Qaeda leader provided about $500,000 to initially finance the plan. Mohammad wanted terrorists to attempt to take over at least four airliners. He wanted multiple hijackings in case one or more of the al Qaeda groups failed to seize their targeted aircraft. He also argued that having simultaneous hijackings would confuse U.S. security officials and complicate the American response.

Mohammad envisioned teams of four to five hijackers. Two of the hijackers would seize control of the airline cockpit. These terrorists would have to have flight training and be able to fly the aircraft. The remaining hijackers would be tasked with gaining control of the cabin and keeping the passengers and crew under control. The terrorists would try to convince the passengers that they would not be harmed if they cooperated.

Al Qaeda leaders initially feared that the most significant difficulty facing the terrorists would be the ability to gain flight instruction. However, the terrorists were able to enroll in civilian flight schools in the United States. Over the next two years, the attackers traveled to the United States, where some received flight training. Initially 26 terrorists attempted to enter the United States, but only 20 were able to get into the country. Consequently, al Qaeda leaders decided to hijack four airliners.

In preparation for any potential U.S. military reprisals because of the attacks, al Qaeda sought to cement its relationship with the Taliban and make sure that the regime's leadership would continue to support al Qaeda. On April 16, 2001, Mullah Mohammad Rabbani, the prime minister of Afghanistan and the number two figure in the Taliban died of liver cancer. Rabbani, who helped establish the Taliban, was the leader of the moderate faction of the organization. He was replaced by an anti-Western hardliner, Mullah Mohammed Omar. Bin Laden perceived the change in leadership as a signal that the Taliban would be more supportive of attacks on the West. In addition, on September 9, Ahmad Shah Massoud, the leader of the Northern Alliance, was assassinated by al Qaeda. Massoud was perceived as one of the few anti-Taliban leaders who could rally Afghans to fight the regime. His death was seen as a major blow to the Northern Alliance. Massoud's death also removed a figure that the United States might supply with weapons or assistance to fight the Taliban or al Qaeda in Afghanistan.

The Hijackers

By the summer of 2001, the al Qaeda terrorists were in the United States and in the final stages of their hijacking preparations. The leader of the terrorist cell was Mohammad Atta. Atta, an Egyptian, became associated with radical Islamic extremists in the early 1990s and even more closely linked while studying in Hamburg, Germany. Several of the 9/11 hijackers became acquaintances while attending the Al-Quds Mosque in Hamburg. The mosque was founded in 1993 and quickly became a center for radical, extremist Islam. Several members of the mosque formed what became known as the Hamburg Cell, an al Qaeda terrorist group.

Atta traveled to Afghanistan in the 1990s, where he met bin Laden and Khalid Sheikh Mohammad. Mohammad recruited Atta for the 9/11 attacks. After receiving flight training in the United States in 2000, Atta helped coordinate the arrival of the other hijackers and the logistics of the attack. He traveled to Spain in July 2001 and met with al Qaeda leaders who gave the final okay for the attacks.

Atta and most of the hijackers had attended college. The majority came from affluent or middle-class families. Most spent some time in Western Europe. They all seemed to have become disillusioned at an early age with their home governments and with the culture and society of the West. Fifteen of the 19 eventual hijackers were Saudi Arabian, two were from the United Arab Emirates (UAE), one was from Lebanon, and one was from Egypt. Most had received some training in al Qaeda camps in Afghanistan, and some had fought alongside the Taliban or with Bosnian and Chechen rebels. The hijackers selected to be pilots were Atta (Egypt), Marwan al-Shehhi (UAE), Hani Hanjour (Saudi Arabia), and Ziad Jarrah (Lebanon). The other hijackers were Khalid al-Mihdhar, Nawaf al-Hazmi, Satam al-Suqami, Waleed M. al-Shehri, Wail al-Shehri, Abdulaziz Alomari, Majed Moqed, Salem al-Hamzi, Ahmed al-Ghamdi, Hamza al-Ghamdi, Mohald al-Shehri, Saeed al-Ghamdi, Ahmed al-Haznawi, Ahmed al-Nami (all from Saudi Arabia), and Fayez Banihammad (UAE).

On August 16, 2001, Zacarias Moussaoui, a French citizen of Moroccan origin, was arrested for immigration violations. There was some evidence that Moussaoui was to have been one of the hijackers and was commonly known as the "twentieth hijacker," since only 19 of the original 20 participated in the attack. Moussaoui had apparently already been removed from the plot before his arrest because of tensions with the other hijackers. Nonetheless, he was convicted of terrorism and sentenced to life in prison in 2006.

The Targets

The targets for the 9/11 attacks were carefully chosen for their symbolism and for the maximum potential impact of their loss. The targets for two of the planes were to be the Twin Towers of the WTC. The WTC was perceived as the center of the U.S. financial system. The WTC consisted of seven buildings, and its centerpiece was the Twin Towers. The 110 stories of the Twin Towers rose more than 1,350 feet above the ground and were briefly the tallest buildings in the world when they opened in 1972. Since the failed 1993 bombing of the WTC, bin Laden had been obsessed with conducting another attack against the facility. The failure of the original strike to do significant damage was seen as an embarrassment for al Qaeda. The WTC buildings were the home to numerous financial and banking firms, ranging from Bank of America to Lehman Brothers investment firm to the Bank of Taiwan. On any given day, the buildings contained more than 50,000 workers and visitors (the towers were significant tourist attractions). Bin Laden believed that the attacks would devastate the financial markets and cause an economic implosion in the United States. Two of the four hijacked planes were used in the attacks on the WTC.

The next target for the hijackers was the Pentagon located just outside of Washington, D.C. The Pentagon is the headquarters of the U.S. Department of Defense and the heart of the U.S. military. Constructed during World War II, the massive structure is the largest office building in the world with more than 6.5 million square feet of space. The five-sided building has five floors and is home to approximately 25,000 military and civilian workers. Beginning in 1998, the Pentagon was undergoing a massive renovation at the time of the 9/11 attacks. The strike against the Pentagon was designed to embarrass the U.S. military and provide retaliation for U.S. cruise missile attacks against al Qaeda facilities in Afghanistan in 1998. Bin Laden and other al Qaeda leaders also believed that the attack might make it more difficult for the United States to launch an immediate retaliatory strike.

There remains some controversy over the final target of the attacks. Evidence exists that either the White House or the Capitol (the home of the U.S. Congress) could have been the final objective. What is clear is that al Qaeda sought to strike at the nation's political structures, along with its attacks on the economic and financial centers.

In choosing the date for the attack, bin Laden wanted to strike quickly after the 2000 attack on the USS *Cole* failed to sink the ship. In addition, the 1993 WTC attack occurred just over one month after President Bill Clinton entered office. Bin Laden believed that the newness of Clinton's administration prevented him from taking stronger action. In 2001, the United States again had a new president. Bin Laden initially proposed May 12, 2001, as the date for the strikes, the six-month anniversary of the *Cole* attack. However, preparations were not finalized and the date had to be pushed back until September.

On November 7, 2000, Texas governor George W. Bush, the son of former president George H. W. Bush, was elected president of the United States (see Chapter 9). Bush defeated incumbent vice president Al Gore in contested balloting in which Gore received the majority of the popular vote, but Bush secured the majority of the Electoral College votes after a lengthy recount and legal process that was not settled until December. Because of the circumstances of his election, Bush was perceived by some al Qaeda leaders as a weak president who would be unlikely to rally the American people.

Warnings of the Attack

There were a variety of signs and evidence of the attack prior to 9/11. On a broad level, the new Bush administration understood the potential danger from al Qaeda. In January 2001, just after entering office, National Security Advisor Condoleezza Rice ordered a review of terrorist threats to the United States, with a particular emphasis on al Qaeda. Meanwhile, Bush reorganized the National Security Council so that the ad hoc interagency groups that had overseen issues such as counterterrorism were replaced by formal structures known as Policy Coordination Committees. This was part of a broader effort by Bush to simplify the decision-making structures involved in national security issues.

As early as 1998, the Federal Bureau of Investigation (FBI), the nation's leading counterterrorism organization, launched investigations into men of Middle Eastern origins who were attending flight school in the United States. Meanwhile, in August of the same year, the CIA received intelligence of a possible plot to hijack an airplane and fly it into the WTC. At the time, the FBI and the CIA (and other U.S. intelligence and law enforcement agencies) did not communicate or share intelligence on most issues. This was the result of legislation put in place in the 1970s after it was revealed that the CIA had conducted surveillance within the United States. By April 2001, the CIA had intelligence that al Qaeda was planning a major attack on the United States, but it lacked specifics on the target or the nature of the strike. Meanwhile, the Federal Aviation Administration (FAA) also received information that an al Qaeda attack was imminent and it warned airlines in April to take extra precautions, but the warning expired in August. Throughout this period, there were also sketchy reports from informants and intelligence sources about the attack, but most were too general to be useful in identifying specific targets or the date of an attack. The United States also received intelligence information from a range of countries, including Italy, Germany, and Israel, about possible al Qaeda attacks. In July, FBI agent Kenneth Williams, stationed in Phoenix, wrote a memo suggesting that the agency investigate Middle Easterners in the United States enrolled in flight schools. Williams was alarmed by what he perceived to be a high number of such students.

Despite the emerging evidence and numerous small clues, U.S. officials failed to recognize the potential danger the nation faced. The main problem was that law enforcement agencies and intelligence services were not sharing information, so that officials did not have the whole range of information—they could not put together all of the pieces of the puzzle. The attacks would prompt dramatic reforms in the nation's law enforcement and intelligence communities.

September 11, 2001

The Hijackings

On the morning of 9/11, the 19 al Qaeda terrorists boarded four U.S. flights: American Airlines Flight 11 from Boston to Los Angeles, United Airlines Flight

175 from Boston to Los Angeles, United Airlines Flight 93 from Newark to San Francisco, and American Airlines Flight 77 from Washington to Los Angeles. There were five hijackers aboard Flight 11, Flight 175, and Flight 77. There were four hijackers on Flight 93. Atta led the team that boarded Flight 11, which was the first plane hijacked.

The first hijacking began at approximately 8:15 a.m. on Flight 11. Atta, along with al-Suqami, Waleed M. al-Shehri, Wail al-Shehri, and Alomari, took control of the plane. Atta began to fly the plane. Air traffic controllers soon realized that something was wrong with the flight, because the plane stopped replying to routine communications and then veered off course. The terrorists used mace, box cutters, and other knife-like weapons to seize control of the airplane. On all of the flights, the pilots and other crew members were killed in the initial hijacking. At least one passenger also died in the initial attack, while other passengers were believed to have been injured. In order to keep the passengers under control, the terrorists claimed that there was a bomb aboard each of the planes and moved the passengers and remaining crew members to the rear of the airplanes.

The terrorists had carefully selected their weapons, most of which were, at that time, legal to carry on airplanes. Only one of the hijackers received any additional security screening as they boarded the aircraft. In Newark, one of the bags of hijacker al-Haznawi was checked for explosives. Otherwise, security officials would later report there was nothing suspicious about the 19 hijackers. Al-Mihdhar and Nawaf al-Hamzi were both on the FBI terrorist list, but were able to buy tickets and board the planes without alerting law enforcement officials.

Flight 175 was the second craft hijacked, at about 8:45 a.m., while Flight 77 became the third, about 10 minutes later. The final craft to be taken over was Flight 93 at about 9:30 a.m. Al-Shehhi took over the controls of Flight 175, with Ahmed al-Ghamdi, Hamza al-Ghamdi, Banihammad, and al-Shehri as the other hijackers. Hanjour was the pilot for Flight 77, and the other hijackers were al-Mihdhar, Moqed, Nawaq al-Hamzi, and Salem al-Hamzi. Flight 93 was piloted by Jarrah, along with Saeed al-Ghamdi, al-Haznawi, and al-Nami.

During the hijackings, the U.S. military scrambled two F-15 fighter jets to intercept American Airlines Flight 11; however, they were unable to locate the aircraft before it was flown into the WTC. The aircraft subsequently began patrols over New York, as additional military aircraft were placed in alert and all military bases in the United States went to high alert.

The WTC

Flight 11 was flown into the North Tower of the WTC at 8:46 a.m., hitting between the 93rd and 99th floors. All of the hijackers and the remaining passengers and crew members were killed when the plane struck the building. The impact caused a massive explosion and fire. Since the hijacking occurred early in the transcontinental flight, the plane was full of highly volatile airline fuel. The crash and the resultant blaze cut off the stairs and elevators for those trapped above the impact site. More than 1,350 people were caught on the upper floors. People on the lower floors began to evacuate the building. Helicopters were unable to take any people from the roof or upper floors of the building because of the flames and smoke. As the fires spread, some of those trapped on the upper floors leapt to their deaths rather than burn.

After the attack on the North Tower, some of the occupants of the South Tower began to evacuate. About 17–18 minutes later, at 9:03 a.m., Flight 175 crashed into the South Tower of the WTC between the 77th and 85th floors, immediately killing all on board. Another massive fire spread quickly through the building. Unlike the North Tower, at least one stairway to the upper floors remained open after the crash. This allowed some on the upper floors to escape. However, at least 650 people were killed on the upper floors because of the impact or the resultant fires.

As the Twin Towers burned, almost half of New York's firefighters and other emergency responders responded to the attacks. In spite of the fires and great danger, many entered the burning buildings to assist in the evacuations and treat the injured. More than 10,000 people were able to evacuate the Twin Towers. Meanwhile, the extreme heat of the fires began to melt the steel superstructure of the buildings.

The South Tower collapsed at 9:59 am, while the North Tower fell at 10:28 am. The collapse of the buildings caused a massive dust and smoke cloud in Manhattan. Meanwhile, other fires were started by debris from the buildings. A smaller building, WTC 7, subsequently collapsed after burning through the afternoon. Four other buildings of the WTC were also destroyed by the fires. Hospitals, clinics, and emergency workers were mobilized throughout the city, but few casualties survived the collapse of the buildings.

The Pentagon

After being taken by the terrorists, Flight 77 was flown into the Pentagon at 9:37 a.m. The plane struck the first floor at ground level, killing all onboard and igniting a massive fire with temperatures of more than 1,000° Fahrenheit. The airplane flew into an area that was undergoing renovations and therefore partially unoccupied. In addition, structural upgrades, including blast-resistant windows and steel reinforcements in the walls, helped minimize casualties. Nonetheless, the plane drove more than 300 feet into the building. The impact caused part of the outer rings of the building to collapse.

Military and civilian workers within the building immediately began rescue and evacuation efforts for those injured in the attack. Firefighters from surrounding communities quickly responded to the blaze. Although there were concerns that further sections of the building would collapse, firefighters were able to contain the blaze by the next day, although smaller fires continued in some areas for several days.

The Pentagon was the center of U.S. military operations, and Secretary of Defense Donald Rumsfeld refused to leave the building and instead maintained operations from areas that were unaffected by the attack. Despite the blaze and the subsequent recovery and restoration efforts, the Pentagon continued to function without interruption.

Flight 93

Passengers and the surviving crew members on Flight 93 became aware of the hijackers' intentions through cell phone and air phone calls. They discovered the news about the attacks on the WTC and the Pentagon. The passengers and remaining crew decided to attempt to retake control of the airplane.

Using plates, boiling water, and other improvised weapons, the passengers rushed the hijackers in the cabin at about 9:57 a.m. Moments before the attack, passenger Todd Beamer was speaking to a phone company representative, the line remained open, and the operator later reported that the last words she heard Beamer say was "Let's roll," as the passengers began their assault. The phrase would later emerge as one of the mottos for the U.S. response to the terrorist attacks.

The terrorist pilot undertook evasive maneuvers to throw the passengers off balance, including rocking the plane from side to side and up and down. However, the passengers were undaunted. By 10:02 a.m., the passengers were able to fight their way into the cabin as Jarrah took the plane into a dive rather than surrender control of the airplane. The flight crashed in an open field near Shanksville, Pennsylvania, at 10:03 a.m., in the midst of the struggle to retake the craft. Investigations subsequently determined that the target of Flight 93 was either the White House or the Capitol.

Casualties

The attacks killed 2,996 people, including the 19 terrorists, and were the largest and most deadly terrorist strikes in history. Not including the hijackers, 87 people died on Flight 11, 60 on Flight 175, and 2,605 in or near the WTC. Among those killed in New York were 411 emergency responders. Excluding the terrorists, 59 people were killed on Flight 77 and 125 at the Pentagon. There were 40 passengers and crew on Flight 93. Approximately 7,000 people were injured in the attacks.

Since many international firms had branches in the WTC, there were a significant number of foreign nationals killed on 9/11. Not including the hijackers, 372 citizens of other countries lost their lives during the attacks on the WTC. The largest number were British, 66; followed by Indian, 41; South Korean, 28; and Canadian and Japanese, 24 each.

Within one week, the United States had identified the 19 hijackers, while on the day following the attacks bin Laden and al Qaeda were named as the perpetrators of the attack. The United States relied on existing evidence that had been collected, as well as intelligence gained through monitoring al Qaeda communications. The United States distributed evidence to various allies, international organizations, and other groups on al Qaeda's guilt. The Bush administration also undertook an effort to rally the American people for possible military action against al Qaeda and the Taliban.

The Economic Impact of 9/11

The Damages

One of the goals of al Qaeda in the 9/11 attacks was to disrupt the U.S. and global economy. Bin Laden and other al Qaeda officials hoped an economic shock would drive the United States into recession and force it to reduce military spending and withdraw deployments from the Middle East and Persian Gulf. Al Qaeda also believed that a strong enough shock to the U.S. economy would permanently end the nation's global economic dominance.

The 9/11 terrorist attacks cost the United States an estimated $109 billion in direct economic losses and resulted in the loss of more than 270,000 jobs. In national terms, this was a loss of about 1 percent of Gross Domestic Product (GDP). Total losses from the attacks, including reductions in the value of the stock market, rose to almost $1 trillion. Worldwide the attacks cost about $300 billion in direct losses, and global economic growth declined from 4.1 percent in 2000 to 1.4 percent in 2001 (although not all the decline was attributable to the terrorist attacks).

The attacks especially affected some economic sectors. For instance, insurance costs alone were $40 billion in claim payouts. Revenues for the airline industry declined by $10 billion, or 20 percent. In response, insurance companies increased premiums by an average of 5 percent for all policy holders. Major stock indices lost between 15 and 20 percent of their value. Tourism and the travel industry were particularly hard hit. Visits by foreign tourists declined by 12 percent in 2001 and 4 percent in 2002. Domestically, Americans were reluctant to fly. To help the travel and tourism sector, Congress adopted an aid package that provided some $15 billion. More broadly, the U.S. government responded to the economic damage by lowering interest rates and providing more than $25 billion to New York City to aid the recovery.

The Economic Response

The Bush administration also undertook a broad campaign to encourage consumer spending by Americans. Bush and other administration officials repeatedly urged Americans to go about their lives and not allow the attacks to alter behavior.

The strategy reflected the importance of consumer spending (which accounts for approximately two-thirds of the U.S. economy). After the attacks, the government did offer a version of the EE series savings bond known as the Patriot Bond, but there was no large-scale campaign to have citizens shift spending to investment in bonds to finance increased military expenditures.

The country was on the verge of a recession on 9/11, as economic growth slowed and the unemployment rate rose. However, economic growth resumed in October and GDP increased by 2.7 percent in the final quarter of 2001. The economic rebound was the result of a number of factors, including a "Patriotic Rally" in stocks which allowed most stock indices to recover their losses. In addition, increases in government spending as a result of recovery and rebuilding efforts and new military expenditures in Operation Enduring Freedom spurred growth, as did the broader resilience of the U.S. economy, which was bolstered by monetary policy which lowered interest rates and provided other stimuli to the economy. Worldwide economic growth increased to 1.9 percent in 2002, led by the U.S. recovery and significant economic growth in China. The attacks did accelerated global defense spending. For instance, defense spending by the United States, Canada, and Europe increased from $486 billion in 2001 to $539 billion in 2002 (the largest increase was on the part of the United States, which spent $307.8 billion in 2001 and $328.7 billion in 2002).

The American Response

New York

Lessons from the 1993 WTC bombing led to improvements in safety and evacuation techniques that saved a considerable number of lives during the 2001 attacks. Emergency responders not only were able to get a large number of people out of the Twin Towers and other buildings of the WTC, but also managed a massive evacuation of the area surrounding the site of the attack. Large sections of Manhattan remained closed over the next weeks, including initially tunnels and bridges, in case of additional attacks.

New York mayor Rudy Giuliani emerged as a national hero during the attacks. When Flight 11 struck the North Tower, Giuliani rushed to the scene and set up a command center to oversee the rescue and recovery efforts as Flight 175 crashed into the South Tower. The mayor's leadership and advocacy for New York earned him the respect and admiration of most Americans. He became known as "America's Mayor." Giuliani in turn was lavish in his praise of New York's first responders. At a press conference on September 12, Giuliani declared, "We have, without any doubt, the best Police Department, the best Fire Department, the best police officers, the best fire officers, the best emergency workers of any place in the whole world. And, although today's tragedy is going to be enormous, and there's no way to minimize it, if it weren't for them, this tragedy would be far worse. . . . I can tell you that whatever the number of casualties, without our Police Department, our Fire Department, our EMS, and the kinds of people we have, many of whom lost their lives, there would be double or triple the number of casualties."[1]

The site of the WTC attack became known as "Ground Zero." Millions visited the site, where they were able to watch debris removal at an elevated observation area. As a tribute to the victims, 88 spotlights were arranged to project two vertical beams of light into the night sky. Known as the Tribute in Light, the beams were first displayed in March 2002. A design for a permanent memorial at the site was selected in 2004, and construction began in 2006. Meanwhile, a range of U.S. officials from Bush to Giuliani to New York governor George Pataki pledged to rebuild the WTC. In addition to rebuilding smaller structures that were destroyed or damaged in the attack, the Twin Towers were scheduled to be replaced by a single structure, known initially as the Freedom Tower. The building was designed to be 1776 feet high (including its antennae) in honor of the year that the Declaration of Independence was signed. Construction began in 2006, and the building was scheduled to be open in 2013.

President Bush

At the time of the first of the 9/11 attacks, Bush was in the midst of a visit to an elementary school in Sarasota, Florida. He was informed of the first attack, and then began reading to a group of children in their classroom. The president continued the classroom visitation for approximately 15 minutes, later explaining that he did not want to frighten or alarm the children. Bush then moved to room in the school where he was briefed by staffers. He then participated in a teleconference with his national security advisors. By 9:30 a.m., the decision was made that the FAA would ground all commercial flights and not allow any more takeoffs in an effort to prevent additional attacks. Later, all flights in the air were ordered to immediately land. Many foreign flights bound for the United States were redirected to Canada. Concurrently, all military bases were placed on high alert.

Bush subsequently addressed the nation at about 9:30 a.m. and asked the nation for a moment of silence in recognition of the loss of lives. Many government buildings and offices in Washington, D.C., were ordered closed and evacuated, including the Capitol. The president and his staffers traveled on Air Force One first to Barksdale Air Force Base in Louisiana, and then to Offutt Air Force Base in Omaha, Nebraska. Meanwhile, Vice President Dick Cheney was moved to a nuclear bomb–proof underground shelter in Washington, D.C., in case of a further attack. By 10:30 a.m., after Flight 93 crashed, the government issued a shoot-down order that permitted the military to shoot down any commercial aircraft that had been hijacked and posed a threat. Bush delivered a brief, taped statement to the public around 1:00 p.m. He arrived back at the White House at 6:54 pm and delivered a second live address to the American people. Bush began by stating, "Today, our fellow citizens, our way of life, our very freedom came under attack in a series of deliberate and deadly terrorist acts"; and later declared that "America was targeted for attack because we're the brightest beacon for freedom and opportunity in the world. And no one will keep that light from shining."[2]

There was criticism of Bush for his actions on the day of attack for not communicating more deeply with the American people during the day and for not returning to Washington more quickly. However, people quickly rallied around the president and the symbols of the United States. Within one week of the 9/11 attacks, Bush's approval rating rose to 90 percent among the American people. Bush made a number of public appearances and statements that resonated with Americans. For instance, on September 14, while touring Ground Zero in New York, Bush was using a bullhorn to address the recovery workers when someone called out that they could not hear the president. Bush responded, "I can hear you. The rest of the world hears you. And the people who knocked these buildings down will hear all of us soon."

On September 20, Bush addressed the nation and called for the Taliban to surrender bin Laden. He attempted to reassure Muslims that any military action would not be a war against Islam, but an effort only to punish the perpetrators of the attacks. Bush used the term "war on terror," which was subsequently used to describe the broad counterterrorism campaign led by the United States. Bush declared, "Our war on terror begins with al Qaeda, but it does not end there. It will not end until every terrorist group of global reach has been found, stopped and defeated."[3]

The United States was simultaneously working with allies such as Saudi Arabia and the United Arab Emirates to convince the Taliban to turn over the al Qaeda leader. The president began to make a case that the United States was engaged in a global struggle against international terrorism, a campaign that will resemble the Cold War in depth and breadth. On September 23, Bush signed Executive Order 13224. The order further reduced the ability of terrorists, or people who support terrorism, from carrying out a range of financial transactions in the United States.

On October 8, Bush created the Office of Homeland Security through Executive Order 13228. The new office was created to coordinate all domestic counterterrorism activities among 40 different federal bodies, including the response and recovery from the attacks. Specifically Bush wanted the new body to overcome the divisions between the existing law enforcement and intelligence agencies and to enhance intelligence and information sharing. Former Pennsylvania governor Tom Ridge was appointed to lead the new body. Ridge's position was a cabinet-level position. Meanwhile, terrorism czar Richard Clarke's position was enhanced. Clarke was charged with improving the country's cybersecurity and critical infrastructure against potential terrorist attacks. Bush also created a Homeland Security Council to parallel the National Security Council.

The Anthrax Attacks

While the nation was in the midst of recovering from the 9/11 attacks, a new terrorist campaign began. On September 18, five letters contaminated with anthrax spores were mailed to news organizations in the United States. Anthrax is a highly dangerous and usually fatal disease. The letters were received by the news departments of the television broadcasters ABC, CBS, and NBC, and the newspapers the *New York Post* and the *National Enquirer*. On October 9, contaminated letters were received at the offices of Senator Tom Daschle and Senator Patrick Leahy (both Democrats). The letters containing the anthrax contained anti-American and anti-Israeli phrases, including "Death to America" and "Death to Israel."

Five people were killed, and 17 others sickened. The letters originated from within the United States and added to public fears in the wake of the 9/11 attacks, especially since a number of anthrax hoax letters were subsequently mailed. The FBI estimated that the investigation and clean-up after the attacks cost $1 billion. Initial suspicions were that al Qaeda or some other international terrorist group was responsible for the attacks. However, evidence indicated that the letters originated from within the United States. A subsequent investigation concluded that Bruce Ivins, a biodefense researcher, was the most likely perpetrator of the attacks. Ivins committed suicide on July 27, 2008, in the midst of the investigation. Meanwhile, the postal service deployed detection devices at its regional sorting centers.

Protecting the Homeland

Bush granted the military the ability to call 50,000 reservists and National Guard troops to active duty on September 14. That number was expanded, and by the end of the year some 67,000 would be activated. Many of these troops were temporarily deployed to airports to provide additional security and to reassure Americans that it was safe to travel by air. By year's end, U.S. defense spending was $307.8 billion or 3 percent of GDP because of increased security costs and the military campaigns launched in the aftermath of the 9/11 attacks.

On September 14, Congress passed a joint resolution authorizing the use of force against those responsible for the 9/11 attacks. Bush signed the act into law four days later. The measure passed the House of Representatives on a vote of 420 in favor and one opposed. The lone dissenter was Representative Barbara Lee of California, who argued that the measure was too broad and granted the president too much power. Lee asserted that Congress should wait for more evidence linking al Qaeda to the attacks. The Senate endorsed the resolution 98–0. The resolution provided the legal framework for subsequent military action against the Taliban and al Qaeda.

Congress also crafted legislation designed to prevent another attack on the scale of the 9/11 strikes. The resultant new law was formally known as the Uniting and Strengthening America by Providing Appropriate Tools Required to Intercept and

Obstruct Terrorism Act of 2001 (the USA PATRIOT Act, or Patriot Act). Bush signed the Patriot Act on October 26. The Patriot Act was a massive measure, consisting of 342 pages, and divided into 10 broad areas. The new law was designed to improve counterterrorism capabilities among law enforcement agencies and to enhance homeland security. It eliminated or reduced restrictions on how the United States gathers both domestic and international intelligence. The law also broadened the scope of what was considered a terrorist act, increased the powers of law enforcement groups to detain terrorism suspects and illegal immigrants, and enhanced the authority of the Treasury Department to monitor and prevent financial transactions by terrorist groups and their supporters.

Under the terms of the act, U.S. domestic law enforcement agencies were directed to exchange information and intelligence on the noncriminal activities of suspected terrorists and other criminals. The measure also clarified the definition of domestic terrorism to make it easier to prosecute suspects. It further introduced new penalties for biological terrorism (this was in response to the 2001 anthrax attacks).

The most controversial aspects of the law were the increased abilities of law enforcement to monitor domestic communications, including e-mails, voicemail, and phone calls, and the ability to access a variety of personal records. Law enforcement bodies were given an expanded power to conduct "sneak and peak" warrants that were designed to allow the seizure of information or materials before that evidence can be destroyed.

Domestic law enforcement agencies were granted an increased ability to seize materials, records, or other items when national security was deemed to be at risk. Many of the provisions of the act were challenged in court. The act also increased funding for border security. Many of the provisions of the act were set to expire in 2005, but most were reauthorized with changes.

Other countries such as Canada, the United Kingdom, and Germany also enacted new antiterrorism measures that were similar to the Patriot Act.

In addition to the Patriot Act, Congress also passed additional legislation to specifically improve airline security. On November 19, the Aviation and Transportation Security Act became law. The legislation established the Transportation Safety Administration (TSA). The TSA was tasked to take over passenger and baggage screening, which had been overseen by the individual airlines. The TSA standardized airline security and increased the resources devoted to passenger security. The TSA was initially part of the Department of Transportation, but was transferred to the Department of Homeland Security after the creation of that body in 2002.

The Victims of Terrorism Relief Act of 2001 (the act was actually signed into law on January 23, 2002) reduced some of the restrictions that were placed on charitable and volunteer organizations and foundations in order to expand aid to victims of the 9/11 attacks. The new law allowed organizations to provide immediate assistance to victims of manmade or natural disasters without financial background checks.

The Shoe Bomber

In spite of the new airline security measures, al Qaeda attempted a bombing of a flight from Paris to Miami. There was a single terrorist involved: Richard Reid, a British citizen who had traveled to Afghanistan and Pakistan in 1999 and 2000, where he joined al Qaeda and received terrorist training. Bin Laden believed that Reid would receive less scrutiny than someone of Middle Eastern origin. On December 22, 2001, Reid boarded American Airlines Flight 63 in Paris. Reid's shoes had plastic explosives in them, and he was supposed to detonate the bombs in a suicide attack. However, Reid was unable to detonate the explosives. Passengers alerted flight attendants that Reid was endeavoring to light a match, and the would-be terrorist was subsequently subdued by passengers and crew. Reid came to be known as the "Shoe Bomber." He pled guilty to terrorism in 2003 and was sentenced to life in prison. Reid's abortive suicide attack led to new inspections of shoes and footwear for airline passengers.

Popular Culture and 9/11

Public Reactions

In the aftermath of the 9/11 attacks, there was a dramatic increase in patriotism and nationalism in the United States. One of the most played songs on radio was Lee Greenwood's "God Bless the USA," a patriotic tune originally released during the 1991 Persian Gulf War. Many homes and businesses displayed American flags and pro-American bumper stickers or signs. The number of volunteers for the U.S. military increased dramatically. In addition, people lined up to donate blood or clothing, or to provide other materials or assistance. Charitable giving also rose significantly, especially to foundations and organizations that provided assistance to the victims and families of victims of the terrorist attacks.

On September 21, CBS aired a telethon titled *America: A Tribute to Heroes*, which was hosted by George Clooney. The event included performances by a range of musical artists from a variety of genres, including Bruce Springsteen, U2, Neil Young, Willie Nelson, Faith Hill, Stevie Wonder, Dave Matthews, Wyclef Jean, and Alicia Keys, among others. The show raised more than $100 million for victims and their families, including sales of the CD and DVD from the telethon.

A number of television dramas addressed the 9/11 attacks and their impact, including highly rated programming such as *NYPD Blue*. Daytime and late-night talk shows addressed the attacks directly. For instance, following the strikes, on September 17, *Late Night with David Letterman* became the first late-night talk show host to return to the air. He presented a noncomedic episode, and then slowly reintroduced comedy over the succeeding weeks.

Hollywood was less quick to react, and there are few productions which are directly based on the attacks. Notable exceptions include the Oliver Stone film *World Trade Center*, released in 2006 and starring Nicolas Cage as one of the last two survivors who were rescued from the wreckage of the WTC; or *United 93*, which tells the story of the air traffic controllers, passengers, crew, and hijackers involved in Flight 93, which crashed in Pennsylvania. Many major Hollywood studios were unwilling to address the attacks because of the potential for a public backlash if films did not resonate with domestic audiences. There were specific fears that films would not be seen as handling the subject in a sensitive fashion. Independent and foreign filmmakers did produce a number of projects on the attacks, but they generally failed to attract widespread audiences in the United States.

There were a number of documentaries released about the attacks. *9/11* was a 2002 documentary which chronicled the attacks using footage of firefighters who were involved in the response to the strikes. The documentary was aired on television in 2002. Michael Moore's award-winning 2004 documentary *Fahrenheit 9/11* was a critical exploration of the Bush administration and focused more on the Iraq War than the 9/11 attacks.

The 9/11 attacks produced a number of conspiracy theories. Most fall into one of two categories. The first is that the Bush administration or elements of the U.S. intelligence community were aware in advance of the attacks and allowed them to happen. The second group of conspiracy theorists contends that the WTC and the Pentagon were destroyed by explosives planted by government operatives. Both groups argue that the attacks were carried out in order to create public support for military campaigns in Afghanistan and Iraq to expand or protect American economic or energy interests in the Middle East. Experts and scholars dismissed these ideas, and their proponents failed to produce compelling evidence.

A variety of spontaneous memorials were created after the attacks. These include areas where flowers and other tributes were gathered. In New York, boards were posted with photographs and messages as people searched, often in vain, for loved ones missing as a result of the WTC attack. At the Pentagon, a massive American flag was displayed on the side of the building where the aircraft struck. In addition, on a hill overlooking the facility, people gathered to place mementos and remembrances. In 2002, a formal memorial was opened within the building, which included victims' names, pictures, and biographical information, alongside a chapel. A larger memorial was created outside of the building consisting of 184 benches inscribed with the names of the victims of the attack. The memorial was formally opened on September 11, 2008. Unidentified remains from the Pentagon attack were buried at Arlington National Cemetery at a separate memorial to the victims. In Shanksville, Pennsylvania, the site of the crash of Flight 93, a temporary memorial fence was built. Visitors left mementos, ranging from photographs to clothing, at the site. In September 2002, Congress approved plans for a permanent memorial, and construction began in 2009, with the first phase of the site completed prior to the 10th anniversary of the crash.

The Media

Various media outlets broadcast vivid images of the 9/11 attacks. Many Americans and others around the world viewed footage of the airplanes striking the WTC and the subsequent collapse of the Twin Towers. There is also footage of victims of the attacks on the WTC falling to their deaths from the buildings.

In the immediate aftermath of the attack, there was a dramatic increase in "rally-around-the-flag" journalism in which reporters and journalists were highly supportive of the United States and its actions. Most media outlets and entertainment channels initially provided around-the-clock coverage of the attacks and the U.S. response. The actions of the media, especially domestic media networks, gained significant approval from the public. For instance, in polls taken after the 9/11 attacks, the percentage of the public that perceived the media as biased decreased from 59 percent to 47 percent, while the percentage of people who believed the press was pro-American rose from 43 percent to 69 percent. Over time, the media began to be more questioning, and critical at times, of the U.S. response to the attacks.

Fox News eclipsed CNN in market share and became the most watched cable news network by the end of 2001. Meanwhile, Al Jazeera broadcast an increasing number of statements and messages from al Qaeda leaders and other terrorist groups. It also broadcast graphic images of terrorist acts, including executions.

The International Response

Allies and Enemies

Condemnation of the attacks was swift by countries that were traditional allies of the United States and even those with tense relations with the United States. For instance, Iran's supreme leader, Ayatollah Ali Khamenei, denounced the attacks (although he also warned that the United States should not undertake military action in response). There were official and spontaneous demonstrations of support for the United States from around the world. More than 100 world leaders contacted the administration to express condolences or support in the aftermath of the bombings. In London, the band at Buckingham Palace played "The Star-Spangled Banner" during the changing of the guards on the day after the attack. In Seoul, South Korea, groups gathered outside of the U.S. Embassy to pray. The French news journal *Le Monde*, a publication that was often critical of the United States and U.S. foreign policy, ran a headline that exclaimed, "We Are All Americans!" The accompanying story declared, "We are all Americans! We are all New Yorkers, just as surely as John F. Kennedy declared himself to be a Berliner in 1962 when he visited Berlin. Indeed, just as in the gravest moments of our own history, how can we not feel profound solidarity with those people, that country, the United States, to whom we are so close and to whom we owe our freedom, and therefore our solidarity?"[4]

The day after the attacks, senior Taliban leaders met to develop a response. It was unlikely that many Taliban officials knew in advance of the attacks; however, after 9/11, al Qaeda's role in the strikes was discussed between the terrorist group and members of the regime. Moderates within the Taliban, such as Foreign Minister Wakil Ahmed Muttawakil and Information Minister Qudratulla Jamal, contended that the organization should turn over bin Laden rather than risk a military response from the United States. However, hardliners, led by Taliban leader Mullah Omar, argued that the regime should deny knowledge of or involvement in the attacks. There was a mistaken perception that the United States might engage in aerial or missile attacks, but that it would not invade for fear of suffering the same fate as the Soviet Union. Consequently, Mullah Omar and other senior Taliban officials condemned the attacks publically, but refused to cooperate with the United States in extraditing bin Laden or other al Qaeda figures. In an effort to appeal to Muslims, the Taliban argued that bin Laden was a guest who had asked for sanctuary, and therefore under Afghan and Islamic custom, he could not be turned over to the United States. The Taliban did offer several times to turn bin Laden over to a neutral Islamic country for trial, but the offer was apparently a delaying tactic and no countries were willing to take the al Qaeda leader.

International Organizations

On September 12, the UN Security Council unanimously adopted Resolution 1368, which condemned the 9/11 attacks and called upon all nations to assist in identifying the perpetrators and bringing them to justice. It also called for all states to increase efforts to combat terrorism. This measure was followed on September 28 by Resolution 1373, which enacted new measures to prevent the financing of terrorist groups and also encouraged countries to increase intelligence and law enforcement cooperation.

Also on September 12, less than 36 hours after the attack, the North Atlantic Treaty Organization (NATO) invoked its collective defense clause for the first time in its history. The action required the then-19 NATO members to come to the aid of the United States. The NATO members agreed to increase intelligence and counterterrorism cooperation and collaboration. NATO also issued a broad statement of support for the U.S.-led war on terror. The alliance also agreed to grant the United States and its coalition allies access to NATO bases, airfields, ports, and overflight rights in any military campaign against the Taliban.

Australia and New Zealand invoked the Australia, New Zealand and United States Pact (ANZUS) to provide military support for the United States. Other international organizations, including the European Union, the Organization of

American States, and the United Nations, also pledged to assist the United States. By September 30, there were 46 multilateral declarations of support for the United States. In addition, more than 100 countries provided intelligence information or increased cooperation with the United States, while 30 states increased law enforcement collaboration. More than 30 countries offered military support to the United States, and the United States acquired the right to use foreign air or military bases in countries ranging from Tajikistan and Uzbekistan to Kuwait and Oman.

Bilateral Cooperation

Following the 9/11 terrorist attacks, foreign states increased cooperation with the United States in counterterrorism efforts. As a result the U.S. Treasury Department was able to freeze 20 overseas bank accounts linked to al Qaeda. Worldwide, more than 200 people were arrested because of ties to al Qaeda or links to the 9/11 attacks.

Pakistan withdrew its support for the Taliban, and its president, Pervez Musharraf, pledged cooperation with the United States and its allies. In return, the United States ended sanctions put in place on India and Pakistan after those two countries detonated nuclear weapons in 1998. The United States also agreed to forgive $600 million of Pakistan's debt. The Bush administration secured additional aid for Pakistan from other states, such as Japan. On September 25, Saudi Arabia also ended diplomatic and political relations with the Taliban, as did the United Arab Emirates.

The United Kingdom emerged as the closest ally of the United States in the post-9/11 era. The United Kingdom and the United States had been very close allies since World War II, and their interaction had evolved into what was commonly known as the "special relationship," a phrase that highlighted the close cultural, political, and military ties between the United States and the United Kingdom. The two countries were already cooperating closely on efforts to contain the Saddam regime in Iraq and worked together frequently on counterterrorism efforts. In addition, a large number of Britons were killed in the 9/11 attacks. British prime minister Tony Blair was very vocal in his support for the United States and his condemnation of al Qaeda: "[T]here is nothing hidden about bin Laden's agenda. He openly espouses the language of terror; has described terrorizing Americans as a 'religious and logical obligation'; and in February 1998 signed a fatwa stating that 'the killing of Americans and their civilian and military allies is a religious duty.'"[5] Blair and Bush developed a very close relationship during the 9/11 crisis, and that closeness continued throughout the tenure of the two leaders.

In addition to pledging close political, military, and diplomatic support, the British initiated negotiations with Iran to ensure that country would either support the anti-Taliban coalition or at least remain neutral during any military action. Iran had supported anti-Taliban Shiite fighters in Afghanistan in response to the regime's suppression of Shiites. Iran continued to provide military support to its allies in Afghanistan and initially refrained from action against the coalition. Poland organized a conference between the United States and 17 Eastern and Central European states that resulted in agreements to increase intelligence and law enforcement cooperation, better monitor the movement of peoples, and curb money laundering.

Of particular importance was the cooperation provided by Turkey. As a Muslim state, Turkey's involvement in the U.S.-led anti-Taliban coalition provided credibility to the effort to develop an anti-Taliban and anti-al Qaeda military alliance. Turkey's geographic proximity to Afghanistan was vitally important since U.S. air units were allowed to use bases in Turkey and Turkish airspace. Similar cooperation by states in Central Asia, including Kyrgyzstan, Uzbekistan, and Tajikistan, was also very important. Such cooperation would not have been possible without support from Russia, which initially perceived collaboration on Afghanistan as a way to suppress al Qaeda–trained terrorists in Russian areas such as Chechnya.

Polls taken in the first weeks after the attacks revealed widespread international support for the United States, including U.S. military action. For instance, 80 percent of Danes, 70 percent of Britons, 73 percent of the French, 70 percent of the Portuguese, and 66 percent of both Italians and the Dutch supported military action by their countries in concert with the United States. Germany, which had constitutional limitations on the deployment of military forces overseas, approved the use of troops to support the U.S.-led coalition when its legislature voted 565 to 40 in favor of military action.

By the end of September, there was considerable international support for military action against the Taliban and al Qaeda. The United States set about developing a coalition of nations willing to provide military, economic, or political support for such an alliance. The United States and its allies began deploying military units in and around Afghanistan in anticipation of an anti-Taliban campaign. Meanwhile, negotiations continued with the Taliban in a largely unsuccessful effort to convince the regime to turn over bin Laden and his senior aides for prosecution.

Conclusion

Al Qaeda executed a devastating attack on the United States, using commercial airliners and targeting symbols of America's economic, military, and political power. The attack demonstrated the global reach of the terrorist organization and its ability to exploit weaknesses in the contemporary United States, including the ease of air travel at that time. However, al Qaeda underestimated the resilience of the American people and economy. Far from retreating from the threat of terrorism, Americans rallied around their government and its officials. The terrorists also misjudged the tenacity of Bush and other U.S. leaders. The United States moved quickly to identify the perpetrators of the attacks and to gain international support for efforts to either prosecute those responsible or undertake military action to punish them. Within a month of the attacks, the United States had developed a military coalition and plans to utilize that alliance to attack the Taliban and al Qaeda. The U.S. military mission would be codename Operation Enduring Freedom and would be initiated less than one month after the 9/11 attacks with broad domestic and international support.

Notes

1. Rudy Giuliani, "Giuliani on Rescue Efforts," September 12, 2001, reprinted by the *Washington Post*.

2. George W. Bush, "9/11 Address to the Nation," September 11, 2001.

3. George W. Bush, "Address to the Nation," September 20, 2001.

4. Jean-Marie Colombani, "We Are All Americans," *Le Monde*, September 12, 2001, 1; reprinted in *World Press Review* 48, no. 11 (November 2001), pp. 10–11.

5. Tony Blair, House of Commons Debate, October 4, 2001, c672; quoted in House of Commons Library, "Operation Enduring Freedom and the Conflict in Afghanistan: An Update," Research Paper 01/81, October 31, 2001.

3

Operation Enduring Freedom and the Invasion of Afghanistan

In the aftermath of the 9/11 terrorist attacks, U.S. president Bush sought swift action to ensure that the perpetrators of the strikes did not escape justice. Bush and other administration officials were aware that prior efforts to destroy or damage al Qaeda, including cruise missile attacks in response to the 1998 Embassy Bombings, had not only not harmed the global terrorist network but also in some ways made the organization stronger by allowing it to survive against the military might of what was supposed to be the most powerful country in the world. The United States also could not allow an attack of the magnitude of the 9/11 bombings to go unpunished for fear of encouraging other terrorist attacks. At the same time, there was considerable trepidation and uncertainty about the outcome of any military campaign in Afghanistan. The Soviets, and before them the British, had military disasters in Afghanistan, at times when the two former superpowers were at the peak of their power and influence. Because of its rugged terrain and fearsome population, Afghanistan had become known as the "graveyard of empires." Some officials in the United States were concerned that the 9/11 attacks were actually a deliberate provocation to get the United States to deploy troops to Afghanistan, where they would face defeat by the former Mujahedeen as had the Soviets. Consequently, U.S. military leaders sought to develop a strategy that would maximize American advantages in technology and firepower, while minimizing the risk to U.S. troops. The U.S. military also had to act quickly, both in response to the need to avenge the 9/11 attacks and in an effort to avoid the worst extremes of the deadly Afghan winter. Their plans culminated in Operation Enduring Freedom, the invasion of Afghanistan.

The U.S. Strategy

The day after the 9/11 attacks, U.S. secretary of defense Donald Rumsfeld ordered Pentagon officials to begin developing possible plans to carry out military strikes in retaliation for the terrorist bombings. Once it became clear that bin Laden and al Qaeda were responsible, U.S. military officials quickly developed a plan to invade Afghanistan since it was assumed the Taliban would be unwilling to turn over the al Qaeda leader for prosecution. Meanwhile, Bush made it clear that if the United States invaded Afghanistan, he wanted the military action to accomplish five goals. First, the invasion had to destroy the existing al Qaeda terrorist network in Afghanistan, including eliminating bases and training facilities. Second, bin Laden and other senior al Qaeda leaders had to be killed or captured. Third, a moderate, pro-Western, democratic government had to be established in the hope that it would prevent future terrorist activities. Fourth, U.S. casualties had to be kept to a minimum. Fifth, and finally, the invasion had to provide humanitarian assistance to the Afghan people and create the conditions for future economic development. The last guideline came in response to a growing humanitarian crisis in the country. In May, in response to starvation and famine, the United States provided $43 million in food aid for the United Nations to distribute in Afghanistan through the World Food Program. By August 2001, the United Nations estimated that more than 5–6 million Afghans were at risk of starvation because of food shortages and that the country was in desperate need of more than 2.3 million tons of food.[1] The food scarcity was the result of the accumulation of damage on agricultural lands from 20 years of fighting and strife, and increasing pressure from the Taliban to grow opium poppies instead of food crops.

U.S. officials developed a plan that incorporated the president's guidelines and presented it to senior defense leaders on September 21. Rumsfeld approved the strategy on October 1, and the president gave his consent the following day. The original proposal was code named Operation Infinite Justice, but the name was changed to Enduring Freedom so as not to offend Muslims, since in Islam infinite justice can only come from God.

The proposed campaign emphasized the deployment of a limited number of special operations forces to bolster local anti-Taliban forces, especially the Northern Alliance. The special operations forces would provide weapons, training, and advice to the local troops. Operating in small groups, they would also provide state-of the-art communications and intelligence capabilities. Their presence would allow the outnumbered and outgunned Northern Alliance to call on precision aerial and cruise missile strikes by coalition aircraft and ships. The anti-Taliban forces would also benefit from advanced satellites, reconnaissance aircraft, and other intelligence capabilities. The U.S. strategy to limit the deployment of non-Afghan troops was part of an effort to avoid the mistakes made by the Soviets during their occupation. Specifically, U.S. planners did not want to appear to the Afghan people as conquerors or occupiers for fear that the Taliban could use nationalism to rally the people against the coalition. Instead, by having anti-Taliban Afghan forces lead the offensive, it would appear that the coalition was supporting a popular uprising against a brutal regime. The United States also sought to minimize coalition casualties and make it easier for U.S. troops to withdraw from the country once the Taliban had been dislodged from power.

The U.S. strategy involved four distinct phases. In the first phase, the coalition would launch a broad aerial campaign against the Taliban. Special operations forces were tasked to make contact with the Northern Alliance and provide weapons and training. In addition, the coalition would destroy the enemy's air units, air defenses, communications capabilities, and headquarters units. Defense officials initially estimated this phase would last one month. The second phase would be the initial ground assault led by Northern Alliance troops. The key objective was the capture of the strategic city of Mazar-e-Sharif. The third aspect of the campaign would be the capture of the major cities, including Kabul, Kandahar, and Jalalabad. The fourth and final phase of the war would consist of operations to capture, destroy, or dismantle any remaining terrorist camps or Taliban bases.

In addition to deploying U.S. and coalition special operations forces, CIA and other intelligence agency operatives were sent into Afghanistan. These intelligence officers used cash bribes, weapons, and other equipment as incentives to convince tribal leaders to side with the coalition. Several senior anti-Taliban leaders, including Rashid Dostum and Abdul Sayyaff, each were given more than $1 million personally to support the coalition. Many of these agents, and indeed, many of the special operations forces troops, arrived in Afghanistan weeks before the invasion began. Most of the work and accomplishments of the covert operatives were secret and would remain largely unknown to the American public and the rest of the world. Pentagon planners hoped that the covert operatives would be able to incite a broad anti-Taliban uprising.

NATO invoked its collective defense clause on September 12. This would have allowed the United States to make the invasion a NATO mission and increase international legitimacy. However, U.S. military planners made the strategic decision not to conduct the assault as a NATO operation. Instead, coalition forces were under U.S. command, and the United States shaped the direction and tactics of the campaign. This was done to avoid delays in decision making and troop deployment and to ensure a unity of command that would operate under U.S. leadership. Nonetheless, the United States relied on NATO and other alliance structures for support in Afghanistan and other operations that were part of Operation Enduring Freedom.

On October 8, NATO dispatched Airborne Warning and Control System (AWACS) airplanes to the United States in order to allow U.S. AWACS to be sent to Afghanistan. On October 10, a NATO naval force was stationed in the Mediterranean to conduct counterterrorism operations. The flotilla, the Standing Naval Force Mediterranean (STANAVFORMED), included nine ships from eight NATO members. This force rotated with the 11 ships of the Standing Naval Force Atlantic (STANAVFORLANT), every three months, beginning on December 6. NATO also agreed to reduce its ongoing peacekeeping missions in the Balkans in order to allow approximately 1,000 U.S. forces currently serving in the region to be sent to Afghanistan.

On November 13, NATO began to develop contingency plans to provide humanitarian assistance to the Afghan people once the Taliban were defeated. The NATO plans became the core of the subsequent UN peacekeeping effort in Afghanistan. On December 7, NATO and Russia officials met to develop new mechanisms for cooperation in the war on terror, building on U.S-Russian cooperation in counterterrorism efforts.

The Opposing Forces

The Taliban and Northern Alliance

On the eve of the invasion, the Taliban army was actually relatively small. It had about 45,000–50,000 troops and about 10,000 allied militia troops, along with 650 tanks, more than 1,000 artillery pieces, and 76 aircraft. The majority of the weapons and military equipment was old, mostly from the period of the Soviet occupation. There were also about 5,000 al Qaeda fighters and their allies. Many of the Taliban forces were deployed in the northern areas of the country where they had been fighting the Northern Alliance for the past six years. Many of the Taliban were former Mujahedeen with lengthy combat experience. There were a considerable number of Taliban and al Qaeda soldiers who were not native Afghans. This had fostered resentment among the Afghan people, especially toward the al Qaeda fighters. Nonetheless, morale among the Taliban and al Qaeda was very high. Many of the fighters believed they were about to fight a holy war against the United States. Taliban and al Qaeda leaders also maintained that the United States would suffer the same fate as the Soviet Union.

At the time of the invasion, the Northern Alliance numbered approximately 15,000 troops, but the majority of the soldiers were ill equipped and undertrained. There were also an unknown number of anti-Taliban guerillas and militias in some areas throughout the country under the control of local warlords. There was an elite group of Northern Alliance troops known as the Zarbati that numbered about 900–1,000 soldiers. The Zarbati were better armed and trained than the majority of the Northern Alliance troops and were generally used as shock troops during attacks. Like their Taliban counterparts, many of the Northern Alliance fighters were former Mujahedeen and best suited to guerilla warfare.

The relationship between the United States and the Northern Alliance turned out to be a key difference between the American invasion and the earlier Soviet occupation. By cultivating Afghan allies ahead of the military attack, the coalition ensured that it would have some support during its operations. It also secured valuable intelligence and, as noted, allowed the coalition to minimize its troop deployments.

The Coalition

Against the Taliban and al Qaeda was arrayed a considerable military force in terms of weaponry and firepower. The United States had deployed two aircraft carrier battle groups and an amphibious landing group by the end of September. Although there was a large U.S. naval and air deployment to the region to support Operation Enduring Freedom, only about 4,000 U.S. ground troops and special operations forces were sent into Afghanistan between October and December 2001. Meanwhile, the coalition naval forces numbered more than 80 ships (the majority were American).

Many allies of the United States contributed military support for Operation Enduring Freedom. Ultimately, more than 68 countries participated in Operation Enduring Freedom in one form or another. British submarines fired cruise missiles in the opening salvos of the war, and a naval task force, including an aircraft carrier, conducted operations throughout the campaign. British special operations forces, ground troops, and air units were deployed in several areas of Afghanistan. French air units flew missions from Tajikistan, and a French naval force supported operations from the Indian Ocean. France also deployed about 2,000 troops in the region. Canada also deployed air, sea, and ground units, including 2,000 troops. As a Muslim nation, Turkey's support was critical. Ankara provided extensive intelligence cooperation and supported a U.S. decision to not stop the military campaign when the Muslim holy month of Ramadan began. It also provided the main air bases for U.S. missions. Turkey sent 90 special operations forces to train the Northern Alliance. They also engaged in counterterrorism efforts. Australia deployed naval and air units and 1,560 soldiers. Other countries ranging from Belgium to Germany to Japan to New Zealand to South Korea offered various forms of military support during Operation Enduring Freedom.

A variety of non-NATO allies participated in Operation Enduring Freedom. Russia, the former Cold War enemy of the United States, supported the coalition in a variety of ways. Following negotiations between the United States and Russia, Moscow agreed to sell military equipment to anti-Taliban Afghan groups (most of the former Mujahedeen were armed with Soviet-era equipment). The United States provided the funds for the groups to buy Russian tanks, artillery, ammunition, and small arms. Russia also offered intelligence and even deployed a field hospital to Kabul to treat civilians. Russia did not initially object to the establishment of U.S. military bases in countries that were formerly part of the Soviet Union. Subsequently, the United States built bases or used existing facilities in Kyrgyzstan, Tajikistan, and Uzbekistan. The Manas Air Base in Bishkek, Kyrgyzstan, became one of the main bases for U.S. and coalition air operations against the Taliban. The coalition began using the facility in September. Eventually the United States utilized air bases in more than 40 countries to move supplies and troops or to conduct aerial attacks against the Taliban and al Qaeda.

Relations between Bush and Russian president Vladimir Putin were initially close in the aftermath of the 9/11 attacks. In October 2001 the two leaders issued a joint statement on their counterterrorism cooperation. Bush and Putin called for "a sustained global coalition to defeat international terrorism. Nations must make use of diplomatic, political, law enforcement, financial, intelligence, and military means to root out terrorists and their sponsors and bring them to justice. . . . The leaders of the two countries view U.S.-Russian cooperation as a critical effort in the global fight against terrorism."[2]

Operation Enduring Freedom

Bush demanded that the Taliban turn over bin Laden and cease support for al Qaeda. In his September 20, 2001, address to the American people, Bush issued an ultimatum to the Taliban. Bush listed a series of very specific demands on the Taliban: "Deliver to United States authorities all the leaders of al Qaeda who hide in your land. Release all foreign nationals, including American citizens, you have unjustly imprisoned. Protect foreign journalists, diplomats and aid workers in your country. Close immediately and permanently every terrorist training camp in Afghanistan, and hand over every terrorist, and every person in their support structure, to appropriate authorities. Give the United States full access to terrorist training camps, so we can make sure they are no longer operating."[3] Bush closed his ultimatum with a warning: "These demands are not open to negotiation or discussion. The Taliban must act, and act immediately. They will hand over the terrorists, or they will share in their fate."[4]

As noted in Chapter 2, the Taliban refused to turn over bin Laden, despite mediation efforts by Pakistan and other Muslim countries, and the threat of attack by the U.S.-led coalition. One argument made by the Taliban was that they had no extradition treaty with the United States. The Taliban did offer to turn over bin Laden to another Islamic country for trial, but the United States rejected their conditions as delaying tactics. The coalition initiated military operations on October 7.

The Campaign Opens

On October 7, U.S. and coalition forces launched aerial and cruise missile attacks on Afghanistan at the start of Operation Enduring Freedom. The first strike included 15 long-range bombers, 25 U.S. aircraft carrier planes, and 50 cruise missiles fired from coalition vessels. The attacks targeted the small Taliban air force, anti-aircraft installations, supply depots, and military headquarters. The strikes were the beginning of the military phase of the invasion of Afghanistan and the concurrent war on terror. The U.S.-led coalition was composed mainly of American troops, but included air, ground, and naval forces from 30 countries, including traditional U.S. allies such as Australia, France, and the United Kingdom.

In the first wave of attacks, approximately 1,000 additional coalition special operations forces soldiers were deployed to Afghanistan to operate alongside anti-Taliban forces. The majority of coalition forces were American. Coalition troops used aerial reconnaissance, unmanned drones, and airstrikes to support their Afghan allies. The U.S. military strategy was innovative and sought to take maximum advantage of American strengths, communications technology, and sophisticated weaponry, and deny the Taliban their advantages, including superior numbers and knowledge of the terrain. Consequently, U.S. planners developed tactics that emphasized U.S. communications and firepower superiority. Small, mobile special operations teams were deployed with Afghan allies. When the coalition forces encountered Taliban forces, they were able to call for massive aerial and cruise missiles attacks on those forces and pinpoint the enemy positions through Global Position System (GPS) and laser-guided technology. The "over-the-horizon" capabilities compensated for the limited artillery and tanks of the Northern Alliance. They also allowed the anti-Taliban forces to move quicker and react faster to changes on the battlefield.

The result was devastating for the Taliban, whose superiority in manpower, armor, and artillery was quickly obliterated during combat with the coalition. The Taliban attempted to fight as a conventional army, but were unable to build or create appropriate trenches, bunkers, or shelters that would shield them from air attacks. Initially, many of the Taliban forces were caught in the open field by coalition air units or artillery or missile strikes. Instead, the Taliban and their allies began to use caves or bunkers that dated from the Soviet occupation. Approximately 70 percent of the munitions used were precision guided, which increased the efficiency of the coalition strikes and minimized civilian casualties. Conventional ground troops of the coalition were deployed beginning in mid-October. By November 1, coalition air units had conducted more than 2,000 combat sorties. They had also gained complete air superiority. To ensure that air units could respond quickly, coalition planes flew to pre-designated grids to patrol. They remained in the air over the area until they were relieved by replacements or until ground units requested airstrikes. As a result, coalition ground forces could call in airstrikes at a moment's notice.

In an effort to undermine support for the Taliban and to assist the Afghan people during the combat, the coalition initiated air drops of food, medicine, and other humanitarian supplies. By November, more than 1 million ration packets had been delivered to the Afghan people. Meanwhile, the Taliban on October 10 called on Islamic nations to come to their aid to fight the United States and its allies. No countries responded to the appeal, although several thousand individual fighters and extremists traveled to Afghanistan to fight the coalition.

Coalition troops also undertook specific operations to weaken the enemy, independent of their anti-Taliban allies. For instance, on October 19, 300 U.S. Army Rangers and other special operations forces were inserted into Afghanistan and captured an airfield near Kandahar. They went on to raid the main headquarters of Taliban leader Mullah Omar. The coalition forces acquired significant intelligence about the Taliban forces and deployments. There were only minor coalition casualties. In December, about 1,300 U.S. Marines were inserted, again, near Kandahar to conduct attacks against the Taliban in the region.

The coalition endeavored to incite a popular uprising against the Taliban. Abdul Haq, a prominent anti-Taliban Pashtun leader, was sent into the southern region of the country to rally anti-Taliban factions. However, Haq was captured and killed on October 26. His loss was a major blow to the coalition, which had supported Haq as a possible post-Taliban Afghan leader.

The Breakthrough

Despite coalition advantages in air superiority and weaponry, the Northern Alliance moved slowly in the opening weeks of the campaign. Rivalry between the warlords and generals in the Northern Alliance made coordinating the movement of troops and planning attacks difficult. However, by November 2, allied airstrikes against Taliban frontline positions had devastated the defensive installations and inflicted large casualties. The success of the air campaign and the ability of the coalition special operations forces to concentrate missile and aerial bombs on enemy positions encouraged the Northern Alliance and other anti-Taliban groups. After being initially reluctant to undertake large attacks, the Northern Alliance grew bolder in their attacks. Taliban fighters began to withdraw from their positions or even deserted in the face of constant bombing campaigns. The collapse of the main Taliban lines in northern Afghanistan paved the way for the Northern Alliance to advance. In an unsuccessful effort to free up more troops to fight against the coalition, the Taliban began to move its forces from garrisons in towns and cities to the front lines. Al Qaeda and other foreign volunteers took over garrison duties. This further undermined support for the regime among the Afghan people, who resented the foreign fighters.

In the midst of the campaign, bin Laden claimed that al Qaeda had chemical and biological weapons. In addition, during the first weeks of November, the Taliban began to withdraw its forces from the front lines in the north to areas in the south and east of the country.

The first major city the coalition attacked was Mazar-e-Sharif, the main supply hub for Taliban forces in northern Afghanistan. On November 9, Mazar-e-Sharif was captured by anti-Taliban forces led by Uzbek leader Abdul Rashid Dostum, and supported by U.S. special operations forces and air units. The actual battle for the city lasted less than two hours. The fall of the town marked a turning point in the war as Taliban forces began to collapse or retreat.

Within four days, the Northern Alliance had captured Kabul after the Taliban withdrew rather than fight for the city. Kanduz was captured on November 26. Northern Alliance commanders began to allow captured Taliban fighters and their allies to return to their villages rather than keep them captive (this leniency toward prisoners of war had been common during the civil war). U.S. commanders attempted to prevent the practice because they wanted to interrogate prisoners and for fear that the former Taliban would fight again in the future. Nevertheless, the practice continued.

The main base of support for the Taliban was in the southeast of the country, centered on the city of Kandahar. Anti-Taliban Pashtun militias advanced on Kandahar from the north, and other allied militias under Gul Agha Shirzai fought their way from the south so that Kandahar was surrounded on three sides by the first week of December. On December 9, Kandahar surrendered after negotiations with the anti-Taliban Pashtun leaders. However, bin Laden and Taliban leader Mullah Omar remained at large. Many of the Taliban escaped to the remote northwest areas of Pakistan. As the Northern Alliance advanced, they were hailed in many villages and towns as liberators from the harsh Taliban regime. However, in some areas, ethnic tensions between Pashtuns and Uzbek or Tajik members of the Northern Alliance muted any potential victory celebrations. Some villagers hid former Taliban fighters and officials as the coalition moved into areas with large Pashtun populations. Despite the success of the allied advance, a large number of former Taliban fighters had returned to their villages and towns, creating a large population of former warriors who could potentially rise up against the post-Taliban government.

After the fall of Kandahar, the fourth and last phase of the initial invasion commenced. Coalition forces began to seek out al Qaeda and Taliban bases to destroy the facilities and any remaining weapons or supplies.

Tora Bora

The last major combat of the invasion was a coalition operation designed to capture bin Laden. Coalition air and ground units, supported by anti-Taliban militia, attacked the main al Qaeda headquarters at Tora Bora in the northeast of the country. Bin Laden and other senior al Qaeda leaders were thought to be at the site, and coalition officials believed that the terrorist group would make a last stand at their headquarters. The base consisted of a series of cave complexes in a mountainous region near the border with Pakistan. It had originally been constructed during the Soviet occupation and then repeatedly enlarged in the 1990s after al Qaeda was allowed to take over the facilities. The al Qaeda force numbered somewhere between 1,000 and 1,500 fighters. The attacking coalition forces included about 100 American, British and German special operations forces, and about 2,000 Northern Alliance and anti-Taliban militia troops, supported by a large number of helicopters and aircraft.

The offensive began on December 2, as coalition special operations forces units were inserted near Tora Bora and began reconnaissance operations. The main assault got underway on December 12. The fighting was marked by intense combat as the coalition forces had to fight cave by cave to dislodge the al Qaeda fighters. By December 17, the coalition had control over the complex. The Northern Alliance and anti-Taliban militia led the attack. Although coalition forces captured the area and killed approximately 400–600 Taliban and al Qaeda fighters, bin Laden and several hundred supporters escaped into Pakistan, where they continued operations. Coalition officers were criticized for not encircling Tora Bora to prevent the escape of any of the al Qaeda fighters and for using local fighters instead of U.S. troops for the assault. Coalition leaders countered that they mistakenly believed that Pakistan was going to do a better job of sealing their border with troops to prevent the crossover of any fighters.

Casualties

From October 2001 through January 2002, the United States lost 56 service members killed in Afghanistan and about 200 wounded. The Northern Alliance had approximately 600 killed and about 1,200 injured. There were approximately 4,000 Taliban dead, with an unknown number wounded. Between 600 and 800 al Qaeda fighters were killed. More than 7,000 Taliban and al Qaeda fighters were taken prisoner. Finally, some 1,300 Afghan civilians were killed during the fighting. A large number of Taliban and al Qaeda leaders were able to cross the border into remote areas of Pakistan, where they continued operations against the coalition and the new Afghan government.

Coalition Operations 2002–2004

After the battle of Tora Bora, coalition military planners undertook a wide effort to identify any remaining Taliban or al Qaeda bases in Afghanistan. The harsh Afghan winter prevented any major operations, but coalition air and intelligence units undertook repeated reconnaissance missions.

The Taliban and al Qaeda increasingly used terrorist tactics, including suicide attacks, assassinations, and strikes against civilians and government officials. For instance, on February 14, 2002, al Qaeda operatives assassinated Abdul Rahman, the new minister of culture and tourism, at the Kabul Airport.

The coalition was able to identify a large Taliban enclave in the Shah-i-Kot Valley in the southeast of Afghanistan. The mountainous region had been a Mujahedeen base during the Soviet occupation, and after the fall of the Taliban a significant number of fighters had retreated to the area and enlarged the existing network of caves and underground bunkers. By the spring of 2002, there were approximately 2,000 Taliban and al Qaeda fighters in the area. To defeat the force, the coalition deployed a force that included about 1,500 Afghan militiamen, 1,000 U.S. troops, and 200 special operations soldiers from a variety of countries ranging from Australia to Canada to Norway. The special operations troops operated in small teams to identify the enemy emplacements and then called in coalition air strikes or artillery. The campaign began on March 2, 2002, and was dubbed Operation Anaconda.

The firepower unleashed on the Taliban was immense. More than 3,500 bombs were dropped over a two-week period. Fifteen coalition soldiers were killed in the fighting, including eight Americans. Approximately 340 Taliban and al Qaeda fighters were also killed. However, communications problems among the coalition forces meant that, once again, the majority of the enemy soldiers were able to escape and make their way to Pakistan, where they joined with other Taliban forces. After Operation Anaconda, estimates were that only about 1,000 Taliban or al Qaeda fighters remained in Afghanistan, although more than 4,000 were in Pakistan.

In order to kill or capture the remaining enemy forces, the coalition carried out a series of smaller operations through the spring and summer of 2002. In addition to American ground troops, soldiers from Australia and the United Kingdom took the lead in anti-Taliban missions. The coalition forces were able to capture large weapons supplies and kill or capture more than 400 Taliban fighters and their allies.

Meanwhile, the Taliban and al Qaeda began to launch attacks on coalition and Afghan national troops in the summer of 2002. The Taliban and their allies resorted to the tactics that the Mujahedeen had employed during the Soviet occupation. Small bands of fighters, numbering between 10 and 50, attacked coalition and government outposts, convoys, and patrols. Often they would fire mortars or rockets at bases, and then withdraw before they could be targeted by the coalition. As the summer drew to a close, the majority of the Taliban and their allies withdrew across the border into Pakistan, where they remained through the winter.

In an effort to improve security around the country and to expand the authority of the Hamid Karzai government, the coalition began to deploy Provincial Reconstruction Teams (PRT) around Afghanistan in 2002. The PRTs were tasked to improve the security, infrastructure, and stability of regions. They were well funded and had the authority to spend money on a range of projects. Funding for the PRTs came from the U.S. State Department and other foreign donors. The teams consisted of 100–200 members, including both military and civilian personnel. They consist of combat troops, engineers, medical officers, agricultural experts, and so forth. The first PRT was deployed to Gardez in the Paktia Province. It consisted of U.S. troops and a small number of civilians. The PRT coordinated the rebuilding of schools, government buildings, clinics, and roadways. Despite their humanitarian efforts, as more of the PRTs were deployed, they increasingly became the target of attacks by the Taliban and al Qaeda. Eventually, other coalition partners, besides the United States, took the lead of other PRTs.

In the spring of 2003, Taliban teams again infiltrated Afghanistan to undertake attacks against the coalition and Afghan government. A growing number of their fighters were foreign, as more Pakistanis and other foreign-born Muslims travelled to the region to fight, just as they had during the Soviet occupation. The coalition responded with targeted operations against suspected Taliban bases or hide-outs. Many Afghans opposed the harsh nature of the Taliban regime, and the coalition generally received productive intelligence from local sources. In addition, Khalid Sheikh Mohammad was captured in Pakistan in March (see Chapter 4). The coalition used information gained from Mohammad to identify and capture a large number of weapons stores and Taliban bases, including several facilities the Taliban had secretly established near coalition sites.

Coalition military activity increased dramatically prior to the invasion of Iraq that began on March 19, 2003 (see Chapter 7). Some American military units were moved from Afghanistan to the fighting in Iraq, and the coalition wanted to keep the Taliban and al Qaeda off balance through continued attacks. U.S. troops and Afghan soldiers undertook a major campaign, Operation Mountain Viper, in September 2003. The offensive was directed against forces loyal to warlord Gulbuddin Hekmatyar, a former anti-Taliban general who switched sides after feuding with the post-Taliban interim government and emerged as the leader of an Afghan terrorist group, Hezb-e-Islami. In July, Hekmatyar even backed an unsuccessful assassination attempt against President Karzai.

Hekmatyar's defection was the most significant in a growing trend whereby a growing number of warlords and tribal leaders abandoned the new Afghan government and joined the Taliban. This trend accelerated as the government and coalition began an initiative to suppress the drug trade, thereby threatening the main source of income for many of the warlords.

The coalition launched a preemptive strike, Operation Mountain Blizzard, in January 2004 in the midst of the winter. Coalition planners hoped to catch the Taliban and their allies unprepared and disrupt the pattern whereby the insurgents would recuperate and rearm during the winter and attack in the spring. The effort led to the destruction of large stores of weapons and ammunition. Intelligence from the offensive led to Operation Mountain Storm, the largest coalition campaign since the initial invasion. Mountain Storm began in March and involved more than 13,000 coalition and Afghan troops. The attack coincided with a parallel campaign by the Pakistani military to destroy Taliban bases in that country. The effort was also undertaken in an effort to minimize attacks and to provide stability ahead of planned elections in Afghanistan in the fall of 2004.

By 2004, the fighting in Afghanistan had increasingly become an insurgency. The Taliban and al Qaeda were engaged in a guerilla campaign that mirrored the earlier anti-Soviet struggle. They also adopted tactics that were used by the ongoing insurgency in Iraq, including the use of homemade or improvised explosive devices and roadside bombs. Throughout this period, the coalition and the small Afghan Army lacked an adequate number of troops to fully secure the country's borders or to suppress warlords and tribal chieftains that opposed the central government. Nonetheless, coalition forces grew steadily. There were approximately 9,700 U.S. troops in Afghanistan by the end of 2002. There were another 2,650 support personnel deployed in the region (including other counterterrorism operations that were part of Operation Enduring Freedom). That number increased to 13,100 U.S. service personnel in Afghanistan, supported by 9,400 other military troops in the region or engaged in Operation Enduring Freedom missions elsewhere in 2003. By 2004, 18,300 U.S. service members were in the country in 2004, with 1,100 support personnel.

The Post-Taliban Government

As Pentagon officials planned the military invasion, U.S. diplomats endeavored to craft an Afghan political coalition to rule after the fall of the Taliban. After the death of Haq, the anti-Taliban Pashtun leader, the United States turned to another moderate Pashtun figure, Hamid Karzai. Karzai was from the Kandahar region and was generally well respected among Pashtuns. The United States sought a Pashtun leader to organize a post-Taliban government because Washington was afraid that a government dominated by the Northern Alliance would alienate the Pashtun majority and lead to another civil war.

After the fall of Kabul in November, a conference of anti-Taliban leaders met in Bonn, Germany, under the auspices of the United Nations. The Bonn Conference was sponsored by the coalition, but every effort was made to ensure that Afghans controlled the event so that whatever post-Taliban arrangements were made, they would enjoy broad popular support. The conference was led by former Afghan king Zahir Shah, who had been deposed in the 1970s. The king remained a popular and well-respected figure to many Afghans. The meeting included representatives from the Northern Alliance, the Peshawar Group (anti-Taliban Afghan Pashtuns who were in exile in Pakistan), the pro-monarchy Rome Group (supporters of the former king), and pro-Iranian Shiite Hazaras.

At the meeting, Karzai was chosen as the interim leader of Afghanistan with U.S. support. The factions also accepted the deployment of a UN peacekeeping force to help stabilize the country. The UN force would operate concurrently with U.S.-led forces. The attendees endorsed a plan whereby the post-Taliban government would be based loosely on the 1964 constitution and would represent all factions of Afghan society.

On December 22, Karzai was inaugurated as leader of a 30-member coalition government. Anti-Taliban Uzbek leader Rashid Dostum initially threatened to boycott the government. The general argued that the new government did not adequately represent the country's diverse ethnic groups. Dostum specifically wanted a larger number of Uzbeks and Tajiks in the government. Dostum was appointed defense minister and a deputy chair of the administration on December 26, and he subsequently endorsed the government.

The Interim Government

In June 2002, a Loya Jirga (a grand meeting of tribal elders, clerics, and other political and social leaders) was convened to create a new transitional government. The new government had a two-year mandate while a new constitution was created and adopted. Karzai was elected president of the transitional government with

80 percent of the vote of the delegates after all of the other leading candidates withdrew in a show of support for the interim leader. The Loya Jirga was also supposed to create an interim legislature, but the attendees were unable to agree on the design or composition of the assembly.

The interim government faced a range of challenges. The rising insurgency created an increasing number of Afghan refugees. By January 2003, human rights groups estimated there were 4 million displaced Afghans. In February, the United Nations issued a report that Afghanistan remained the world's leading producer of opium despite the fall of the Taliban. Regional warlords were increasingly active in cultivating poppies and worked with the Taliban on the drug trade.

During the spring of 2003, the Taliban launched an increasing number of attacks on coalition forces. They also expanded their numbers through recruiting drives among the Pashtun population in Afghanistan. Meanwhile, more and more foreign fighters, especially Pakistanis, joined the insurgency. They stop using large formations or groupings and instead deployed bands of 40–50 fighters to engage in guerilla warfare against the coalition and government targets through ambushes or attacks on outposts and patrols. Concurrently, a rising number of civilian deaths were attributable to coalition airstrikes, undermining efforts to win the hearts and minds of the population. The increase in violence prompted the United Nations to suspend its demining program in 10 provinces in May, although the world body resumed its program in July. Attacks against the government and coalition expanded through the summer. For instance, al Qaeda terrorists detonated a bomb outside the U.S. consulate in Karachi on June 14, killing 11 people. On July 6, Afghan vice president Haji Abdul Qadir was killed by gunmen believed to be affiliated with al Qaeda.

Karzai appointed a 33-member group in April to draft the new constitution. The group completed its work in November. On December 14, a new Loya Jirga began deliberations over the proposed constitution. Former Afghan president Sebghatul-lah Mojaddedi was elected chair of the conference.

The constitutional Loya Jirga approved a new constitution on January 4, 2004. The 160 articles of the constitution created an executive branch led by the president, a bicameral legislature, and a judicial system with a supreme court. The lower house of the legislature was the 250-member Wolessi Jirga (House of the People), and the upper house was the 102-member Meshranao Jirga (House of Elders). The lower house was directly elected, while one-third of the upper house was chosen by district councils, one-third by provincial councils, and the final third by the president. Islam was proclaimed as the state religion, but civil law governs the land. Individual liberties, including the rights to life, liberty, and freedom of expression, are guaranteed. The constitution divided the country into 34 provinces, split into smaller districts with elected bodies. One of several controversial provisions granted the power to appoint provincial governors to the president. Critics charged that Karzai used this authority to reward warlords and other supporters. Karzai signed the constitution on January 26.

Elections and the New Government

After decades of strife and conflict, the Afghan economy was devastated. Karzai and other Afghan leaders sought substantial aid and assistance from the United States and other Western nations. An international conference of donor states pledged $8.2 billion in reconstruction assistance for Afghanistan in April 2004. The summit also endorsed an economic plan developed by the Karzai government which emphasized improvements in tax collections and infrastructure projects. However, the scale and complexity of the reconstruction effort, combined with the dangers of the ongoing insurgency, made development progress difficult.

Meanwhile, in preparation for elections scheduled for the fall, on August 20, 2004, a yearlong, nationwide voter registration drive was completed. More than 10.6 million were registered to vote amid Taliban and al Qaeda attacks that left 12 election workers dead. The Taliban had pledged to disrupt the elections in an effort to undermine the government.

In elections on October 9, 2004, Hamid Karzai was elected president of Afghanistan with 55.4 percent of the vote against more than a dozen other candidates. The balloting marked the first time that Afghanistan elected its national leader. The Taliban threatened to disrupt the balloting, but there were only minor incidents. With an estimated voter turnout of 70 percent, the election was seen as a major accomplishment in the country's efforts to become democratic. Karzai was inaugurated on December 7, and he appointed a new cabinet on December 23. Ahmad Zia Masoud, an ethnic Tajik, and Mohammad Karim Khalili, a Hazara, became vice presidents. The newly elected president asserted that the government's main priorities were to improve the economy and enhance security. In his inauguration speech, Karzai stressed that the government and its coalition allies continued to face significant threats. The president declared, "Our fight against terrorism is not yet over," and that "the relationship between terrorism and narcotics and the continued threat of extremism in the world at large are a source of continued concern."[5] Karzai pledged to take action against the opium poppy producers who had become the main source of money for the Taliban and other anti-government insurgents.

Warlords and Corruption

The Karzai government suffered from several weaknesses. First, and foremost, since the central government did not have enough troops or security forces to patrol the entire country, Karzai had to rely on alliances with local warlords. These tribal and ethnic leaders exercised informal control over large areas of

Afghanistan. When Karzai endeavored to bring the warlords under his control, he received no support from the United States, which sought to avoid the impression that it favored one faction over another. The result was that the Afghan president's political authority was undermined. The brutality and corruption of the warlords also eroded public support for the central government since people associated the excesses of the leaders with Karzai and his administration. Matters were made worse as warlords sometimes used the coalition to attack rivals or rebellious villages. It was not uncommon for some warlords to report that their rivals were Taliban in hopes of eliciting coalition military action against those enemies.

At the same time, the Karzai regime itself was riddled with corruption. Less than half of the foreign aid that initially flowed into Afghanistan was actually spent on projects or distributed to the Afghan people. The rest disappeared in the form of bribes, graft, or cost overruns. The high level of corruption further reduced the Afghan people's confidence in the central government.

The International Security Assistance Force

After the Bonn Conference, the United Nations adopted Resolution 1386 on December 20 which formally endorsed the peacekeeping force in Afghanistan, the International Security Assistance Force (ISAF). The United States heartily supported the creation of ISAF. American military commanders wanted to concentrate on combat missions and allow the Europeans and other countries that had more experience in humanitarian operations to lead the peacekeeping mission. Several nations in Europe, including the British and French, had long experience with peacekeeping operations in the Balkans and Africa. U.S. defense officials also hoped that ISAF would grow large enough that American troops could be withdrawn and the burden of security could be ultimately transferred to the international peacekeeping force.

ISAF was initially deployed to undertake humanitarian operations and provide general security in the country while coalition forces led by the United States continued anti-Taliban and al Qaeda military missions. The United States would retain overall command of both the coalition's anti-Taliban and anti-al Qaeda operations to ensure that the two missions did not undertake operations in the same area or duplicate efforts. This division of labor created some controversy between the United States and the United Kingdom on one hand, and Germany and France on the other. The French and Germans sought to have the ISAF mission completely independent. They asserted that combining the two would undermine peace-building efforts by ISAF. Despite objections, the original proposal was implemented and the United States oversaw both the combat and peacekeeping operations in Afghanistan.

The UN force was originally authorized to consist of 6,000 troops, but the number grew over time, and was led by the United Kingdom for its initial three months; thereafter, lead countries rotated every six months, beginning with Turkey, then transitioning to Germany, and so forth. ISAF initially included troops from the United Kingdom, Austria, Belgium, Denmark, Finland, France, Germany, Greece, Italy, the Netherlands, New Zealand, Norway, Portugal, Romania, Spain, Sweden, and Turkey. The majority of the troops were initially from the United Kingdom, with 1,800; followed by Germany, with 800; and France, with 550; the other contributors deployed smaller forces. The small overall size of ISAF and the often small individual country contributions were the result of reluctance by contributing nations to have large numbers of troops stationed in Afghanistan since they were fearful of casualties.

The first members of ISAF began to arrive in Afghanistan in January 2002. In May, their mandate was extended. By year's end, ISAF numbered 4,500 troops from 19 countries. Meanwhile, the United States had approximately 7,000 troops in Afghanistan undertaking anti-insurgency operations.

ISAF was headquartered in Kabul and at first concentrated on providing security for the capital and the new Karzai government. The troops also undertook engineering projects such as road and bridge repair and construction, building repair or construction, and providing humanitarian aid and medical assistance. To facilitate these types of operations, about half of the initial troops in ISAF were engineering, logistics, or medical personnel. ISAF troops also began training a new national army for Afghanistan.

The United Nations voted in October 2002 to expand ISAF's mission outside of Kabul province. The international force subsequently began to slowly deploy missions to other provinces around the country. The United Nations also repeatedly extended ISAF's mandate, including a 2010 resolution that extended the mission through 2011.

The NATO Mission

By mid-2002, ISAF faced increasing difficulty in convincing nations to take on the lead role of commanding the UN force. As a result, negotiations began between the United Nations and NATO, over the alliance taking command of the mission. Most of the nations participating in ISAF were members of the alliance and NATO agreed to accept the responsibility of the mission. On August 11, 2003, NATO assumed command of ISAF, but the mission continued to operate under the auspices of the United Nations. In October 2003, the UN Security Council, through Resolution 1510, expanded ISAF's area of responsibility outside of Kabul. NATO agreed that ISAF would eventually expand to provide security for all of Afghanistan, but it planned its expansion in stages. ISAF initially expanded from Kabul into the relatively peaceful areas of northern Afghanistan. By 2004, it was active in nine provinces in the north. The slow pace of ISAF expansion would later be criticized for allowing the Taliban and other anti-militia forces to regroup and reestablish presences in provinces throughout the country. However, the main constraint of ISAF was a lack of troops. The force was completely dependent on voluntary deployments of troops by individual countries. Many of the NATO members found their militaries overstretched, especially since several NATO partners had troops operating with ISAF and with the U.S.-led coalition forces in Afghanistan, while after the start of the 2003 Iraq War, they also had deployments in Iraq.

Through the remainder of 2003 and into 2004, NATO took command of the existing PRTs and began to deploy additional teams. PRTs became increasingly active in training local police forces. They also worked to support local government officials and increase the legitimacy and popularity of the Karzai government. Through the PRTs and joint Afghan-coalition initiatives, new public services and infrastructure were available, ranging from roads to schools to electricity to medical care. However, the limited number of PRTs constrained the program's ability to make significant changes throughout the country. NATO would spend the next several years expanding the number and geographic range of the PRTs in an effort to maintain the support of the Afghan population in the face of an increasing insurgency by the Taliban, al Qaeda, and local warlords.

Conclusion

Operation Enduring Freedom brought together military units from around the globe to fight the Taliban and al Qaeda. The campaign highlighted the technological and firepower superiority of the U.S.-led forces. Its unorthodox reliance on existing anti-Taliban factions in Afghanistan minimized the deployment of U.S. and coalition troops. It also ended in a quick victory for the United States in the aftermath of the 9/11 attacks. Operation Enduring Freedom accomplished several of the objectives identified by Bush prior to the invasion. The invasion removed the Taliban regime from power in Afghanistan and installed the first democratically elected government in Afghanistan's long, troubled history. The military campaign dismantled al Qaeda's network of terrorist training camps and facilities with minimal coalition casualties. The invasion also expanded the amount of humanitarian aid and assistance available to Afghanistan's desperate population. While the operation destroyed existing terrorist bases, a large number of Taliban and al Qaeda were able to cross the border into Pakistan and establish new centers of operations. From these bases, the Taliban and al Qaeda launched an insurgency against the Karzai government and the coalition, using the tactics and techniques that had been utilized by the Mujahedeen. Al Qaeda also continued to launch attacks against the United States and Western targets throughout the world. As the United States was preparing for the invasion of Iraq, the insurgency expanded throughout the country, leading the United States and its allies to deploy an increasing number of troops in the country (see Chapter 8).

Notes

1. United Nations, Office of the United Nations Coordinator for Afghanistan, "The Deepening Crisis in Afghanistan: Update on the Plans and Needs of the Assistance Community to Respond to Drought, Conflict and Displacement in Afghanistan," August (New York: United Nations, 2001).

2. White House, Office of the Press Secretary, "Joint Statement on Counterterrorism by the President of the United States and the President of Russia," Shanghai, China, October 21, 2001.

3. George W. Bush, "Address to the Nation," September 20, 2001.

4. Bush, "Address to the Nation," 2001.

5. John Lancaster, "At Inauguration, Karzai Vows Action on Tough Issues," *Washington Post*, December 8, 2004, p. A13.

4

Civil Liberties and the War on Terror

The 9/11 terrorist attacks demonstrated the potential for terrorists to use the openness and freedom of American society to conduct strikes against the country. In the immediate aftermath of 9/11, many Americans called for increased security to prevent future attacks. The government quickly acted to increase precautions and security in a range of areas. However, the government's efforts were criticized on two very different grounds. Some argued that the United States was not doing enough to protect its citizens, borders, and critical infrastructure such as utility or transport systems. Proponents of this view asserted that the United States needed to devote more resources to homeland security. At the same time, others argued that government actions increasingly infringed on the individual rights and civil liberties of Americans. This group contended that the actions of the administration of President George W. Bush endangered the very foundations of U.S. political culture and would, ironically, result in a terrorist victory because their attack caused the United States to become a very different country. However, the trend whereby personal freedoms were eroded in exchange for greater societal safety was not a new dynamic in the United States. Often when the country faced significant internal or external threats, the government had suspended some civil rights. Terrorist attacks prior to the 9/11 strikes had already led to new laws, regulations, and restrictions, and the 9/11 attacks accelerated this trend.

Terrorism and Civil Liberties

Civil liberties are the basic rights that protect individuals or groups from government persecution. These freedoms place limitations on what governments can do to individuals. In the United States, a variety of civil liberties are enshrined in the Constitution, the nation's basic law. Among well-known civil liberties are the rights to privacy, freedom of speech, a fair and speedy trial, equality before the law, and freedom from unreasonable search or seizure.

During periods of extreme national danger, some civil liberties have been suspended. Political leaders, the courts, and other sections of U.S. society have generally accepted limitations on civil liberties in exchange for greater security during times of war or conflict. However, in retrospect, many of the instances in which curtailments of civil liberties were undertaken were overreactions to potential threats and did not significantly enhance U.S. domestic security. For instance, in April 1861, President Abraham Lincoln suspended the right of habeas corpus (Latin for "you have the body"). Habeas corpus is a court order or writ by which a judicial body can force officials to bring a person before the court to determine whether or not that person is being held lawfully. Courts, individuals, or other parties may file writs of habeas corpus to challenge someone's detention. Lincoln's suspension of the right meant that the government could arrest and detain people without judicial recourse. During World War I, the government placed severe limitations on freedom of speech and freedom of the press, including restrictions on the right to criticize government actions as a result of the Espionage Act (1917) and the Sedition Act (1918). The Sedition Act specifically forbade "unloyal" language or speech directed at the United States. Through the acts, more than 2,000 aliens were deported because of ties to the United States' enemies during World War I or due to anti-government actions or speech. The laws were also the basis for a series of raids against suspects known as the Palmer Raids (after then–Attorney General Alexander Palmer). On January 2, 1920, more than 6,000 people were arrested across the United States in a coordinated, nationwide campaign to detain people who were suspected of anti-government activities.

On the eve of World War II in 1940, the government enacted the Alien Registration Act (commonly known as the Smith Act for Congressman Howard Smith, one of its authors). This law forbade anyone from engaging in efforts or participating in groups that advocated the overthrow of the U.S. government, including developing or distributing materials that were seditious. The Smith Act was used as the basis for the internment of more than 120,000 Japanese Americans on the West Coast of the United States. President Franklin D. Roosevelt authorized the imprisonment in February 1942, following the Japanese attack on Pearl Harbor on December 7, 1941. The Japanese Americans were detained during a period of hysteria and extreme xenophobia that followed the surprise attack in Hawaii that killed more than 2,400 U.S. service members and civilians. The internment was challenged in court, but in the case *Korematsu v. United States* (1944), the Supreme Court ruled that the government had the authority to take such actions to protect the homeland. In the 1980s, the government apologized for its actions and paid reparations to those detained or their families.

The Smith Act and other legislation was also utilized in the 1950s to arrest communists and other suspected subversives during a period of extreme anti-communism at the dawn of the Cold War. However, from the 1950s through the 1980s, a series of civil rights measures and Supreme Court decisions reduced the power of the government. For instance, in 1957, in the Supreme Court case *Yates v. United States*, the justices ruled that the First Amendment did not allow the government to criminalize political ideas, only actions that were based on those ideas. Consequently, the government could not prosecute someone for simply belonging to a group such as the Communist Party, but only if that person engaged in illegal activities or called for people to undertake illicit actions. In *Brandenburg v. Ohio* (1969), the court ruled that the Smith Act and similar sedition measures were unconstitutional. Later, the Civil Liberties Act of 1988 was the vehicle for the formal apology to Japanese Americans for the World War II internment program, and it contained measures to prevent similar large-scale internments in the future.

In addition, a succession of court cases expanded the civil liberties of those detained for both political and non-political crimes. For example, in 1963, in *Gideon v. Wainwright*, the courts ruled that everyone had the right to a lawyer in criminal cases. As a result, the poor or indigent could have a court-appointed attorney if they could not otherwise afford counsel. One of several other milestone cases was the 1966 *Miranda v. Arizona* decision, in which the Supreme Court held that police must inform suspects of their constitutional rights before interrogating them.

By the late 1970s, there was a well-established constitutional and legal framework to protect civil liberties. However, the rise in terrorism led the government to enact a series of laws designed to better protect Americans. Civil libertarian groups, including the American Civil Liberties Union (ACLU), were critical of aspects of many of these measures, arguing that efforts to increase security had the unintended consequence of reducing the civil liberties of individuals and groups.

Counterterrorism Measures prior to 9/11

Prior to the 9/11 attacks, some civil libertarians already criticized a succession of laws and policies that were enacted during the period between 1970 and 2001. After the 1973 Munich Massacre, the United States began installing metal detectors and X-ray machines to scan passengers and baggage before they boarded airplanes. Initially, some objected to the baggage screenings as a violation of privacy, but the procedure became routine and accepted by the overwhelming majority of Americans. In May 1980, the Federal Bureau of Investigation (FBI) created the nation's first counterterrorism task force in New York City in response to both domestic and international terrorism. Other actions and measures were more controversial.

In 1992, federal agents went to serve an arrest warrant on Randy Weaver, an anti-government extremist, who had refused to participate in a trial where he was charged with the illegal possession of weapons. During the incident at Ruby Ridge, Idaho, federal marksmen shot Weaver, and killed his wife and 13-year-old son. Subsequent investigations were highly critical of the federal agencies involved, including the Bureau of Alcohol, Tobacco, and Firearms (ATF), the FBI, and the U.S. Marshal Service, for violating the civil liberties of Weaver and his family and for using excessive deadly force. More than a dozen federal agents were punished for their actions. The following year, federal agencies were again criticized for excessive force during a stand-off at a compound in Waco, Texas, with a fringe religious group, the Branch Davidians, led by David Koresh. On April 19, Koresh and 74 of his followers, including 25 children, died in a fire that erupted when FBI agents attempted to storm the compound. These two incidents fueled anti-government sentiment in the United States and led to an increase in the militia movement, a far-right extremist movement known for its belief that the federal government had become too powerful. The events led the federal government to standardize rules about the use of deadly force.

Meanwhile, in 1995, President Clinton signed an executive order authorizing rendition (the non-judicial transfer of a suspect from one country to another). The practice bypassed the U.S. legal system and allowed the United States to move suspected foreign terrorists or other criminals without court approval. The practice was most commonly used to avoid the public disclosure of the capture of a suspect, and thereby avoid alerting terrorist networks that they have been compromised. Critics charged that the practice was also used to allow the torture of suspects by means that would not be permitted under U.S. law. Suspected terrorists captured by the United States were turned over to countries such as Saudi Arabia, which tortured the individuals to obtain information which was then passed on to U.S. intelligence services.

Oklahoma City Bombing

A domestic terrorist attack in 1995 dramatically altered U.S. domestic counter-terrorism efforts. On April 19 of that year, Timothy McVeigh and Terry Nichols, American right-wing militia extremists, used a truck bomb, loaded with explosives and fertilizer, to destroy most of the Alfred P. Murrah Federal Building in Oklahoma City, killing 168 and injuring more than 680, in the worst domestic terrorist attack in U.S. history. The attack became known as the Oklahoma City Bombing. The two conspirators acted because they were angered by what they perceived to be the excessive power of the federal government following the Ruby Ridge and Branch Davidian incidents. Both Nichols and McVeigh were apprehended and tried for their crimes. Nichols was sentenced to life in prison for his role in the attack, and McVeigh was executed in June 2001.

The attacks shocked the nation. Many initially believed that the strikes were perpetrated by a foreign terrorist group because they could not believe Americans could do this to their fellow citizens. In addressing the American people on the day of the bombing, Clinton strongly condemned the attacks. He declared that "the bombing in Oklahoma City was an attack on innocent children and defenseless citizens. It was an act of cowardice, and it was evil. The United States will not tolerate it. And I will not allow the people of this country to be intimidated by evil cowards."[1] This theme that terrorists were "evil" and were "cowards" would be repeated by Clinton in remarks following other terrorist incidents and would later be used by Bush in framing the war on terror.

Days after the attacks, the Clinton administration launched a $1.5 billion anti-terrorism initiative that included new resources for domestic law enforcement to carry out counterterrorism operations. The FBI was also granted increased surveillance powers to monitor suspected terrorists. On April 24, 1996, Clinton signed into law the Antiterrorism and Effective Death Penalty Act. The measure was initiated because of the Oklahoma City Bombing, but many of the aspects of the law also dealt with foreign terrorism. The law limited the appeals process for some capital convictions in the United States, making it easier to put to death convicted terrorists. It also expanded the ability of U.S. citizens to sue foreign governments that supported terrorism, and gave the federal government new powers to restrict terrorists' access to funding sources and weapons and materials. Specifically, the government now had the authority to criminalize specific groups by labeling them as "Foreign Terrorist Organizations." The new measure also made it easier to deport or extradite suspected terrorists by creating a special court that was able to use secret evidence against those suspected of ties to terrorism. Finally, potential immigrants with links to terrorist groups were forbidden entry into the United States.

During the debate over passage of the act, the Clinton administration sought more sweeping security powers, including an expansion of the government's power to monitor telephone conversations of suspected terrorists. The government also asked Congress to expand the statue of limitations on terrorism cases and grant it greater access to hotel records.[2]

Civil libertarians were highly critical of the limitations placed on the appeals process for cases involving the death penalty. The law, along with a 1995 Supreme Court decision, limited the ability of those convicted to request a habeas corpus review of their conviction, and mandated that this habeas corpus review had to be filed within a year of the final appeal of the original conviction. The law also forced federal courts to accept habeas corpus decisions by state courts. In the past, the federal judicial system had served as an additional step to review decisions for mistakes or errors. Despite criticisms, the Supreme Court subsequently upheld the new provisions of the law.

Federal Counterterrorism Efforts

In the years after the Oklahoma City Bombing, new terrorist attacks were undertaken on U.S. targets overseas, including the 1996 Khobar Towers Bombing and the 1998 Embassy Bombings (see Chapter 1). In response, the Clinton administration endeavored to increase U.S. counterterrorism capabilities. The list of organizations that the United States recognized as terrorist groups was expanded. The FBI's counterterrorism budget was doubled by 2000, and the number of agents assigned to counterterrorism was increased by more than 800, including the assignment of more than 130 agents to overseas posts. The number of FBI overseas offices was doubled from 22 to 44, with new offices in areas such as Egypt, Israel, and Pakistan. By the time Clinton left office in 2001, counterterrorism spending in the United States had increased 205 percent since he began his presidency in 1993.

In June 1995, Clinton issued a secret order (Presidential Decision Direction 39 or PDD 39) which laid out U.S. counterterrorism strategy. It declared that the United States would not negotiate with terrorists, and designated the State Department as the lead agency to respond to international terrorism and the FBI as the lead for domestic counterterrorism efforts. The directive also called for increased cooperation and collaboration among domestic law enforcement and the nation's intelligence agencies. The document promised that the administration would seek greater power to develop effective counterterrorism programs. The document states, "Within the United States, we shall vigorously apply U.S. laws and seek new legislation to prevent terrorist groups from operating in the United States or using it as a base for recruitment, training, fund raising or other related activities."[3] The 1996 antiterrorism measure was a manifestation of this effort. Nonetheless, U.S. counterterrorism efforts continued to be hampered by a lack of resources and a failure to coordinate efforts and intelligence across agencies. Clinton would follow PDD 39 with PDD 62, which reinforced the call for increase cooperation between federal agencies to suppress terrorism. However, like the previous directive, the order did not substantially increase collaboration among the different federal intelligence and law enforcement bodies.

In reaction to the foreign attacks, in January 1999, the U.S. issued a comprehensive indictment of bin Laden and other senior al Qaeda leaders for their roles in the 1998 Embassy Bombings and other terrorist attacks. The following year, al Qaeda was added to the list of foreign terrorist organizations, while three groups were eliminated. The new list totaled 28 groups at that time.

9/11 and Civil Liberties

The 9/11 attacks led to dramatic reassessments of many aspects of U.S. security and law enforcement. The ease with which the al Qaeda terrorists were able to enter the United States, receive pilot training, and then board and take over the four aircraft resulted in calls for increased border security and enhanced airlines screenings. Concurrently, law enforcement agencies and intelligence services launched a massive investigation to ensure that additional al Qaeda attacks would not occur. The 2001 anthrax attacks and the failed Shoe Bomber (see Chapter 2) further bolstered public and congressional calls for enhanced domestic security.

Public Attitudes

In the aftermath of the attacks, the public demanded the government take greater action to secure the homeland from terrorist attacks. Public opinion polls after the strikes showed that Americans believed that the government could have done more to prevent the attacks. An ABC News poll taken two days after 9/11 found that 65 percent of the people thought the government should have taken more steps to stop the terrorists.[4] In addition, many Americans were initially willing to accept intrusions on their civil rights in exchange for greater security. For instance, a *Los Angeles Times* survey found that most Americans were more afraid of terrorists who would use the United States' freedoms against its people than they were concerned about efforts to limit civil liberties. Some 57 percent of the public cited the "abusers of freedom" as more of a threat than those that would constrain freedoms.[5] Consequently increased security measures at airports or other public facilities elicited little public outcry. Public support for increased security meant that legislation to enhance homeland security enjoyed fairly wide support in Congress.

Despite the initial backing for increased security measures, however, Americans tend to be distrustful of government. This is especially true in regard to civil liberties. Although the public generally remained supportive of security initiatives by the Bush administration, there was growing opposition to measures that eroded civil liberties. Opposition was initially spearheaded by groups such as the ACLU and various media outlets. Nonetheless, as the war on terror expanded, more Americans questioned the growing intrusiveness of the federal government. Opposition to some aspects of domestic security measures even created a strange political coalition that brought together some liberals and conservatives, who criticized the loss, and potential loss, of individual and group freedoms.

The Initial Government Response

From the day of the attacks, the FBI and other law enforcement agencies mobilized to prevent further terrorist strikes. The FBI dramatically expanded its program to monitor wireless communications, especially mobile phones and e-mail. Typically search warrants were required for this type of monitoring, but the FBI engaged in lengthy communications eavesdropping for periods ranging from 18 months to five years without proper authorization. An internal investigation into the program found more than 250 violations on the part of the FBI. In addition, on September 13, the National Security Agency (NSA) began to monitor all international phone calls. Intelligence leaders argued that had the program been in place prior to the 9/11 attacks, they would have been able to discover the plans ahead of time because the hijackers did communicate with al Qaeda figures in telephone conversations.

The 1978 Foreign Service Intelligence Act (FISA) required that U.S. intelligence agencies obtain a warrant from a special three-member court, the Foreign

Service Intelligence Court, before undertaking surveillance on American soil. The court's proceedings were not open to the public; therefore, intelligence officials could reveal secret information to the judges without fear of jeopardizing ongoing intelligence operations. However, after the 9/11 attacks, the Bush administration asserted that the FISA process was too cumbersome to allow it to react quickly to potential threats. Bush issued an executive order that authorized the NSA to undertake electronic surveillance of phone calls, e-mails, text messages, and other communications without a FISA warrant.

The warrantless surveillance programs were designed as preventative measures. The material gathered were generally not part of ongoing criminal investigations, but rather an effort by agents to collect information about future attacks in order to prevent them. In addition to warrantless wiretaps of specific individuals, the government also undertook a range of data-mining programs. These initiatives used advanced detection capabilities to search for specific keywords in electronic communications, including e-mail, text messages, and other network-based communications.

The Bush administration did endeavor to convince Congress to grant the federal government the authority to undertake warrantless wiretaps as part of the 2001 resolution that granted the president the ability to use military force against the perpetrators of the 9/11 attacks. Congress refused to grant the administration specific approval to carry out wiretaps without judicial permission. The Bush administration later argued that broad language in the legislation actually granted the government permission to undertake a variety of programs that infringed on civil liberties. The 2001 measure stated that the "President is authorized to use all necessary and appropriate force against those nations, organizations, or persons he determines planned, authorized, committed, or aided the terrorist attacks that occurred on September 11, 2001, or harbored such organizations or persons, in order to prevent any future acts of international terrorism against the United States by such nations, organizations or persons."[6] The specific phrase "all necessary and appropriate force" would emerge as the terminology used to justify a range of efforts.

The existence of the warrantless surveillance program was not made public until 2005, when it was revealed by the *New York Times*. The revelations provoked a broad backlash from civil liberties groups, Congress, and even the public. The administration worked with Congress to revise the original FISA measure. On August 3, 2007, Congress enacted the Protect America Act of 2007, which expanded the powers of intelligence agencies to conduct electronic espionage. The new measure loosened requirements for warrants for electronic espionage, allowing the government up to 72 hours of surveillance before agents had to obtain a warrant. In addition, any communications that included foreign actors, even if they involved a U.S. location, no longer needed a warrant. The act also expanded the types of data that could be collected without a FISA warrant. The act had a sunset provision in which many of its components automatically expired. In 2008, Congress amended the act so that most of the aspects of the Protect America Act were abolished, although existing investigations were allowed to continue until 2012.

Terrorism Alert System

As part of the effort to prevent further attacks, the Bush administration also developed a system to better inform the public when intelligence or other information indicated a strike was possible. The logic was that an informed public would be better able to recognize danger signs or people or things that were out of place. The public would report these warning signals to officials. A five-tiered color-coded system was developed to indicate the danger level. Green indicated a "low" threat level, blue was "guarded," yellow "elevated," orange "high," and red "severe." The colors and their corresponding threat levels were tied to specific security measures. For instance, an increased threat level automatically triggered enhanced security measures for passengers boarding airplanes.

The color system proved effective in triggering increased or decreased security procedures, but it was never fully successful with the public. Because it was impractical to share the intelligence that might prompt an elevation in the threat level, many Americans never really accepted the system or understood its intent. Many also poked fun at the system or made jokes about it. The public had a similar reaction to attempts by the government to convince Americans to prepare their homes for the possibility of a chemical or biological attack, including efforts to prompt citizens to have an emergency kit ready in the event of a strike.

The Patriot Act

The Patriot Act (see Chapter 2) was passed by overwhelming majorities in both houses of Congress. The House of Representatives adopted the measure on a vote of 357 in favor and 66 opposed, and 98 in favor and one opposed in the Senate. The new law enhanced the police and surveillance powers of the federal government. It began by expanding the definition of terrorism to include more crimes and it redefined what constituted a terrorist organization. The act also simplified the procedures that allowed law enforcement officials to use existing tools and laws that had been developed to suppress organized crime against terrorist groups. This included wiretaps and statues such as the Racketeer Influenced and Corrupt Organization (RICO) law. RICO had been used successfully to prosecute mafia- and gang-related cases by allowing law enforcement to arrest people for participation in the groups. During the Senate debate on the Patriot Act, future Vice President Joe Biden exclaimed that "the FBI could get a wiretap to investigate the mafia, but they could not get one to investigate terrorists. To put it bluntly, that was crazy! What's good for the mob should be good for terrorists."[7] The Patriot Act eased the differences. For instance, with the new law, officials could use roving wiretaps that authorized them to monitor the communications of an individual person, rather than an individual communications device. Instead of monitoring a specific phone, law enforcement could monitor all communications by a suspect, no matter what device was used. This technique had been used by police and federal officials against organized crime for many years with great success. The act also permitted authorities to ask the Federal Intelligence Surveillance Court for subpoenas to examine business, financial, or banking records of suspected terrorists when it would not be appropriate for such an investigation to be overseen by a normal grand jury. This was most often the case when intelligence sources or techniques would be compromised if information became public or a matter of open records during a trial.

The Patriot Act made the Justice Department the lead federal organization in counterterrorism efforts. Prior to the new law, a number of federal bodies had oversight over specific areas that could be related to terrorism. For example, the ATF (part of the Treasury Department) had jurisdiction over cases involving weapons, while the Coast Guard (Department of Defense) had oversight over protecting the waterways. The act further removed some existing legal barriers to sharing information between U.S. intelligence agencies. For example, prior to the act, the CIA and domestic intelligence agencies were forbidden from exchanging some information on American citizens.[8]

Prior to the Patriot Act, U.S. law enforcement bodies could only obtain search warrants in the district or area in which they were based. If activity occurred in several localities or states, officials would be required to obtain multiple search warrants. However, the new measure changed that requirement in regard to acts of terrorism in order to allow officials to seek warrants in the area where terrorist activities or events occurred, regardless of where the warrants would ultimately be served.

In addition, the act increased the penalties for a range of terrorist activities, including harboring terrorists, and eliminated the statute of limitations on most terrorist activities. Finally, the new law made terrorist strikes on mass transit systems or biological strikes federal offenses.

Concerns over the Patriot Act

There were a number of controversial aspects of the Patriot Act that worried civil libertarians. Normally, when a dwelling or facility was searched by law enforcement, officials had to present a search warrant before entering the dwelling or building. However, the act permitted the government to conduct "sneak and peak" warrants whereby officials could enter a facility and conduct a search without notifying the owner or occupant. It also gave the government the ability to enter a space and install listening devices or cameras to record illicit activity. Law enforcement was only authorized to utilize "sneak and peak" warrants when there was either an immediate danger of terrorist attack or if a traditional search warrant would tip off the suspects in such a way as to make it more difficult for officials to prevent an attack or other activity. In addition, after a reasonable period of time, suspects were supposed to be informed of the warrant.[9]

The act also allowed the government to request records normally kept by public institutions such as libraries or businesses. Federal agencies were authorized to send notifications requesting this information without a warrant or other judicial oversight. This part of the measure was deeply opposed by civil libertarians and libraries. In response, many libraries posted warning notices that patron records might be turned over to federal agents. Libraries also began destroying patron records so they would not be forced to turn them over to law enforcement agencies. From 2001 through 2005, federal agents requested records from more than 200 libraries.

Because of the controversial nature of many of the aspects of the Patriot Act, the original bill contained sunset provisions that automatically ended areas of the measures on December 31, 2005. In March 2006, Congress passed revisions to the act. In addition, courts overturned some parts of the act as unconstitutional.

Meanwhile, on December 17, 2004, the Intelligence Reform and Terrorism Prevention Act was signed into law. The measure created the National Counterterrorism Center, which drew on the resources of existing agencies to develop antiterrorism policies and actions. The legislation also established the office of the Director of National Intelligence (DNI). The DNI was tasked to coordinate all of the nation's intelligence agencies and facilitate information sharing in order to avoid the mistakes that led to the 9/11 attacks. The Privacy and Civil Liberties Oversight Board was also created as a means to ensure that intelligence efforts and counterterrorism programs did not infringe on individual rights or civil liberties. John Negroponte was appointed the first DNI and assumed office on April 25, 2005.

Homeland Security Act

Also in November 2002, Congress passed the Homeland Security Act. The measure was enacted to enhance the powers and capabilities of domestic law enforcement and counterterrorism efforts. The law expanded the scope and size of the Office of Homeland Security and converted the agency into a cabinet-level body. The resultant Department of Homeland Security (DHS) was the largest reorganization of the federal bureaucracy since the establishment of the Department of Defense in 1947. The new DHS centralized homeland security and brought together agencies that had been part of numerous different federal bodies. The consolidation was designed to reduce redundancies and enhance information sharing between different agencies. It was also hoped that the reorganization would provide a unified command system and prevent interagency rivalry.

To better coordinate homeland security efforts across all levels of government, the Bush administration also created the Homeland Security Council (HSC) in October 2001 and Congress formalized the body through the 2002 Homeland Security Act. This body was similar to the National Security Council, which had been created in 1947 to oversee U.S. foreign and security policy. The act created the position of homeland security advisor to provide counsel and advice to the chief executive on matters of domestic security. Members of the HSC include the president, vice president, attorney general, and secretaries of Homeland Security, Defense, Treasury, Transportation, and Health and Human Resources, in addition to other agency directors. Other officials participate when necessary or appropriate.

The newly created DHS combined 22 existing federal agencies, including the Coast Guard, Secret Service, Customs and Border Protection, Immigration and Customs Enforcement, and Transportation Security Administration. The new department eventually had more than 200,000 employees, making it the third largest federal agency behind the Defense Department and the Department of Veterans Affairs. DHS was divided into four directorates: Border and Transportation Security, Emergency Preparedness and Response, Science and Technology, and Information Analysis and Infrastructure Protection. Each directorate was tasked to oversee specific aspects of homeland security. For instance, transportation security, including airline safety, was the responsibility of Border and Transportation Security. Former governor Tom Ridge, who was the head of the Office of Homeland Security, became the first secretary of the DHS.

Some civil libertarians criticized the new department for a lack of transparency and for overzealousness. For instance, the ACLU and other groups sued DHS over an automated tracking system which developed a risk assessment on travelers, including Americans, based on a variety of risk factors. The system was designed to identify potential terrorists, but it also grounded substantial numbers of innocent travelers. Democratic senator Ted Kennedy of Massachusetts was even flagged by the system in 2004. Public and congressional pressure led Bush to order DHS to discard the system and develop a new one. The ACLU led another lawsuit in 2006 against the successor program, leading to additional reforms. In 2008, the ACLU would also lead other groups in a suit against DHS for refusing to turn over records on searches and detentions at border crossings. Tensions between homeland security officials and civil libertarians reflected broader societal and political concerns over the erosion of personal and group rights in an effort to make people safer.

Signing Statements

Civil libertarians repeatedly condemned the Bush administration's use of signing statements. Signing statements are written directives that presidents issue in response to a new piece of legislation. The statements are supposed to help federal agencies or employees understand the implications of new laws, but presidents may also issue declarations that are more political in nature and object to passages or components of bills. In some cases, signing statements challenge the validity of a law and endeavor to limit its impact or scope.

Chief executives began to use signing statements in the 19th century, but late-20th-century presidents, beginning with Reagan, dramatically expanded their use. A report by the Congressional Research Service found that Reagan had 250 signing statements, and 86 (34 percent) had objections to provisions in legislation. George H. W. Bush had 228 statements, and 107 (47 percent) objected to aspects of laws, while Clinton had more statements (381) but fewer protests (70, 18 percent). George W. Bush issued 161 statements during his presidency, with 120 (71 percent) opposing components of legislation. Significantly, many of Bush's signing statements contained multiple objections, meaning that Bush challenged more than 1,100 aspects of laws, far more than any of his predecessors. Critics charged Bush used signing statements to weaken or ignore parts of legislation that his administration did not agree with.[10]

Enemy Combatants

The United States also initiated international counterterrorism programs that had implications for civil liberties in the United States. As noted, the U.S. government had previously engaged in rendition. The Bush administration expanded the use of the practice and began to develop overseas prisons and interrogation facilities. On September 17, President Bush authorized the creation of what became known as "black sites." These were areas where the CIA and other intelligence agencies took prisoners for questioning using methods that were often not legal in the United States. Black sites were established in at least eight countries, ranging from Egypt to Poland to Afghanistan. The existence of these facilities became known following an investigative report by the *Washington Post*, a U.S. newspaper, in 2005. The Bush administration publicly acknowledged their existence the following year and ended the program, transferring the remaining prisoners from the black sites to other detention facilities. One prisoner, Khalid El-Masri, was a German citizen who was abducted by the CIA in 2004 and taken to a black site in Albania, where he was interrogated and tortured. The CIA discovered he was not the individual they sought, and he was released. El-Masri later brought a civil lawsuit against the United States government. Successive U.S. courts, including the Supreme Court, rejected his suit after the Bush administration argued that allowing the lawsuit to go to trial would harm American national security.

Enemy Combatants

After the U.S.-led coalition invaded Afghanistan, the Bush administration decided to hold al Qaeda fighters and other terrorists captured in Afghanistan at a detention facility in Guantanamo Bay, Cuba, where the United States had a naval base (the site had previously been used as a camp for Haitian refugees in the 1990s). The administration sought to avoid housing the prisoners at detention facilities in the United States. Officials were concerned that there would be domestic and international pressure to treat those detained as civilian prisoners subject to U.S. legal protections and standards. American intelligence officials wanted to isolate and interrogate the prisoners without interference from legal counsels. There was also concern over escapes or the potential that terrorists might strike at court proceedings or prisons that housed terrorist leaders. On December 28, 2001, John Yoo and Patrick Philbin of the Justice Department prepared a memorandum that contended that U.S. courts would not have jurisdiction over detainees held at Guantanamo Bay. A key argument, one that was later challenged by civil libertarians, was that Guantanamo Bay was outside of the territorial sovereignty of the United States and therefore could not be subject to American law. Yoo and Philbin asserted that even though the United States had rights to the facilities at Guantanamo Bay due to a 99-year lease, the territory was still officially Cuban. In January 2002, the first wave of prisoners arrived at Guantanamo. Ultimately, more than 750 detainees would be sent to the facility.

The Bush administration never recognized the Taliban as the legitimate government of Afghanistan. Consequently, the United States did not recognize Taliban fighters as legitimate soldiers, subject to rules and norms of international law. On January 18, 2002, the United States adopted a policy whereby captured fighters are designated as "detainees" or "enemy combatants." Under international law, an enemy combatant was a fighter or other enemy agent that could be detained for the duration of an armed conflict. Enemy combatants were typically civilians, and they were distinct from prisoners of war who were captured while serving in uniform in an armed conflict. The United States designated all members of al Qaeda, the Taliban, and those who were affiliated with, or agents of, either organization as enemy combatants.

Enemy combatants could be divided into two broad categories: (1) lawful or (2) unlawful. Lawful enemy combatants were granted the same status as military prisoners of war under international law. They were entitled to a range of protections under the Geneva Conventions, but could be detained for the duration of a conflict. An example of a lawful enemy combatant would be a government official or a police officer in an enemy regime. The category also includes civilians who worked for enemy military forces as cooks, as drivers, or in other support positions.

Unlawful enemy combatants were those who engaged in combat or other activities but were not in the military. They were not eligible for prisoner of war status as defined by the Geneva Conventions or under U.S. law. In conflicts throughout the 20th century, it was common for unlawful combatants to be subject to military trials and, potentially, execution if found to be fighting out of uniform. For instance, civilian guerilla forces or partisans could be classified as unlawful combatants.

Military commanders or the president have the authority to make decisions on who is a lawful or unlawful enemy combatant. The Bush administration decided to classify all al Qaeda and Taliban fighters as unlawful enemy combatants. The administration argued that al Qaeda fighters were terrorists and therefore not associated with legitimate government. Likewise, since the Taliban was not recognized by most of the international community as the legitimate rulers of Afghanistan, they were also not soldiers under the Geneva Conventions. The Bush administration also argued that since most of the al Qaeda and Taliban did not wear uniforms or engage in traditional military operations, they were not soldiers in the customary sense.

The Bush administration also determined that any Americans captured fighting alongside the Taliban or al Qaeda would be designated as unlawful enemy combatants and therefore not subject to normal U.S. legal procedures. The action was protested by civil liberties groups and human rights activists, who argued that the prisoners should be treated as captured soldiers or tried under U.S. law. In March 2002, the Bush administration announced that the prisoners at Guantanamo Bay would be tried by special military tribunals.

On November 25, 2001, John Walker Lindh was captured by Northern Alliance forces. Lindh had converted to Islam and then traveled to Yemen and Pakistan before joining the Taliban in Afghanistan. He was turned over to U.S. forces after being wounded during a prison uprising in December. Lindh was charged with crimes ranging from offering material support to terrorists to conspiracy to murder Americans. He pled guilty to two charges and was sentenced to 20 years in prison in October 2002. Civil libertarians criticized the government's management of the case, arguing that Lindh was denied his constitutional rights when he was first turned over to U.S. forces, including the right to counsel. Groups such as the ACLU asserted that U.S. citizens captured in Afghanistan should not be designated as enemy combatants, but should be granted the full range of constitutional protections available to other Americans charged with criminal offenses.

The Supreme Court and Enemy Combatants

A series of court cases refined the status of prisoners over the next few years. The first case, *Rasul v. Bush*, was filed in February 2002 and decided by the Supreme Court in 2004. In the 6–3 ruling, the high Court held that the U.S. judicial system had the authority to determine whether non-citizens who had been designated unlawful enemy combatants were being legally detained. In *Hamdi v. Rumsfeld*, filed in June 2002 and decided in 2004, the Court accepted the government's argument that it had the power to detain unlawful enemy combatants, but that U.S. citizens who were charged with that designation had the right to challenge that status in civilian courts.

In 2005, in response to both domestic and international criticism, Congress enacted the Detainee Treatment Act. The law forbade the U.S. government from subjecting enemy combatants to cruel or unusual treatment. It also denied detainees the ability to challenge their status before U.S. courts. The Bush administration opposed some aspects of the law and subsequently issued a signing statement asserting that the president had a duty to protect the country from further attacks. Critics of the signing statement argued that Bush was endeavoring to preserve the ability to violate the law if U.S. officials deemed it necessary to torture a detainee in order to protect Americans.

Meanwhile in 2006, in *Hamdan v. Rumsfeld*, the Supreme Court ruled that the military tribunals created by the Bush administration to try unlawful enemy combatants were illegal, and violated both domestic law and international law, including the Geneva Conventions.

Following *Hamdan v. Rumsfeld*, Congress enacted the Military Commissions Act, which was signed by Bush on October 17, 2006. The new way attempted to address problems cited by the Supreme Court when it rejected the initial government plan for military tribunals. The act permitted military tribunals or commissions, but called for them to be based on existing military jurisprudence, including rules that were used in a court martial. The act permitted alien unlawful enemy combatants to be tried, but not American citizens. It also allowed the military commissions to deny habeas corpus to alien unlawful enemy combatants. Consequently, the detainees could not challenge the legitimacy of their captivity.

The Military Commissions Act became the basis for trials of unlawful enemy combatants when the first cases began in 2007. The Supreme Court in 2008 in *Boumediene v. Bush* rejected the original Bush administration argument that Guantanamo Bay was not subject to U.S. sovereignty. Instead the Court determined that American constitutional protections had to be extended to those held at Guantanamo. On October 28, 2009, Congress amended the Military Commissions Act so that it was in accordance with *Boumediene v. Bush*.

Domestic Terrorism and Homeland Security

The widespread suspicion and wariness that pervaded American society in the aftermath of the 9/11 attacks were exacerbated by additional terrorist threats besides the aforementioned anthrax attacks and Shoe Bomber. Although the public and government officials tended to be mainly concerned with the potential for another major al Qaeda attack, the FBI and other law enforcement agencies reported that the majority of terrorist threats and incidents between 2002 and 2009 originated from domestic groups. The majority of the attacks and planned strikes were minor and were perpetrated by groups ranging from environmental and animal rights activists to pro-independence Puerto Rican groups.[11] Ironically, the actual number of terrorist attacks within the United States peaked in 1998, before declining in the period from 1999 to 2001, before rising slightly in 2002, and then declining dramatically as the result of increased security efforts and the decision by some domestic groups to abandon armed strikes as a tactic to achieve their goals.

Terrorist activity at home and abroad escalated people's fears. Between 2001 and 2009, in the United States there were 46 separate terrorist plots or attempted attacks that involved 125 people and were linked to radical Islam.[12] About half of these events involved single individuals. Less than a week after the 9/11 attacks, law enforcement arrested four Muslim immigrants in Detroit on charges they planned to attack Disneyland. They were described as a "sleep cell"—a group of individuals who are planted in a host country and remain dormant for a period of time before undertaking an attack. The arrest of the Detroit Sleeper Cell stoked fears throughout the United States that there were other groups of extremists laying low and preparing for future attacks. Other groups of Muslim extremists were discovered and arrested in areas such as Lackawanna, New York (the Lackawanna Six or Buffalo Six), in September 2002 and Portland, Oregon, in October 2002 (the Portland Six).

Meanwhile, on May 8, 2002, Jose Padilla, a convert to Islam who was suspected by law enforcement officials to be associated with Muslim extremists, was arrested in Chicago on suspicion of terrorism. Padilla was returning to the United States from the Middle East when he was arrested, and evidence initially indicated that he was involved in a plan to detonate a "dirty bomb" (an explosive device with radioactive materials whose detonation would contaminate surroundings). Concern over a potential dirty bomb attack led to new security measures at vulnerable facilities, including power plants, water reservoirs and treatment centers, and airports. It also prompted concerns among Congress and the public over port and airlines security to prevent radioactive materials from being brought into the United States. Security at nuclear power plants and nuclear waste storage facilities was also bolstered to deter the theft of radioactive materials. Padilla was initially held as an enemy combatant, but later charged with conspiracy to commit terrorism. He was convicted in 2007 and sentenced to 17 years in prison.

Attacks against U.S. interests and facilities overseas also continued. On June 14, 2002, al Qaeda terrorists detonated a bomb outside the U.S. consulate in Karachi, Pakistan. Eleven people were killed, and scores were injured. On October 6, in an attack reminiscent of the strike against the USS *Cole*, an explosives-laden boat rammed into the side of a French oil tanker, the *Limburg*, off of the coast of Yemen. The al Qaeda attack killed one crew member and wounded four others. At least 90,000 barrels of oil were spilled into the Gulf of Aden, raising fears that al Qaeda would continue to strike oil tankers in the region. Oil firms rerouted shipping away from the Gulf of Aden, causing massive economic losses to Yemen.

Back in the United States, over a two-week period at the beginning of October 2002, a series of sniper attacks occurred in the greater Washington, D.C., metro area. Thirteen people were shot, and 10 died from their wounds. The shootings caused panic and fear throughout the region, especially as law enforcement officials initially appeared unable to stop the attacks or discover a motive or pattern to the shootings. John Allen Muhammad, a Muslim convert, and Lee Boyd Malvo were arrested and convicted for the attacks, which came to be known as the "D.C. Sniper" incident. The two fired at random victims, using high-powered hunting rifles, from a specially modified car that allowed one shooter to fire from the trunk of the vehicle without being detected.

The continuing terrorist incidents, and the threat of additional strikes, created an atmosphere of fear and uncertainty in the United States. Muslim Americans and people of Middle Eastern or South Asian ethnicity were viewed with suspicion by some. One result was an increase in racial profiling, an illicit procedure in which individuals are targeted for questioning, arrest, or detention, initially because of their race or ethnicity.

Racial Profiling

In the aftermath of the 9/11 attacks, civil libertarians and minority groups raised concerns over racial profiling of Arab Americans and immigrants. Although the Bush administration issued guidelines warning government agencies and law enforcement officers against racial profiling, following the 9/11 attacks, the Justice Department detained approximately 1,200 Arabs, South Asians, and other Muslims who were regarded as suspicious. Most were quickly released, but many remained in custody for an extended period. In November, the Justice Department initiated a program to interview 5,000 individuals who had entered the United States from countries linked to terrorist activities.

In March, 2002, the Justice Department initiated interviews with approximately 3,000 more Arab, Muslim, and South Asian immigrants or registered aliens for information on potential terrorism, and requested help from local police departments to carry out the questioning. Some local departments opted out of the program, fearing that it would undermine trust in confidence among the Muslim community. Civil liberties groups were highly critical of initiatives which targeted specific religious or ethnic groups, arguing that the government's actions exacerbated prejudice toward and suspicion of minority groups. Furthermore, by alienating Muslims or South Asians, the government undermined its ability to gain vital intelligence about potential terrorist activity within the United States.

Conclusion

While the Bush administration endeavored to improve homeland security in order to defend against future terrorist attacks, the public grew increasingly uncomfortable with the erosion of civil liberties. Concurrently, Americans were more accepting of the threat of terrorism. For many Americans, the threat of terrorism became just one of a number of other safety risks. Terrorism also became more abstract to many people. A 2005 poll by Quinnipiac University found that 85 percent of Americans believed that there would be additional large-scale terrorist attacks on the United States; however, 85 percent also believed that their own communities and families were "very safe" or "somewhat safe" from attacks.[13] As the memories of the 9/11 attacks receded, Americans were increasingly less willing to trade freedoms for safety. The Quinnipiac poll also found that Americans by a margin of 61 percent to 33 percent did not want increased security to violate their civil liberties.[14]

When the war on terror began, the public, political leaders, and segments of American society rallied around President Bush and his administration. As time went by, the support began to weaken. Bush's public approval ratings were 90 percent in the immediate aftermath of the 9/11 attacks, but they began to decline as people became more critical of the administration's management of the war on terror. As the war on terror expanded, questions over the direction and scope of the nation's response emerged. This was especially true as the United States embarked on the next phase of the war on terror, the invasion of Iraq.

Notes

1. Bill Clinton, *Remarks on the Bombing of the Alfred P. Murrah Federal Building in Oklahoma City, Oklahoma on April 19, 1995*, Public Papers of the Presidents of the United States of America (Washington, D.C.: Federal Register Division, National Archives and Records Service, General Services Administration, 1995), 552.

2. Bill Clinton, *Statement on Signing the Antiterrorrism and Effective Death Penalty Act of 1996 on April 24, 1996*, Public Papers of the Presidents of the United States of America (Washington, D.C.: Federal Register Division, National Archives and Records Service, General Services Administration, 1996), 630–32.

3. White House, "Presidential Decision Directive 39," June 21, 1995, reprinted by the Federation of American Scientists.

4. Gary Langer, "Standing United: American Public Closes Ranks behind Bush and Anti-Terror Measures," *ABC News*, September 15, 2001.

5. Jill Darling Richardson, "Poll Analysis: Concern Growing over Loss of Civil Liberties," *Los Angeles Times*, December 21, 2001.

6. U.S. Congress, "Authorization to Use Military Force," 107th Congress, 1st Session, September 18, 2001.

7. U.S. Congress, Senate, *Congressional Record*, October 25, 2001, S11048.

8. Restrictions were placed on the CIA in the 1970s that required the approval of senior administration officials, including the attorney general, before the agency could collect intelligence on U.S. citizens. Furthermore the CIA could only investigate an American if they were suspected of espionage or terrorism or other forms of treason. In 1981, President Reagan issued Executive Order 12333, which called for domestic agencies to cooperate with the CIA when the organization requested permission to conduct domestic intelligence. Executive Order 12333 also placed additional prohibitions against U.S. government officials involvement in assassination efforts.

9. For a more thorough examination of sneak and peak warrants and the Patriot Act, see James Beckman, *Comparative Legal Approaches to Homeland Security* (Aldershot: Ashgate, 2007).

10. T. J. Halstead, "Presidential Signing Statements: Constitutional and Institutional Implications," in *Congressional Research Service Report*, September 17 (Washington, D.C.: Congressional Research Service, 2007).

11. Neil Reedy and Justin Miller, "The Evolution of Homeland Security and the War on Terror," in Tom Lansford, Robert P. Watson, and Jack Covarrubias, eds., *America's War on Terror*, 2nd ed. (Aldershot: Ashgate, 2009), 130.

12. Toni Johnson, "The Threat of Homegrown Islamist Terrorism," Council on Foreign Relations Backgrounder, December 10, 2010.

13. Quinnipiac University, "U.S. Voters Want Anti-Terror Funds Based on Need," poll, July 25, 2005.

14. Quinnipiac University, "U.S. Voters."

5

Operation Iraqi Freedom

As discussed in Chapter 1, from the 1991 Gulf War through the 1990s, relations between the United States and Iraq remained tense. In the aftermath of the 9/11 attacks, U.S. intelligence services investigated possible links between Iraq and al Qaeda and other terrorist organizations. American security officials were particularly apprehensive over the possibility that the regime of Saddam Hussein might transfer or sell WMDs to a terrorist organization. Concern over Iraq led the United States to redouble efforts to isolate Iraq. The United States led an international effort to force Iraq to allow UN personnel to resume inspections and monitoring of the country's weapons of mass destruction (WMD) programs. Although the Saddam regime allowed UN inspectors back into Iraq, the United States and a coalition of nations charged that the Iraqis were not fully complying with existing UN resolutions. The Bush administration endeavored to build a broad coalition, but mainly nations, including key allies such as France and Germany, opposed military action. In March 2003, the United States and its allies invaded Iraq. Although the U.S.-led forces quickly overwhelmed the Iraqi military and overthrew the Saddam regime, an insurgency emerged that caused more casualties than did the initial invasion and created instability throughout the country.

Iraq and Preemption

Immediately after the 9/11 terrorist attacks, Czech intelligence officials provided information to the United States that hijacker Mohammad Atta met with Iraqi intelligence agents. U.S. intelligence also discovered contacts between other al Qaeda officials and Iraq, but no direct evidence of Iraqi involvement in the strikes. Allied officials also cited Iraq's support for Palestinian terrorist groups, including a program whereby Iraq paid $10,000 to the families of suicide bombers who died in attacks against Israel, as proof of the regime's ties to global terrorism. Meanwhile, on September 20, U.S. and UK aircraft attacked surface-to-air-missiles sites in Iraq after the installations targeted allied aircraft patrolling the no-fly zone. Over the next two months, the Bush administration was primarily focused on the military campaign in Afghanistan, but senior officials also worked to craft an overarching national security strategy that emphasized the threat of terrorism to the United States and world stability.

On January 29, 2002, Bush delivered a State of the Union address. During the speech, the president listed Iran, Iraq, and North Korea as part of an "axis of evil," and he accused the nations of threatening world peace by supporting terrorism, intimidating neighboring states, and seeking to acquire weapons of mass destruction. This marked the beginning of a broad diplomatic, political, and military effort to make a case for war against Iraq if it did not comply with existing UN resolutions. Bush stated,

> Iraq continues to flaunt its hostility toward America and to support terror. The Iraqi regime has plotted to develop anthrax, and nerve gas, and nuclear weapons for over a decade. This is a regime that has already used poison gas to murder thousands of its own citizens—leaving the bodies of mothers huddled over their dead children. This is a regime that agreed to international inspections—then kicked out the inspectors. This is a regime that has something to hide from the civilized world.[1]

Fresh from toppling the Taliban regime, Bush's address declared to the world that the United States would be increasingly aggressive in seeking to counter threats to global peace. Bush announced, "I will not wait on events, while dangers gather. I will not stand by, as peril draws closer and closer."[2]

The codification of Bush's more aggressive security was the *National Security Strategy of the United States*, published in September 2002. The document was developed by the National Security Council and articulated a policy that became known as the Bush Doctrine. The Bush Doctrine rejected reactive security policies and embraced preemptive military strikes as a means to forestall threats to the United States. Under the Bush Doctrine, the United States declared that it would attack enemies or potential enemies in order to prevent them from harming the United States or its allies. The Bush Doctrine was the means by which the president's 2002 State of the Union Address was put into practice. The *National Security Strategy* contended, "To forestall or prevent such hostile acts by our adversaries, the United States will, if necessary, act preemptively in exercising our inherent right of self-defense. The United States will not resort to force in all cases to preempt emerging threats. Our preference is that nonmilitary actions succeed. And no country should ever use preemption as a pretext for aggression."[3]

Preemption is highly controversial. Article 51 of the UN Charter affirms that all states have the inherent right of self-defense. Under international custom and tradition, preemption is acceptable under very limited circumstances. For instance, a smaller state that is about to be attacked by a larger state or coalition might strike first in an effort to gain a tactical advantage. Central to the acceptance of a preemptive war is the danger of imminent attack. Many domestic and international figures criticized the Bush administration's embrace of preemption; however, the administration contended it was a necessary step to prevent a future catastrophic WMD attack by either a terrorist group or a country.

In addition, the 2002 *National Security Strategy* also addressed a number of other areas. For instance, the new policy document stressed the need for the United States to maintain global military predominance. It asserted that the United States would increase aid and assistance for states adopting democratic governments and endeavor to enhance the economies of poor countries. Finally, the report high-lighted the danger of AIDS to the international community and the need for joint efforts to combat the disease.

The Neo-Conservatives

Of particular concern to officials in the Bush administration was the possibility that Iraq either would use WMDs against the United States and its allies, or would allow terrorist groups to have access to them. Vice President Dick Cheney and officials, including Secretary of Defense Donald Rumsfeld and Deputy Secretary of Defense Paul Wolfowitz, advocated strongly for action to depose Saddam and for the United States to use military power to counter global terrorism.

Many of these hardliner figures in the Bush administration, including Cheney and Wolfowitz, were neo-conservatives. The neo-conservatives (or neo-con) movement emerged in the late 1960s and early 1970s among intellectuals and pundits in the Democratic Party who were dissatisfied with the growing anti-war wing that opposed the Vietnam War. Neo-conservatism was initially marked by staunch anti-communism and a rejection of the expanding role of the federal government. The movement was led by figures such as Irving Kristol (1920–2009). Neo-cons argued that the United States should use its military power to spread democracy and free trade throughout the world. Neo-cons within the administration played a major role in drafting the 2002 *National Security Strategy of the United States* and in advocating war with Iraq.

International Relations and Iraq

Through the winter and spring of 2002, the Bush administration undertook a diplomatic effort to secure support for stronger measures against Iraq, including military action if the country did not open itself to a new round of UN inspections for WMDs. Beginning in March, UN secretary general Kofi Annan attempted unsuccessfully for several months to convince Iraqi leaders to resume WMD inspections. However, Iraq invited UN officials to Baghdad in August to discuss a new round of inspections. The unwillingness of Iraq to resume inspections was one of the principal arguments the Bush administration initially used to assert that the Saddam regime was attempting to hide an ongoing WMD program. In addition, intelligence emerged that indicated Iraq had continued to pursue WMDs after UN inspectors were forced out of the country in 1998.

Iraqi officials vehemently denied the country had WMDs or ongoing WMD programs. Iraqi leaders claimed to oppose UN inspections because they asserted the program was used by the United States and the United Kingdom as a cover to conduct a spying campaign against the Saddam regime. Meanwhile, British prime minister Blair made public an intelligence dossier that reported that the Saddam regime continued an active WMD program.

By the fall of 2002, the majority of the American people supported military action against Iraq, but preferred that the use of force be approved by the United Nations. By September 2002, 58 percent of Americans supported the use of force to remove Saddam from power, with 36 percent opposed.[4] Overseas, opinion was more divided. Throughout the crisis, the government of the United Kingdom remained the closest ally of the United States and staunchly backed military action against Iraq. While allies such as Australia, Italy, and Spain strongly supported the removal of Saddam, other key international powers such as China, France, and Russia opposed military action against Iraq. Relations between the United States and those nations that were against the use of force worsened through the summer and fall of 2002. Much of the goodwill and sympathy that had been directed toward the United States after the 9/11 attacks began to erode.

The First UN Debate

President Bush addressed the United Nations on September 12, 2002. and alleged that Iraq was a major threat to world peace because it violated a range of UN resolutions and continued to support terrorism and pursue WMDs. The speech formally launched an intensive period of lobbying as the United States and the United Kingdom attempted to convince China, France, and Russia of the importance of removing Saddam from power. All five countries were permanent members of the UN Security Council, which meant that any one of them could veto any resolution by the Council.

France and Russia had longstanding economic and political ties with Iraq. The two countries also had a range of energy and trade agreements with Iraq that were suspended or on hold while the Saddam regime was subject to international sanctions because of continuing violations of UN Security Council resolutions. Russia had been Iraq's main arms supplier prior to the 1991 Persian Gulf War. Between 1988 and 1991 alone, Russia sold Iraq $4.1 billion in arms and weapons. UN sanctions after the Persian Gulf War stopped Iraq from buying most arms or weapons, and Russia consistently sought to end the sanctions in order to resume sales to the country. In addition, Russia's non-military trade with Iraq was approximately $1 billion per year through the 1990s and early 2000s. Iraq had a $6 billion foreign debt with France from the 1990s, but the imposition of sanctions after the Persian

Gulf War prevented Iraq from paying money back. After 1991, France became Iraq's largest European trading partner, with annual trade in excess of $1.5 billion. Consequently, both France and Russia had economic incentives to remove the existing sanctions, not add additional restrictions. Concurrently, China generally opposed international efforts to remove recognized governments by military force. China also had significant economic interests in Iraq. China, France, and Russia were Iraq's main suppliers of weapons between 1991 and 2001. Many countries, including France, Germany, Russia, and China had long-term energy exploration contracts in place with Iraq that were scheduled to take effect once UN sanctions were lifted.

Annan reached an agreement with Iraqi officials on September 16 in which the Iraqis pledged to resume UN inspections without any preconditions. The Saddam regime also repeated its denial that it possessed WMDs. The United States and the United Kingdom dismissed the Iraqi offer as a ruse and argued that the government was not sincere in its promise to cooperate. The United States insisted that the UN Security Council adopt a new resolution that threatened military action if Iraq did not fully comply with the existing UN measures passed in the aftermath of the 1991 Persian Gulf War.

On September 22, 2002, Rumsfeld exacerbated tensions between the United States and some of its European allies that opposed military action against Iraq. The secretary of defense characterized the divide between the European states that supported a U.S.-led military campaign against Iraq and those that opposed military action as the difference between "old Europe," exemplified by France and Germany, and new Europe, those Central and Eastern European states that had recently been freed from Soviet oppression and were either new members of, or vying to be members of, Western institutions such as the EU and NATO. Meanwhile, also on September 22, Germany completed federal elections. During the campaign, the incumbent chancellor, Gerhard Schröder of the Social Democrat Party (SPD), ran on an anti-war platform. Polls had Schröder's SPD down considerably until he embraced the anti-war message. The SPD won the election, but lost 47 seats in the parliament.

U.S. Politics

Following his September speech to the United Nations, Bush asked Congress for the authorization to use military force against Iraq. Military and intelligence officials briefed Congress that Iraq likely had an ongoing WMD program and could proliferate weapons or technology to terrorist groups.

The president argued that his administration needed the authority in case military action was necessary before the UN debate was finalized. In addition, U.S. diplomats asserted that if the president already had congressional approval to use force, it would strengthen the negotiating position of the United States at the United Nations.

On October 16, following briefings with U.S. intelligence and military officers, Congress adopted a resolution authorizing the use of force against Iraq. The House of Representatives passed the measure on a vote of 297–133, while the Senate voted 77 in favor and 23 opposed. The vote occurred less than one month ahead of midterm congressional elections, and some members of Congress were hesitant to vote against the measure for fear of being accused of being soft on terrorism. Furthermore, Bush still enjoyed a very high public opinion rating, and some members of Congress also did not want to oppose the president. In the balloting on November 5, the Republicans gained eight seats in the House of Representatives. More importantly, the GOP picked up two seats in the Senate, which gave them control of the chamber. With Republican majorities in both chambers of Congress, Bush faced even fewer domestic challenges in implementing his security policy, including the preemption doctrine.

Nonetheless, a vibrant anti-war movement emerged in the United States. Demonstrations and protests against military action became increasingly common through October and November of 2002, although the majority of Americans continued to support Bush and regime change in Iraq. At the end of 2002, U.S. military spending increased to $328.7 billion, or 3.4 percent of the country's GDP. Anti-war activists and critics of the Bush administration decried the increased military spending and argued that money should be diverted to homeland security and social programs.

Resolution 1441

After Congress gave Bush the authority to use military force against Iraq and the Republicans won the 2002 midterm elections, the UN Security Council debated an Anglo-U.S. draft resolution on Iraq. The main point of contention continued to be the use of force. The United States and the United Kingdom sought a measure that would automatically authorize military action if Iraq did comply with existing UN resolutions. There was concern among some member states that the United States would unilaterally attack Iraq without UN approval. Therefore, states that had opposed military force were willing to support the Anglo-U.S. resolution as a way to give Iraq another opportunity to comply with international measures.

On November 8, 2002, the Security Council unanimously approved Resolution 1441. The measure declared that Iraq remained in violation of previous UN resolutions. It also called for Iraq to disclose all WMDs and WMD programs within 30 days and required the regime to immediately allow UN inspectors back into Iraq. The resolution stated that any further obstruction on the part of Iraq would be an additional breach of UN requirements. If Iraq did not disarm and obey international restrictions on its military programs, the resolution promised "serious consequences." The resolution was a compromise between the Americans and British on one hand, and the Russians and French on the other. The Anglo-American proposal included language that would automatically trigger the authorization to use military force if Iraq failed to comply with the UN mandates, a measure opposed by the Russians and French. The United States agreed to the compromise in order to ensure that all members of the Security Council voted in favor of the measure.

The Iraqi Response

Iraq agreed to fully comply with Resolution 1441. On November 18–19, UNMOVIC officials met with Iraqi leaders in Baghdad to discuss the implementation of new inspections. On November 28, UNMOVIC personnel arrived in Iraq and began their mission. Initially they sought a range of documentation and access to suspicious sites.

On December 7, Iraq provided UNMOVIC with a disclosure report on its WMD program as required by Resolution 1441. Most of the information in the 12,000-page report had already been provided by Iraq, and the regime claimed that all WMDs had been destroyed and all WMD programs had been stopped. U.S. and UK officials were critical of the report and Iraq's willingness to meet the terms of 1441. U.S. Secretary of State Colin Powell rejected the report, claiming that the massive overview "totally fail[ed]" to meet the requirements of 1441 that called for a complete accounting of Iraq's WMDs. On December 28, Iraq gave the United Nations a list of personnel who were associated with its WMD programs.

In mid-December, Saddam met with senior military commanders in Iraq and informed them that the regime no longer had significant stockpiles of WMDs and that the generals had to develop plans to counter any military action by the United States without biological or chemical weapons. Saddam also initiated a program to destroy evidence of the regime's past WMD programs, including facilities and equipment. Western satellite images of activity at Iraqi sites associated with WMDs were mistakenly interpreted by intelligence analysts as efforts to hide actual WMDs.

In January 2003, Saddam increased the bounty paid to the families of Palestinian suicide bombers from $10,000 to $25,000 as part of a broader effort to improve his image among Arabs in the Middle East. The decision was cited by U.S. officials as further evidence of Saddam's support for terrorism.

Support for the Use of Force

Supporters of military action against Saddam argued that military action was necessary before the Iraqi regime used WMDs against the United States or its allies. They also contended that the escalating tension between the United States and Iraq would prompt the Iraqis to proliferate WMDs or WMD materials to terrorist groups. The Saddam regime had a history of using chemical weapons against foes of the regime and against Iran during the Iran-Iraq War. Advocates also argued that Saddam had ignored or cheated on UN resolutions for more than 10 years and that the regime was a threat to other states in the region. Opponents of the use of force based their arguments on the importance of allowing UN inspections to proceed before force was used. The anti-war camp also warned that military action against Iraq could destabilize the region and increase support for radical Islamic terrorists. Of particular worry to some was the potential disruption of oil shipments through the Persian Gulf in the event of conflict. Any interruption in energy supplies could trigger a global economic slowdown.

Although in 2002 the majority of the U.S. public supported the removal of Saddam Hussein, there was a vibrant anti-war movement across the United States. The anti-war activists conducted an escalating series of protests across the country through the winter of 2002 and 2003. A group of antiwar activists challenged the constitutionality of the 2002 Iraq War Resolution, arguing in court that Congress improperly surrendered its authority to declare war to the president. The case, *Doe v. Bush*, was dismissed on February 24, 2003, and then rejected on appeal on March 13. In dismissing the case, the justices of the First Circuit Court of Appeals ruled that Congress had participated in the decision-making process and had acted in accordance with precedent in granting the chief executive the authority to use force.

Meanwhile, elections in Turkey on November 3, 2002, brought the Islamic Justice and Development Party to power. The new government strongly opposed military action against Iraq, as did the Turkish people. Polls indicated that 70–80 percent of the Turkish population were against an invasion. Official and popular opposition complicated U.S. military strategy, which was initially based on a two-front war with invasions from the south through Kuwait and from the north through Turkey. U.S. military planners began to develop alternative strategies in the case of invasion.

A number of U.S. allies supported the American drive to remove Saddam. On January 30, 2003, the leaders of eight NATO members issued a public declaration of support for the United States and for the Bush administration's policy toward Iraq. The document was carried by newspapers and media outlets around the world. The "NATO Eight," as they were dubbed, were the Czech Republic, Hungary, Italy, the Netherlands, Poland, Portugal, Spain, and the United Kingdom. The leaders of the eight countries declared,

> We in Europe have a relationship with the U.S. which has stood the test of time. Thanks in large part to American bravery, generosity and farsightedness, Europe was free from the two forms of tyranny that devastated our continent in the 20th century: Nazism and communism. Thanks, too, to the continued cooperation between Europe and the US we have managed to

guarantee peace and freedom on our continent. The trans-Atlantic relationship must not become a casualty of the current Iraqi regime's persistent attempts to threaten world security. . . . We know that success in the day-to-day battle against terrorism and the proliferation of weapons of mass destruction demands unwavering determination and firm international cohesion on the part of all countries for whom freedom is precious.[5]

Meanwhile, the United States began building a coalition of nations willing to provide diplomatic or military support for an invasion of Iraq. The United States used the phrase "coalition of the willing" to describe those allies willing to undertake military strikes or support armed force. Initially, the most visible support came from the NATO Eight and Australia. Most other states only committed modest or small troop commitments, but they did offer the use of military bases, airspace, ports, and logistics in a manner similar to the support provided by the coalition in Operation Enduring Freedom. Bush tasked Secretary of State Colin Powell to develop the diplomatic coalition for military action and force consensus at the United Nations. Powell undertook an intense series of meetings and negotiations with foreign leaders and diplomats to garner support for the administration. The United States offered financial and military aid and assistance to countries that were willing to support the use of force.

WMD Inspections

In January 2003 Hans Blix, the head of UNMOVIC, issued a report that criticized the Saddam regime for not fully cooperating with the UN inspection effort and noted that Iraq had misled UNMOVIC about some of its WMD programs. The head of the International Atomic Energy Agency, Director General Mohamed El Baradei, filed a separate report on Iraq's nuclear programs. The IAEA report concluded that there was no evidence that Iraq was endeavoring to acquire nuclear weapons. However, it noted that Iraq failed to address questions and concerns over its past nuclear program and that the Saddam government continued to be uncooperative in a number of areas. The UNMOVIC report also highlighted Iraq's continuing lack of full compliance with inspections. It reported that Iraq had missiles that exceed the maximum range allowed under UN Security Council Resolution 687, and that the Saddam regime had continued to acquire missile parts and technology as late as December 2002 (after UNSCOM inspections had resumed). For instance, Iraq imported 380 rocket engines that could be used in prohibited missiles. Blix further noted in the report that Iraq failed to account for large stockpiles of WMDs and WMD equipment that had been discovered or detailed in previous inspections. Specifically, Iraq failed to account for 6,500 chemical bombs or about 1,000 tons of chemical weapons. In addition, UNMOVIC discovered the presence of chemical rocket warheads at a site near Baghdad (Iraq later claimed the warheads were left over from the Iran-Iraq War and had been overlooked). Finally,

UNMOVIC revealed that Iraq continued to import dual-use technology (equipment that may have legitimate commercial or agricultural uses, but could also be used in the manufacture of WMDs).

Blix and El Baradei subsequently reported that Iraq had increased cooperation. Access to additional sites, personnel, and documents had been granted. Both requested more time for the inspections. On March 1, Iraq began destruction of the missiles identified by UNMOVIC as violating Resolution 687. On March 17, Blix issued a follow-up report which described general improvements in cooperation from the Iraqis, but also cited some instances of continuing intransigence. The report also detailed some further discoveries of WMD evidence. The United States was critical of the report, which U.S. officials claimed downplayed Iraqi actions and WMDs.

Transatlantic Rifts

While the Bush administration continued its efforts to build a coalition of the willing, several key allies of the United States grew more strident in their opposition to military action. Germany and France emerged as the leaders of the anti-war faction among the United States' allies. As the United States attempted to gain allies to support the use of force, France and Germany were equally engaged in developing a counteralliance. French president Jacques Chirac was especially ardent in his opposition. Chirac had earlier supported Saddam in the 1980s during the Iran-Iraq War and hoped to resume commercial relations with Iraq. The French president perceived that a strong Iraq was the best way to keep Iran from threatening the stability of the region. In an effort to weaken the U.S. coalition of the willing, Chirac offered aid to countries to oppose military action and issued veiled threats to the Eastern European supporters of the United States that France might block efforts by those countries to join Western institutions such as NATO or the European Union.

France, Germany, and Russia issued a statement on February 11, 2003, calling for additional time for UNMOVIC to continue its inspections. France and Russia, permanent members of the UN Security Council, also threatened to veto any resolution calling for the use of force against Iraq.

Later in February, NATO underwent one of its most significant challenges when Belgium, France, and Germany vetoed a request by Turkey to invoke Article IV of the NATO charter. The clause allowed a NATO member to call together the alliance and request aid or assistance in the presence of a potential threat. Turkey sought support from the NATO allies in case of a U.S.-led invasion of Iraq. Belgium, France, and Germany asserted that the request would increase tensions in the region and was therefore unnecessary. They argued that the invocation of Article IV would make it appear that war was inevitable. However, the three states found themselves isolated by the other NATO members and accused of allowing politics to potentially destroy the cohesion of the alliance. The United States brokered a compromise whereby Turkey was granted assistance, including the deployment of NATO AWACS planes and theater missile defense systems, without the formal invocation of Article IV. Instead, NATO members agreed to provide Turkey the assistance requested as part of a series of bilateral agreements, thereby bypassing NATO and saving the alliance from a very public rift.

Meanwhile, a growing anti-war movement emerged in Europe where majorities in most countries opposed military action without UN authorization. Large protests were held across the continent. On February 15, 2003, the global anti-war day saw massive demonstrations with 3 million people protesting in Rome, 300,000 in Berlin, and 750,000 in London. However, there was a clear divide between public sentiment and government support for the United States in most European states. For instance, Spanish prime minister José Aznar emerged as a significant supporter of military action, partially as a result of his own country's long struggle against Basque separatists who had waged a terrorist campaign against the central government in an effort to gain independence. Aznar supported the Bush administration's efforts to fight terrorism around the globe.

Ten Central and East European states (the Vilnius Group) followed the NATO Eight pronouncement with a public statement of support for the United States after Powell presented the U.S. case for war against Iraq before the United Nations. The Vilnius Group was Albania, Bulgaria, Croatia, Estonia, Latvia, Lithuania, Macedonia, Romania, Slovakia, and Slovenia. Their statement asserted, "Our countries understand the dangers posed by tyranny and the special responsibility of democracies to defend our shared values. The trans-Atlantic community, of which we are a part, must stand together to face the threat posed by the nexus of terrorism and dictators with weapons of mass destruction."[6]

As was the case with the NATO Eight, the Vilnius Group countries offered some troop deployments and various other forms of military assistance. Other states outside of Europe offered the United States a range of non-military support. For instance, Japan offered $1.3 billion in financial assistance to states in the region, including Egypt, Syria, and Jordan, in the event of a conflict. Such action was designed to counter worries that a war could impact the economies of the region.

The Bush administration suffered another major setback with Turkey when, on March 1, the country's parliament voted to deny permission for the United States to utilize Turkish bases for an invasion. The vote was the direct result of the unwillingness of the United States to provide $30 billion in aid as requested by Turkey as part of a series of negotiations. There were also widespread concerns in Turkey that a war might lead to the creation of an independent Kurdish state in northern Iraq (Turkish officials feared that an independent Kurdish state on its border would support Kurdish rebels in Turkey who had been engaged in a decades-long struggle against the Turkish government). The loss of access to Turkish bases meant that the original plan for a two-pronged invasion from the north and south would have to be altered on the eve of the conflict. Also on

March 1, a summit of Arab leaders called for the Saddam regime to end its WMD programs and to disarm as regional leaders hoped that Iraq would be more open to UN inspections and therefore avoid a war.

Countdown to War

After the release of a January UNMOVIC report that was critical of Iraq, the United States, Spain, and the United Kingdom attempted to gain support for a resolution authorizing the use of force against Iraq for noncompliance with past UN resolutions. Military action remains staunchly opposed by Russia, France, and Germany.

By February, the United States and its allies began to assert that UN inspectors do not need to find a "smoking gun" that proved Iraq was engaged in clandestine WMD programs; instead, Iraqi non-compliance with past resolutions was enough to justify armed action. On February 5, the foreign ministers of the Security Council presented statements on the escalating crisis. U.S. secretary of state Powell presented the U.S. case for armed action against Iraq, including charges that the Saddam regime continued to pursue WMDs. Powell offered a variety of evidence before the United Nations. Some of the evidence included pictures of, and communications about, Iraqi activity at former WMD sites.

Other foreign ministers argued for more time for the WMD inspections. German foreign minister Joschka Fischer stated, "Despite all the difficulties, U.N. efforts to disarm Iraq in the past were not without success. In the 1990s the inspectors were able to destroy more WMD capacities than the Gulf War. The threat potential of Iraq for the region was thus clearly reduced. The current basis for the inspection is laid down in Resolution 1284 and 1441. The weapons inspectors from UNMOVIC and IAEA ha[ve] further-reaching powers than ever before. They have to be given a real chance and the time they need to fully exhaust their possibilities. . . . The dangers of a military action and its consequences are plain to see."[7]

On March 7, the United States, Spain, and the United Kingdom introduced a resolution that would authorize the use of force unless Iraq took enough steps so that the Security Council would certify by March 17 that Iraq had met all of the requirements of UN Resolution 1441. Security Council members France, Russia, and China issued a statement on March 15 asserting that inspections should continue and that there was no need to resort to force at this point. On March 16, the leaders of the United States, Spain, Portugal, and the United Kingdom met in the Azores. Bush, Blair, and Aznar held a press conference and again presented their case for war. They also argued that diplomatic efforts to end the crisis had failed and conceded that war was imminent. After the summit, the authorization to use force was withdrawn on March 17. Of particular concern to the anti-Saddam coalition was the approaching Iraqi summer and the potential that a war would be fought during the brutal heat of June, July, and August. The UNMOVIC inspectors left Iraq in mid-March, when it became clear that a U.S.-led invasion of Iraq was imminent.

German and French opposition to military action against Iraq created a backlash against the two countries in the United States. Congress initiated hearings on the issue, and there were proposals put forward to enact restrictions on French wine and bottled water, and to withdraw U.S. forces from bases in Germany. After some restaurants renamed French fries "freedom fries," the U.S. House of Representatives followed suit and food vendors were required to rename French fries and French toast (the policy was reversed in 2006).

On March 17, Canadian prime minister Jean Chrétien issued a public statement that Canada would not join the coalition in any military action against Iraq. That day, Bush promulgated an ultimatum to Iraq, demanding that Saddam and his sons Uday and Qusay Hussein leave Iraq within 48 hours or face military action by the United States and its allies. Two days later, the United States conducted a preemptive cruise missile strike in an effort to kill Saddam Hussein and his top aides, who were at Dora Farms, just outside of Baghdad. The attack marked the start of combat in the Iraq War, and on the following day the coalition launched widespread aerial and cruise missile attacks against targets that had been pre-spotted by GPS and special operations forces.

In an address to the nation on the evening of March 20, Bush announced the invasion of Iraq. The president stated, "Our nation enters this conflict reluctantly, yet our purpose is sure. The people of the United States and our friends and allies will not live at the mercy of an outlaw regime that threatens the peace with weapons of mass murder. We will meet that threat now with our army, air force, navy, coastguard and marines so that we do not have to meet it later with armies of firefighters and police and doctors on the streets of our cities."[8] Bush's comments about fighting terrorists overseas so that Americans did not have to fight them within the United States became one of the administration's main arguments for continuing military operations in Iraq after the fall of Saddam.

Operation Iraqi Freedom

In September 2002, the United States began to pre-deploy tanks and other mechanized vehicles in Kuwait for potential military action against Iraq. Ground forces were also deployed to the region, and the United States gained permission from the British to upgrade air force facilities on the island of Diego Garcia in order to base B-2 bombers there within striking distance of Iraq. By November, the United States had four aircraft carrier battle groups in the region. Two additional battle groups were dispatched in January 2003.

Iraqi Preparations

In preparation for a potential invasion by the United States and its allies, the Iraqi government divided the country into four regions, each under the personal command of one of Saddam's closest allies or relatives. At the time, Saddam was more concerned with an internal revolt than an external invasion. Consequently, he concentrated forces near the autonomous Kurdish areas and in the Shiite regions of southern Iraq. Saddam also deployed units along the border with Iran for fear that Tehran might attempt to take advantage of coalition military action to invade Iraq. These decisions split Iraqi forces.

Tactical command among the Iraqi forces was concentrated in the hands of senior officers, which limited the freedom of action of field officers and meant that Iraqi forces would fight a mainly defensive and static war. Saddam's senior military officers were chosen for their loyalty to the regime instead of their military capabilities. Some units, the Republican Guard and the Special Republican Guard, were given priority for weapons, equipment, and supplies, causing morale to be very low among most regular Iraqi Army units.

Prewar Iraqi military strategy was initially based on the faulty assumption that the coalition would not use significant ground troops in an invasion for fear of casualties that could undermine domestic support in the United States. Saddam believed that only limited numbers of troops would be deployed, and he hoped to draw those coalition forces into urban areas where Iraqi generals believed they could inflict massive casualties. Militia and reserve forces were called to duty or provided additional weapons and training. The most significant of these groups was the Saddam Fedayeen (translated loosely as "Saddam's martyrs" or "Saddam's men of sacrifice"), a paramilitary force created in 1995 and under the command of Saddam's son Qusay. The force numbered approximately 40,000 and was well armed and trained (members were typically recruited in their early teens). Saddam Fedayeen troops were deployed to bolster regular Iraqi Army units and ensure they did not retreat or desert.

The Coalition of the Willing

The United States provided the overwhelming majority of coalition troops and military assets in the invasion, and it developed the coalition's military strategy for the invasion, code named Operation Iraqi Freedom. The United States initially planned for a two-front attack, with allied forces invading from the north through Turkey and the south from Kuwait. However, Turkey's refusal in March to allow the United States access to its bases prompted a last-minute readjustment to strategy. The southern invasion became the main thrust of the coalition invasion, while airborne and special operations forces were parachuted into northern Iraq to work with anti-Saddam Kurdish forces to create a smaller second front. Meanwhile, a

U.S. Army division that was supposed to be deployed to Turkey was rerouted to Kuwait.

Prior to the invasion, senior U.S. Army leaders, including Army chief-of-staff general Eric Shinseki and the commander of the invasion, General Tommy Franks, argued that the attacking force needed to be larger in size to overcome Iraqi defenses and to provide security once the Saddam regime was toppled. Rumsfeld rejected these arguments and contended that U.S. advantages in technology and firepower would compensate for the Iraqi numerical superiority. U.S. commanders were also concerned about the weather. Temperatures during the summer in Iraq could rise to 120° Fahrenheit (48° Celsius). If coalition forces faced a chemical or biological attack, troops would have to wear special protective clothing that would magnify the temperatures. The high temperatures could also take a significant toll on vehicles, leading to higher incidents of overheating or engine wear. In addition, beginning usually around April, a dry, hot wind, known as the Sharga, produced massive sandstorms and gusts of wind capable of overturning vehicles. Such conditions would erode U.S. advantages in precision-guided weapons and communications. They would also make it difficult to conduct air strikes.

Central to U.S. strategy was the concept of "shock and awe," a military strike of such intensity and volume that it destroyed both the enemy's ability to resist and its will to fight. Rumsfeld's shock and awe campaign was designed to destroy the enemy's war-fighting, communications, and transportation capabilities, and eliminate senior officers through targeted attacks, leaving the Iraqis unsure how to react or what to do next. In addition to a massive aerial and cruise missile bombardment, special operations forces were to be inserted to attack strategic targets and create chaos behind enemy lines. For shock and awe to be effective, an attack force had to be able to hit multiple targets simultaneously in order to paralyze the enemy and overwhelm their ability to respond to multiple threats.

In an effort to maximize positive news coverage, the coalition allowed reporters and journalists to be embedded with military units. About 600 reporters participated in the program; the majority were British or American. Critics of the program asserted that being in close quarters with the military caused the journalists to be biased and report more favorably on the coalition's military operations.

The Invasion

Coalition forces began psychological operations in early 2003. Senior Iraqi political and military leaders were approached through secret communications and assured that they would be able to surrender and promised safety after the war. In addition, clandestine operations provided weapons, cash, and communications equipment to Kurdish forces in the north and Shiite groups in the south. Special operations forces endeavored to provoke an uprising in the south which would occur simultaneously with an invasion. Covert operations also conducted pre-invasion reconnaissance missions to gain information on Iraqi deployments and defenses.

The U.S.-led coalition numbered about 300,000, far less than the number engaged in the 1991 Persian Gulf War. The majority of troops were American, but the British deployed 45,000 and the Australians 2,000. About 200 Polish special forces troops also participated, as did small numbers of special operations forces from other countries, while countries such as Denmark and Spain provided troops that did not participate in combat, but offered logistical and other support. Iraqi forces numbered approximately 450,000, including the Saddam Fedayeen. Years of arms embargos and sanctions degraded the Iraqi military so that only about 700 of its 2,600 tanks were modern and comparable to their coalition counterparts. In addition, of Iraq's 300 aircraft, only 150 were flyable and many of those were obsolete compared with the fighters and bombers of the United States and its allies (Iraq also had about 375 helicopters). The Iraqi Navy consisted of six patrol boats. U.S. invasion plans assumed that the coalition would quickly establish air and naval superiority. Nonetheless, traditional military doctrine asserted that attacking forces should outnumber defenders by a 3–1 margin, or higher in challenging terrain such as urban areas or the jungle. In addition, Iraqi forces had been preparing for a possible invasion since 1991.

During the first two days of the shock and awe campaign, the coalition launched more than 3,000 bombs or missiles against Iraqi targets. Nonetheless, the shock and awe campaign never reached the scale envisioned by U.S. military planners. British military officers were able to successfully argue for the elimination of about half of the planned strikes on infrastructure targets such as power plants or water treatment facilities, asserting that the attacks would turn the population against the coalition and make reconstruction more difficult. Still, aerial and cruise missile attacks were highly effective against Iraqi military targets. After one strike on Republican guards units outside of Baghdad, only 19 out of 850 tanks remained in operation, and only 40 of 550 artillery pieces could still fire.

In the first week of the invasion, British airborne units and Polish special operations forces captured the Ramallah oil fields and most offshore rigs before Iraqis were able to set fire to the oilrigs as they had done in 1991 in an effort to interfere with coalition air operations. Only 44 oilrigs were set ablaze during the war, and most were quickly contained.

On March 23, a U.S. supply column was ambushed and 12 soldiers killed. Army private first class Jessica Lynch was captured along with five other soldiers. Lynch was later rescued in a special operations mission on April 1. The military portrayed Lynch as a hero, and her rescue as a daring operation. However, information later surfaced that Iraqi forces had left the area before U.S. troops retrieved Lynch and that footage from the episode had been staged. Lynch admitted that her weapon jammed and she did not fight against the Iraqis during her capture, undermining military claims that she was a hero.

Coalition airborne units landed in the Kurdish areas of northern Iraq and linked up with anti-Saddam peshmerga. They captured oil fields in the region and undertook combined attacks against Iraqi forces and Ansar al-Islam fighters who had a network of camps and bases in the region. By March 30, the combined coalition-peshmerga forces captured the main Ansar al-Islam bases and launched assaults on the major cities of Kirkuk and Mosul. Kirkuk was captured on April 10, and Mosul the following day.

As allied forces advance, Saddam remained distrustful of his top military leaders and prevented meaningful communications between them. This prevented individual commanders from having an accurate view of the progress of the war. He was afraid that senior officers would use the invasion as an opportunity to overthrow his regime. In some cases, officers were not given accurate maps for fear that troops would loot Saddam's palaces if they knew their locations. Saddam also insisted that commanders receive his permission before moving troops or undertaking attacks. This caused significant delays when responding to coalition movements. Even as coalition forces neared Baghdad in April, Saddam was reluctant to redeploy forces from Kurdish areas or Shiite regions for fear of rebellion.

The Breakthrough

The southern invasion was a two-pronged assault with the British, Poles, Australians, and U.S. Marines conducting an amphibious assault in the southeast to capture the Faw Peninsula in one thrust. The British-led offensive quickly overran Iraqi positions. Coalition naval forces bombarded coastal positions and conducted minesweeping missions to open Iraqi waters to allied naval vessels. By March 28, the coalition was landing ships and supplies at the port of Umm Qasr. The coalition surrounded Basra, but efforts to incite an anti-Saddam rebellion among the Shiites in the region failed. The British choose to keep the city under siege rather than advance and engage in urban combat against the Iraqi forces. Meanwhile, British and U.S. Marine armored units moved northward in the eastern pincer of the campaign.

The second prong of the invasion was an armored assault in the southwest with Baghdad as its objective. Coalition units moved rapidly into Iraq, but the speed of the advance overwhelmed the allied logistical system. Coalition forces advanced more than 200 miles in less than three weeks in one of the fastest military incursions in modern history. Frontline units could not be supplied in a timely fashion with gasoline and ammunition, a situation that worsened when massive sandstorms reduced visibility and made roads impassable. Irregular Iraqi units, especially troops of the Saddam Fedayeen, began attacking coalition supply columns, creating further logistical problems. Coalition forces halted briefly on March 29 to allow the lead units to be resupplied. On April 1, the western prong recommenced its advance and quickly overran Iraqi units. By April 3, U.S. armored forces advanced to Saddam Hussein International Airport on the outskirts of Baghdad, and the next day an armored column moved into the city. Concurrently, the British captured Basra and U.S. troops gain Karbala. By April 9, coalition forces had control of Baghdad. That day, Iraqis and U.S. soldiers tore down a large statue of Saddam in Firdos Square in Baghdad. Video footage of the event was transmitted around the world. The episode became an iconic moment in the fall of the regime. The last major fighting of the initial invasion occurred on April 15, when coalition forces capture Tikrit, Saddam's hometown and the center of his power. Saddam and most of the senior regime figures went into hiding rather than surrender.

On May 1, from the deck of an aircraft carrier, Bush announced the end of major combat operations in Iraq. The declaration proved to be premature as an insurgency ultimately killed more coalition troops over the next few years than the number killed in the opening phase of the war. The success of the initial invasion gave administration officials a false sense of accomplishment. The 2003 Iraq War cost $40 billion and lasted 26 days, while the 1991 Persian Gulf War cost $78 billion and lasted 48 days. Casualties were initially smaller in the 2003 conflict than in the 1991 war. Bush's approval ratings were above 60 percent, although they were at their peak and declined through most of the remainder of his presidency.

By the end of 2003, 580 coalition troops had been killed in Iraq from the following countries: the United States, 486; the United Kingdom, 53; Italy, 17; Spain, 10; Bulgaria, 5; Ukraine, 3; Poland, 2; Thailand, 2; Czech Republic, 1; and Denmark, 1. Iraqi military deaths were estimated to be 6,300, and civilian losses were approximately 3,750.

Conclusion

On April 21, retired U.S. general Jay Garner arrived in Iraq to oversee reconstruction efforts and the transition to Iraqi civilian rule. Garner oversaw the formation of the Coalition Provisional Authority (CPA), which was created to serve as the interim government of Iraq until the country transitioned to its own government. The CPA superseded the Office for Reconstruction and Humanitarian Assistance (ORHA) which had been created in January to serve as the initial government in a post-Saddam Iraq. On May 11, former ambassador L. Paul Bremer was appointed to lead the CPA after Garner was unable to contain increasing lawlessness in Baghdad and other major cities.

Grand Ayatollah Sayyid Ali al-Sistani, the leading Shiite cleric in Iraq, urged his supporters to engage in the political process and avoid violence. Sistani emerged as the leading figure for the nation's Shiites. For the Shiites, who had been repressed under Saddam, the removal of Sunni-dominated government presented an opportunity to exert influence over the future of Iraq. However, a growing anti-American insurgency drew in a growing number of both Sunnis and

Shiites. Many Sunnis, who were former officials or government employees in the Saddam regime, continue to fight against the coalition. Meanwhile, the inability of the CPA to maintain order in Iraq undermined confidence among Shiites.

In spite of the bitter disagreements prior to the war, the Iraqi occupation by United States and its allies was endorsed by the UN Security Council in May with a resolution that authorized the coalition to begin reconstruction efforts. The Council also ended sanctions against Iraq and terminated the UN WMD inspection program. Even those nations that had opposed the U.S.-led invasion recognized the importance of maintaining stability in Iraq and sought a quick exit by the United States.

In April, the first teams from the Iraq Survey Group (ISG) were sent to Iraq. The ISG was an international body of WMD experts who searched Iraq for evidence of banned weapons. At its peak there were more than 1,400 members of the ISG; the majority were Americans, Australians, and Britons. It was initially led by American David Kay, who was formally the United Nations' chief WMD inspector in Iraq after the Persian Gulf War. In October, ISG issued its first interim report. Search teams found no evidence of current WMDs, but did find documents, materials, and equipment related to Iraq's earlier WMD programs. The ISG spent $400 million in 2003 to search for WMDs in Iraq.

The failure to find WMDs undermined the basic rationale for the conflict and called into question the appropriateness of preemptive war. The credibility of the United States was undermined, especially in the Arab world. An increasing number of foreign fighters traveled to Iraq and joined anti-coalition forces in the insurgency. Meanwhile, the United States continued to face growing challenges in its global war on terror.

Notes

1. George W. Bush, "State of the Union Address," January 29, 2002.

2. Bush, "State of the Union Address," 2002.

3. U.S. National Security Council, *The National Security Strategy of the United States*, September (Washington, D.C.: National Security Council, 2002).

4. Gallup Poll, September 5–8, 2002.

5. José Maria Aznar, Jose-Manuel Durão Barroso, Silvio Berlusconi, Tony Blair, Vaclav Havel, Peter Medgyessy, Leszek Miller, and Anders Fogh Rasmussen, "United We Stand," January 30, 2003.

6. Albania, Bulgaria, Croatia, Estonia, Latvia, Lithuania, Macedonia, Romania, Slovakia, and Slovenia, "Statement of the Vilnius Group Countries in Response to the Presentation by the United States Secretary of State to the United Nations Security Council Concerning Iraq," New York February 5, 2003.

7. Joschka Fischer, "UN Address: The German Response," United Nations, New York, February 5, 2003.

8. George W. Bush, "Address to the Nation," March 20, 2003.

6

The Global War on Terror

The military campaigns in Afghanistan and Iraq emerged as the main components of the American struggle against international terrorism, but the U.S.-led war on terror was global in scope. After the 9/11 attacks, U.S. political and military leaders envisioned the war on terror to be a long-term, multifaceted effort similar in scope and intensity to the Cold War (1945–1991) between the United States and its allies on one hand, and the Soviet Union and its satellites on the other. The Bush administration pursued the struggle against terrorism on multiple fronts. As discussed in Chapters 3 and 5, America's traditional NATO allies, led by the United Kingdom, as well as non-NATO partners ranging from Australia to Canada to Japan, all endorsed Operation Enduring Freedom and provided varying degrees of support for the United States.

While military action was often the most visible indication of the conflict, the United States also worked to increase law enforcement and intelligence cooperation with nations around the world and improve international efforts to suppress terrorist financing. One of the more controversial aspects of the expansion of the war on terror was a decision by Bush in October 2001 to allow U.S. intelligence agencies to assassinate terrorists. The United States subsequently began to use unmanned aerial drones to undertake targeted strikes against terrorist leaders.

In the immediate aftermath of the 9/11 attacks, the war on terror had a series of successes. Governments agreed to designate a number of groups as terrorist organizations or supporters of terrorism. International intelligence collaboration between law enforcement agencies grew dramatically, and a number of terrorists were killed or captured. However, terrorists across the globe continued to conduct large-scale attacks on civilian targets. Bin Laden and other senior al Qaeda leaders remained at large and continued to inspire new attacks. Insurgencies in Afghanistan and Iraq drew new volunteers for terrorist groups. In addition, the Arab-Israeli conflict exacerbated tensions in the Middle East, while groups such as Hamas and Hezbollah continued to sponsor suicide attacks on Israel. Nonetheless, the overall number of terrorist attacks declined globally after the onset of the war on terror, and even as the number rebounded after 2003, the majority of new strikes were in Afghanistan and Iraq (terrorism in Afghanistan and Iraq is discussed in Chapters 3, 7, and 8).

Arab-Israeli Conflict

The Arab-Israeli conflict was a major factor in the rise of radical Islamic terrorism in the 1970s and 1980s (see Chapter 1). The struggle continued to influence anti-Western Islamic terrorism after the 9/11 attacks. U.S. and European support for Israel was cited by bin Laden and other extremists as justification for attacks on Western targets because of Israeli suppression of the Palestinian people.

During the summer of 2001, Hamas launched a new terrorist offensive against Israel, marked by a dramatic increase in the number of suicide attacks. However, the Palestinian government condemned the 9/11 attacks and endeavored to distance themselves from al Qaeda and the Taliban. Under pressure from the United States, Israel and the Palestinians agreed to a temporary cease-fire. However, on October 17, 2001, Rehavam Zeevi, the Israeli tourism minister, was assassinated by a Palestinian terrorist group. By December, Hamas had resumed suicide attacks against the Israelis.

One goal of the Bush administration was to end, or at least diminish, the Arab-Israeli conflict in order to remove the struggle as a motivator for future terrorism. Bush and senior U.S. leaders began to develop a statement of support for a two-state solution in the Arab-Israeli conflict. This would be a major shift in U.S. policy and would publicly commit the United States to the creation of an independent Palestinian state alongside Israel. On November 10, Bush embraced, in a speech to the United Nations, the idea of a separate Palestine. Bush announced that the United States "is working toward the day when two states, Israel and Palestine, live peacefully together within secure and recognized borders."[1]

The UN Security Council adopted Resolution 1397 on March 12. The resolution reaffirmed the United Nations' commitment to a two-state solution in the Arab-Israeli conflict, Israel and an independent Palestine. The measure, supported by the United States, passed on a vote of 14–0, with Syria abstaining. The United Nations also called on all parties in the conflict to end violence. On March 29, the UN Security Council followed up with Resolution 1402, which called for Israel to withdraw from Palestinian areas and for the Palestinians to cease terrorist attacks against Israel.

However, in response to a growing number of terrorist attacks, Israel launched Operation Defensive Shield in March 2002, the largest Israeli military campaign since the Yom Kippur War. Israeli forces invaded the West Bank, an area under Palestinian control, and surrounded the compound of Palestinian leader Yasser Arafat, virtually imprisoning him. The offensive met with international criticism. Thirty Israeli soldiers and 240 Palestinians were killed, in addition to more than 2,000 Palestinians detained or arrested. Civilian deaths, caused by both sides, created renewed anger and condemnation of Israel by Muslim leaders. Israel withdrew most forces in May. Following the offensive, Palestinian attacks against Israel declined by more than 50 percent and civilian casualties dropped by more than 35 percent, but the campaign undermined the power and credibility of Arafat. This provided an opportunity for more militant groups, such as Hamas, to gain influence among the Palestinians.

In March, in the midst of the fighting, King Abdullah of Jordan proposed a new peace plan at a summit of Arab leaders. Among the proposals was the creation of an independent Palestinian state. The United States supported the initiative, but it was ultimately rejected by Israel. Bush developed a compromise plan, but, however, withdrew it after new suicide bombings killed 26 in Israel. The attacks weakened U.S. support for Palestinian leader Yasser Arafat. Washington still endorsed the creation of a Palestinian state, but called upon the Palestinians to elect new leaders and establish a democratic government, as well as renounce terrorism. Bush contended that only when peace was restored in the Middle East would a Palestinian state be viable.

In March 2003, Arafat appointed Mahmoud Abbas as prime minister of the Palestinian National Authority (PNA). Abbas was perceived by the United States and Israel as a moderate, and Arafat hoped his appointment would help restart negotiations. Arafat, the longtime leader of the Palestinians, died on November 11, 2004. Arafat had founded the Fatah Party in 1959, emerged as chair of the Palestinian Liberation Organization, and then became the president of the PNA. In 1994 Arafat received the Nobel Peace Prize, along with Israeli leaders Yitzaak Rabin and Shimon Peres, for his role in the Oslo peace process (see Chapter 1). However, his tenure as PNA president was marked by corruption and the rise of Hamas as a rival organization to Fatah.

After Arafat died, Abbas was elected president of the PNA. However, a growing internal power struggle between those who supported Abbas (Fatah) and those supporting Hamas undermined his authority. Hamas continued to conduct terrorist attacks against Israel in order to weaken Abbas. The Bush administration became increasingly critical of Abbas for his inability to reduce terrorist attacks.

After Hezbollah guerillas attacked an Israeli patrol near the border with Lebanon, Israel launched an invasion of southern Lebanon in July 2006, in what became known as the 2006 Lebanon War. The conflict increased tensions and anti-Western sentiment throughout the Middle East and undermined support for the pro-Western government of Lebanon. The war killed 121 Israeli soldiers, approximately 500 Hezbollah fighters, and more than 1,000 civilians. A UN ceasefire ended the war. The measure called for an Israeli withdrawal, the disarming of Hezbollah, and the deployment of a UN peacekeeping force to southern Lebanon.

By the end of the Bush administration in 2009, the Arab-Israeli conflict remained a significant source of tension in the Middle East. It also served as a recruiting issue for radical extremist Islamic groups. U.S. efforts to foster a negotiated settlement in the conflict were unsuccessful, and American support for Israel continued to motivate anti-Western terrorists.

The Global Campaign

Prior to the 9/11 attacks, al Qaeda offered support to a number of terrorist groups around the globe, including organizations in Europe, the Philippines, and Yemen. Concurrently, Iranian-backed groups such as Hamas and Hezbollah continued to sponsor terrorist attacks on Israel. Following the 9/11 strikes, the United States offered military and other assistance to countries fighting terrorist campaigns as part of Operation Enduring Freedom. By 2003, U.S. officials estimated that military operations as part of the war on terror cost the United States approximately $4.5 billion per month. While some U.S. initiatives proved highly successful, others were mixed or even exacerbated existing terrorist threats. For example, new U.S. efforts to restrict financing for terrorist organizations resulted in the movement of funds from legitimate banking and business enterprises into the informal hawala system, making it more difficult to track the movement of monies (hawala is a financial system common in Muslim cultures in Africa, Asia, and the Middle East in which money is transferred from one broker to another, instead of traditional loans).

Central Asia

Because of their proximity to Afghanistan, several states in Central Asia were among the first countries involved in Operation Enduring Freedom. In December 2001, U.S. military personnel were deployed to Kyrgyzstan to establish a coalition air base near the Kyrgyz capital of Bishkek. The facility was built at Manas International Airport and became one of the main bases that allied aircraft used to attack al Qaeda and Taliban positions in Afghanistan. The base also served as a transit site to fly troops and equipment into the region.

Uzbekistan also granted the U.S. military access to one of its large air facilities, following a visit by Rumsfeld in October 2001. The United States subsequently began using a former Soviet air base at Khanabad to conduct air attacks and transport operations. In July 2005, following U.S. criticism of Uzbekistan's government over its human rights record and failure to democratize, Americans were asked to withdraw from the base by November. U.S. and coalition forces continued to use a smaller NATO base in the country.

The Bush administration rescinded a 1993 prohibition on the sale or transfer of military equipment to Tajikistan after the 9/11 attacks. The United States subsequently provided arms and funding for Tajik special operations forces to support Afghanistan's Northern Alliance, which had a large proportion of ethnic Tajiks in its ranks. The United States also supported an arrangement whereby Russian troops were deployed along the Tajik border to prevent the infiltration of al Qaeda or other terrorist groups (the Tajik government agreed to the deployment after Russia wrote off $300 million in debts owed from the Soviet period). In return, Tajikistan allowed the coalition the use of several military facilities.

Turkmenistan is constitutionally neutral, and after the 9/11 attacks the government refused U.S. requests for access to military facilities. However, coalition forces were allowed to fly through Turkmen airspace and travel across the country when delivering humanitarian aid and equipment. The United States and Turkmenistan also initiated a training program whereby allied forces trained Turkmen security troops and conducted joint counterterrorism exercises.

Pakistan

When the British colony of India became independent in 1947, it split into two countries, India and Pakistan. A third nation, Bangladesh, became independent from Pakistan in 1972, following a bitter civil war. Hindu is the dominant religion in India, while Islam is the dominant religion in Pakistan. India and Pakistan have disputed the area of Kashmir since 1947. Pakistan controls the northwest, while India controls the southwest (in 1963, China took control of some areas of the northeast). India and Pakistan fought a series of wars over Kashmir, including a brief two-month conflict in 1999. The bitter conflict over Kashmir prompted successive Pakistani governments to covertly support Islamic groups fighting against India in the region. Some of these groups formed ties with other Islamic terrorist networks. India and some Western governments repeatedly accused the Pakistani intelligence services of providing training, weapons, and other support for anti-Indian groups. However, the importance of Pakistani support for the Mujahedeen during the Soviet occupation of Afghanistan led U.S. administrations to provide economic and military aid to Islamabad. Sanctions were put in place by the United States in 1998 after India and Pakistan conducted nuclear tests.

After U.S.-led coalition forces defeated the Taliban and al Qaeda, many fighters fled into neighboring Pakistan. As noted in Chapter 3, they established new bases among the clans and tribes in the northwest region of the country and launched attacks into Afghanistan. Pakistan had hosted training centers for the Mujahedeen (see Chapter 1) during the Soviet occupation of Afghanistan, and there were a number of madrassahs that indoctrinated students in fundamentalist Sunni Islam. Some of these students joined international terrorist groups such as al Qaeda, while others joined groups fighting for Kashmir to be part of Pakistan.

Pakistan endorsed the U.S.-led war on terror and provided a variety of support for Operation Enduring Freedom. The main allied land supply route into Afghanistan was through Pakistan, and the U.S.-led coalition, and later NATO-led forces, depended on the roadway for receiving the bulk of their supplies and equipment.

While Pakistan was a supporter of Operation Enduring Freedom, U.S. relations with the country were complicated by the presence of the madrassahs, terrorist training camps, and various Islamic terrorist groups. In addition, in 1999, a military coup put General Pervez Musharraf in power. Consequently, U.S. support for Pakistan meant support for an undemocratic regime. The Bush administration attempted to pressure Musharraf to suppress the madrassahs and terrorist groups. Such groups enjoyed very strong support among the military and intelligence services that were Musharraf's main backers. Nonetheless, in January 2002, Musharraf ordered that the madrassahs be brought in under government oversight and banned a number of Islamic terrorist groups. Also bowing to U.S. pressure, Musharraf restored the constitution and held legislative elections in 2002. Musharraf's political group won the most seats in the balloting for the national assembly, but a coalition of Muslim political parties, the United Coalition of Action (Muttahida Majlis-e-Amal, or MMA), won a majority of seats in several provinces. The MMA opposed Pakistani participation in Operation Enduring Freedom, as well as military and intelligence cooperation with the United States. This complicated Musharraf's efforts to suppress the newly formed al Qaeda and Taliban bases in the northwest of Pakistan. Military and police efforts to combat the Taliban and al Qaeda were generally unsuccessful, even with covert intelligence and military support from the United States. Local and regional leaders refused to cooperate with national security forces and often forewarned terrorist groups of upcoming offensives or arrests.

Meanwhile, there were a series of attacks against Americans and Westerners in Pakistan. For example, Daniel Pearl was an American journalist for *The Wall Street Journal* who was in Pakistan working on a story about the Shoe Bomber, Richard Reid. On January 23, 2002, Pearl was kidnapped by terrorists in Karachi. The terrorists issued a range of demands, including the release of convicted terrorists held by the Pakistani government. They accused Pearl, who was Jewish, of being a covert U.S. intelligence operative. On February 1, Pearl was beheaded. A videotape of his murder was released to the press on February 21. Pearl's body was discovered on May 16. Four Kashmiri separatists were arrested for the crime by Pakistani authorities, and all were convicted. The leader of the group, Ahmad Omar Saeed Sheikh, was sentenced to death, and the others to life in prison. Khalid Sheikh Mohammad, one of the masterminds of the 9/11 attacks, later confessed to beheading Pearl.

On March 1, 2003, Khalid Sheikh Mohammad was captured in Pakistan. After his arrest, Pakistan turned Mohammad over to the United States. He was sent into captivity at Guantanamo Bay. During subsequent interrogations, Mohammad provided a wealth of intelligence on past and ongoing al Qaeda operations to U.S. officials, including an effort by al Qaeda to acquire nuclear materials to build a dirty bomb. Mohammad later charged that U.S. intelligence agents tortured him and other detainees at Guantanamo Bay. In 2008, Mohammad was charged for his role in the 9/11 attacks. Meanwhile, over a two-week period in December 2003, Musharraf survived two assassinations attempts.

The Bush administration designated Pakistan a "major non-NATO ally" in 2004, putting the country on par with traditional U.S. allies such as Australia and Japan. The United States also removed remaining economic sanctions that had been placed on Pakistan after the country's 1998 nuclear tests. In return, Pakistan increased intelligence cooperation with the United States, although some U.S. critics charged that Pakistani intelligence officials continued to covertly provide support to fundamentalist Islamic groups. Pakistan transferred more than 700 suspected terrorists and insurgents over to the United States.

In 2006, Musharraf attempted a new strategy and negotiated a peace agreement with tribal leaders in the northwest by which the region was granted increased autonomy in exchange for pledges to suppress al Qaeda and the Taliban at the local level. Tribal chieftains further agreed to expel foreign fighters end support for insurgents in Afghanistan. The government agreed to withdraw about 70,000 troops from the area and release a number of prisoners. Existing al Qaeda or Taliban fighters were granted an amnesty if they agree to lay down their arms. The ceasefire proved ineffective as al Qaeda and the Taliban used the withdrawal of government forces to expand their network of bases.

In July 2007, government forces captured a mosque in Islamabad that was being used by militants in the capital to organize attacks and promote radical Islam. The siege left 100 dead, including Abdul Rashid Ghazi, a fundamentalist cleric with ties to insurgent groups in Pakistan. Musharraf received praise from the Bush administration and other Western governments for his efforts to suppress Islamic terrorist groups; however, tribal leaders in the northwest annulled their year-old ceasefire with the government, prompting new fighting in the region. The Taliban and other terrorist groups launched new strikes throughout the country and formed a new coalition of approximately 20 Islamic groups under the banner of Student Movement of Pakistan (Tehrik-e-Taliban, or TTP). The TTP was led by Baitullah Mehsud. It launched attacks throughout the Swat Valley in a campaign that killed more than 1,500 civilians. The TTP particularly targeted schools, destroying more than 180 facilities. By 2009, the TTP controlled about 90 percent of the Swat Valley.

Meanwhile, Musharraf faced growing discontent with his rule, especially after the regime dismissed the chief justice of the nation's supreme court. In an effort to reach out to opposition groups, the president resigned from the military and allowed former Prime Minister Benazir Bhutto to return from exile. After she landed in Pakistan on October 18, 2007, suicide bombers attacked the crowds who came out to cheer her convoy, killing 145 and injuring more than 300. On November 3, Musharraf declared martial law. More than 5,000 militants and suspected terrorists were arrested.

Although she survived the attack, Bhutto was subsequently killed on December 27 in another suicide attack. Bhutto's death united the political opposition in Pakistan. Musharraf postponed legislative elections scheduled for January for a month because of rising terrorism. In balloting on February 18, 2008, no party won a majority in the parliament, but a coalition government was formed and impeachment proceedings were launched against Musharraf. Musharraf resigned on August 18 and went into exile in the United Kingdom. Bhutto's husband, Asif Ali Zardari, was elected president. Zardari endeavored to negotiate with the TTP and other Islamic militant groups. Meanwhile, the United States increasingly undertook military and intelligence operations inside Pakistan. U.S. special operations forces repeatedly crossed the border into Pakistan from Afghanistan to target Taliban and al Qaeda figures and facilities. The United States also conducted an increasing number of strikes by unmanned aerial drones. Nonetheless, terrorist attacks continued to increase. In 2008 alone, there were more than 1,800 attacks throughout the country. One of the most significant was a truck bombing of the Marriott Hotel in Islamabad on September 20, 2008, in which 54 people were killed and more than 260 were injured. The Taliban denied responsibility, but U.S. intelligence uncovered evidence that al Qaeda was behind the strikes. Attacks continued to rise in October, with more than 300 people killed that month alone. Meanwhile, the United States increased pressure on Pakistan to undertake a broad military and law enforcement offensive against the Taliban and al Qaeda (see Chapter 10).

Central and South America

Central and South America emerged as a front in the war on terror because of U.S. concerns that terrorists could infiltrate the United States through Mexico or the Caribbean or form alliances with overseas terror networks. In addition, U.S. officials were worried that terrorist groups might become active in the drug trade and use funds to finance attacks. By 2001, a number of insurgent groups in Latin America, including the Revolutionary Armed Forces of Colombia (Fuerzas Armadas Revolucionarias de Colombia, or FARC) and the Shining Path (Sendero Luminoso) of Peru, had become involved in both the drug trade and kidnappings. In addition, the groups had formed links with other international terrorist groups. For instance, in the 1990s, FARC and the Irish Republican Army (IRA) collaborated on training and the acquisition of weapons and supplies. U.S. intelligence officials had identified an alarming trend whereby groups in the region had brought in experienced terrorists from Iran, Lebanon, Libya, Syria, and Yemen to help train local recruits and offer advice on operations.

In order to suppress domestic terrorist groups after 2001, the United States increased counterterrorism and anti-drug funding throughout the region. The most significant U.S. effort was Plan Colombia, an expansion of an effort began in 2000 under the Clinton administration in which the United States provided increased military aid to suppress the drug trade. U.S. military personnel were also deployed to the region to train Colombian security forces. The program also increased the social and economic assistance the United States provided to Colombia. The number of American troops in the country eventually rose to 500. Under the Bush administration, funding for the Plan Colombia initially decreased from $765 million in 2000 to $243 million in 2001, but after the 9/11 attacks the funding rose steadily to $641 million by 2005.

In addition to indigenous terrorist groups, Middle Eastern terrorist organizations such as Hamas and Hezbollah conducted strikes in the 1990s. For instance, in 1992, Hezbollah terrorists bombed the Israeli Embassy in Buenos Aires, Argentina, killing more than 30 people. Two years later, Hezbollah bombed the Argentine-Israeli Mutual Association in Buenos Aries. That attack killed more than 80. By 2000, U.S. counterterrorism officials were mainly concerned with a region that bordered Argentina, Brazil, and Paraguay, which was home to a significant Muslim population. Although there were links to Iranian-sponsored terrorist groups in the region, including Hamas and Hezbollah, intelligence reports indicated that there were no al Qaeda–affiliated organizations in the area.[2]

A number of countries in Central and South America deployed troops as part of either Operation Enduring Freedom or Operation Iraqi Freedom. For instance, El Salvador, Honduras, and Nicaragua all provided small troop contingents for Operation Iraqi Freedom, averaging about 300 soldiers per nation.

Eastern Europe and the Caucasus

Many nations in Eastern Europe and the Caucasus offered varying degrees of support for Operation Enduring Freedom or Operation Iraqi Freedom. Nations including the Vilnius 10 hoped to cultivate closer relations with the United States and other Western nations and perceived that support for the war on terror would lead to membership in organizations such as NATO. In addition, the Bush administration offered a variety of incentives for countries to support the war on terror, ranging from economic aid to military assistance.

The United States deployed Special Forces units and military trainers to Georgia in October 2001. Although not a central front in the war on terror, Georgian officials requested aid because of Chechen rebels who were fighting for independence against Russia. The United States also provided military equipment. The deployment was criticized by Russian officials, who complained that the United States was attempting to gain influence in an area that had traditionally been within Moscow's sphere of influence.

Tensions between the United States and Russia worsened following the "Rose Revolution" in 2003, in which the pro-Russian former Soviet foreign minister Eduard Shevardnadze was deposed. Georgian elections on January 4, 2004, brought the U.S.-educated and pro-Western Mikhail Saakashvili to power. Saakashvili increased ties with the United States, which continued to provide military training, weapons, and an increasingly large amount of foreign aid. During a speech in the Georgian capital of Tbilisi in May 2005, Bush declared before an enthusiastic crowd of 100,000 that the country was a "beacon of liberty for the region and the world." Saakahvili hoped the growing relationship with the United States would serve as a counter to Russia influence in the region.

One manifestation of the close relationship between the United States and Georgia was Georgian participation in the U.S.-led coalitions in Iraq and Afghanistan. Georgia sent soldiers to Iraq in August 2003, and the deployment eventually numbered some 2,000. The country dispatched 175 troops to Afghanistan in 2009 before increasing that number to 1,000 in 2010.

Bush pushed for Georgia to become part of NATO, but in 2008 the alliance rejected U.S. proposals to quickly grant membership to the country. In August 2008, Russia dispatched troops to Georgia in support of two breakaway provinces. The United States, NATO, and the European Union condemned the incursion, but took no direct action against Moscow other than suspending Russian participation in various NATO organs.

Armenia traditionally had close relations with Russia. As a result of a border dispute with Azerbaijan, Armenia looked to Russia for military and diplomatic support. However, the country also sought stronger ties with the United States after the 9/11 terrorist attacks. While Russia continued to maintain some 8,000 troops in Armenia, in 2004 the United States provided $75 million in economic aid and $2.5 million in military assistance. Armenia subsequently deployed a 50-member military unit to Iraq from 2005 to 2008.

After the 9/11 attacks, Azerbaijan announced its support for the war on terror and allowed the coalition use of its airspace to send supplies to Afghanistan. In return, in 2002, the Bush administration ended economic sanctions on Azerbaijan that were enacted during the country's border war with Armenia. The United States also provided military and economic aid and granted Azerbaijan "most favored nation" trade status. Azerbaijan sent troops to Afghanistan as part of the International Security Assistance Force (ISAF) in 2002. In 2003, the country deployed 250 soldiers to Iraq. The troops were withdrawn in 2008.

Eastern European nations, from Bosnia-Herzegovina to Ukraine, deployed troops in Operation Enduring Freedom and Operation Iraqi Freedom. These deployments ranged from the 24 soldiers Moldova dispatched as part of the coalition of the willing in Iraq in September 2003 to Ukraine's 1,650 troops.

The Broader Middle East, North Africa, and the Persian Gulf

U.S. allies in the Middle East, including Egypt, Jordan, and the states of the Persian Gulf (Bahrain, Kuwait, Oman, Qatar, Saudi Arabia, and the United Arab Emirates), condemned the 9/11 attacks and offered various forms of cooperation with the United States. For instance, U.S. air units flew resupply missions to Afghanistan during the initial combat phase of Operation Enduring Freedom from

Qatar. Approximately 15–20 flights per day went through the Al-Udeid air base, which was home to 6,500 U.S. military personnel and defense contractors. Qatar also led the way in cooperative efforts with the United States to deny funding for terrorist organizations, enacting a strict money-laundering law after the 9/11 attacks and closing suspicious foreign bank accounts. Bahrain provided vessels to support the naval activities of Operation Enduring Freedom, while special operations forces from the United Arab Emirates were deployed to Afghanistan, as was an Egyptian military medical unit.

Saudi Arabia, which had been one of the largest sources of funding for Islamic extremists groups, also began to crack down on money laundering, closing accounts of questionable charitable groups and auditing accounts of extremist groups. In 2003, the Bush administration negotiated new restrictions by the Saudi government on financing Islamic groups, and the FBI and IRS were allowed to establish offices in Riyadh to coordinate U.S.-Saudi efforts to suppress the financing of terrorist groups. Other nations throughout the region also worked with U.S. intelligence agencies to track and arrest terrorists. Reports also charged that the Bush administration established secret detention centers in states including Egypt, Morocco, and Jordan, where suspects could be tortured outside of the laws of the United States.

U.S.-Jordanian intelligence cooperation had been strong since the 1990s (see Chapter 1), and became closer following the 2000 Millennium Bombing Plot. Jordan deployed a military medical unit in Afghanistan as part of Operation Enduring Freedom in December 2001, and they established a medical treatment facility in Mazar-e-Sharif.

The Arab states in the broader Middle East often faced a difficult balancing act during the war on terror. Popular opinion in the countries was highly anti-Israeli and often anti-American. For instance, after the onset of Operation Enduring Freedom, a poll found that only 30 percent of Saudis backed the U.S.-led war on terror, while 57 percent opposed American efforts to suppress terrorism.[3] Official support for the United States was often met by increased popular discontent, ranging from street protests to an increase in terrorism and insurgencies. Conversely, many of the governments in the region were highly critical of the Bush administration for not supporting Gulf initiatives to resolve the Arab-Israeli conflict. Regimes typically avoided public manifestations of support for the war on terror, but generally increased intelligence and law enforcement cooperation with the United States.

Many terrorist groups, including al Qaeda, that conducted campaigns against the United States and the West also targeted Middle Eastern and Persian Gulf states. The volume of attacks increased significantly after the onset of the 2003 Iraq War. For instance, on May 12, 2003, three housing compounds in Riyadh, Saudi Arabia, were attacked by suicide bombers. The attacks left 34 dead and more than 100 wounded. Eleven suspected al Qaeda terrorists were subsequently arrested for plotting the attacks (nine suicide bombers were killed in the strikes). The Saudi government subsequently launched a major campaign to suppress al Qaeda and other terrorist groups. More than 350 religious officials were removed from their positions, and more than 600 suspected terrorists or terrorist supporters were arrested. In November 2005, three hotels were attacked in Amman, Jordan, by suicide bombers, killing 60 and wounding more than 100. The rise in terrorism led to increased intelligence cooperation with the United States. Meanwhile the war divided the region. Some states such as Bahrain, Kuwait, and Qatar allowed the United States to use facilities to launch the invasion of Iraq. Kuwait was the staging area for the ground offensive against Iraq. Both the Kuwaiti government and the Kuwaiti people supported the invasion and the subsequent ouster of the Saddam regime because of Iraq's invasion of their country in 1990. Qatar hosted the main facilities for U.S. Central Command, the main headquarters for coalition forces in the initial phase of the invasion. Later the main U.S. air operations center in the region was transferred from Saudi Arabia to Qatar.

However, there was often popular unrest over government support for the Iraq invasion. For example, there were large demonstrations in January 2003 in Bahrain prior to the invasion. Many in the region feared that the Iraq invasion would reduce the ability of the Iraq to serve as a balance to Shiite Iran. The resultant insurgency in Iraq increased radicalism and terrorism in the region. Just as Muslims had traveled to Afghanistan in the 1980s to fight the Soviets, Arabs from around the Middle East went to Iraq to fight the U.S.-led coalition (see Chapter 7).

After the 9/11 attacks, Algeria pledged its support for the war on terror and increased intelligence and security cooperation with the United States. In 2003, the government even forbade domestic protests against the U.S.-led invasion of Iraq. The increased ties between Algeria and the United States helped erode the country's diplomatic isolation that had existed since the 1990s following a military takeover of the government. In 2006, al Qaeda–allied domestic terrorist groups increased attacks in Algeria after the government offered a ceasefire to insurgents, including a promise of amnesty for past attacks. The terrorist campaign was designed to undercut domestic support for the regime.

Morocco and Tunisia also endorsed the U.S.-led war on terror. Morocco and the United States conducted joint military exercises, and the Kingdom was even praised by Secretary of Defense Rumsfeld in 2006 for its cooperation with the United States during a trip to the region. Meanwhile, in 2004, Morocco and the United States signed a free trade agreement. Between 2004 and 2008, trade between the two countries almost doubled. Domestic critics in Morocco charged that the economic agreement was a bribe by Washington to gain the Kingdom's support in the war on terror. Morocco was the target of a series of al Qaeda–linked terrorist attacks, including the 2003 Casablanca car bombings which left 45 dead and hundreds injured. Fourteen suicide bombers targeted Western hotels, restaurants, and a Jewish cemetery. Tunisia was the recipient of increased U.S. military assistance, beginning in 2006, in response to its support for American counterterrorism efforts.

Syria and Lebanon

The United States had long considered Syria a state sponsor of terrorism and had various forms of sanctions in place because of the country's support for Hezbollah and interference in Lebanon. In the immediate aftermath of the 9/11 attacks, both countries shared intelligence on terrorist groups, including al Qaeda. However, Syria opposed the 2003 Iraq War. Both countries were ruled by the Ba'athist Party (*Ba'ath* means "resurrection" in Arabic), an Arab secular, socialist political movement. In addition, Syrian leaders feared that toppling Saddam in Iraq would prompt the United States to attempt regime change in Syria. After the U.S.-led invasion began in March 2003, Syria allowed anti-coalition fighters to cross the border into Iraq and provided logistical and military assistance to insurgents in Iraq. Consequently, the Bush administration imposed new sanctions on the country designed to end Syria's financial support for terrorist groups.

On February 14, 2005, former Lebanese prime minister Rafik Hariri was assassinated. Hariri was a staunch opponent of Syria, which had occupied Lebanon since the 1970s. His death was blamed on Syrian intelligence officials, and the United States and other Western powers called for Syria to withdraw. Meanwhile, domestic protests against Syria spread throughout Lebanon. In what became known as the Cedar Revolution, the pro-Syrian government resigned on February 28 and a pro-Western bloc won legislative elections. Syria withdrew its forces in April under international pressure. U.S. officials touted the Cedar Revolution as a manifestation of the success of the Bush Doctrine.

Syria continued to support anti-American insurgents in Iraq, and in February 2008 Bush issued an executive order that placed additional sanctions on the country. In addition, the United States took military action to destroy the smuggling network that existed on the Syrian side of the border with Iraq. In October, U.S. special operations forces and ground troops conducted an incursion into Syria. Eight Syrians were killed, and several facilities were destroyed. Syria protested that the attack was a violation of international law, while the insurgent networks shifted their operations to other areas.

Libya

Libyan leader Muammar Gaddafi utilized the war on terror to improve his international image and distance his regime from terrorism. Libya provided intelligence information to the United States and endorsed the war on terror. Gaddafi also ended overt support for several terrorist groups. Concurrently, the regime accelerated negotiations with the West over compensation for past terrorist acts. In August 2003, Libya and the United States announced an agreement whereby Libya did not admit direct involvement in the 1988 Lockerbie Bombing (see Chapter 1), but accepted responsibility for the actions of any of its officials. Libya also agreed to pay $10 million to the families of the 270 people killed in the attack. Libya also agreed to pay $170 million to the 170 families of those killed in a 1989 bombing that destroyed a French passenger plane over Niger, and $35 million to the victims and their families of the 1986 Berlin Disco bombing. After the agreements, the United Nations rescinded sanctions against Libya in September 2004.

In 2003, the U.S.-led invasion of Iraq prompted Libyan leader Gaddafi to enter into negotiations with the United States and the United Kingdom over his country's WMD program. On December 19, Gaddafi announced an end to Libya's chemical and nuclear weapons programs and invited UN weapons inspectors to oversee the destruction of WMDs and equipment. Inspectors discovered that Libya had an advanced nuclear program and was endeavoring to enrich uranium for use in nuclear weapons. The country had also produced 23 tons of materials to make mustard gas and acquired the munitions to deliver the chemical weapon. Libya also agreed to destroy its arsenal of medium- to long-range missiles capable of delivering WMD warheads. U.S., British, and Russian officials oversaw the destruction of the WMD components under UN supervision. The United States spent about $2.5 million to assist Libya. Libya later signed and ratified the Chemical Weapons Convention in 2004. In February 2004, the United States ended some economic sanctions against the country, and most additional restrictions were lifted in April. Full diplomatic relations between Libya and the United States were restored in 2006, and Bush appointed the first U.S. ambassador to Libya in more than 35 years. Libya was taken off of the State Department's list of state sponsors of terrorism. U.S. energy companies subsequently negotiated a range of agreements with the government, totaling almost $5 billion in oil and natural gas exploration and production. The European Union also ended sanctions against Libya, and some European countries even resumed weapons sales to the regime. In 2007, the Bush administration reversed a longstanding U.S. policy of opposing a nonpermanent seat for Libya on the UN Security Council (Libya became a member of the Security Council in January 2008). The administration also worked to exempt Libya from a 2008 law that permitted American citizens to sue to gain access to or payments from U.S. assets of countries that had sponsored terrorism. The Bush administration hoped that Libya would emerge as an example of the benefits of renouncing terrorism and the pursuit of WMDs and that countries such as Iran and North Korea would follow suit (neither did). Meanwhile, relations between Libya and the United States deteriorated after the election of Barack Obama in 2008 (see Chapter 10).

The Asia-Pacific

The Philippines

The Abu Sayyaf Group was an al Qaeda–affiliated Islamic terrorist group in the Philippines. The organization had received some funding from al Qaeda, and some Abu Sayyaf members had been trained in the Middle East. Abu Sayyaf sought independence in the southern Philippines and the creation of an Islamic theocratic state. In 2001, it numbered approximately 1,000 fighters. They carried out a series of bombings and assassinations of government officials through the late 1990s and early 2000s. The group also conducted numerous kidnappings for ransom which they used to finance operations. Between 1998 and 2002, the group kidnapped more than 50 foreign nationals and Filipinos. In a number of instances, Libya paid the ransom for those kidnapped in what Western intelligence agencies described as backdoor method to funnel money to the terrorist group. In one example in 2000, Libya secured the release of a group of European hostages with an offer of $25 million to the group.

On May 27, 2001, the Abu Sayyaf Group attacked a popular beach resort for foreign tourists on Palawan Island in the Philippines and took 16 people hostage, including three Americans, Guillermo Sobero and Martin and Gracia Burnham. Sobero was later beheaded, while the Burnhams remained in captivity until June 7, 2002, when Philippine security forces identified their location and launched a campaign to secure their release. Martin Burnham was killed during the rescue.

In an effort to help the Filipino government suppress Abu Sayyaf, in 2002, 1,200 U.S. special forces troops and military trainers were deployed to the Philippines as part of Operation Enduring Freedom (the Filipino campaign was designated Operation Enduring Eagle). The United States also provided the Philippines with military equipment and financial aid. U.S. troops assisted Filipino security forces in operations against the Abu Sayyaf Group and another Islamic terrorist organization, Jemaah Islamiyah. By the end of 2002, approximately 500 Abu Sayyaf fighters had been killed or captured and the group's main bases had been identified and overrun. In addition, a number of senior leaders had been killed or captured. The number of U.S. troops was reduced to 600 in 2005. The following year, Abu Sayyaf's leader, Khaffady Janjalani, who was wanted by the FBI for terrorist activities, was killed in a battle with government security forces. The number of active fighters was estimated to have declined to 100 by 2008.

In many ways, Operation Enduring Eagle was the most successful aspect of the war on terror outside of Afghanistan or Iraq. Besides suppressing terrorism, U.S. forces also conducted a range of humanitarian missions, including building schools, hospitals, and clinics, as well as working on infrastructure programs to improve water quality and sanitation. The Philippines deployed a small contingent of about 50 troops to Iraq from 2003 to 2004.

Indonesia

Indonesia is the largest Muslim country in the world, with a population of 240 million. Although Indonesia condemned the 9/11 attacks, the country initially took few steps to suppress extremist Islamic groups and refused to even acknowledge that an al Qaeda–linked group, Jemaah Islamiyah, was operating in the country despite warnings by American, Australian, and other Western intelligence officials. In addition, there were widespread protests and demonstrations throughout the country in November 2001 following the U.S.-led invasion of Afghanistan. Nonetheless, Indonesia's counterterrorism policies changed dramatically in 2002.

In the largest terrorist attack in Indonesian history, on October 12, 2002, Jemaah Islamiyah exploded two bombs outside of popular tourist nightclubs on the island of Bali. The strikes killed 202 people and injured more than 200 others. The majority of people killed were foreign tourists, including 88 Australians. A third bomb was detonated outside of the U.S. consulate, but it caused little damage. Three members of Jemaah Islamiyah were executed for their role in the attack. The Bali attacks demonstrated the capability of al Qaeda–linked groups to conduct major terrorist attacks and showed that although the al Qaeda network had been destroyed in Afghanistan, its allies and affiliated groups could continue to undertake major strikes. On August 5, 2003, a car bomb was detonated at the Marriott Hotel in Jakarta, Indonesia. Thirteen people were killed and 149 injured in the attack that was perpetuated by Jemaah Islamiyah. Although the hotel was mainly frequented by Westerners and tourists, most of those killed and hurt were Indonesians.

Tourism was an important sector of the Indonesian economy, and the government undertook significant action after the attacks in order to suppress terrorism and reassure foreign visitors. Bush would subsequently describe Indonesia as an important ally in the global campaign against terrorism. In May 2005, the United States ended some military sanctions that had been put in place in 1991 in response to the government's repression in East Timor (the area became the independent country of Timor-Leste in 2002). In November 2005, the United States resumed military sales to Indonesia.

Somalia and the Horn of Africa

Since the early 1990s, Somalia had been a haven for some Islamic extremist groups. By September 2001, the country was in the midst of a longstanding civil war. The instability and strife created conditions that allowed terrorist groups to establish bases in Somalia. In an effort to contain the instability, the U.S. military established the Combined and Joint Task Force—Horn of Africa in 2002 (CJTF-HOA). Officially, the command was part of Operation Enduring Freedom and included troops and naval and air units from coalition partners such as Australia, Canada, France, Germany, Pakistan, Turkey, and the United Kingdom. The United States negotiated an agreement to create a base and headquarters for CJTF-HOA in Djibouti, and at its peak the facility housed some 2,000 coalition forces.

Fighting in Somalia and Ethiopia had created a large number of refugees who traveled to Djibouti. Because of concerns that Islamic extremists had entered the country among the refugees, Djibouti expelled more than 80,000 illegal immigrants in 2003. During the expulsions, the government arrested more than

200 people suspected of ties to terrorist groups in cooperation with coalition intelligence officers.

With support from the United States, a temporary peace plan for Somalia was finalized in 2004. The agreement called for the creation of a transitional government and initially received the support of most Somali factions. However, an Islamic political and military movement, the Islamic Union, continued fighting against the new unity government. The Islamic Union was accused by the Bush administration of having ties to al Qaeda and other terrorist groups, and the organization became part of the Islamic Courts Union which waged a civil war against the transitional government from 2006 to 2009. The leader of the movement, Sheikh Hassan Dahir Aweys, was listed on the U.S. terrorism watch list. Ethiopian troops intervened in 2006 and helped suppress the Courts Union, and an 8,000-member African Union peacekeeping force was subsequently deployed to Mogadishu. Meanwhile the military wing of the Courts Union, Al Shabaab ("The Youth"), launched a terrorist campaign against the transitional government, international peacekeepers, foreign aid workers, and UN personnel.

Coalition forces in Africa conducted three main missions in the region. First, naval units patrolled the waters off of the Horn of Africa to interdict suspicious vessels. For instance, coalition naval units near the Horn of Africa stopped a North Korean ship on December 9, 2002. The ship was carrying Scud missiles and warheads and was believed to be destined for Yemen. In addition, a dramatic increase in piracy in the waters off of Somalia led to the deployment of international naval forces to protect commercial shipping. The Somali-based pirates hijacked commercial freighters and tankers and held the ships and crew for ransom. By 2008, there was, on average, more than 100 pirate attacks per year, with more than 40 successful hijackings annually. The United States secured permission from the Somali transitional government to deploy international naval forces in Somali waters, an agreement that was endorsed by the UN Security Council on June 2, 2008. Increased patrols led to a decline in attacks and hijackings after 2008.

Second, allied troops trained military and security units in Djibouti, Ethiopia, and Kenya in counterterrorism tactics and worked to improve intelligence gathering and cooperation among the nations and the United States. A separate program, the Pan Sahel Initiative, provided military training for forces from Chad, Mali, Mauritania, and Niger from 2002 to 2004. The United States developed partnerships with Algeria, Burkina Faso, Morocco, Tunisia, Chad, Mali, Mauritania, Niger, Nigeria, and Senegal to train security forces and increase law enforcement and intelligence capabilities. Although an expansion of Operation Enduring Freedom, the Trans-Saharan initiative was led by the State Department, not the Department of Defense, and was officially designed to increase stability throughout the region, instead of focusing primarily on counterterrorism.

Third, and finally, coalition forces carried some covert operations against terrorist groups or bases in the area. The majority of these missions were in Somalia and

Yemen. Some operations involved the CIA and other intelligence agencies; other missions were undertaken by the military. For instance, in November 2002, the CIA used an unmanned aerial drone to attack a car carrying Abu Ali al-Harithi, one of the architects of the 2000 *Cole* attack. Harithi was killed in the strike, which involved cooperation between the U.S. and Yemeni government. The success of the attack prompted the CIA to expand the use of aerial drones to strike terrorist leaders and facilities. However, in February 2006, 23 al Qaeda prisoners escaped from a Yemeni prison, including 13 figures who were convicted for participating in the 2000 attack on the USS *Cole*. The escape underscored the influence of al Qaeda in the country. Meanwhile, on January 8, 2007, U.S. aircraft fired on suspected al Qaeda positions in Somalia during the ongoing civil war between the country's transitional government and the Islamic Courts Union (the United States conducted three other airstrikes over the course of the year). Aden Hashi Ayro, the commander of *Al Shabaab*, was killed during a U.S. aerial attack on May 1, 2008.

The growing importance of Africa in the war on terror prompted the Bush administration to create a new military command for the continent, U.S. Africa Command (AFRICOM) in 2007. AFRICOM became one of six regional U.S. military commands around the world. It was tasked with coordinating U.S. and coalition counterterrorism operations in Africa and overseeing other military missions in the region that were not associated with the war on terror. Nonetheless, by the end of the Bush administration, al Qaeda and other terrorist groups still maintained significant cells in both Somali and Yemen.

Yemen

Following the 2000 attack on the USS *Cole*, the United States increased pressure on Yemen to suppress radical Islamic groups and bolster intelligence and covert operations in the region. After the 9/11 attacks, the Yemeni government announced that it would cooperate with the U.S.-led war on terror. The government further increased military and intelligence cooperation with the United States and began to close religious schools and centers that were perceived to be recruiting centers for Islamic terrorist groups. Known Islamic radicals were arrested, and a number of foreigners were expelled. By 2005, more than 500 suspected terrorists or Islamic radicals had been detained. However, the government offensive was met with broad resistance by opposition groups, such as the Islamic Islah Party, which opposed the growing relationship with the United States. Beginning in 2004, a Shiite rebellion killed thousands and lasted for four years. Within the country, terrorist strikes grew in size and scope. In February 2006, more than 20 al Qaeda prisoners escaped from a Yemeni prison. The government granted tacit approval for the United States to undertake strikes by unmanned aerial drones against al Qaeda figures in the country.

Conclusion

The Bush administration sought to develop the war on terror as a global campaign in which the United States and its allies used a range of tactics and methods to suppress terrorism. Multiple countries increased intelligence and law enforcement cooperation with the United States. Heightened collaboration was important in the apprehension of terrorist leaders such as Khalid Sheikh Mohammad. In addition, the Bush administration worked with the United Nations and individual countries to reduce the flow of money to terrorist groups by cracking down on money laundering and the illicit movement of funds through informal networks such as the hawala system. These efforts clearly made it more difficult for groups such as al Qaeda to operate, but the campaign did not stop terrorism or completely destroy the ability of al Qaeda and its allies to carry out large-scale attacks.

The military aspects of the global war on terror also produced mixed results. Troop contributions to the U.S.-led military campaigns in Afghanistan and Iraq were the most visible signs of cooperation with the United States. However, many states provided access to bases, the use of airspace, and other forms of military support. Coalition military campaigns in Afghanistan and Iraq were both initially highly successful, but insurgencies in both countries soon undermined the broader global counterterrorism efforts, and by 2004 Iraq emerged as the main center of the struggle between the United States and its partners and al Qaeda and its allies.

Notes

1. George W. Bush, "Speech to the United Nations," November 10, 2001.

2. Mark P. Sullivan, *Latin America: Terrorism Issues* (Washington, D.C.: Congressional Research Service, 2010), 4.

3. Zogby International, "The 10 Nation 'Impressions of America' Poll Report," August 7, 2002.

7

The Insurgency in Iraq

Introduction

By the end of April 2003, U.S.-led forces had conquered most of Iraq and toppled the regime of Saddam Hussein. However, the initial military victory proved fleeting as a multifaceted insurgency spread throughout much of the country. The insurgency began as resistance to the U.S.-led coalition and the interim Iraqi government, but it soon included a sectarian conflict between Sunnis and Shiites. Matters were complicated by the initial failure to capture Saddam or many of the senior regime officials. The insurgency lasted from late 2003 through 2008, and more U.S. and allied service personnel were killed in the fighting than died in the initial invasion. The fighting undermined the domestic popularity of President Bush in the United States and eroded support for the occupation.

The Bush administration attempted a number of strategies to suppress the insurgency and create a stable, democratic government. Critics charged that the United States initially did not have an adequate plan to establish a post-Saddam government, and that the United States underestimated the ability of al Qaeda and other terrorist groups to build networks within the country. Meanwhile, the controversies surrounding the invasion, including disputes over the need for military action and the presence of weapons of mass destruction (WMDs) in Iraq, complicated efforts by the United States to garner international support for its efforts in Iraq. Nonetheless, Iraqis participated in a series of elections that were the freest and fairest in the history of the nation. Eventually, a strong central government emerged and the insurgency was suppressed by a combination of a troop "surge" by American and allied forces and a broad anti-terrorist campaign that garnered the support of Sunni chieftains. By 2008, the insurgency had been largely suppressed, although al Qaeda and other groups continued to conduct attacks throughout the country. The waning of the insurgency prompted the beginning of troop withdrawals from Iraq and a reorientation of U.S. military efforts to Afghanistan (see Chapter 8).

The Beginnings of the Insurgency

After the United States captured Baghdad, U.S. planners hoped to quickly install an interim Iraqi government as the coalition had done in Afghanistan. However, Iraq was even more divided among religious and ethnic lines. Although 97 percent of Iraqis were Muslim, they were divided by religion: 60 percent of the people were Shiite, while 35 percent were Sunni, and there was also a small Christian population. Although Shiites were the majority people, the government and economic system was traditionally dominated by the Sunni elite. In addition, Iraqis were divided by ethnicity, with 75 percent of the people Arab, 20 percent Kurdish, and the remaining 5 percent Turkmen or Assyrian. Since the end of the 1990s, the Kurdish areas of the north had been semi-autonomous with their own elected government. Both the Shiites and the Kurds had faced brutal repression under the Saddam regime. The challenge for the United States and its allies was to help the Iraqis create an inclusive government that did not alienate any of the major groups.

Since the 1990s, the United States had provided significant monetary and technical assistance to an Iraqi resistance organization, the Shiite-dominated Iraqi National Congress. Formed in exile in 1992, the group was led by Ahmed Chalabi. It provided considerable intelligence to the United States prior to the invasion and was seen as the nucleus of a post-Saddam government. However, after the fall of the Saddam regime, it became apparent that some information provided by the Iraqi National Congress, especially intelligence relating to WMDs, was false. In addition, the organization did not have the clout within Iraq that U.S. officials had initially believed and the coalition instead sought to create an interim government that included exile groups, including the Iraqi National Congress, as well as domestic opposition groups.

The End and Beginning of Combat

As noted in Chapter 5, on May 1, 2003, Bush declared that the main fighting in Iraq was over. Speaking from the deck of the U.S. aircraft carrier the *Abraham Lincoln*, Bush declared to the world, "Major combat operations in Iraq have ended. In the battle of Iraq, the United States and our allies have prevailed. And now our coalition is engaged in securing and reconstructing that country."[1] However, the coalition forces had not captured Saddam, his two sons, or most of the senior members of the regime. Some Iraqi military forces and paramilitary groups, including the Saddam Fedayeen (see Chapter 5), continued to fight coalition forces in the vain hope that Saddam or other Ba'athists could be returned to power. The initial inability to capture the Iraqi leader undermined Iraqi support for the coalition as people feared Saddam and his supporters still had the power or ability harm or kill opponents of the regime.

U.S. forces developed a list of its 55 most wanted Iraqi leaders and placed their pictures on a deck of playing cards. For instance, Saddam Hussein was the ace of spades, while his sons Uday and Qusay were the aces of hearts and clubs, respectively. The cards were designed to make it easy for coalition forces to identify wanted Iraqis.

On May 11, former ambassador L. Paul Bremer arrived in Iraq to oversee the Coalition Provisional Authority (CPA). His main task included the reconstruction of Iraq and the formation of an Iraqi government. In one of his first acts, on May 23, Bremer issued an order that formally dissolved the Iraqi Army and other components of the Saddam regime. Bremer hoped to create a new security force and government that would enjoy the trust of the Iraqi people, especially the Shiite majority and the Kurds, both groups which had been brutally suppressed under the Sunni-dominated Ba'athist regime of Saddam. The program came to be known as "de-Ba'athification." The dismissal of the Ba'athist security forces created two problems for the U.S.-led coalition. First, many of the newly dismissed security forces joined the insurgency. They had lost their careers, status, and income, and directed their resentment and anger against the coalition. Second, the rapid dismantling of the security forces created a vacuum. Iraqi soldiers and police officers no longer patrolled the streets or guarded installations. Most coalition forces were still engaged in fighting Saddam loyalists and not engaged in routine police functions. As a result, there was widespread looting and vandalism of businesses, government facilities, and homes. The core of the insurgency initially was an area that came to be known as the "Sunni Triangle," a rough geographic triangle that ran northwest from Baghdad in the South to Tikrit in the north and then southwest to Ramadi. The area had a large Sunni population, some of whom remained loyal to Saddam after the invasion.

In an effort to contain the growing chaos, coalition forces launched Operation Desert Scorpion. The campaign was designed to suppress attacks against coalition forces and installations. U.S. military leaders also hoped to capture former regime figures that were wanted or that were suspected of participating in the insurgency, including Saddam and his sons. Finally, the operation was tasked to collect and destroy weapons and munitions that remained from the invasion. As coalition forces advanced into Iraq in March and April, many Iraqi soldiers and security forces simply deserted their posts, taking their weapons with them. Iraqi military bases and camps were also abandoned, leaving a large amount of weaponry behind. As a result, insurgents and anti-U.S. fighters had an easy time acquiring arms and munitions. The campaign captured large caches of weapons and killed or captured more than 100 insurgents, but it failed to stem the rising violence.

The Coalition of the Willing

U.S. military officials planned for a gradual withdrawal of American combat forces, with the concurrent deployment of troops from coalition partners and the creation of Iraqi national security forces. Ultimately more than 30 countries contributed troops to Operation Enduring Freedom. The majority of these forces were deployed as part of what was dubbed the Multinational Force (MNF). Most of the contributors to the MNF only deployed small numbers of troops. Besides the United States, the largest contributors were the United Kingdom with 46,000 troops; South Korea, 3,600; Italy, 3,200; Poland, 2,500; and Australia and Georgia with 2,000 each. Other countries that maintained at least 1,000 troops during their peak deployments included the Netherlands, Spain, and the Ukraine. Many countries in the coalition sent noncombat forces, including medical, engineering, and civil police units. Coalition partners also placed restrictions on the deployment of their forces and insisted that the units not be stationed in the midst of heavy combat zones. Even British forces were stationed in the less dangerous southern areas, away from the Sunni Triangle. These factors complicated coalition planning efforts and meant that the majority of combat operations were undertaken by U.S. soldiers.

The CPA initially planned to train 75,000 Iraqi police officers and a 40,000-member army. These numbers grew as the coalition endeavored to rebuild both the Iraqi military and civilian police forces. However, by April 2004, there were only about 5,000 soldiers in the Iraqi military. However, the post-Saddam Iraqi military ultimately grew to number more than 500,000.

Al Qaeda and Sectarian Strife

At some point during the summer of 2002, Abu Musab al-Zarqawi arrived in northern Iraq where he became active with the Islamic extremist group Ansar al-Islam. The group fought Kurds in the area. Zarqawi was wanted by Jordan, Iraq, and the United States for his terrorist activities, and the United States offered a $25 million bounty for his capture. Zarqawi had traveled to Afghanistan in 1989 to join the Mujahedeen and later became active in radical Islamic terrorist groups. He was jailed in Jordan from 1992 to 1999, and then returned to Afghanistan and joined al Qaeda. After the U.S. invasion, Zarqawi became the leader of al Qaeda in Iraq. When the coalition captured Baghdad, he and his supporters began to conduct attacks on U.S. and allied personnel and facilities. The broader al Qaeda network provided funding for Zarqawi and sent recruits to join its Iraqi affiliate. The number of foreign fighters increased dramatically as time went by. By 2005, there were an estimated 5,000 foreign fighters in Iraq. Zarqawi also recruited Iraqi Sunnis, forming a special group of Iraqi suicide bombers titled the Ansar platoon. On August 7, 2003, a car bomb was detonated outside the Jordanian Embassy in Baghdad. The attack killed 14. It was the first suicide bombing in the Iraqi capital since the invasion.

Under Zarqawi, insurgents began to shift tactics. Instead of directly attacking coalition forces, insurgents increasing resorted to suicide attacks with car or truck bombs. They also utilized remote-controlled roadside bombs to target coalition convoys. The large amount of leftover ordnance after the major combat operations provided insurgents and terrorists a ready supply of munitions. They used the munitions to create homemade remote-controlled bombs that were labeled improvised explosive devices (IEDs) by the coalition. As the insurgency spread, IEDs were responsible for the major of deaths and injuries among coalition soldiers (by 2004, IEDs were responsible for approximately 70 percent of coalition casualties). Insurgents also kidnapped foreign workers, journalists, and officials, often torturing or murdering those taken.

Meanwhile, in June 2003, a Shiite cleric, Muqtada al-Sadr, established a paramilitary force in Baghdad, the Mahdi Army. The force initially numbered several hundred, but it grew rapidly to more than 10,000. The Mahdi Army emerged as a powerful political force in Iraqi politics and initially battled Sunni insurgents and Saddam loyalists. However, the Mahdi fighters also resisted coalition forces as they endeavored to gain control over Baghdad.

Meanwhile, on August 19, a truck bomb exploded at the UN headquarters in Baghdad in an attack by al Qaeda. The strike killed 23, including the head of the UN mission in Iraq, Sergio Viera DeMello. More than 100 were wounded. The attack prompted the United Nations to withdraw most of its personnel from Iraq. The same day, a suicide bomber killed 20 and injured 140 in Jerusalem, Israel.

Al Qaeda endeavored to exploit tensions between Shiites and Sunnis in Iraq in order to spark a civil war. Terrorists targeted Shiite mosques and leaders. For instance, on August 29, a suicide bomber killed 90 at a prominent Shiite mosque in Najaf, including a senior Shiite leader, Ayatollah Mohammad Baqr al-Hakim. Later, on October 27, a wave of suicide bombings in Baghdad killed 35 and injured more than 200. The strikes targeted the Red Cross/Crescent headquarters in Baghdad and three police stations. The attacks marked the beginning of what became known as the Ramadan offensive. Over the next month, there was a marked increase in suicide strikes and attacks on coalition forces. On November 2, two U.S. helicopters were hit by surface-to-air-missiles, killing 16 and wounding 20, in the largest single-day loss of life since May. Ten days later, a suicide bomber struck the headquarters of Italian coalition forces in Nasiriyah. The attack killed 19 Italians and 14 Iraqis.

In response to the al Qaeda attacks, Shiite groups, including the Mahdi Army, began to strike back at Sunni groups. Mixed Sunni-Shiite neighborhoods became increasingly segregated as militia groups forced people of other ethnicity or religious affiliation out of the area.

During the summer of 2003, the coalition did have some successes. On July 22, Saddam's sons, Uday and Qusay Hussein, were killed during a battle with U.S. troops in Mosul. An informant revealed the hiding place of the two to U.S. troops, and American special operations forces attempted to capture the brothers. However, a gun battle ensued and the two brothers, along with a bodyguard and

Qusay's 14-year-old son, were killed. The two brothers had been in hiding since the fall of Baghdad.

Ali Hassan al-Majid, nicknamed "Chemical Ali" because of his role in using chemical weapons against the Kurds, was captured by coalition forces on August 22, 2003. Majid was the fifth most-wanted figure in Iraq after the fall of Saddam. He had been Saddam's defense minister, minister of the interior, and intelligence director. Majid was tried and convicted by an Iraqi court for genocide and crimes against humanity and sentenced to death in June 2007. He was executed on January 25, 2010.

After coalition forces received intelligence about Saddam's whereabouts, an operation dubbed Red Dawn was launched, involving 600 U.S. troops. On December 13, they discovered the former Iraqi leader hiding in a small underground bunker near his hometown of Tikrit. Saddam was turned over to the interim Iraqi government for prosecution, along with 11 other members of his regime in June 2004. By January 2004, coalition troops had killed or captured 42 of the 55 most-wanted Iraqis. However, by September of that year, 1,000 U.S. soldiers had died in Iraq, including those lost in the initial invasion.

Meanwhile, by the end of 2003, coalition forces discovered more than 50 mass graves containing the bodies of Iraqis who had been executed during Saddam's regime. Estimates were that 300,000–500,000 Iraqis were killed by the regime during Saddam's reign.

The Interim Iraqi Government

As part of the effort to facilitate Iraqis taking on greater responsibility for governing their country, and to blunt anti-coalition nationalism, the CPA appointed an interim civilian government, the Iraqi Governing Council (IGC), on July 13, 2003. The IGC consisted of 25 members who were hand-picked by Bremer and the CPA. The Iraqis were all anti-Saddam figures. Careful attention was paid to make sure that the IGC reflected the ethnic divisions in Iraq. There were 13 Shiites, 5 Sunnis, 5 Kurds, 1 Christian, and 1 Turkmen. Three of the members were women. The IGC had a rotating presidency so that each of the groups would have the opportunity to lead the body. The interim government was tasked to begin drafting a new constitution for the country and to organize elections. The council was recognized by the Arab League in September as Iraq's legitimate government. Most other countries and international organizations also accepted the IGC as Iraq's government.

The IGC worked through the fall of 2003 and the winter of 2004 to draft an interim constitution. Shiites sought to have Islamic law (sharia) be the basis for the constitution, while Kurds wanted a federal system in which the provinces had significant power. Specifically, the Kurds sought a provision whereby any three provinces could collectively veto any clause of a future permanent constitution with a two-thirds vote by its citizens. The measure was known as the

"Kurdish veto." Iraq's senior Shiite religious leaders accepted the Kurdish veto in exchange for the direct election of representatives to a proposed legislature, the Transitional National Assembly (TNA).

The IGC and the United States formally approved the interim constitution on March 8, 2004. On May 17, Izzedin Salim, the IGC chair and a leading moderate Shiite, was assassinated by al Qaeda in a car bombing. The high-profile killing exacerbated tensions between Shiites and Sunnis. In June the IGC was replaced by the Iraqi Interim Government (IIG) after the United Nations endorsed the transfer of sovereignty from the CPA to the new, temporary government. On June 7, the United Nations adopted Resolution 1546, which affirmed the authority and legitimacy of Iraq's interim government. The United States officially transferred sovereignty to the interim government on June 28, and Bremer departed Iraq the same day. Bush acknowledged the transition in a note in which he wrote, "Let freedom reign." During negotiations over the IIG, Ayad Allawi, a leader of the Iraqi National Accord, a moderate Shiite political party, was selected as the prime minister. Ghazi Ajil al-Yawar, a Sunni, was appointed to the ceremonial post of president. Even after the compromise that created the new government, the divisions remained between the factions. Disagreements slowed preparations to create the TNA.

Elections for the 275-member TNA were scheduled for January 30, 2005. Al Qaeda and other terrorist groups threatened to disrupt the balloting through attacks on polling stations, voters, and candidates. Rising violence between Shiites and Sunnis prompted Muhsin Abd al-Hamid, the leader of the largest Sunni political grouping, the Iraqi Islamic Party, to call on his followers to boycott the elections. Despite the threats, voter turnout was approximately 60 percent of eligible voters and the balloting was the freest and fairest in Iraqi history. The polling was the first time that women were allowed to vote in Iraq. Because the main Sunni groups boycotted the elections, the largest Shiite party, the United Iraqi Alliance (UIA), won a majority with 140 seats; followed by the main Kurdish party, the Democratic Patriotic Alliance of Kurdistan (DPAK), winning 75; and a multireligious party, the Iraqi List, led by incumbent prime minister Allawi, won 40 (the remaining seats were won by small parties). There were concurrent elections for the Kurdish assembly and other regional legislatures.

After lengthy and often raucous negotiations, on April 6, 2005, the TNA elected Jalal Talabani, a Kurd of the DPAK, as the president, along with one Sunni and one Shiite vice president. Talabani subsequently appointed a Shiite, Ibrahim al-Jaafari of the UIA, as prime minister of a new cabinet that was sworn in on May 3. Because of the boycott, many Sunnis felt they were largely excluded from political power. This sentiment further increased tensions between the religious communities, but Sunni leaders also learned a valuable lesson and participated in later elections.

A committee of the TNA completed a draft constitution which was approved in a referendum on October 15 by a vote of 78.6 percent in favor and 21.4 percent opposed. The new constitution established Iraq as a federal, parliamentary democracy. The government was divided into three branches: an executive headed by a president, a bicameral legislature, and an independent judiciary with a supreme court as the highest appellate body. The legislature elected both the prime minister and the president. Islam was enshrined as the state religion, but religious freedom was guaranteed for other beliefs. Arabic and Kurdish were the state languages, but minorities were permitted linguistic autonomy, especially in education. The basic law also guaranteed a range of individual liberties.

On December 15, elections were conducted for the new national assembly, the Council of Representatives. After perceiving that they were shut out of the political process because of their boycott of the previous legislative balloting, Sunni groups participated in the elections, which had a voter turnout rate of 79.6 percent. Despite threats from insurgency groups and al Qaeda, there was little violence. Despite some criticism of voter fraud, international observers certified the balloting as generally free and fair. The United Iraqi Alliance again won the largest share of the seats, with 128 of the 275. It formed a new coalition government, led by Prime Minister Nouri al-Maliki, a Shiite.

Rising Violence

The first months of 2004 were marked by extreme violence. On January 22, the CIA issued a report that Iraq was on the verge of a civil war between the Shiites, Sunnis, and Kurds. The following month, U.S. intelligence officials discovered evidence that al Qaeda and other Sunni terrorists groups were endeavoring to foster a religious civil war in Iraq. On February 2, two al Qaeda suicide bombers attacked Kurdish political party headquarters in Irbil. The attacks killed 117 and injured more than 130. Eight days later, a suicide car bomb killed 53 at a police station in Iskandariya. The next day, another suicide car bomb killed 47 in Baghdad at an army recruiting station. On March 2, 171 people died in two suicide attacks in Baghdad and Karbala. Two weeks later, another powerful car bomb killed 28 and wounded 45 in Baghdad.

In addition to using weapons and munitions found in Iraq, insurgent groups were able to move arms through Syria into Iraq. Border security between the two countries remained problematic until 2008. A small number of Shiite groups in Iraq also received support from Iran.

On March 31, four U.S. contractors working for the defense firm Blackwater were captured by insurgents in Fallujah. The Americans were tortured, killed, and then hung from a bridge. A video of the grisly incident was broadcast. In response, on April 4, coalition forces launched Operation Vigilant Resolve, an offensive against insurgents in Fallujah, in April. Over the course of the next month, coalition forces engaged in tough, urban combat. As civilian casualties mounted, the United States announced a ceasefire and then withdrawal. Twenty-seven U.S. troops were killed, along with more than 180 insurgents and approximately 600 civilians. However, continued insurgent attacks prompted a second, larger offensive in November. This time, coalition forces took complete control of the city. The coalition suffered 109 killed. There were more than 1,200 insurgents killed and 1,500 captured, with at least 800 civilian deaths.

In the midst of Vigilant Resolve, al Qaeda and other groups in Iraq continued their attacks. Two Japanese aid workers and a Japanese journalist were kidnapped on April 8. Their captives demanded that Japan withdrew its troops from Iraq. Although the Japanese government refused the demands, the hostages were released a week later. Meanwhile, al Qaeda launched three suicide attacks in Basra and Zubeir, killing 73, including 17 children, on April 21.

Coalition and Iraqi authorities concurrently attempted to suppress the Mahdi Army. In response, Sadr urged his followers to action and Mahdi militiamen began to take control of police stations and other public buildings. There were also minor clashes with coalition forces. By early April, Sadr's supporters had control of several Iraqi towns. Coalition forces launched a campaign to retake areas under control of the Mahdi militia. Most areas were retaken quickly; however, clashes grew increasingly violent. By May, coalition troops had Mahdi fighters contained in four areas, including Najaf, Karbala, Diwaniyah, and Basra. Negotiations led to a tenuous truce, but fighting resumed in May. By the end of the month, only Karbala remained under Mahdi control. Sadr called on his followers to stop fighting on June 6. He subsequently endeavored to form a political party and enter Iraqi politics, but fighting resumed in August when Mahdi militiamen attacked an Iraqi police outpost. By August 13, the militia fighters had been mostly defeated by the coalition troops and Iraqi security forces. A group of Mahdi fighters had retreated to the Iman Ali Shrine in Najaf. Because of the holy nature of the site, coalition forces did not attack the remaining fighters, and the stand-off was ended through the intervention of the Grand Ayatollah Sistani, who convinced the Mahdi militiamen to withdraw and enter into a ceasefire with the government and coalition. The incident demonstrated the growing political power of Sistani, a fact recognized by the Bush administration, which henceforth endeavored to work closely with the grand ayatollah, and the president often asked his advisors, "Where's Sistani on this?"[2]

U.S. Troop Strength

The violence prompted U.S. military officials to delay a planned withdrawal of American combat forces. In June 2004, U.S. troop strength in Iraq was supposed to be reduced from 135,000 to 115,000. However, Rumsfeld authorized an extension of the deployment of the troops, including National Guard and Reserve units. U.S.

troop strength in Iraq would increase as time went by. By December 2005, there were 156,200 U.S. military personnel in Iraq. That number decreased in 2006 to 136,900, before rising again in December 2007 to 165,700. By December 2008, U.S. military personnel had begun to be redeployed from Iraq and the Persian Gulf, and the number dropped to 148,500 before falling further (see Chapter 10).[3]

On May 11, 2005, Bush approved a supplemental appropriations bill that provided $76 billion for the ongoing conflicts in Afghanistan and Iraq. This was in addition to the $496.3 billion defense budget. In June the Army National Guard reported that it repeatedly missed its monthly recruitment goals, leaving the Guard about 19,000 soldiers under strength. The regular Army also missed its recruiting goal by about 9,000 soldiers, the first time it had missed its projected recruit number since 1999. Meanwhile, analysts estimated that the Army needed to be increased by 30,000–50,000 troops in order to end lengthy deployments by Army Reservists and National Guard troops in Afghanistan and Iraq. More than 250,000 Guardsmen and 202,000 Reservists were deployed to Afghanistan and Iraq between 2001 and 2008, compared with 1.2 million regulars from the Army. During this period, on average, there were more than 11,500 Guardsmen and 6,500 Reservists in Iraq, and 5,600 Guardsmen and 1,600 Reservists in Afghanistan.

Between 2005 and 2008, the costs of deploying troops in Afghanistan and Iraq increased substantially because of the ongoing insurgencies in both countries. In Iraq, the cost of deployment of a brigade (approximately 4,000 troops) increased by 57 percent over a three-year period because of the additional costs of combat operations, including the need for replacement equipment, ammunition, and higher fuel usage. The cost to deploy a brigade in Afghanistan increased by 50 percent during the same period. There were also further expenditures necessary when units returned to the United States to repair and replace equipment.[4]

Continuing violence elevated the number of U.S. troops dead in Iraq to 2,000 by the time of the Iraqi constitutional referendum in October 2005. Iraqi civilian deaths from suicide bombings, and other terrorist attacks averaged 9.9 per day during 2005. More than 10,000 Iraqi civilians died during the year as a result of the insurgency.

Weapons and Tactics

The increasing number of civilian and coalition casualties resulted from two factors. First, insurgent groups were able to operate throughout the country, moving quickly from one area to the next and both waging a guerilla-style military campaign against the coalition and undertaking terrorist attacks against the civilian population. By 2005, it was clear that the combination of American, coalition, and existing Iraqi troops was not enough to contain the insurgents, who were estimated to number about 25,000–50,000, including religious militias. The coalition forces were unable to secure Iraq's borders or provide security in urban areas. Critics urged the Bush administration to deploy more troops in Iraq, but the administration was reluctant to increase the number of U.S. forces because of the growing domestic unpopularity of the war in the United States. Some estimates were that the coalition would need an additional 150,000–200,000 troops to stabilize Iraq and suppress the insurgency. In addition, as casualties mounted, members of the coalition of the willing began to withdraw their forces from Iraq.

Second, the weapons and tactics of the American forces, who undertook the majority of the combat missions, were not initially suited to counter the tactics of the insurgents. For instance, the most commonly used vehicle of U.S. troops was the High Mobility Multipurpose Wheeled Vehicle, known as the Humvee. The Humvees were fast and highly mobile, but lightly armored. They were highly vulnerable to IEDs, mines, and rocket-propelled grenades. Increasing casualties from Humvee attacks prompted a growing chorus of criticism of the military by Congress, veterans, and military analysts. In response, in 2004, the Defense Department began to retrofit Humvees with kits that added additional armor to the vehicles; however, manufacturers were initially unprepared to meet the needs of the additional armor kits. As late as 2007, it was estimated that more than 4,000 Humvees in Iraq needed the upgraded armor kits. The U.S. military had to establish 11 sites throughout Iraq to retrofit Humvees with better armor. The services also began to purchase more heavily armored infantry vehicles to replace Humvees.

U.S. forces were criticized for not developing better relations within Iraqi communities and among tribal leaders. American forces typically were stationed in bases and would conduct patrols from a central location. Other coalition members, particularly the British, dispersed forces among communities and undertook more systemic efforts to build relationships with local and regional leaders in order to build trust and confidence.

Abu Ghraib

On April 28, 2004, graphic images of prisoner abuse at the U.S.-run Abu Ghraib detention center in Baghdad were first reported in the media. Abu Ghraib was one of the largest prisoner of war facilities in Iraq. U.S. personnel stationed at the facility took pictures of various physical, sexual, and psychological abuse taking place at the site. In addition, evidence emerged that U.S. intelligence officers tortured prisoners. The news program *60 Minutes II* broadcast an investigation of the abuse, prompting international condemnation. The story caused deep anger in the Arab world and undermined U.S. claims that its presence in Iraq promoted democracy and human rights. Eleven U.S. soldiers were convicted for their actions at the prison, and the commanding officer of U.S. detention facilities in Iraq, Brigadier General Janis Karpinski, was demoted.

Rumsfeld offered to resign over the scandal, but Bush asked him to remain in office. Bush delivered an apology over the abuse scandal on May 5 on Al Hurra, a U.S.-financed Arab language media outlet. Bush stated that the actions were "abhorrent abuses" and that the United States "will do to ourselves what we expect of others. And when we say, 'You've got human rights abuses, take care of the problem,' we will do the same thing. We are taking care of the problem. And it is unpleasant for Americans to see that some citizens, some soldiers have acted this way, because it doesn't—again, I keep repeating, but it's true: It doesn't reflect how we think. This is not America. America is a country of justice and law and freedom and treating people with respect."[5]

A documentary, *Ghosts of Abu Ghraib*, about the prisoner abuse scandal premiered at the 2006 Sundance Film Festival and was later broadcast on HBO. *Standard Operating Procedure*, another documentary on the topic, was released the following year. Meanwhile, a number of films and documentaries were released in Arabic.

On May 11, an American businessman, Nicholas Berg, was beheaded by al Qaeda members. The execution was videotaped and then shown online. Al Qaeda claimed the murder was in retaliation for the Abu Ghraib scandal.

Resentment toward the U.S.-led coalition grew after an incident on May 19 in which American forces mistakenly attacked a civilian wedding party. False intelligence identified the house where the celebration was taking place as an insurgent safe house. The strike killed 42 people and was dubbed the Mukaradeeb Wedding Massacre. The attack was one of a growing number of episodes in which civilians were killed by coalition forces and U.S. security contractors. Suicide attacks in June kill more than 250 Iraqis.

Al Qaida's International Offensive

Al Qaeda attacks outside of Iraq also impacted the insurgency and complicated the efforts of the coalition. On March 11, 2004, al Qaeda terrorists detonated bombs on three commuter trains in Madrid, Spain. The attacks killed 201 and wounded more than 1,400. The conservative Spanish government of José Maria Aznar, a staunch supporter of the U.S.-led war in Iraq, initially blamed Basque separatists. However, evidence emerged that the strikes were the work of Islamic terrorists. In elections three days after the attack, the ruling conservatives were defeated and a socialist government led by José Luis Rodriguez Zapatero was installed. Zapatero had campaigned on a pledge to withdraw the 1,300 Spanish troops from Iraq. The last Spanish troops left Iraq on April 28.

The withdrawal created tensions between the United States and Spain which were partially resolved through an increase in Spanish troops in Afghanistan. Nonetheless, U.S. security officials argued that the withdrawal would embolden al Qaeda and lead to more attacks against coalition partners as the terrorist group sought to pressure governments to withdraw troops. On July 7, 2005, al Qaeda suicide bombers detonated three bombs on the London subway and a fourth on a bus. The attack killed 56 and wounded more than 700. However, the Blair government refused to withdraw British troops from Afghanistan or Iraq. On July 7, Angelo de la Cruz, a Philippine citizen, was abducted by insurgents. The Philippine government, which had already planned to withdraw a small 51-member military unit, agreed to end its military mission a month early and secured the release of Cruz on July 20.

The Search for WMDs

In October 2003, the Iraq Survey Group (ISG) issued a preliminary overview on its search for WMDs in Iraq. ISG head David Kay reported that it had not found stockpiles of WMDs. Instead, Iraq's WMD program had been inactive for several years. The group found plans, documents, and some facilities that had remained hidden from UN inspections, but the Iraqis appeared to have just maintained the capabilities to restart WMD programs. The most significant find were biological weapons laboratories with strains of botulinum, but not stockpiles of the material to make biological weapons.

Kay resigned as the leader of the ISG on January 23, 2004, after publicly declaring that he did not believe that the group would discover WMDs and that pre-war intelligence about Iraq's WMD programs was inaccurate. He was replaced by Charles Duelfer. On September 30, the ISG issued its main report. The ISG found no evidence that Iraq had stockpiles of WMDs or an active and ongoing WMD program at the time of the invasion. The ISG found only a small number of VX and mustard gas warheads that it concluded were likely left over from the Iran-Iraq War. Instead, the investigation found that Saddam had ended his chemical weapons program in 1991 and his biological weapons program in 1995, and the regime had only retained small amounts of either type of weapons, most of which were destroyed by successive UN programs. Iraq retained the capability, including facilities, personnel, and equipment, to restart production of chemical and biological weapons, but evidence indicated Saddam sought to preserve these capabilities to restart WMD programs only after UN sanctions had been lifted. By November, ISG's main investigations have been completed and its teams began to be withdrawn from Iraq. The report undermined the Bush administration's rationale for invading Iraq to prevent the use or proliferation of WMDs and further eroded public support for the continuing U.S.-led military mission in the country. The ISG spent $600 million in its final two years searching for Iraqi WMDs.

Former UNMOVIC chief Blix asserted on March 5, 2004, that the Iraq War was illegal since the coalition did not allow the United Nations to conduct a full round of inspections in Iraq. Blix was the latest addition to a growing number of international officials who disputed the legality of the conflict. In April, the UN

Security Council adopted Resolution 1540, which called on all member states to make the proliferation of WMDs a crime and to enhance border and transportation security to prevent proliferation. The U.S. sponsored the measure. Meanwhile, UN secretary general Annan on September 16, when questioned by a reporter, noted that he believed the Iraq War was not in line with international law and therefore was illegal.

In January 2005, the ISG withdrew its remaining inspection teams from Iraq. The ISG issued an additional, follow-up report in March. It found no evidence that Iraq transferred significant WMDs or WMD technology to Syria, but warned that it was likely that small amounts of equipment, especially biological weapons capabilities, may have been moved. It also warned that scientists and technicians who worked on Iraq's earlier WMD programs could be reemployed to develop WMDs by insurgents, terrorists, or other states. Critics of the invasion asserted that the report indicated that the war had likely accelerated WMD proliferation in the region, rather than suppressing the spread of WMDs.

The IAEI and its chief, El Baradei, were awarded the Nobel Prize for Peace on October 7, 2005, for their efforts to stop the proliferation of nuclear weapons. The choice was seen as an effort to promote peaceful conflict resolution over the use of force and a rebuke of the Bush administration. On December 14, Bush announced that the decision to go to war with Iraq was based on inaccurate intelligence and information. He accepted full responsibility for the mistakes, but argued that the removal of Saddam justified the invasion.

The Tipping Point

U.S. forces in Iraq endeavored to train more Iraqi security forces, with plans to increase the number of troops to 200,000 in 2006. However violence continued to increase throughout the country. On February 22, 2006, Sunni insurgents bombed a revered Shiite shrine in Samarra. The attack prompted a wave of Sunni-Shiite violence throughout the country. For instance, a week later, 60 people were killed in suicide bombings in Baghdad.

By the end of 2006, 3,000 U.S. service members had died in Iraq. The growing number of casualties dramatically undermined public support for the war. Congress formed the Iraq Study Group on March 15. The bipartisan group consisted of 10 senior and well-known foreign policy and political officials, including former secretaries of state James A. Baker III and Lawrence Eagleburger, and former defense secretary William J. Perry. The group was tasked to provide an analysis of past and current U.S. strategy toward Iraq, as well as make recommendations for future action. The group issued its final report on December 6. Among its key recommendations were that the United States should begin a phased withdrawal from Iraq and that the United States needed to devote more military forces and resources to Afghanistan. The group also endorsed an expanded role for diplomacy in easing the civil war in Iraq, including opening negotiations with Iran and Syria. Rising violence in Iraq was partially responsible for Republicans losing control of both houses of Congress in the 2006 midterm elections (see Chapter 9). Rumsfeld resigned as secretary of defense on November 8, and was replaced by Robert Gates.

Meanwhile, more than 20,000 Iraqis died in 2006 alone. The coalition did enjoy some success in its efforts to suppress the insurgency. On June 7, intelligence revealed that Zarqawi was at a site in Baquba. U.S. aircraft launched a bombing raid that killed the al Qaeda leader. Although al Qaeda continued to launch attacks, the death of Zarqawi was a serious blow to the terrorist organization. After a lengthy and complicated trial, former Iraqi leader Saddam Hussein was convicted on November 5 of his role in the execution of 149 Shiites who took part in an assassination plot in the 1990s. Saddam was executed by hanging on December 30.

In 2007, coalition and Iraqi forces launched a series of offensives against al Qaeda and other insurgent groups. In an effort to quell the continuing insurgency, on January 10, Bush announced plans to deploy an additional 20,000 combat troops to Iraq in what became known as the "surge." In announcing the additional troops, Bush told the nation that "the situation in Iraq is unacceptable to the American people, and it is unacceptable to me. Our troops in Iraq have fought bravely. They have done everything we have asked them to do. Where mistakes have been made, the responsibility rests with me."[6]

Bush also appointed a new military commander in Iraq, General David Petraeus. Petraeus had served in the initial invasion of Iraq, and then commanded multinational coalition forces in Iraq. He was credited with building a high degree of trust and confidence between the coalition and Iraqis in the areas under his command. Petraeus oversaw the military operations associated with the surge.

With support personnel, the surge included some 28,000 additional soldiers. Bush also extended the tours of some units already deployed in Iraq. It took until June before the additional troops were in place and ready to begin operations. With the extra forces, the coalition undertook a range of new insurgency campaigns, beginning with Operation Phantom Thunder, launched on June 16. Phantom Thunder was the largest coalition offensive since the war began and included 28,000 coalition and Iraqi troops. The campaign ended on August 14. Iraqi security forces played a major role in the operation, which was partially designed to demonstrate the growing effectiveness of the Iraqi soldiers. The United States lost 140, while Iraqi security had approximately 240 killed. There were an estimated 1,190 insurgents killed, and more than 6,700 captured. The coalition and its Iraqi allies also captured a large amount of weapons and bomb-making equipment.

While the surge contributed to growing stability in Iraq, relations with Turkey deteriorated after Turkish military units crossed the border into northern Iraq in October 2007 in pursuit of Kurdish rebels. Additional cross-border intrusions led Washington to issue warnings to Turkey in 2008.

On January 8, 2008, U.S. and Iraqi forces initiated a large offensive in Mosul against al Qaeda–led insurgents. The campaign was very successful, and by the end of the month, al Qaeda in Iraq only had a significant presence in Diyala Province. On July 29, U.S. and pro-government Sunni militias attacked the remaining al Qaeda stronghold. By mid-August, coalition forces had captured or killed more than 4,000 al Qaeda fighters and other insurgents, including 24 senior leaders. They also discovered more than 3,000 weapons and explosive caches. After the campaign, there was a dramatic decrease in violence across Iraq. Civilian deaths in Iraq due to the insurgency declined dramatically from approximately 18,000 in 2007 to 8,000 in 2008 and then 3,500 in 2009.

While military pressure was essential in suppressing the insurgency, political measures proved just as important. In late 2005 and early 2006, Sunni tribal leaders in Anbar province turned against al Qaeda and other Sunni insurgent groups. The movement was known as the Anbar Awakening (the movement was also known as the "Sons of Iraq"). With the support of the Maliki government, Sunni militias began to form Awakening Councils throughout Iraq and cooperate with coalition forces. Sunni militia members were paid $300 per month to serve with coalition troops. Initially, 10,000 militia troops were employed— a figure that rose to 54,000. The Councils also provided valuable intelligence and information on Sunni insurgents. The Councils evolved into a political movement and participated in the 2010 legislative elections. By 2011, there were more than 100,000 Sunni members of Awakening Councils.

In addition in 2008, the Iraqi parliament reversed the de-Ba'athification measures that had restricted former members of the Saddam regime from serving in the government, police, or military. The change allowed an estimated 30,000 former regime members to join the government or security forces. It also further reduced tensions between the Sunni and Shiite communities.

Benchmarks and Political Progress

Improvements in Iraq's internal security led the government to request that the United States develop a timeline for the withdrawal of coalition forces from Iraq. The Bush administration also faced mounting domestic pressure, especially after the 2006 elections, to withdraw troops. The Bush administration was reluctant to commit to a specific timetable for withdrawal, arguing that if insurgents knew the schedule for redeployment, they would use the timetable to plan their strategy and tactics. Instead, the Bush administration agreed to develop a series of benchmarks or milestones that could be used to assess whether coalition forces could be withdrawn.

Ultimately, the United States developed 18 goals that ranged from conducting successful elections to repeal of the de-Ba'athification laws to passage of an oil revenue-sharing law that would allow the different regions of Iraq to share in the sales of energy resources. In September 2007, the Bush administration issued a report that Iraq had met or made significant progress on 11 of the 18 benchmarks. The remaining seven were mostly political measures that remained deadlocked in parliament.

By the end of 2007, security had dramatically improved in Iraq. The British turned security operations for Basra, Iraq's second-largest city, over to the Iraqis on December 16, 2007. In addition, in 2008, the United States began to withdraw combat troops. On September 1, 2008, the United States turned Anbar province, once the heart of the insurgency, over to Iraqi security forces.

Economic Costs

As a result of the war and the insurgency, Iraq's GDP declined by 3 percent in 2003 and then fell 21.8 percent the following year. However, GDP grew by 52.3 percent in 2005, mainly as the result of massive foreign assistance and the resumption of oil and natural gas production. After the fall of Saddam, the United States pledged $20 billion for Iraqi reconstruction, and the European Union and other international donors promised another $18 billion. The continuing insurgency, which included attacks on energy production sites and pipelines, constrained economic growth in 2006, when GDP fell by 3.0 percent, before rising by 2.4 percent (2007), 5.9 percent (2008), 7.8 percent (2009), and 4.5 percent (2010). Meanwhile, inflation, which had grown to 70 percent in 2006, declined to 14 percent in 2008, before falling to 2.8 percent in 2009. In spite of the insurgency, Iraq continued to receive substantial economic aid and assistance from foreign donors. For instance in 2010, the International Monetary Fund provided Iraq with $5.98 billion in loans and grants to help the country repay its foreign debt and rebuild its infrastructure.

By the end of 2003, U.S. defense expenditures were $404.9 billion or 3.7 percent of GDP. This did not include all of the costs of military operations in Afghanistan and Iraq which were largely funded through separate appropriations. By 2008, defense expenditures were $800 billion or 5.6 percent of GDP (including all defense appropriations and outlays for Operations Enduring Freedom and Iraqi Freedom). From 2003 through 2008, there were 4,221 U.S. service personnel killed in Iraq. The British lost 178 killed, while 139 coalition members from other countries died in Iraq. Estimates were that more than 60,000 Iraqi civilians died during the insurgency, along with more than 9,800 members of the Iraqi security forces (including civilian police).

Conclusion

In 2008, fighting continued in Iraq. In March a series of battles ensued as Iraqi security forces attempt to assert control over areas held by the Mahdi Army. Nonetheless, violence in Iraq had declined to pre-2004 levels. It had a stable, democratic government, albeit one that continued to face significant tensions between Iraq's three major groups—the Shiites, Sunnis, and Kurds. However, even as violence waned, a growing insurgency in Afghanistan forced the United States and is allies to refocus attention on the country at the center of Operation Enduring Freedom. Critics charged that the focus on Iraq allowed the Taliban and al Qaeda to regroup in Afghanistan and not only threaten that country but also destabilize Pakistan.

2008 also marked the end of the second presidential term of George W. Bush. In the United States, presidential and congressional elections dominated domestic politics even as fighting in Afghanistan intensified (see Chapter 9). Although the United States had greater international support in Afghanistan, the insurgency in the country presented a number of different challenges than the coalition of the willing had faced in Iraq. As the insurgency spread through Afghanistan, questions emerged over not only the ability of coalition forces to defeat the Taliban and al Qaeda, but also the stability and legitimacy of the Afghan government.

Notes

1. George W. Bush, "Speech," April 1, 2003.

2. Bob Woodward, *State of Denial: Bush at War, Part III* (New York: Simon & Schuster, 2006), 322–3.

3. Amy Belasco, "The Cost of Iraq, Afghanistan, and Other Global War on Terror Operations since 9/11," Congressional Research Service, September 2, 2010, 42–3.

4. Belasco, "The Cost of Iraq," 24–9.

5. "George W. Bush Interview," Al Hurra, May 5, 2004.

6. George W. Bush, "Address," January 10, 2007.

8

The Insurgency in Afghanistan

Introduction

The U.S.-led coalition quickly defeated the Taliban and al Qaeda in 2001, and the country initially seemed to be making considerable political progress, marked by democratic elections and the creation of a new democratic and constitutional government. However, by 2004, a broad insurgency threatened to engulf the country. Opposing the coalition and the U.S.-backed government of Hamid Karzai were two main groups: a loose alliance between the Taliban and al Qaeda, based in Pakistan; and a growing number of regional warlords who challenged the authority and legitimacy of the government in Kabul. Complicating international efforts to suppress the insurgency was a growing drug trade which financed both groups of insurgents, and the ability of anti-government fighters to establish bases and networks in neighboring Pakistan.

The United States worked closely with international organizations such as the United Nations and NATO to support the Karzai government and promote stability in Afghanistan. However, the concurrent conflict in Iraq constrained the ability of the United States to expand its troop presence in the country. Meanwhile, U.S. allies limited the military personnel and resources devoted to Operation Enduring Freedom. By the time that security had stabilized in Iraq to the point that it allowed the redeployment of U.S. forces to Afghanistan, the insurgency had spread throughout the country. In addition, as the insurgency in Iraq was suppressed, an increasing number of foreign fighters traveled to Afghanistan, making the country, again, the central front in the war on terror. Meanwhile, the legitimacy of the Karzai government was increasingly diminished by corruption and inefficiency.

The Insurgency

In the immediate aftermath of the invasion of Afghanistan and the fall of the Taliban regime, anti-government and anti-coalition attacks were mainly led by the Taliban and al Qaeda. Operating from bases in Pakistan, the groups launched a guerilla campaign against the Karzai government and the U.S.-led international forces (see Chapter 3). The insurgency spread into Pakistan as well, with the Taliban conducting a joint campaign against both the Afghan and Pakistani governments. One result was an increasing number of Pakistani Taliban members fighting in Afghanistan. A number of other factors also led to increased violence in Afghanistan, especially after 2004.

The 2003 invasion of Iraq angered many Muslims, both Shiite and Sunni, across the region. There was a significant increase in the number of foreign fighters who traveled to Pakistan to train with the Taliban after the beginning of the U.S.-led campaign against Saddam Hussein. Some fighters and terrorists trained in Pakistan and then went to Iraq to fight against coalition forces, while others remained in Pakistan and joined anti-U.S. efforts in Afghanistan.

Meanwhile, as time passed, other groups in Afghanistan joined the insurgency. In some cases, new fighting broke out between rival ethnic groups, mainly between the majority Pashtun population and minority groups such as the Tajiks, Uzbeks, Turkmen, and Hazaras (who were mainly Shiite, unlike other segments of the Afghan population who were mainly Sunni). In addition, regional warlords began to challenge the authority of the Karzai regime. The reemergence of the drug trade in Afghanistan exacerbated tensions between the central government and the warlords, especially as government and coalition forces undertook a succession of campaigns to suppress drug trafficking.

Afghans had a long tradition of fighting amongst themselves. The country was divided along religious and ethnic lines. There were also regional divisions. However, Afghans were also nationalistic and had an equally long tradition of uniting to fight foreign invaders. The manner in which Afghans united under the Mujahedeen during the Soviet Occupation exemplified this trend. While the U.S. -led coalition was initially welcomed by most Afghans, resentment toward what many perceived to be a foreign occupation grew after 2002. This trend was worsened by civilian deaths during coalition operations, especially airstrikes.

Common among the Pashtun people of Afghanistan and Pakistan was the Pashtunwali ("way of the Pashtuns") code. The code was a series of traditional ethical and moral guidelines at the core of Pashtun society. One of the central tenets of Pashtunwali was the notion of justice. Males in a family or clan were expected to seek collective compensation or revenge if a member of their group was wronged. Within Afghanistan, the code meant that blood feuds between tribes were common. The deaths of civilians, because of government or coalition operations, prompted some clan members to join the insurgency in order to exact revenge (the code also motivated Pashtuns to fight against the Taliban and al Qaeda following terrorist attacks on civilians). The code also emphasized the importance of sanctuary, which obligated clans to provide a safe haven for those who faced persecution by their enemies. Taliban members invoked the code at various times during anti-government or anti-coalition missions.

The Taliban and Al Qaeda

After the U.S.-led coalition defeated the Taliban, Mullah Omar reorganized the group's leadership. He formed a 10-member governing council and declared a jihad against all foreign troops in Afghanistan. There was a moderate faction within the Taliban that urged a negotiated settlement with the Karzai government, especially after the president permitted former members of the Taliban regime to participate in the 2005 legislative elections and released a number of Taliban who had been held in captivity since the 2001 invasion.

Omar repeatedly rejected overtures from the central government, even after Karzai offered to give senior Taliban members cabinet positions in the Afghan government in 2007. By that year, the Taliban had become increasingly divided. The most extreme faction, led by Jalaluddin Haqqani, operated from bases in Pakistan and undertook attacks in southeastern Afghanistan. They cooperated closely with the Pakistani Taliban and had very close ties with al Qaeda. Other small groups operating elsewhere in Afghanistan often had only very loose connections with the Taliban leadership (these groups were often referred to as the "neo-Taliban"). Meanwhile, in March 2008, moderate Afghan Taliban leaders called for negotiations with both the Afghan and Pakistani governments.

The moderate Taliban faction grew increasingly critical of terrorist attacks against civilian targets. While even moderates strongly supported military action to force the U.S.-led coalition to withdraw troops from Afghanistan, strikes against civilians were denounced as un-Islamic and antithetical to the Pashtunwali code. Some Taliban leaders criticized attacks on civilians as cowardly and dishonorable. This group continued to engage in efforts to develop a negotiated settlement that would result in the departure of foreign troops and the integration of the Taliban into Afghanistan's government and security forces.

By 2004, the Taliban and al Qaeda began to shift tactics in their ongoing insurgency against the United States, ISAF, and the Afghan government. As had happened in Iraq (see Chapter 7), insurgents increasingly used terrorist tactics against international troops and aid workers, and Afghan security forces. The Taliban publically announced the start of the suicide bombing campaign in January 2004, issuing a statement that declared that the organization would continue to conduct suicide attacks until all foreign troops withdrew from Afghanistan. The number of suicide attacks increased dramatically from 2004 to 2005. The attacks became more specific, with the terrorists targeting army and police recruiting and training facilities, schools, medical facilities, and hotels or other sites frequented by Westerners. For instance, on May 7, 2005, a suicide bomber blew himself up at a hotel in Kabul, killing a UN worker and an Afghani citizen, and injuring five others. In June, another suicide bomber attacked a funeral procession, killing 19 and wounding more than 50. From November 14 to 18 in Kabul, there were five separate suicide attacks. On January 15, 2006, a suicide bombing attack against a Canadian convoy killed three, including a diplomat, and injured 14. The next day, two suicide attacks in Spin Boldak in Kandahar province killed 26 and wounded more than 40. The attacks undermined confidence in the government and the coalition.

The Taliban and al Qaeda continued to attack coalition bases, convoys, and patrols, using guerilla-style hit-and-run tactics. The insurgents often ambushed coalition forces or fired mortars or rockets at military facilities, and then attempted to retreat before a counterattack was launched. U.S. and ISAF troops were generally better armed and equipped than the insurgents and had better communications and intelligence capabilities, including night vision gear. Coalition forces also enjoyed a substantial "over-the-horizon" advantage—they could call in airstrikes or artillery or missile barrages when attacked. Usually, if coalition forces and insurgents met in a pitched battle, the Taliban and al Qaeda fighters suffered heavy casualties.

Meanwhile, the Taliban continued the military pattern that had emerged after the 2001 U.S.-led campaign. The group would launch attacks from bases in Pakistan during the spring and summer, and then withdraw across the border during the harsh Afghan winter. During the cold months, the Taliban and its allies would rearm and resupply, train new recruits, and plan operations for the upcoming year. The majority of Taliban and al Qaeda bases were located among sympathetic tribes along the northwest frontier between the two countries (see Chapter 5). The Taliban and the Pakistani tribes were linked by blood or had longstanding relationships dating back to the Soviet occupation. The Pakistani tribal leaders funneled money and supplies to the Taliban and al Qaeda, in some cases with the tacit support of Pakistani security officials and intelligence officers.

In response, U.S. and coalition special forces units conducted cross-border incursions into Pakistan to obtain intelligence. The United States also launched attacks by unmanned aerial drones against Taliban and al Qaeda leaders near the Afghan-Pakistani border. Although such raids and attacks had occurred with some frequency since 2003, the first publically acknowledged raid into Pakistan occurred on September 3, 2008, when U.S. Navy SEALS were inserted about one mile inside Pakistan, near Angor Adda. The U.S. special operations forces captured a number of Taliban leaders. Intelligence from the raid was used by the United States to conduct a series of strikes by unmanned aerial drones over the next week. The Pakistani government bitterly protested the violation of its sovereignty publicly, but tacitly tolerated the attacks and allowed other minor U.S. incursions.

The Warlords

Most regional warlords supported the U.S.-led invasion and the toppling of the Taliban government, and their militias often fought alongside American troops. However, after the fall of the Taliban, the warlords endeavored to reassert control over their tribal areas. Some warlords were hereditary clan or tribal leaders, while others rose to power as military or religious leaders. The warlords exercised significant authority and influence in their areas. Meanwhile, Karzai's power was concentrated in and around Kabul, and he was, therefore, dependent on the goodwill and cooperation of the warlords.

Many warlords supported Karzai, in exchange for political positions and de facto recognition of their authority from the central government. For instance, Dostum, the Uzbek leader who led the coalition attack on Mazar-e-Sharif in November 2001, was appointed deputy defense minister by Karzai (see Chapter 3), then made a general in the Afghan Army in 2003. However, Uzbek forces under Dostum's control fought a series of battles with rival Tajiks in 2003 and 2004. U.S. military officials negotiated a truce in the strife, but Dostum's fighters subsequently launched new attacks on militia forces loyal to Akbar Bai, a former ally of the general. In addition, the Uzbek general campaigned as a presidential candidate against Karzai in the 2004 elections (he received 10 percent of the vote). After Karzai won reelection, he appointed Dostum as chief of staff of the army in a bid to gain his loyalty. However, tensions between Dostum and the president prompted the general's resignation in 2008 (Dostum then went into exile in Turkey). Furthermore, a number of the general's political allies were removed from the government. Dostum was reappointed as army chief of staff in 2009 in exchange for his support of Karzai's reelection bid (see Chapter 10).

The main non-Taliban anti-government group in Afghanistan was the Hizb-i-Islami (Islamic Party), founded in 1977. Led by former Mujahedeen leader and former prime minister Gulbuddin Hekmatyar, Hizb-i-Islami was an ultra-orthodox Sunni religious grouping, composed mainly of Pashtuns. Hekmatyar and his group allied with the Northern Alliance and fought against the Taliban prior to 2001. However, Hizb-i-Islami opposed the U.S.-led invasion and the Karzai government. Hekmatyar called for the withdrawal of all foreign forces from Afghanistan and denounced the Pakistani government for cooperating with the United States. Hizb-i-Islami fighters conducted small-scale attacks on government and coalition forces in 2002, prompting the CIA to undertake an unsuccessful attack against Hekmatyar using an unmanned aerial drone in May 2002. Hizb-i-Islami retaliated with an equally unsuccessful assassination attempt directed at Karzai in September of that year. Hekmatyar subsequently went into exile in Iran and called for a jihad against the United States. He was forced from Iran and returned to Afghanistan, where he rejected an offer by the president for amnesty for Hizb-i-Islami fighters.

By 2006, Hizb-i-Islami had become allied with the Taliban and cooperated with the group in attacks against both the government and coalition. The increasing number of suicide attacks and strikes against civilian targets alienated many of Hekmatyar's supporters. By 2007, divisions appeared within Hizb-i-Islami, with a growing moderate faction of the grouping arguing for a negotiated settlement with the Karzai government. The government opened new talks with Hizb-i-Islami members in 2008, but a hardliner faction of the grouping, led by Hekmatyar, continued to cooperate with the Taliban and al Qaeda. The moderate faction came to be known as the Hizb-i-Islami—Afghanistan. It was led by Abdul Hadi Arghandiwal, who joined the Karzai government as economics minister in 2008. Hekmatyar's faction was dubbed the Hizb-i-Islami—Hekmatyari.

Other warlords supported Karzai, but participated in the drug trade or in other activities that undermined the peace and stability of Afghanistan. For instance, Gul Agha Sherzai, a former Mujahedeen leader, fought alongside coalition forces in the capture of Kandahar in 2001. However, in 2002 he forced from office the governor of Kandahar province who had been appointed by Karzai (Sherzai then assumed the post himself). His tenure was marked by extreme corruption. For example, he forced foreign aid organizations to pay bribes in order to operate in the province. In 2003, Karzai removed Sherzai from the governorship, but a year later appointed him governor of Nangarhar province. Sherzai subsequently emerged as an important ally of Karzai. The Taliban tried to assassinate the governor in July, and the attack drew him closer to the president. However, Sherzai also became increasingly involved in the drug trade and was accused, again, of corruption.

Corruption among other warlords created instability and prompted fighting between local groups. For example, Ismail Khan was a legendary Mujahedeen and Islamic scholar. During the post–Soviet Occupation civil war, he joined the Northern Alliance. Khan was considered to be so pious that when the Taliban captured him in 2000, he was not executed as were other opponents of the regime. After the fall of the Taliban, he became governor of Herat. Khan essentially ignored the central government. He imposed his own laws and refused to send taxes or tariffs to Kabul, spending the funds instead in Herat or diverting them for his own use. Resistance to his rule became widespread, prompting local tribes and militias to turn against the regime. After his forces were defeated in a series of battles with rival militias in 2004, Khan resigned and was appointed to a position in the Karzai government. Afghan army and coalition forces had to be deployed to Herat to restore order in the midst of the ongoing intertribal strife.

United National Front

In addition to warlords, there also emerged a democratic opposition to Karzai. A coalition known as the National Understanding Front was launched in 2005 as a collection of 11 political parties that were opposed to Karzai. The Front was led by Mohammad Yunos Qanuni, who placed second to Karzai in the 2004 presidential balloting (Qanuni was the speaker of the lower house in the Afghan parliament). The Front was superseded in 2007 by a new coalition, the United National Front (UNF), led by former president Rabbani (see Chapter 1). Rabbani argued for national reconciliation and advocated negotiations with the Taliban to end the insurgency. Former foreign minister Abdullah Abdullah was chosen as the UNF's presidential candidate for the 2009 elections (see Chapter 10).

U.S. and Coalition Troops and Strategy

The United States and its allies steadily increased their military presence in Afghanistan to counter growing violence. The number of U.S. combat troops in Afghanistan increased from 18,300 in 2004 to 48,250 in 2008. ISAF's strength was 6,500 in 2004 and grew to 51,350 in 2008. In 2004, the Afghan national army number approximately 10,000 soldiers, with an additional 20,000 police officers. However, the quality of the government's security forces was mixed, and the force suffered from a significant number of desertions (by 2004, one-third of the original army recruits had deserted). In an effort to retain recruits, monthly pay was increased from $50 to $70 in 2004. The Afghan army had increased in size to about 60,000 soldiers by 2008. That year, the United States announced a plan to double the size of the force to 120,000 by 2013, through a $20 billion program. The initiative also provided better arms and equipment for the force. Meanwhile, the Taliban and al Qaeda numbers grew from approximately 7,000–12,000 in 2004 to 25,000 in 2008.

In an effort to increase cooperation between the Afghan government and the coalition, on May 23, 2005, Karzai and Bush announced that their two nations had formed a strategic partnership in the war on terror. One practical manifestation of the enhanced relationship was that Afghan military facilities were opened to use by U.S. and ISAF forces. Coalition partners further agreed to expand training of Afghan security forces. However, revelations over prisoner abuse by U.S. forces and intelligence operatives at Afghan detention centers in 2005 caused new tensions between the allies. The scandal was less severe or widespread than the one that occurred at Abu Ghraib in Iraq (see Chapter 7), but it led to protests and demonstrations against American and ISAF troops. U.S. newspapers reported that two prisoner who had died at a detention facility in Bagram had been tortured by American soldiers. Other abuses were subsequently reported. Fifteen U.S. soldiers were charged for various crimes, and seven were convicted of crimes ranging from assault to detainee abuse to making false statements.

The United States endeavored to use its air superiority to attack bands of Taliban or al Qaeda fighters and to target individual insurgent leaders. In May 2007, the Taliban's main military commander, Mullah Dadullah, was killed by special operations forces in the Helmand province. He was temporarily replaced by his brother, Mansur Dadullah, but Omar dismissed Mansur in December 2007 following a dispute over tactics and strategy.

The Afghan Government

The constitution that was approved in 2004 created a bicameral legislature, the Shoray-i-Milli ("National Assembly"). The upper house of the Assembly was the

Meshrano Jirga ("House of Elders"). The House of Elders consisted of 102 members. One-third, 34, of the members of the House were appointed by the president, one-third were elected by councils representing each of the nation's 34 provinces, and the remaining members were elected by district councils. The constitution mandated that at least 17 members had to be women. In addition, seats were reserved for ethnic minorities and the disabled. The lower chamber was the Wolesi Jirga ("House of the People"). The House of the People had 249 members, with each province electing two or more representatives, depending on population. In addition, women were guaranteed a minimum of 68 seats, while nomads were allocated 10 seats.

Afghanistan conducted parliamentary and regional elections on September 18, 2005, after repeated delays. Candidates ran as independents, without party affiliations listed on the ballots. The Taliban and al Qaeda attempted to disrupt the balloting, and at least four candidates were killed during the campaign. Nonetheless, more than 6 million Afghans voted. Although there were instances of fraud, the voting was the freest in Afghanistan since 1949. Women won 28 percent of the seats in the lower house, a dramatic reversal of the Taliban period when women were not even allowed to work outside of the home. Although the provincial elections for the House of Elders took place as scheduled on September 18, balloting for the district representatives was postponed because of a dispute over electoral boundaries.

Candidates allied with regional warlords won a majority of seats in both houses of the assembly. This allowed the warlords to exert significant political pressure on Karzai. The president appointed a number of warlords and their allies to government posts. As a result, the warlord bloc supported Karzai and his pro-American policies, but the president's relationship with the regional leaders undermined public confidence in the government. Many of the warlords who endorsed Karzai were known both within Afghanistan and to the outside world for their corruption, including bribery, fraud, and the misappropriation of foreign aid and assistance. The government's increasing ties to warlords also eroded international confidence in Karzai. Officials within the Bush administration questioned the capability of the president and his cabinet to conduct needed reforms and address security concerns such as the rise in the drug trade.

After the 2005 legislative elections, tensions emerged between the president and the legislature. The lower chamber became divided along regional lines with lawmakers from the north supporting Islamic conservatives. Karzai appointed a new cabinet on December 23, but the legislature delayed confirmation of many of the members until May 2, 2006. Five of Karzai's appointees were rejected by the Assembly because of opposition by Islamic conservatives. In 2007, the Assembly impeached two ministers after Iran began to force Afghan refugees to return to Afghanistan. The Afghan Supreme Court ruled that the impeachments were unconstitutional. Also in 2007, the legislature approved a very restrictive media law, but Karzai refused to sign the measure. In a second, more moderate measure, however, the president also declined to endorse the law. Incidents such as this were demonstrative of a growing rift between the moderate Karzai and conservative lawmakers.

Karzai meanwhile faced growing international pressure to undertake an anticorruption campaign and initiate reforms. In January and February 2006, more than 70 countries and international donor institutions met in London to discuss Afghanistan at a conference co-hosted by the United Nations and the British and Afghan governments. A five-year agreement, the Afghanistan Compact, was negotiated by the delegates. The accord promised $10.5 billion in aid to Afghanistan in exchange for political and economic reforms. Karzai pledged to abolish regional militias, curb the power of the warlords, and suppress the drug trade. In order to improve the nation's security and fight the insurgency, the president agreed to increase the size of the Afghan Army to 70,000 by 2009. The Afghan leader also promised to enact economic reforms and appoint judges based on merit and ability, rather than religious affiliation. The government consented to a series of reforms proposed by the donor states, including increased transparency and greater oversight of government accounting.

Legislative opposition limited Karzai's ability to undertake the promised reforms. For instance, even with support from the U.S.-led coalition, the insurgency spread and efforts to suppress the drug trade were not successful. In addition, Karzai was unable to constrain the power of the warlords. Because of the insurgency, the drug trade, and the continuing power of regional leaders, economic reforms only had limited impact.

A survey found that Afghanistan has large reserves of oil, natural gas, and coal. Further geological reports discovered deposits of a variety of precious minerals, ranging from gold to gemstones, as well as copper, iron, and cobalt. Estimates were that the country had more than $1 trillion in potential energy and mineral reserves. However, the insurgency kept most foreign firms from investing in the country, while domestic companies did not have the capital or resources to exploit the energy or mineral reserves. In 2006, the International Monetary Fund (IMF) approved a $1.2 billion, three-year loan to the government. Foreign investment in Afghanistan declined by more than 50 percent in 2007 as international companies withdrew staff and resources because of rising violence in the country. In addition, the Taliban began to impose a 50 percent tax on companies operating in Afghanistan. Failure to pay the extortion prompted attacks by the Taliban. A year later, a Chinese firm became the first major international company to make a major investment in Afghanistan. The firm pledged to invest $3 billion over a five-year period to establish a copper-mining operation. Another donor conference in June 2008 raised more than $15 billion in additional international aid for Afghanistan. Donor states and organizations charged that past aid had often been mismanaged. The groups demanded greater accountability for the new assistance.

The increased foreign aid caused Afghanistan's GDP to expand by more than 20 percent the following year.

Diplomacy, Pakistan, Iran, and the Insurgency

In March 2006, Bush, Karzai, and Musharraf met to coordinate efforts to suppress Taliban bases in Pakistan. Karzai pressed for stronger action by the Pakistani government to stop Taliban and al Qaeda incursions into Afghanistan. Over the next few years, the Bush administration continued to pressure Pakistan for stronger action against the Taliban and al Qaeda. As aforementioned, the United States also increased its troop presence in Afghanistan and worked with its allies to expand ISAF's troop strength.

On March 12, 2006, former Afghan president Sibghatullah Mojaddedi survived an assassination attempt when two attacks detonated a car bomb alongside his vehicle. Mojaddedi and other Afghan officials blamed Pakistan's intelligence services for the attack, not al Qaeda. Mojaddedi was a vocal critic of Pakistan's inability to destroy the Taliban network. The former president and other Afghan officials asserted that Pakistani intelligence and military officials supported the Taliban as a way to destabilize Afghanistan and gain influence in the region. The two countries had a longstanding dispute over the 1,600-mile-long Durand Line, the border between the two which had been established in the 1890s. Afghanistan never officially recognized the boundary because it split the Pashtuns and the Balochs into two different countries. Some areas along the border were poorly defined and had been claimed by both countries, and there had been minor military skirmishes over territory since Pakistan became an independent country in 1947. In 2007, Pakistani forces crossed the border and built a fence system on Afghan territory. Pakistani authorities claimed the barrier was designed to prevent Taliban incursions into Afghanistan, but the Karzai government rejected the assertion and argued the effort was an attempt to establish control over Afghan territory. Afghan troops dismantled the fence. Pakistani and Afghan troops exchanged fire several times during the incident. Both countries have also accused the other government of not taking sufficient steps to reduce smuggling along the border.

In 2007, the United States became increasingly concerned over the involvement of Iran in Afghanistan. Iran traditionally had close ties with the Hazara ethnic group in Afghanistan. Intelligence indicated that Iran was supplying weapons and funding to Hazara militia groups. In April 2007, coalition forces captured a shipment of Iranian arms in Afghanistan, including mortars and high explosives, bound for Taliban insurgents. Iran denied responsibility for the arms. Nonetheless, Iranian president Mahmoud Ahmedinejad paid a state visit to Afghanistan in August and met with Karzai. The two leaders discussed economic cooperation and signed a number of agreements. Iran continued to provide support to Hazara groups, and coalition troops later captured additional Iranian arms shipments.

Provincial Reconstruction Teams

The first Provincial Reconstruction Teams (PRTs) were formed in 2002 (see Chapter 3); however, by 2004, these units emerged as a key component of coalition strategy. The PRTs were responsible for facilitating local and regional reconstruction projects, ranging from building schools, clinics, and hospitals to road construction and irrigation improvements. Each PRT was under the command of a senior military officer who oversaw projects and was authorized to initiate ventures that cost $25,000 or less. Efforts costing more had to be approved by central headquarters. The PRTs typically consisted of about 100 members, including military personnel and civilian aid specialists. Team members were engineers, medical personnel, accountants, and other specialists. Security was often an issue with the teams. By 2011, there were 27 PRTs deployed throughout Afghanistan. Both the U.S. military and ISAF used PRTs.

To protect the PRTs, coalition forces were stationed with the units. Later, Afghan Army troops were also deployed with the PRTs. At times the teams were regularly targeted by insurgents. For instance, one of the first PRTs, in Gardez, was attacked more than 30 times during its first two years of operation. The insurgents routinely fired rockets and mortars into the camp. The Taliban and al Qaeda also targeted Afghans who cooperated with the coalition. Insurgents used a variety of terrorist tactics against local officials, including assassinations, kidnappings, and suicide attacks.

The PRTs also attempted to expand the reach and authority of the Karzai government. However, the teams often found their programs resisted by local warlords who did welcome infrastructure improvements but resisted efforts to extend the scope of the central government's power. Nonetheless, the PRTs help dramatically broaden educational opportunities in Afghanistan. For example, under the Taliban, only 900,000 youths (all males) were enrolled in schools, a figure that rose to 5 million children (male and female) by 2008.

The PRTs were tasked with not only improving infrastructure but also promoting economic development. In 2002, there were also an estimated 5 million Afghan refugees in Pakistan and other neighboring countries. Many of these displaced people began to return to their homes after the fall of the Taliban; however, renewed fighting created new refugees and prompted significant internal migrations. Afghanistan also suffered a series of extraordinarily harsh winters in 2002 and 2003, further straining the country. The teams endeavored to build networks of roads and bridges to connect villages, towns, and cities to make it easier to move goods back and forth. Decades of conflict left more than 3 million Afghans, out of a population of 26 million, unemployed. One of the poorest countries in the world, Afghanistan's per capita income was $800 in 2009. It was estimated in 2008 that more than 50 percent of the population lived in poverty, while 75 percent of the population did not have access to safe drinking water. In addition, 80 percent of the population was engaged in agriculture (mainly subsistence farming). The country produced few cash exports except opium poppies.

The Drug Trade

The insurgency and the drug trade were inexorably intertwined. As the Taliban and al Qaeda increased their operations, the groups needed additional funds. Opium poppy production offered a convenient method to raise cash quickly. That money could be used to purchase weapons, fund operations, and train new recruits. Insurgents could also bribe local tribal leaders to gain their cooperation and prevent them from providing intelligence to government or coalition forces. The drug trade also created relationships between the insurgents and Afghan warlords. This undermined incentives for the warlords to cooperate with the government or the coalition. In fact, efforts by U.S.-led forces to suppress poppy production prompted some warlords to turn against the Karzai regime.

After the fall of the Taliban, poppy production rose dramatically. The United Nations estimated that poppy production in 2001 was 185 metric tons. Production rose to 3,400 metric tons in 2002, 3,600 in 2003, and 4,200 in 2004.[1] From 2004 to 2005, the area under poppy cultivation increased by 49 percent, and then expanded by 59 percent the following year, rising to 165,000 hectares. By 2006, Afghanistan accounted for 92 percent of the world's opium production, producing a crop worth $2.7 billion (meanwhile, legal exports were worth $600 million that same year).

Of course, the real value in the drug trade lay outside of Afghanistan. Once opium had been converted into heroin, its value increased by more than 100 times. One kilogram of opium could be processed into about 150–300 grams of heroin, depending on the purity of the drug (heroin sold on the streets typically had a purity of 35–60 percent). The United Nations estimated that the average price of a gram of heroin was $160. Within Afghanistan, drug use increased dramatically after 2001. International agencies estimated that 5–7 percent of the Afghan population regularly used drugs. Opium was the most commonly used drug among addicts. Efforts to curb both use among Afghans and production for export faced enormous challenges.

Eradication Efforts

The United Kingdom initially took the lead in developing a national poppy eradication program for Afghanistan. U.S. military and political officials wanted to concentrate on ending the Taliban and al Qaeda insurgency and were satisfied to leave anti-drug initiatives to other nations. The British developed a three-year program that was supposed to replace poppy production with other forms of farming. The program sought to not create a backlash among Afghans, so widespread aerial spraying or other chemical eradication operations were not used. Officials also tried to work with local and regional leaders to gain their trust and confidence.

NATO troops were initially ordered to ignore the drug trade. However, many warlords continued to engage in the expanding drug trade, and coalition counter-drug efforts failed. Nonetheless, many European nations continued to resist more aggressive counternarcotic efforts. In an address in 2006, Benita Ferrero-Waldner, a European commissioner, argued that one of the main problems with contemporary efforts to eradicate the drug trade in Afghanistan is that they were too narrow and needed to be coordinated with other countries. Ferrero-Waldner declared,

> We need to focus on **improving cooperation between countries along the drug trafficking routes** [bold in original], starting with Afghanistan and moving along the three principal trafficking routes. Aided by donors, individual countries are making enormous efforts to crack down on traffickers by improving border management, training law enforcers and the judiciary, and targeting illegal smuggling of chemical precursors. These efforts must continue, but above all, we must help countries to cooperate more effectively together. We need initiatives covering several countries and regions along the drug routes, so strengthening regional coordination. Crossborder problems require cross-border solutions.[2]

In 2005, opium production declined slightly, falling to 4,100 metric tons, but production then skyrocketed over the next two years, rising to 6,100 metric tons in 2006, and then peaking at 8,200 metric tons the next year.

By 2006, the U.S. Drug Enforcement Agency (DEA) became the lead agency in counternarcotic initiatives. The coalition was spending about $500 million per year to end the drug trade. About one-third of the budget was spent on eradication efforts which included the use of pesticides to destroy the crop. Small aircraft were used to spray suspected poppy fields with a commonly used weed and grass killer. The technique was highly effective but very unpopular among Afghans. Many believed that the spray was poisonous to both plants and humans and that it would inflict long-term damage on croplands. Opposition by the Karzai government led to a shift toward ground eradication, which included the use of tractors and manual destruction of the crop. These methods were often dangerous and exposed counternarcotic forces to attack and booby traps, including landmines and improvised explosive devices (IEDs). About one-third of the budget was spent on efforts to promote alternative crop production by farmers, and the remaining third was allocated to patrols, arrests, and anti-smuggling efforts.

Meanwhile, efforts to promote cultivation of alternative crops were generally unsuccessful. First, other crops did not pay as well as opium poppies. In addition, many other crops proved more difficult to grow, needing more fertilizer or irrigation. Second, farmers faced pressure, including violence, from local warlords or insurgents if they abandoned poppy cultivation. Efforts to arrest and prosecute drug traffickers were undermined by corruption among local police. Even when coalition forces or Afghan national police detained suspected drug traffickers, they were frequently released by sympathetic or corrupt judges. There were also instances of political pressure being brought on police and judges as officials in the Karzai regime endeavored to retain the loyalty of regional warlords and clan leaders. There were also tensions within the coalition over the use of resources. For instance, U.S. military leaders were reluctant to allow the DEA and Afghan anti-drug units the use of helicopters, arguing that the aircraft were needed for anti-insurgency operations.

Despite the challenges, counternarcotic efforts began to have some success in 2008. That year, the United States developed a comprehensive strategy that endeavored to coordinate counternarcotic efforts across the DEA, the U.S. military, and other agencies. In the northern provinces, alternative crop programs proved successful as farmers rejected opium production and instead grew crops such as wheat, cotton, and various vegetables. Corruption in the northern and northeastern areas was also generally lower, and a number of regional governors and local leaders were committed to eradicating the drug trade. One U.S. program rewarded districts that eradicated poppy production with accelerated development initiatives including new schools, clinics, and roads. As a result, opium production fell to 7,700 metric tons in 2008 from its 2007 peak (it fell further to 6,900 metric tons in 2009). Drug production became increasingly concentrated in the southern region, which was also the heart of the insurgency. The United Nations noted that "total opium cultivation in 2008 in Afghanistan is estimated at 157,000 hectares (ha), a 19% reduction compared to 2007. Unlike previous years, 98% of the total cultivation is confined to seven provinces with security problems: five of these provinces are in the south and two in the west of Afghanistan."[3] Afghan and coalition military increasingly undertook counternarcotic operations in order to deny the Taliban funds to finance the insurgency.

Coalition Offensives and NATO

In 2006, NATO announced that it would increase its troop strength in Afghanistan from 8,500 to 16,000. The deployment marked a turning point for ISAF, which had concentrated on reconstruction and development programs. Henceforth, the international troops increasingly undertook combat operations. Beginning in May, U.S.-led forces launched a major offensive against the Taliban in the southern provinces in Afghanistan. Dubbed Mountain Thrust, the campaign was the largest operation since the initial invasion and included more than 11,000 coalition and Afghan troops. Mountain Thrust was designed to suppress the Taliban and al Qaeda in the restive Helmand Province. From the best estimates, there were 2,000–2,500 insurgents in the region. Coalition forces captured their main objectives, but lost 155, including 24 Americans, while more than

1,110 insurgents were killed and more than 380 captured. During the offensive, the Taliban showed great resilience, even temporarily capturing several towns, despite massive allied aerial and missile strikes. In addition, after Mountain Thrust, the Taliban launched a series of counterattacks. The number of terrorist attacks also increased significantly. On September 10, the governor of Paktia province was killed in a suicide attack.

The Taliban and al Qaeda adopted tactics that had been used by the insurgents in Iraq. In addition to a rise in suicide-bombing attacks, there was an increasing use of IEDs and remote-detonated roadside bombs. The insurgents also employed more sophisticated weaponry, including armor-piercing rounds and guided anti-aircraft missiles. The tactics and weaponry contributed to the rise in casualties among coalition troops.

In the aftermath of Mountain Thrust, NATO took command of the southern region of Afghanistan on July 31, 2006. In discussing the expansion of NATO's role in Afghan, NATO Secretary General Jaap de Hoop Scheffer declared,

[L]et me underscore the guiding principle that security cannot be achieved by military means alone. While ISAF will fulfill its tasks in security matters, we cannot succeed without adequate civil governance, rule of law and economic and community development. Institution building, development, reconstruction, and human capacity building mutually reinforce the security efforts. That is why we [NATO] will continue to work closely with the Government of Afghanistan, the United Nations, the EU, the G-8 nations, individual donor nations and many others as strategic Partners in fulfilling the aspirations of the Afghan people and their freely elected representatives.[4]

As additional international troops arrived in the region, NATO forces undertook a major offensive in southern Afghanistan in September in response to rising Taliban and al Qaeda violence. In order to support the operation, NATO leaders agreed to increase the number of troops in Afghanistan by an additional 2,500. However, disagreements emerged within the alliance. Some NATO partners, including Belgium, Germany, and France, argued that the alliance should concentrate on reconstruction and economic development, while the United States and the United Kingdom contended that violence had to be reduced and the country stabilized before development efforts could be successful. Differences in approach continued to affect NATO throughout its mission in Afghanistan.

On September 21, NATO defense ministers, meeting in Brussels, agreed to take responsibility for the security of all of Afghanistan. On October 5, NATO formally took command of coalition forces in the country. The unification of command ended the division in Afghanistan whereby U.S.-led forces and NATO troops operated semi-independently of each other (a small U.S. force did continue training Afghan troops in a mission outside of ISAF). The consolidation was designed to reduce redundancies and allow coalition forces to work closer together and make better use of resources and intelligence. The United States continued to supply the bulk of the combat forces and undertook the majority of the combat operations. Also, the overall NATO commander in the country was an American, with a British deputy. The first U.S. commander of ISAF was General Dan McNeill. By the end of 2006, ISAF included more than 32,000 troops from 40 countries.

By December 2007, the United States had 24,600 troops in Afghanistan, a figure that rose to 32,500 the following year.[5] In 2007 and 2008, ISAF launched preemptive offensives in the winter in an effort to disrupt insurgents. The coalition also undertook campaigns in the spring. In 2007, Operation Achilles deployed 6,000 ISAF troops and 1,000 Afghan national forces in Helmand province. As with past offensives, the operation killed a large number of insurgents, but failed to completely quell the insurgency. Subsequent operations would also fail to suppress the insurgency. For instance, on February 27, 2007, a suicide bomber killed 23 at an attack at Bagram Air Force base during a visit by U.S. vice president Dick Cheney. Then, on April 27, Karzai survived an assassination attempt when insurgents attacked a military parade in Kabul. The Taliban launched a series of increasingly bold counterattacks on government and coalition forces beginning in the spring and continuing through the summer, including a large-scale attack on a NATO convoy that was struck by a suicide car bomb on May 18, and a suicide attack on the Bagram air base the following day. They also attacked a prison in Kandahar and freed more than 1,200, including at least 400 Taliban fighters.

More than 5,000 people died in 2008, including 2,100 civilians. By the end of the year, estimates were that the Taliban controlled about 10 percent of the country, the central government controlled 30 percent, and the rest of Afghanistan was under the power of warlords. In addition, both the coalition and government faced increasing opposition from the Afghan population. In Kabul and other major cities, protests grew against coalition military strikes. On April 30, large demonstrations took place following U.S. strikes that killed an estimated 130 Taliban fighters (protestors claimed that many of the dead were civilians).

Casualties among foreign troops rose steadily through the early 2000s. From 2004 to 2005, the number of U.S. or coalition troops killed in Afghanistan rose from 60 to 131 (including 52 Americans in 2004 and 99 in 2005). In 2006, there were 191 ISAF troops killed (including 99 Americans), a figure that rose to 232 (117 Americans) in 2007 and 295 (155 Americans) in 2008.

Nevertheless, the coalitions had some successes. Mullah Akhtar Osmani, the number four senior Taliban leader, was killed in a U.S. airstrike on December 19, 2006. The group's third most senior leader, Mullah Obaidullah Akhund, was captured in Pakistan in March 2007. Meanwhile, the IMF announced in 2008 that Afghanistan met the requirements to qualify for the Heavily Indebted Poor Countries initiative, an international debt-relief program. Consequently, 96 percent of Afghanistan's $1.6 billion debt was eliminated.

Conclusion

By the end of 2008, the insurgency in Afghanistan had grown dramatically, while the concurrent Taliban campaign across the border threatened the stability of Pakistan. For most of the tenure of the Bush administration, the United States officially opposed negotiations with the Taliban without the surrender of senior Taliban leaders and the renunciation of violence and terrorism by the group. In fact, in 2002, when former Taliban foreign minister Maulvi Wakil Ahmad Mutawakkil attempted to negotiate with the United States, he was arrested and sent to Guantanamo Bay for more than four years. There were covert efforts to convince individual Taliban leaders to defect and join the Karzai government. These initiatives met with only minimal success. However, by the summer of 2008, the administration, under pressure from the Karzai government, became more receptive to talks between the Afghan government and moderate Taliban leaders. One of the proponents of negotiations was General David Petraeus, who asserted that one key to reducing violence in Iraq had been the ability of the central government to co-opt Sunni leaders through the Sunni Awakening movement (see Chapter 7). The U.S. general argued that a similar approach could be used in Afghanistan to gain the support of regional and local leaders and turn them against Taliban extremists, al Qaeda, and warlords.

As Bush left office, incoming president Barack Obama took over an increasingly unpopular war. During his presidential campaign, Obama had argued for the need to develop new strategies for both Afghanistan and Iraq. However, once in office, the new chief executive faced competing pressures and interests, both domestically and internationally. Ultimately, Obama's Afghanistan strategy involved a series of compromises between the anti-war wing of the Democratic Party, U.S. defense and intelligence officials, and foreign leaders. Meanwhile, Obama's election and subsequent security policies were also the culmination of a number of trends in U.S. domestic politics.

Notes

1. United Nations Office on Drugs and Crime, "Afghanistan Opium Survey 2010: Summary Findings," September (New York: United Nations, 2010), 15.

2. Benita Ferrero-Waldner, "Drug Trafficking: The Priorities for the Future," speech, Moscow, June 28, 2006.

3. United Nations Office on Drugs and Crime, "Afghanistan Opium Survey 2008: Executive Summary," August (New York: United Nations, 2008), 3.

4. Jaap de Hoop Scheffer, "Secretary General's Intervention at the London Conference," speech, London, January 31, 2006.

5. Amy Belasco, "The Cost of Iraq, Afghanistan, and Other Global War on Terror Operations since 9/11," Congressional Research Service, September 2, 2010, 43.

9

U.S. Politics, the War on Terror, and Iraq

The war on terror and the Iraq War dominated U.S. politics throughout the first decade of the 21st century. The conflicts were the main issues in the national elections of 2002 and 2004, and played a major role in balloting in 2006 and 2008. Americans responded to the 9/11 attacks with renewed patriotism and a newfound sense of unity. The war on terror and the subsequent Iraq War defined the presidency of George W. Bush and shaped the early years of the tenure of Barack Obama. The conflicts also prompted discussion and debate over issues ranging from immigration to globalization to homeland security to the United States' role in the world.

For many Americans, the attacks shattered a sense of invulnerability and a concurrent feeling of exceptionalism from the rest of the world. Not since the surprise Japanese attack on Pearl Harbor on December 7, 1941, had the United States been struck such a devastating blow. Americans rallied behind their political leaders and government. President Bush's approval ratings soared to record levels. This was especially significant because of the disputed nature of the 2000 presidential balloting in which Bush won the majority of the Electoral College vote but lost the popular vote. However, debate and disagreement over the scope of homeland security, combined with questions over the appropriateness of military action against Iraq in 2002, eroded confidence in the president and his administration. Domestic issues, including the government's response to Hurricane Katrina and an economic recession that began in 2008, further undermined confidence. By the time Bush left office in 2009, his approval ratings were among the lowest of any modern president.

The 2000 Election

The 2000 election was the closest and most controversial presidential contest in more than 100 years. The balloting pitted Texas governor George W. Bush against Vice President Al Gore. Democrats had controlled the White House for eight years under President Bill Clinton. However, in the 1994 midterm elections, the Republicans regained control of both houses of Congress for the first time since the 1950s, and had maintained majorities in both the House of Representatives and the Senate through the rest of the decade. Clinton's vice president, Gore, secured the Democratic nomination for the 2000 balloting, defeating New Jersey senator Bill Bradley, his main competitor. Gore was a moderate Democrat who served as a U.S. representative from his home state of Tennessee from 1977 to 1985, and then as a U.S. senator from Tennessee from 1985 until he was sworn in as vice president in 1993. Gore's running mate was moderate Democratic senator Joe Lieberman of Connecticut, the first Jewish American vice presidential candidate.

Bush, the son of former president George H. W. Bush, defeated Arizona senator John McCain to represent the Republican Party in 2000. Bush had worked in the oil industry and was a co-owner of the Texas Rangers baseball team before he was elected governor of Texas in 1994. A popular and centrist Republican, Bush was reelected governor in 1998 by a landslide. In order to counter criticisms that he did not have significant national experience, Bush chose Dick Cheney as his vice presidential candidate. Cheney had been secretary of defense under Bush's father and had overseen the military aspects of the 1991 Persian Gulf War.

The campaign focused mainly on domestic matters, but Bush's lack of foreign policy experience was also an issue. After the attack on the U.S. naval vessel *Cole* on October 12, 2000 (see Chapter 1), terrorism emerged as an increasingly significant campaign matter. Bush criticized the Clinton administration's failure to kill or capture bin Laden, and both candidates promised tougher action to curb international terrorism.

On election night on November 7, 2000, Gore won the popular vote by 500,000 ballots; however, Bush appeared to win the Electoral College balloting. A bitter controversy followed over a recount of votes in Florida, where Bush's brother Jeb Bush was governor. Initial reports indicated that Bush won Florida, and its 25 electoral votes, by a slim margin. However, the Gore campaign sought a recount of votes in heavily Democratic districts in southeast Florida. The liberal Florida Supreme Court approved the recount, but the Bush campaign appealed and the U.S. Supreme Court ordered the recount stopped in December since, among other considerations, it was only a partial recount. Gore conceded and Bush won the Electoral College vote 271–266. Only once before in American history had the son of a former president also been elected chief executive of the nation (John Quincy Adams, the son of John Adams, was elected president in 1824).

In his inaugural address on January 20, 2001, Bush concentrated on attempting to heal the rifts that emerged because of the disputed election. In addition, most of his themes dealt with domestic policy. Bush did speak broadly about the United

States' role in the world and especially about the efforts of the nation to promote democracy:

> We have a place, all of us, in a long story; a story we continue, but whose end we will not see. It is the story of a new world that became a friend and liberator of the old. The story of a slave-holding society that became a servant of freedom. The story of a power that went into world to protect but not possess, to defend but not to conquer. It is the American story; a story of flawed and fallible people, united across the generations by grand and enduring ideals. . . .
>
> Through much of the last century, America's faith in freedom and democracy was a rock in a raging sea. Now it is a seed upon the wind, taking root in many nations. Our democratic faith is more than the creed of our country, it is the inborn hope of our humanity; an ideal we carry but do not own, a trust we bear and pass along. And even after nearly 225 years, we have a long way yet to travel.[1]

The effort to spread democracy was a constant theme in Bush's two terms as president.

True to his inaugural address, Bush initially concentrated on domestic politics after he was sworn into office in January 2001. He worked with Democrats to enact the bipartisan No Child Left Behind Act, an educational measure that was designed to improve primary and secondary education. Among other features, the law required state testing for students as a means to increase accountability among schools. However, Bush alienated the left and some moderates when the Republican-controlled Congress enacted $1.35 trillion in tax cuts over a 10-year period. Disenchantment over the tax cuts led Republican senator Jim Jeffords of Vermont to leave the party and become an independent in May 2001. Jeffords's defection ended Republican control of the Senate (the chamber had a 50–50 tie between the parties, but as vice president, Cheney was constitutionally required to cast the deciding vote when there was a tie in the 100-member Senate). Jeffords agreed to caucus with the Democrats, which gave them a 51–49 edge in the upper chamber.

In order to compensate for his lack of foreign and security policy experience, Bush appointed a number of well-known and respected figures to senior positions in his cabinet, including former Chairman of the Joints Chiefs of Staff Colin Powell as secretary of state. Powell became the first African American to hold the senior cabinet post. Donald Rumsfeld, who had served as secretary of defense in the 1970s under President Gerald Ford, was again appointed to that post. As noted in Chapter 5, with the exception of Powell, most of the president's foreign and security policy team were neo-conservatives who sought to reshape global politics through the spread of democracy and other U.S. interests.

Bush's First Term and the War on Terror

As noted in Chapter 2, the Bush administration was aware of the potential dangers posed by global terrorism and had begun to review the Clinton-era policies prior to

9/11. After the terrorist attacks, the government undertook broad reforms (as noted in Chapter 4) in homeland and foreign security policies. Congress and the American public were initially very supportive of these reforms, although civil libertarians expressed concern over the expansion of government powers under the Homeland Security Act.

Bush's Wartime Presidency

In the American governmental system, the president has wide latitude in the realm of security and defense policy. This is especially significant since the U.S. political system is built around a system of checks and balances, with the expectation that one branch of government can act as a balancer or "check" on another. The president is the commander-in-chief of the military and appoints the senior military officers (with confirmation by the Senate). The day-to-day operations of the military are overseen by the secretary of defense, another presidential appointee, who reports directly to the chief executive. The president also traditionally sets the direction and tone of U.S. foreign and security policy. In the 20th century, and especially after World War II, Congress typically granted successive presidents a high degree of deference in the development and implementation of policy. There are two main constraints on the president's conduct of security policy. First, the 1973 War Powers Act mandates that a chief executive cannot commit U.S. troops to combat for more than 90 days (including a 30-day withdrawal period) without the approval of Congress. The measure was passed in the wake of the Vietnam War and was designed to prevent the nation from being pulled into conflicts without debate and discussion by the legislature. However, since 1973, Congress has not voted no on, or denied, requests from presidents to use force. As aforementioned, when Bush asked Congress for the ability to deploy the military against the Taliban and al Qaeda in Afghanistan, the authorization was almost unanimously approved (the subsequent request to use force in Iraq was also approved by an overwhelming majority of both houses). Consequently, the act has not been as effective a check on military deployments as it was originally envisioned. Second, Congress controls the budget for the Defense Department and could deny or limit funding for combat operations. However, successive presidents were able to prevent Congress from limiting funding for military operations by designating the spending as outside of the regular defense budget, as emergency or supplemental funding. Presidents have also charged that efforts to limit defense funding could result in service members' lives being put at risk, an accusation that few members of Congress have been able to effectively counter. As a result, congressional budget authority has not proven an effective check against presidential action.

The attacks transformed Bush's presidency. He became the first U.S. president since Franklin D. Roosevelt to be in office during a foreign attack on American soil. As noted, Bush's approval ratings soared to above 90 percent, but he faced a public that demanded swift action against the perpetrators of the terrorist attacks. The public pressure to act quickly gave the president an unusual amount of deference as his administration crafted its response. The result was that Bush had an even greater degree of freedom from political checks and balances than his predecessors.

Bush's predominance in U.S. security matters on the domestic level was reinforced by the global influence and power of the United States. With the end of the Cold War in 1991, the United emerged as the world's sole remaining superpower. Through the 1990s, the military power and capabilities of the United States continued to outpace those of other countries. By 2002, the United States accounted for approximately 50 percent of the world's total military spending. The United States spent almost eight times as much as China and Russia, the number two and three nations in the world in terms of military expenditures. In comparison, during the waning days of the Cold War in the 1983, the United States and the Soviet Union had roughly equal defense expenditures (both spent more than $212 billion that year). Partially because of the large defense outlays, the United States also had an enormous edge over other countries in military weapons and technology. U.S. advantages in communications and laser-guided, precision weaponry had even made it difficult to work with allies in previous conflicts during the 1990s (American technological advances were one reason cited by Rumsfeld to use mainly U.S. forces during the invasion of Afghanistan).

The United States had further emerged as a global leader on a range of issues, including globalization and trade, humanitarian missions, and counterterrorism. One result was a culture of deference toward the United States, not only among the nation's closest allies, but among other nations as well. The brutality of the 9/11 attacks temporarily reinforced this trend and left Bush in a unique position to shape global affairs with tremendous political and military power and authority, both at home and abroad.

Dick Cheney

No discussion of the Bush presidency would be complete without an examination of the role of Vice President Dick Cheney. In the past, vice presidents were often appointed to the post as a reward for seniority or service to their political party. Many vice presidents have had relatively little power or influence. Often vice presidents are chosen to balance the presidential contender in some fashion. For instance, George H. W. Bush chose Senator Dan Quayle (Indiana) as his vice president in 1988, because Quayle was younger and from the Midwest. As aforementioned, Bush chose Cheney because of the latter's experience.

Cheney exerted significant influence within the administration, especially on security matters. Cheney emerged as the leader of the hardliner faction within the administration. He advocated for an aggressive response to the 9/11 attacks. He was also the leading proponent for military action against Iraq. For Cheney and other hawks in the administration, eradicating terrorism and the promotion of democracy were inexorably intertwined. These neo-conservatives believed that democracy and free trade capitalism were the keys to reducing conflict and strife around the globe. They viewed the examples of Germany and Japan after World War II or the wave of democratization that swept Eastern Europe as proof of the primacy of that form of government. Along with the war on terror, Cheney and his supporters in the administration were vocal proponents of supporting democratization movements in countries such as Ukraine and Lebanon.

Cheney dramatically expanded the formal and informal powers of the vice presidency and took on a very active role in the decision-making process. Opponents of the administration were increasingly critical of Cheney after the invasion of Iraq, and the vice president became a focal point for denigration of the administration.

Bipartisanship

The 9/11 attacks produced a "rally-around-the-flag" effect in U.S. politics. Democratic leaders who had been very critical of Bush's domestic policies, including the 2001 tax cuts, publicly supported the president and his administration. The result was the emergence of a temporary broad bipartisan consensus on security policy. Democratic leaders, including Senate party leader Tom Daschle of South Dakota and House party leader Dick Gephardt of Missouri, worked with the White House and Republican leaders in Congress to enact Bush's new security agenda. Concurrently, the Bush administration initially worked closely with Daschle, Gephardt, and other Democratic leaders on the military planning that culminated in Operation Enduring Freedom.

A similar bipartisan consensus on security matters had existed during the Cold War. Beginning with the administration of Harry S. Truman in the aftermath of World War II, Republicans and Democrats generally demonstrated a high degree of cooperation on national security. For instance, Republican leaders in the Senate, led by Senator Arthur Vandenberg of Michigan, endorsed the creation of NATO in 1949. The alliance became the first permanent military alliance in the history of the United States. It also overcame a tradition of isolationism in U.S. foreign and security policy whereby the United States avoided engagement in European issues. Throughout the bipolar conflict, majorities in both parties generally backed successive administrations on security policy, with some notable exceptions, including the Vietnam War and efforts by the Reagan administration in the 1980s to provide arms and financial support to anti-communist rebels in Nicaragua. With the end of the Cold War, U.S. foreign and security policy became increasingly politicized. For instance, there was bitter debate over the resolution to use force against Iraq following its invasion of Kuwait. The authorization to use force passed a closely divided Senate on a vote of 52 in favor and 47 opposed on January 12, 1991.

In writing about the Bush presidency, presidential scholar Gary C. Jacobson notes,

> Bush's [approval] ratings remained above 60 percent for 16 months, the longest streak at this level for any president since Roosevelt during World War II. The terrorist attacks had completely redefined the priorities and purpose of his presidency; Bush was now first and foremost a war president, and in that capacity, he drew overwhelming bipartisan support for his initial responses to the attacks. The public was nearly unanimous in backing the president's decision to use military force to go after Osama bin Laden and his al Qaeda forces in Afghanistan when its Taliban government refused to hand them over. . . . With nearly 90 percent of the public favoring military action against the terrorists, anything less might have actually cost him public support; the administration's main concern while preparing to fight in Afghanistan was to avoid the perception that it was reacting too slowly or with insufficient force.[2]

Because of the tremendous public support for Bush and the almost unheralded amount of power and authority held by the president, the administration initially faced relatively little domestic or international opposition to Operation Enduring Freedom.

Politics and Elections

In the United States, Democrats generally refrained from criticizing Bush's foreign and security policy, including the war on terror from late 2001 through 2002. Instead, the party sought to differentiate between its stance on domestic issues and the positions of Bush and the Republicans. Democratic leaders concentrated on economic policy, social security, and health care. They also criticized the Bush tax cuts for a growing budget deficit that swelled because of the post-9/11 economic slowdown and increased military spending as a result of the war on terror. Before 9/11 the United States had a small budget surplus, but in 2002, the deficit grew to 1.48 percent of GDP and then rose to 3.49 percent of GDP the following year. With midterm elections in 2002 and a presidential election in 2004, Democratic leaders struggled to find winning issues against a president who had historic approval ratings.

One area where the Democrats endeavored to draw distinctions between their positions and those of Bush and the Republicans was homeland security. As noted, various Democratic leaders cautioned against the enactment of what they perceived to be extreme measures that would undermine civil liberties. At the same time, Democrats were critical of the slow pace of reforms within the newly created office, and later department, of homeland security. They called for increased security to protect infrastructure, including ports, transportation networks, and energy plants. Democrats also sought increased funding for state preparedness for emergency response.

Concurrently, the Republicans sought to recapture control of the Senate in the 2002 midterm elections and strengthen their majority in the House of Representatives. Consequently, the GOP endeavored to emphasize national security as the party prepared for the midterm balloting. Campaigning for the congressional polling took place at the same time as the domestic and international debate over potential military conflict with Iraq.

2002 Elections

Historically in midterm elections, the party in power in the White House loses seats in Congress. Prior to the balloting, most congressional Democrats were supportive of Bush's security agenda. Democrats had overwhelmingly voted in favor of the legislation to use force against Afghanistan and for the Homeland Security Act. Nevertheless, national security was a major issue in the 2002 midterm elections. Some Republican candidates accused their Democratic opponents of being soft on terrorism or national security. Democrats charged that Republicans were politicizing national security. During the campaign, Bush criticized Democrats for opposition to his homeland security policies. The president also campaigned diligently for Republican congressional candidates. Bush was able to nationalize the balloting as a referendum on his presidency's management of the war on terror to that point. The potential for war with Iraq was also a major issue.

In an adroit political maneuver, Republicans in Congress arranged for a vote on the Iraq War Resolution on October 16, 2002, less than a month before the election. Democrats were forced to either vote for the measure or face the possibility of being perceived by the public as opposed to the still popular president, as well as weak on national security.

In the balloting, Republicans gained seats in both the House and Senate (recapturing control of the upper chamber). The GOP increased its share of the national vote by 2.3 percent over the 2000 congressional balloting. The Republicans also regained control of the majority of state legislatures for the first time in more than 50 years. Democrats did gain one governorship in the polling, leaving the balance of power among governors 26–24 in favor of the GOP. In addition to Bush's popularity, Republicans were aided by redistricting which occurred following the 2000 census. Population shifts allowed some nominally Republican states, including Texas, to gain seats. In addition, legislatures redrew electoral districts in efforts to benefit whichever party held political power in the state.

Almost immediately after the midterm elections, jockeying for the Democratic nomination for the 2004 presidential campaign began. House Democratic leader Gephardt launched a bid to capture the nomination. In an article in the journal *Foreign Affairs*, Gephardt endeavored to explain his differences with Bush, but he also endorsed the main tenets of Bush security policy, including the war on terror. However, he attempted to portray himself as an international consensus builder who would develop a broad anti-Saddam coalition along the lines developed by Bush's father:

> Before I start, I want to address the question of foreign policy in Iraq, because I know it's on everyone's mind. I believe we must disarm Saddam Hussein, and I'm proud that I wrote the resolution that helped lead the President to finally make his case to the United Nations.
>
> For all our military might, there are too many threats to our security, too many global challenges for America simply to go it alone. We need the friendship and we need the cooperation of our time-honored allies.
>
> We need a President who will lead the world toward that consensus and will lead by real leadership and not merely trying to bully other nations into doing that.[3]

As the prelude to the Iraq War continued and the U.S. presidential campaign began, a vibrant anti-war movement emerged in the United States.

Anti-War Movement

Congress overwhelmingly voted to authorize the use of force against Afghanistan on September 14, 2001. Public opinion polls also indicated overwhelming support for the Bush administration. However, in the aftermath of the attacks there emerged an anti-war movement in the United Sates and other countries. Initially, activists sought to avoid military action and have a non-violent resolution of the conflict. Many opposed to military action in Afghanistan also feared that fighting might have one of two major negative consequences. The first main reason for opposition to war was a concern that the United States would find itself in another conflict that became a quagmire as happened during the U.S. involvement in the Vietnam War (1955–1975). During that war, successive U.S. administrations had difficulty formulating and implementing a long-term strategy for winning the war or achieving the nation's goals. The Vietnam War ended with more than 58,000 Americans killed or missing and undermined the nation's credibility abroad. As the Cold War waned in the 1980s, many compared the Vietnam War to the Soviet Occupation of Afghanistan (dubbing the conflict the "Soviet Union's Vietnam"). Those who opposed the invasion of Afghanistan, and later the Iraq War, asserted that the conflicts had the potential to turn into quagmires such as Vietnam.

The second main motivating factor among the anti-war movement was the concern that the invasions of Afghanistan and Iraq would increase violence and instability and actually lead to an increase in terrorism and anti-American violence. Evidence indicated that many of the foreign Mujahedeen who went to Afghanistan to fight the Soviets returned to their countries with extreme views and became involved in radical groups, including some terrorist organizations, in their home countries. Bin Laden was one example of this trend. Anti-war advocates contended that an invasion of Afghanistan could create a new wave of extremists and terrorists. While there was not a dramatic increase in foreign fighters in Afghanistan after the initial invasion, the numbers grew substantially after 2004. Meanwhile, the number of foreign insurgents in Iraq grew steadily from the earliest months of the invasion onward. In addition, the Afghan and Iraq conflicts also served to rally radical Islamic terrorists around the globe (see Chapter 6).

Besides concerns over negative consequences for the United States, many anti-war activists were opposed to violence because of philosophical or religious reasons. Religious groups such as the Quakers had a long tradition of pacifism and were in the forefront of the anti-war movement. Opponents also contended that any invasion would cause civilian casualties, killing innocent Afghans in response to a terrorist attack that was condemned because of the deaths of so many civilians. Anti-war activists asserted that this was highly illogical.

Many opponents of the Iraq War based their resistance on opposition to the Bush Doctrine. They denounced the notion of preemption. For instance, in a speech on June 3, 2004, billionaire philanthropist and activist George Soros declared that there were "two kinds of sovereignty in the world: U.S. sovereignty, which is inviolate, and the lesser brand suffered by the rest of the world that is subject to the Bush Doctrine."[4] Soros also argued that the United States "went to war in Iraq on false pretences. There was no connection between Saddam Hussein and al-Qaida. There were no weapons of mass destruction. . . . And what I find most galling is the final argument of justification that we went for the sake of the Iraqi people."[5] Soros also echoed many anti-war activists when he contended that "the war on terrorism as conducted by Bush has since caused more innocent victims than the victims of the [9/11] attack on America."[6]

Protests and Protest Movements

One of the first broad anti-war groups that emerged was Act Now to Stop War and End Racism (ANSWER). ANSWER was a coalition of left-of-center groups that emerged in the immediate aftermath of the 9/11 attacks. Its initial purpose was to oppose military action against Afghanistan, but the coalition later worked against a range of U.S. foreign policy initiatives, including arms sales, U.S. support for Israel, and the war on terror. The group organized the first large anti-war protest against the potential use of force against Afghanistan on September 29, 2001. ANSWER brought together approximately 20,000 people in a demonstration in Washington, D.C. ANSWER subsequently convened other protests against Operation Enduring Freedom and led protests against the Iraq War in 2003, including a protest in Washington, D.C., on March 15, 2003, that drew more than 60,000 people. Moveon.org, which was founded in 1998, also emerged as a major opponent of the Iraq War. The organization raised funds and campaigned against members of Congress who supported the war (Moveon.org also campaigned against Bush in the 2004 presidential election).

Many mainstream political organizations and special interest groups were leery about cooperating with ANSWER and similar bodies in the aftermath of the 9/11 attacks out of concern that they would alienate average Americans, who, polls indicated, were strongly supportive of Operation Enduring Freedom in 2001 and 2002. However, with the onset of the Iraq War, an increasing number of political and social movements were highly critical of the use of the military in the war on terror. One result was a substantial increase in the size and fervor of anti-war protests and demonstrations around the country. Groups also began to coordinate with similar anti-war movements overseas, staging global protests on the eve of the invasion.

Once the invasion of Iraq began, anti-war demonstrations became more common. There were widespread protests in major U.S. cities, including Atlanta, Chicago, New York, Seattle, San Francisco, Los Angeles, and Washington, D.C. On March 23, demonstrations in New York drew more than 200,000 people. On March 29, Boston was the site for the largest anti-war demonstration in the city since the Vietnam War. Protests continued throughout the U.S. occupation of Iraq.

The 2004 Elections

Mainly as a result of his historically high approval ratings, Bush did not face a challenge in the Republican primaries and caucuses for the party's nomination for the 2004 presidential election. This allowed Bush to preserve his campaign funds for the general election. Meanwhile, Bush was a prodigious fundraiser. His campaign raised more than $367 million. Bush ran on his leadership in the war on terror and his national security policies.

There was a large field of Democratic candidates, including Gephardt; former Vermont governor Howard Dean; Senators John Kerry (Massachusetts), John Edwards (North Carolina), Bob Graham (Florida), and Joseph Lieberman (Connecticut); as well as retired general Wesley Clarke, Reverend Al Sharpton, Representative Dennis Kucinich (Ohio), and former senator Carol Moseley Braun (Illinois). Dean emerged as the frontrunner. He was highly critical of Bush's national security policy, especially the war in Iraq and the war on terror. Dean argued that the Iraq War diverted attention and resources from the effort to defeat al Qaeda and the Taliban. He also ridiculed the Bush administration for its inability to kill or capture bin Laden. Dean ran television advertisements that criticized his opponents who had supported the Iraq War. The former governor also ran a populist campaign that condemned Bush's economic policies. Dean lost his front-runner status after the Iowa caucuses as other candidates began to emerge as more centrist.

Other Democratic candidates who opposed the Iraq War were Sharpton, Moseley Braun, and Graham, who voted against the 2002 authorization to use force against Iraq. Lieberman was a staunch supporter of the war on terror and the Iraq War and had been one of the sponsors of the Senate version of the resolution that authorized the use of force against Iraq. Lieberman, Gephardt, Edwards, and Kerry voted for the Iraq War resolution. However, Edwards and Kerry were critical of the conduct of the war. They also asserted that the Bush administration had provided bad intelligence and had they known that Iraq did not possess WMDs, they would have opposed the use of force. Like Dean, Edwards also ran a populist campaign that emphasized the growing disparity between the rich and poor in the United States.

After reorganizing his campaign, Kerry eventually secured the nomination. He chose the youthful Edwards as his running mate. Edwards helped balance the ticket because of his youth and the fact that he was a Southerner, while Kerry was from Massachusetts. Kerry was a highly decorated Vietnam War veteran, and Democrats increasingly perceived him as the party's best chance to defeat Bush.

On July 29, 2004, in his acceptance speech at the Democratic National Convention in Boston, Massachusetts, Kerry alluded to his military service when he began his address by stating, "I'm John Kerry, and I'm reporting for duty."[7] The Democratic presidential nominee went on to attempt to reaffirm his patriotism and then to differentiate himself from Bush and his administration:

> We are here tonight because we love our country. We're proud of what America is and what it can become. My fellow Americans, we're here tonight united in one purpose: to make America stronger at home and respected in the world....
>
> I will be a commander in chief who will never mislead us into war. I will have a vice president who will not conduct secret meetings with polluters to rewrite our environmental laws. I will have a secretary of defense who will listen to the best advice of the military leaders. And I will appoint an attorney general who will uphold the Constitution of the United States. My fellow Americans, this is the most important election of our lifetime. The stakes are high. We are a nation at war: a global war on terror against an enemy unlike we've ever known before.[8]

Kerry reminded the country of the 9/11 attacks and the country's response, but continued his criticism of Bush.

> Remember the hours after September 11th when we came together as one to answer the attack against our homeland. We drew strength when our firefighters ran up stairs and risked their lives so that others might live; when rescuers rushed into smoke and fire at the Pentagon; when the men and women of Flight 93 sacrificed themselves to save our nation's Capitol; when flags were hanging from front porches all across America, and strangers became friends. It was the worst day we have ever seen, but it brought out the best in all of us.
>
> I am proud that after September 11th all our people rallied to President Bush's call for unity to meet the danger. There were no Democrats. There were no Republicans. There were only Americans. And how we wish it had stayed that way. Now, I know there that are those who criticize me for seeing complexities, and I do, because some issues just aren't all that simple. Saying there are weapons of mass destruction in Iraq doesn't make it so. Saying we can fight a war on the cheap doesn't make it so. And proclaiming "Mission accomplished" certainly doesn't make it so.
>
> As president, I will ask the hard questions and demand hard evidence. I will immediately reform the intelligence system, so policy is guided by facts and facts are never distorted by politics.
>
> And as president, I will bring back this nation's time-honored tradition: The United States of America never goes to war because we want to; we only go to war because we have to. That is the standard of our nation.[9]

These themes formed the core of the Kerry campaign and were the foundation of the candidate's efforts to defeat Bush.

Bush was renominated as the Republican presidential candidate at the party's convention in New York, New York, on September 2, 2004. In his acceptance speech, the president attempted to accomplish several goals. First, Bush addressed speculation that he had considered replacing Cheney as vice president. The president declared, "In the work we have done and the work we will do, I am fortunate to have a superb vice president. I have counted on Dick Cheney's calm and steady judgment in difficult days, and I'm honored to have him at my side."[10] Second, Bush reminded the nation of the 9/11 attacks and explained his approach to the war on terror by relating an anecdote from his trip to New York after the attack:

> Workers in hard hats were shouting to me, "Whatever it takes." A fellow grabbed me by the arm, and he said, "Do not let me down." Since that day, I wake up every morning thinking about how to better protect our country. I will never relent in defending America, whatever it takes.

So we have fought the terrorists across the Earth, not for pride, not for power, but because the lives of our citizens are at stake.

Our strategy is clear. We have tripled funding for homeland security and trained half a million first responders because we are determined to protect our homeland.

We are transforming our military and reforming and strengthening our intelligence services. We are staying on the offensive, striking terrorists abroad so we do not have to face them here at home.[11]

Bush's point about fighting terrorists overseas so that the United States would not have to fight them on U.S. soil became a central campaign theme. Bush and his supporters contended that Operation Iraqi Freedom drew terrorists and other extremists to Iraq, which had become the central front in the war on terror. Al Qaeda and other terrorist groups concentrated their efforts and resources in Iraq and Afghanistan, where they were confronted by American combat forces. According to Bush, the twin campaigns therefore helped protect the United States and reduce the likelihood of additional terrorist attacks on American soil. Third, Bush presented an overview of what he perceived to be the major accomplishments while in office:

Our strategy is succeeding. Four years ago, Afghanistan was the home base of Al Qaida. Pakistan was a transit point for terrorist groups. Saudi Arabia was fertile ground for terrorist fund-raising. Libya was secretly pursuing nuclear weapons, Iraq was a gathering threat. And Al Qaida was largely unchallenged as it planned attacks.

Today, the government of a free Afghanistan is fighting terror. Pakistan is capturing terrorist leaders. Saudi Arabia is making raids and arrests. Libya is dismantling its weapons programs. The army of a free Iraq is fighting for freedom. And more than three-quarters of Al Qaida's key members and associates have been detained or killed.

We have led, many have joined, and America and the world are safer.[12]

Finally, Bush reminded the nation that Kerry and Edwards had initially supported Operation Iraqi Freedom.

Members of both political parties, including my opponent and his running mate, saw the threat, and voted to authorize the use of force. We went to the United Nations Security Council, which passed a unanimous resolution demanding the dictator disarm, or face serious consequences. Leaders in the Middle East urged him to comply.

After more than a decade of diplomacy, we gave Saddam Hussein another chance, a final chance, to meet his responsibilities to the civilized world. He again refused.

And I faced the kind of decision that comes only to the Oval Office, a decision no president would ask for, but must be prepared to make: Do I forget the lessons of September 11th and take the word of a madman or do I take action to defend our country?

Faced with that choice, I will defend America every time.[13]

Once the general campaign began, outside interest groups campaigned heavily for both parties, producing negative attack ads and false accusations against Bush and Kerry. For instance, groups called into question Kerry's war record in an effort to undermine the senator's standing on military matters. Concurrently, Dan Rather of *CBS News* ran a news story that accused Bush of receiving preferential treatment as a member of the Air National Guard during the Vietnam War (the story proved to be false, and Rather subsequently resigned from CBS). In the end, the election was one of the most negative in recent history.

Kerry's campaign was based on opposition to Bush's conduct of the Iraq War and the war on terror. But the senator attempted to walk a very fine line between being critical but not defeatist. Bush's campaign emphasized his leadership as a war president. Bush initially had a significant lead over Kerry, but after a series of presidential debates, that lead was eroded. Nonetheless, Bush continued to enjoy relatively high approval ratings. He won the election by a margin of 51 percent to 48 percent. The election was the first since 1988 in which a candidate received more than 50 percent of the vote. The Republicans also gained additional seats in the Senate and House of Representatives. Flushed with victory, some Republican leaders began to speak of the party having a near-permanent majority, just as the Democrats had established during the 1930s under Roosevelt.

In his inaugural address on January 20, 2005, Bush linked the war on terror with democratization and his administration's efforts to spread democracy.

So it is the policy of the United States to seek and support the growth of democratic movements and institutions in every nation and culture, with the ultimate goal of ending tyranny in our world.

This is not primarily the task of arms, though we will defend ourselves and our friends by force of arms when necessary. Freedom, by its nature, must be chosen, and defended by citizens, and sustained by the rule of law and the protection of minorities. And when the soul of a nation finally speaks, the institutions that arise may reflect customs and traditions very different from our own. America will not impose our own style of government on the unwilling. Our goal instead is to help others find their voice, attain their freedom, and make their own way.[14]

Partisanship

By the time of the 2004 elections, the country had become increasingly polarized with the war in Iraq and the broader war on terror as the central dividing issues between Americans. Many moderate or centrist Democrats were defeated by more conservative Republicans in the 2002 and 2004 congressional elections. The erosion of a political middle ground was also manifested within the government. In the administration, Powell resigned as secretary of state and was replaced by National Security Advisor Rice. Rice's deputy, Stephen Hadley, was appointed to succeed her as the president's main security advisor. Powell was seen as the leader of the moderate faction within the administration, and his loss seemed to signal an increase in the power and influence of Cheney and Rumsfeld. Rice would subsequently emerge as the leading moderate on security matters within the Cabinet.

In an effort to find a bipartisan solution to end the Iraq War, Congress formed the Iraq Study Group in March 2006 (see Chapter 7). The body was tasked with developing concrete proposals to end the conflict. It issued its recommendations in December in an effort to avoid influencing the November 2006 midterm elections. Many of its recommendations, including proposal to engage Iran and Syria in a diplomatic effort to end the fighting, were rejected by the Bush administration. The Iraqi government also refused to go along with a number of findings, including a call for the central government to maintain a high degree of control over the country's oil revenues. Instead the Iraqis government favored allowing regional governments to retain control over the revenues.

The failure of the Iraq Study Group was emblematic of growing partisanship in the United States. Throughout his presidency, Bush retained a relatively high public approval rating among Republicans; however, his standing among Democrats and independents declined precipitously as the war in Iraq progressed. For instance, in the immediate aftermath of the 9/11 attacks, Bush's approval ratings exceeded 95 percent among Republicans, 90 percent among independents, and 84 percent among Democrats. However, by 2005, almost 80 percent of Republicans continued to approve of his performance, but among Democrats his approval rating had fallen to 7 percent (a figure lower than that of President Richard M. Nixon after he resigned in 1974).[15] Bush's average approval rating among Republicans was 91.5 percent during his first term, the highest average of any Republican president (Dwight D. Eisenhower had averaged 87.6 percent during his two terms). Concurrently, the approval gap between Republicans and Democrats on Bush averaged 78 percent during his first term, the largest average margin of any president to date.[16] By the time of the 2006 congressional elections, Bush's standing among Republicans had also declined. Dissatisfaction among Republicans and the continuing negative perceptions among Democrats resulted in a historic election in which the GOP lost control of Congress.

2006 Elections

In midterm congressional elections on November 7, Republicans lost their majorities in both the Senate and the House of Representatives. The Republicans lost six seats in the Senate to give the Democrats a 51–49 advantage. In the House, the Republicans lost 30 seats to give the Democrats a 233–202 lead. The losses were the result of a combination of factors. For instance, congressional Republicans were wracked by a series of scandals. In 2004, a leading Republican lobbyist, Jack Abramoff, was accused of trading access to Republican politicians in exchange for campaign contributions. He later pled guilty to three felonies, including fraud. Twelve others, including Republican representative Bob Ney (Ohio), were also convicted for their roles in the scandal. In 2005, Republican house majority leader Tom Delay (Texas) resigned his leadership position after he was charged with money laundering for illegally transferring $190,000 in contributions to Republican candidates in the Texas legislature. Delay was convicted in 2010. In addition, it was revealed in October 2006 that Republican representative Mark Foley (Florida) had inappropriate relations with underage male congressional pages and the GOP leadership did not initially take strong action against the congressman. Political scientist and presidential scholar Robert P. Watson called the 109th Congress (2005–2007) "one of the worst in American history."[17] Watson went on to note that "during the 2006 calendar year the Congress was in session a total of less than one hundred days and passed not a single significant piece of legislation despite the presence of a number of serious problems at home and abroad."[18]

Bush and Republicans also faced growing dissatisfaction with the administration's management of the Iraq War. The anti-war movement continued to grow in the United States, and anti-war sentiment became increasingly strident. This motivated those who opposed the Iraq War to turn out to vote. Meanwhile, even among those who backed the war, support became increasingly lukewarm, and voter turnout among Republicans and conservatives was depressed. Public dissatisfaction with the Bush administration extended beyond the Iraq War and the war on terror. The administration's management of the response to Hurricane Katrina in 2005 also undermined public confidence.

Nancy Pelosi, a California Democrat who opposed the Iraq War, was elected speaker of the house. The day after the elections, Rumsfeld resigned as secretary of state. He was replaced by former CIA director and national security advisor Robert Gates. Gates was a far less public figure than his predecessor and less polarizing. He quickly gained the support of leading members of Congress from both parties (Gates would later be asked to remain in office after a new presidential administration entered office in 2009).

One major issue for Democrats was how to be anti-war while still supporting the troops. Anti-war members of the party did not want to appear unpatriotic, but they sought to pressure the administration into withdrawing troops from Iraq. Democrats also sought to pressure Bush into concessions on domestic issues. Bush endeavored to enact broad immigration reform, but his efforts were opposed by conservatives in the Senate who defeated the initiative through a filibuster.

Meanwhile, Bush vetoed 11 measures after the Democrats took control of Congress (Congress overrode four of those vetoes, including two farm bills and a Medicare measure). Bush had the fewest vetoes of any president since Warren G. Harding. This statistic did not reflect a cooperative relationship with Congress, but rather the inability of the Democratic-controlled Congress to enact many of its legislative priorities. Bush and the Democrats did work together on a number of economic measures during the last two years of his tenure as the country slid into a recession, caused by a crisis among mortgage lenders, banks, and other financial institutions. The centerpiece of the government's response was a $700 billion stimulus initiative enacted in 2008. Meanwhile, Bush finalized negotiations to begin the withdrawal of U.S. combat forces from Iraq.

Conclusion

As president, Bush had approval ratings that were among both the highest and lowest in U.S. history. He entered office as president of a divided country following the contested 2000 election, but public attitudes toward Bush soared following the 2001 terrorist attacks. The advent of the Iraq War undermined public confidence in his leadership, especially after the revelations that the Saddam regime did not have the WMD programs that were cited as justification for Operation Iraqi Freedom. When Bush left office, his overall approval rating was 22 percent (Harry S. Truman had the next lowest rating at 32 percent). Nonetheless, even at that point, a majority of Republicans, 57 percent, believed Bush was doing a good job (compared with only 6 percent of Democrats and 18 percent of independents).[19] Interestingly, Bush's rating rose after he left office. A Gallup poll done in 2010 found that Bush's job approval rating had risen to 47 percent.[20]

Succeeding Bush was Barack Obama, the first African American president of the United States and an anti–Iraq War Democrat. Obama promised to withdraw U.S. troops from Iraq and to reinvigorate the American-led campaign in Afghanistan. However, Obama's primary focus upon entering office was domestic politics and the economy. The first two years of the Obama presidency were dominated by the Great Recession and efforts to pass landmark legislation such as comprehensive health care reform. One result was that Obama continued many of the national security policies of the Bush administration, although the tone, rhetoric, and even terms used to describe the nation's counterterrorism campaign were softened.

Notes

1. George W. Bush, "Inaugural Address," Washington, D.C., January 20, 2001.

2. Gary C. Jacobson, *A Divider, Not a Uniter: George W. Bush and the American People* (New York: Pearson Longman, 2007), 83.

3. Richard Gephardt, "We Are All Tied Together in a Single Garment of Destiny," *Foreign Affairs*, February 21, 2003.

4. George Soros, "Take Back America Speech," Washington, D.C., June 3, 2004.

5. Soros, "Take Back America Speech."

6. Ibid.

7. John Kerry, "Acceptance Speech," Boston, Mass., July 29, 2004.

8. Kerry, "Acceptance Speech."

9. Ibid.

10. George W. Bush, "Acceptance Speech," New York, September 2, 2004.

11. Bush, "Acceptance Speech."

12. Ibid.

13. Ibid.

14. George W. Bush, "Inaugural Address," Washington, D.C., January 20, 2005.

15. Jacobson, *A Divider*, 4–5.

16. Ibid, 6–8.

17. Robert P. Watson, ed., *The Roads to Congress 2008* (Lanham, MD: Lexington Books, 2010), 3.

18. Watson, *The Roads to Congress*.

19. CBS News, "Bush's Final Approval Rating: 22 Percent," January 16, 2009.

20. Lydia Saad, "Kennedy Still Highest-Rated Modern President," Gallup Poll, December 6, 2010.

10

The Obama Presidency and the War on Terror

During the 2008 presidential contest, Barack Obama campaigned vigorously against the war in Iraq. His opponent, Republican senator John McCain (Arizona), generally defended the Bush administration's management of the conflict, although the senator did criticize various U.S. actions, including the use of prisoner abuse scandals and the use of torture. McCain, a highly decorated veteran who had been a prisoner of war during the Vietnam War, emphasized his military experience and endeavored to appeal to both Republicans and independents. However, Obama, whose campaign slogan was "Hope and Change," was able to secure the support of most independents by pledging to revive the U.S. economy, reorient the war on terror, and repair the United States' image abroad. On November 4, 2008, Obama was elected president. He received 52.9 percent of the vote, compared with McCain's 45.7 percent. Obama also captured traditional Republican states such as Virginia, North Carolina, and Florida. Meanwhile, Democrats increased their control of both chambers of Congress. In the Senate, the Democrats gained eight seats, giving them a total of 59 seats. Joe Lieberman, a pro-Iraq War Democrat, lost his primary contest, but ran as an independent and won. Lieberman caucused with the Democrats, giving the party 60 seats, a filibuster-proof majority. In the House, Democrats secured an additional 21 seats, giving them 257 seats.

With commanding majorities in Congress and a mandate from voters, Obama came into office with a degree of political power and influence that exceeded that of even Bush in the aftermath of the 9/11 attacks. However, with the country in the midst of a deep economic morass, Obama initially concentrated on domestic matters. His foreign security policy in many ways mirrored that of Bush, and there were few dramatic changes in the United States' war on terror.

The Presidential Transition

Once in office, Obama attempted to repair the public image of the United States at home and abroad. He softened the rhetoric and tone of U.S. foreign policy and pledged to end several controversial aspects of the war on terror. For instance, Obama pledged to accelerate the withdrawal of U.S. troops from Iraq. He also promised to close the detention center at Guantanamo Bay. Obama even stopped the use of the phrase "war on terror." In March 2009, the Department of Defense was directed to stop using "war on terror" and instead use "overseas contingency operations" when referring to military actions against terrorists or the operations in Afghanistan and Iraq. The Obama administration sought to replace the Bush-era concept of a global struggle against international terrorism with the perception that the country was involved in specific conflicts, including Afghanistan, but that it was not waging a long-term, Cold War–style effort against terrorism. Instead, terrorism was just one of many national security threats to the United States. This conceptual approach was radically different from that of the Bush administration, which tended to link issues, such as the promotion of democracy or economic development, as part of the broader struggle against terrorism. While the new administration adopted a different strategic approach, it continued the tactics used by the previous administration.

The new president reached out to the Muslim world in an effort to create a new dialogue and reduce the antipathy toward the United States and the West. Obama chose Egypt to deliver his first major foreign policy speech. In the address on June 4, 2009, the new president declared,

> I have come here to seek a new beginning between the United States and Muslims around the world; one based upon mutual interest and mutual respect; and one based upon the truth that America and Islam are not exclusive, and need not be in competition. Instead, they overlap, and share common principles–principles of justice and progress; tolerance and the dignity of all human beings.
>
> I do so recognizing that change cannot happen overnight. No single speech can eradicate years of mistrust, nor can I answer in the time that I have all the complex questions that brought us to this point. But I am convinced that in order to move forward, we must say openly the things we hold in our hearts, and that too often are said only behind closed doors. There must be a sustained effort to listen to each other; to learn from each other; to respect one another; and to seek common ground. As the Holy Koran tells us, "Be conscious of God and speak always the truth." That is what I will try to do–to speak the truth as best I can, humbled by the task before us, and firm in my belief that the interests we share as human beings are far more powerful than the forces that drive us apart.[1]

Obama's speech was generally well regarded in the Middle East, and opinion surveys indicated that people in the region viewed the new president much more favorably than his predecessor. However, people and leaders in the Middle East also sought concrete actions on the part of the Obama administration. Specifically, leaders in the region pressured the administration to take a larger role in resolving the Arab-Israeli conflict. Obama appointed former senator and Senate majority leader George Mitchell (Maine) as a special envoy for the Palestinian-Israeli conflict. Mitchell had been involved in negotiations that led to a ceasefire and political settlement in Northern Ireland between the Irish Republican Army and the British government. Mitchell was tasked to jumpstart peace negotiations between Israel and the Palestinians. However, Mitchell was unable to make meaningful progress on the conflict. Obama continued the Bush-era policy of supporting a two-state solution with an independent Palestine and Israel; however, critics of the administration charged that the president and his secretary of state, former first lady Hillary Rodham Clinton, did not develop or articulate a clear vision for a settlement. Regional leaders also complained that the United States was not deeply engaged in efforts to resolve the dispute.

One area where the new administration hoped progress could be made was the relationship between the United States and Syria. Syria was seen as an important linchpin in developing a resolution to the Arab-Israeli conflict and to easing the internal conflict in Lebanon. Relations between the United States and Lebanon had grown increasingly strained in the final years of the Bush administration, as U.S. officials blamed the regime of Syrian President Bashar Assad for fomenting unrest in Lebanon and for assassinating pro-Western prime minister Rafic Hariri in 2005. Obama signaled a willingness to reopen diplomatic channels with Syria. In 2009, Assad undertook a government reorganization that removed some hardliner anti-Western figures in a move that many in the Obama administration perceived to be a sign of reform. However, the Obama administration renewed various sanctions against the Assad regime in May of that year. In continuing the punitive measures, the president issued a statement declaring that the sanctions had been put in place "to deal with the unusual and extraordinary threat to the national security, foreign policy, and economy of the United States constituted by the actions of the Government of Syria in supporting terrorism, maintaining its then-existing occupation of Lebanon, pursuing weapons of mass destruction and missile programs, and undermining U.S. and international efforts with respect to the stabilization and reconstruction of Iraq."[2] He further noted that Syria continued to pose a danger to the United States. However, the following month, Obama announced that he would appoint an ambassador to Syria for the first time in more than four years. In addition, Mitchell was directed to undertake negotiations with the Assad regime as part of an effort to resolve the Arab-Israeli conflict. U.S.-Syrian reconciliation efforts were undermined in 2009 when the Iraqi government charged that Syrian intelligence agents were behind two terrorist bombings, one in August and one in October. Both nations recalled their ambassadors over the incidents. In 2010, the Obama administration charged that Syria was supplying missiles to Hezbollah. The munitions were subsequently fired into Israel. One result was that Obama extended sanctions against Syria for another year. The United States did relax some economic sanctions in the telecommunications sector in order to allow U.S. investors to do business in Syria. After Syria's foreign minister met with Clinton in Washington in September, both sides claimed that new negotiations on the Arab-Israeli conflict would begin. Meanwhile, in 2010 Iraq and Syria reestablished diplomatic ties. Talks between Israel and Syria remained stymied over the status of the Golan Heights, preventing any meaningful progress on the broader Arab-Israeli struggle.

The Continuing Global War on Terror

Although the rhetoric and phraseology were different, the Obama administration continued efforts to cooperate and collaborate with allies to suppress international terrorist groups. For example, in 2010, with U.S. military and financial support, Algeria, Mali, Mauritania, and Niger launched a joint military command as part of their effort to combat terrorism in the Saharan and sub-Saharan regions. The Obama administration also affirmed Bush's designation of the Philippines as a major non-NATO ally. Meanwhile, the United States also endeavored to enhance its relationship with Indonesia, which was quickly becoming the hub of anti-Western terrorists in Asia. In July 2009, U.S. defense secretary Robert Gates paid a visit to Indonesia to discuss security ties. His visit was followed by one by Obama. As a result of negotiations, the United States offered to sell advanced F-16 fighter jets to the country. In addition, the U.S. expanded cooperation with Indonesian counterterrorist units, especially after terrorist attacks on Western hotels in Jakarta in July. The attacks prompted a series of counterterrorist strikes that resulted in the deaths of a number of terrorists, including Noordin Mohammed Top, one of the leaders of Jemaah Islamiyah (see Chapter 6).

Iraq

Meanwhile, Iraq remained one of the main issues in U.S. foreign and security policy. By 2008, security conditions in Iraq had improved dramatically. Iraqi security forces had taken on an increasing share of the security of their nation. In July 2008, the remaining U.S. forces that had been part of the 2007 troop surge were withdrawn from Iraq, even as U.S. and Iraqi forces undertook a major offensive that destroyed the last al Qaeda stronghold in the country, killing or capturing more than 4,000 insurgents. Following the election, a framework agreement was signed between the Bush administration and the Iraqi government which called for the withdrawal of U.S. combat forces from Iraq by December 2011. On the eve of Obama's inauguration in January 2009, the United States turned control of the "green zone," the heavily fortified government and military complex in Baghdad which had been overseen by U.S. forces since the Iraqi capital was captured in 2003, over to Iraq.

Iraq also conducted national elections on March 7, 2010, although a lengthy stalemate ensued over the creation of a government. No political party received a majority in the balloting, and former prime minister Allawi created a new political coalition, the Iraqi National Movement (INM). The INM won 91 seats in the election, while Maliki's State of Law Coalition secured 89 seats. Eventually, talks resulted in Maliki's reappointment as prime minister in November and Talabani's reappointment as president.

In a speech at the U.S. Military Academy at West Point, New York, Obama outlined his approach to Iraq and pledged to accelerate the withdrawal of U.S. forces from the country. The president declared that

> in early 2003, the decision was made to wage a second war, in Iraq. The wrenching debate over the Iraq war is well-known and need not be repeated here. It's enough to say that for the next six years, the Iraq war drew the dominant share of our troops, our resources, our diplomacy, and our national attention, and that the decision to go into Iraq caused substantial rifts between America and much of the world.
>
> Today, after extraordinary costs, we are bringing the Iraq war to a responsible end. We will remove our combat brigades from Iraq by the end of next summer, and all of our troops by the end of 2011. That we are doing so is a testament to the character of the men and women in uniform. Thanks to their courage, grit and perseverance, we have given Iraqis a chance to shape their future, and we are successfully leaving Iraq to its people.[3]

By December 2009, 125,000 U.S. troops remained in Iraq. Obama announced a timetable to withdraw troops in February 2009. Essentially, the plan followed the Bush framework agreement that had been signed in November 2008, although it accelerated the redeployment of troops by several months. U.S. combat forces were to be withdrawn from Iraq by August 31, 2010. Approximately 50,000 troops would remain in Iraq after that date to continue training and minor security operations. However, the bulk of those forces were to be withdrawn by the end of 2011 (the date for the final withdrawal under the Bush-era agreement). Anti-war activists criticized the pace as too slow and especially decried the continued deployment of the 50,000 troops after the initial withdrawal date.

U.S. combat troops were withdrawn by August 31, 2010. That day, Vice President Joe Biden and Iraqi prime minister Maliki conducted a ceremony in Baghdad in which the United States formally transferred oversight of Iraq's security to that country's military. Obama addressed the American people to hail the historic milestone. In a televised address on August 31, he declared,

> So tonight, I am announcing that the American combat mission in Iraq has ended. Operation Iraqi Freedom is over, and the Iraqi people now have lead responsibility for the security of their country. . . .

This completes a transition to Iraqi responsibility for their own security. U.S. troops pulled out of Iraq's cities last summer, and Iraqi forces have moved into the lead with considerable skill and commitment to their fellow citizens. Even as Iraq continues to suffer terrorist attacks, security incidents have been near the lowest on record since the war began. And Iraqi forces have taken the fight to al Qaeda, removing much of its leadership in Iraqi-led operations. . . .

This new approach reflects our long-term partnership with Iraq, one based upon mutual interest and mutual respect. Of course, violence will not end with our combat mission. Extremists will continue to set off bombs, attack Iraqi civilians and try to spark sectarian strife. But ultimately, these terrorists will fail to achieve their goals. Iraqis are a proud people. They have rejected sectarian war, and they have no interest in endless destruction. They understand that, in the end, only Iraqis can resolve their differences and police their streets. Only Iraqis can build a democracy within their borders. What America can do, and will do, is provide support for the Iraqi people as both a friend and a partner.[4]

Through 2011, the remaining 50,000 U.S. troops began to be withdrawn. The administration did announce that some U.S. troops could remain after the 2011 deadline to continue to train Iraqi security forces. By March 2011, 4,440 Americans had died in Iraq, along with 318 soldiers from coalition partners.

The invasion of Iraq was a manifestation of the Bush preemption doctrine. In May 2010, Obama modified, but did not reject, preemption. In his national security strategy, Obama asserted that the United States would avoid unilateral action and instead endeavor to use all other approaches before resorting to the use of force.

While the use of force is sometimes necessary, we will exhaust other options before war whenever we can, and carefully weigh the costs and risks of action against the costs and risks of inaction. When force is necessary, we will continue to do so in a way that reflects our values and strengthens our legitimacy, and we will seek broad international support, working with such institutions as NATO and the U.N. Security Council.

The United States must reserve the right to act unilaterally if necessary to defend our nation and our interests, yet we will also seek to adhere to standards that govern the use of force. Doing so strengthens those who act in line with international standards, while isolating and weakening those who do not.[5]

Obama's security strategy did not explicitly reject preemption. Some anti-war activists, human rights groups, and foreign governments criticized the strategy because of its failure to categorically declare that the United States would not engage in preemption. However, critics pointed to the expansion of the use of aerial drones to attack targets in Pakistan, Yemen, or Somalia as proof of the Obama administration's willingness to undertake unilateral and preemptive military action.

Afghanistan

Tensions over the growing U.S. influence in Central Asia led Russia to retaliate in an effort to protect its own influence in the region. For instance, Russia increasingly pressured the Kyrgyzstani government to close the Manas Air Base, which had been used by coalition forces for operations in Afghanistan since the beginning of Operation Enduring Freedom. In February 2009, the Kyrgyzstani parliament voted to close the site. However, following negotiations, the United States agreed to increase payments for using the base to $60 million per year in June, and a new lease was subsequently agreed upon.

In 2009, Karzai was reelected in a contested presidential election marked by widespread fraud and voter intimidation. Karzai led the initial balloting on August 20, and the first reports credited the incumbent with 54.6 percent of the vote. However, opponents challenged the results, citing numerous election violations and electoral fraud. An audit found that Karzai had actually only received 49.7 percent of the vote. Afghan law mandated that the winning candidate had to receive more than 50 percent of the vote. Consequently, a run-off election was scheduled between Karzai and the number two vote getter, former foreign minister Abdullah Abdullah of the United National Front. The Taliban endeavored, unsuccessfully, to organize a boycott of the elections and then launched attacks to disrupt the polling. After a run-off was scheduled for November 7, Abdullah withdrew from the election, claiming that the potential for fraud would make any additional balloting illegitimate. With no opponent, Karzai was declared the winner. The Obama administration unsuccessfully attempted to convince Karzai to form a coalition government that would include leading opposition figures such as Abdullah Abdullah. However, the president rebuffed the pressure. In addition, Karzai forced the removal of American Peter Galbraith, the deputy special representative of the United Nations in Afghanistan, after the latter publicly called for new elections. On November 19, Karzai was inaugurated for a second, full term. Controversy over the elections increased friction with the legislature, which refused to confirm half of Karzai's initial cabinet appointments. Meanwhile, parliamentary elections were delayed until September 2010.

The fraudulent elections also strained relations with the United States. The Obama administration became increasingly critical of the Karzai government and endeavored to pressure the regime into undertaking reforms and enacting anti-corruption measures. Tensions between the two allies were also exacerbated by the growing number of Afghan civilian casualties caused by coalition air or missile strikes. For instance, in September 2009, during anti-Taliban operations, German troops erroneously called for an airstrike that killed 137 Afghan civilians. The incident heightened tensions between NATO-led security forces and Afghan civilians and prompted the resignation of the German defense minister. Afghan security forces and civilians became increasingly reluctant to cooperate with coalition forces. Concurrently, Karzai began to call for the withdrawal of NATO-led forces from Afghanistan.

During his presidential campaign, Obama pledged to send an additional 10,000 U.S. troops to Afghanistan. Once in office, Obama found that Defense Department officials requested that figure be raised to 17,000. After recommendations from U.S. military commanders, Obama decided on December 1 to undertake a significant troop surge in Afghanistan. The United States announced that it would deploy an additional 30,000 troops, bringing the U.S. total in the country to 100,000. The president also promised to begin the withdrawal of the additional troops after 18 months. Obama outlined how he came to his decision to undertake the surge at his December 2009 West Point speech. Speaking directly to the cadets, many of whom would serve in Afghanistan, Obama declared that

Afghanistan is not lost, but for several years it has moved backwards. There's no imminent threat of the government being overthrown, but the Taliban has gained momentum. Al Qaeda has not reemerged in Afghanistan in the same numbers as before 9/11, but they retain their safe havens along the border. And our forces lack the full support they need to effectively train and partner with Afghan security forces and better secure the population. Our new commander in Afghanistan—General McChrystal—has reported that the security situation is more serious than he anticipated. In short: The status quo is not sustainable. As cadets, you volunteered for service during this time of danger. Some of you fought in Afghanistan. Some of you will deploy there. As your Commander-in-Chief, I owe you a mission that is clearly defined, and worthy of your service. And that's why, after the Afghan voting was completed, I insisted on a thorough review of our strategy. Now, let me be clear: There has never been an option before me that called for troop deployments before 2010, so there has been no delay or denial of resources necessary for the conduct of the war during this review period. Instead, the review has allowed me to ask the hard questions, and to explore all the different options, along with my national security team, our military and civilian leadership in Afghanistan, and our key partners. And given the stakes involved, I owed the American people—and our troops—no less. This review is now complete. And as Commander-in-Chief, I have determined that it is in our vital national interest to send an additional 30,000 U.S. troops to Afghanistan. After 18 months, our troops will begin to come home. These are the resources that we need to seize the initiative, while building the Afghan capacity that can allow for a responsible transition of our forces out of Afghanistan.[6]

In the same address, Obama explained the dangers he perceived in Afghanistan and Pakistan. He made it clear that his administration considered the area the central front in the effort against al Qaeda.

If I did not think that the security of the United States and the safety of the American people were at stake in Afghanistan, I would gladly order every single one of our troops home tomorrow. So, no, I do not make this decision lightly. I make this decision because I am convinced that our security is at stake in Afghanistan and Pakistan. This is the epicenter of violent extremism practiced by al Qaeda. It is from here that we were attacked on 9/11, and it is from here that new attacks are being plotted as I speak. This is no idle danger; no hypothetical threat. In the last few months alone, we have apprehended extremists within our borders who were sent here from the border region of Afghanistan and Pakistan to commit new acts of terror. And this danger will only grow if the region slides backwards, and al Qaeda can operate with impunity. We must keep the pressure on al Qaeda, and to do that, we must increase the stability and capacity of our partners in the region. Of course, this burden is not ours alone to bear. This is not just America's war. Since 9/11, al Qaeda's safe havens have been the source of attacks against London and Amman and Bali. The people and governments of both Afghanistan and Pakistan are endangered. And the stakes are even higher within a nuclear-armed Pakistan, because we know that al Qaeda and other extremists seek nuclear weapons, and we have every reason to believe that they would use them.[7]

Anti-war activists argued that Obama's warning of the potential dangers of proliferation of nuclear weapons to terrorist groups was eerily similar to the arguments used by the Bush administration in advocating for war against Iraq.

In addition to increases in U.S. troops, the United States pressured its NATO allies to also bolster their forces in Afghanistan. In April 2009, NATO allies agreed to deploy another 5,000 troops, but the majority of these forces were used for training, not combat operations. Meanwhile, in May, U.S. and Afghan forces had a major victory in their efforts to combat illicit drugs. A counternarcotics operation resulted in the capture of more than 60 insurgents and more than 100 tons of drugs in Helmand province. The seizure was the largest narcotics bust in Afghan history.

The additional U.S. troops were used in a series of offensives against the Taliban and other insurgents in the southern provinces of Afghanistan. In February 2010,

15,000 coalition and Afghan forces launched a massive campaign in the Helmand province. The operation was only marginally successful, and the coalition launched a second, larger mission with more than 25,000 troops in the Kandahar region during the summer and fall. This second offensive disrupted Taliban operations and resulted in the death or capture of more than 500 insurgents. Nonetheless, attacks against coalition forces in 2010 rose to their highest level since 2001.

As part of a broader effort to improve relations between coalition forces and Afghans, in April 2010, NATO adopted the "Afghan First Program." The initiative called for coalition forces to purchase or procure goods and services form local Afghan vendors whenever possible or practical. In announcing the program, NATO issued a statement declaring,

> Increasing local procurement in Afghanistan is considered the most important step in promoting the development of the Afghan private sector and supporting the economic development of the country. The analysis undertaken by NATO demonstrates that purchasing local goods and services has the potential to create an economic stimulus for Afghanistan.
>
> Together, the expenditures of NATO and ISAF Contributing Nations in support of ISAF activities are significant. By reorienting resources towards the Afghan economy, ISAF has the potential to enhance Afghan economic development. While the top priority for all NATO procurement for operations is to ensure efficient, effective missions and the security of the civilian and military personnel, experiences demonstrate that making the maximum use of local goods and services is advantageous for Afghanistan and ISAF Contributing Nations.[8]

The NATO document also highlighted the benefits of the program:

> Procuring goods and services from Afghan companies promotes sustainable economic development by creating jobs, building economic capacities, developing the private and banking sectors, encouraging the development of infrastructure and generating tax revenue to support the delivery of services to the people of Afghanistan. Afghan firms know the market and can often provide quality goods and services at competitive prices. With a shorter supply chain, local procurement is often the best way for the buyer to maximize value and the timely delivery of needed goods and services. Increased local procurement allows local businesses to grow, gain experience, and generate jobs in the industrial, commercial, service and agricultural sectors.[9]

Meanwhile, in an effort to reduce the growing violence, Karzai called together some 1,600 political and tribal leaders at a summit in Kabul in June 2010. The attendees were unable to develop a broad, comprehensive plan to resolve conflicts in the country. However, the assembly did agree that the government should create a national peace and reconciliation commission. It also endorsed a proposal to open negotiations with moderate Taliban and insurgent leaders in an effort to convince them to end their armed struggle and engage in the political process. The Taliban attempted to disrupt the summit with a suicide attack. The incident prompted Karzai to replace the minister of the interior.

In May 2010, the number of U.S. troops in Afghanistan exceeded the number of American forces in Iraq for the first time since the invasion of Iraq in 2003. At the end of 2010, there were 48 nations that contributed 132,000 troops to ISAF. The United States was the largest single contributor of troops, with 98,000 soldiers in Afghanistan (including 8,000 troops outside of ISAF's command). Other major contributors included the United Kingdom, 9,500; Germany, 4,900; France, 3,970; Italy, 3,800; and Canada, 2,900. A number of countries had deployments of less than 50 troops, including Armenia, 40; Austria, 3; Bosnia and Herzegovina, 45; Iceland, 2; Ireland, 7; Luxembourg, 9; Malaysia, 30; Montenegro, 36; Singapore, 48; Ukraine, 20; and the United Arab Emirates, 35. NATO oversaw 28 provincial reconstruction teams. In June 2010, there were 66 U.S. service members killed in Afghanistan, a dubious and new casualty record. By March 2011, 1,504 U.S. service members had been killed in Afghanistan, along with 863 soldiers from coalition partners.

Scandals and Leaks

Obama appointed General Stanley McChrystal as the new military commander in Afghanistan in May 2009. McChrystal replaced General David McKiernan, who the administration perceived had not able to develop an effective counterinsurgency strategy. McKiernan's removal marked the first time that a field commander had been replaced by a president since the Korean War. McChrystal had been an Army ranger and a member of the Special Forces. The general had overseen operations that had targeted insurgent leaders in Iraq in 2007 and was credited with helping make the troop surge in Iraq a success. Obama hoped his new commander would invigorate U.S. efforts in Afghanistan by developing a more effective counterinsurgency strategy in the country. McChrystal won the praise and admiration of Afghan officials, including Karzai, and was credited with undertaking a more aggressive and effective approach toward the suppression of the Taliban and al Qaeda. He was also instrumental in convincing Obama to undertake the Afghan troop surge. After his appointment, McChrystal reported to the president that if troop strength in Afghanistan was not increased, the Taliban would have effective control of the majority of the country in less than a year.

In June 2010, an article in *Rolling Stone* was published in which the general and his staff criticized Obama, Vice President Biden, and a range of other U.S. officials. The article undermined Obama and made the president seem disengaged from, and overwhelmed by, the Afghan conflict. Karzai endeavored unsuccessfully to convince Obama to retain McChrystal, but the president dismissed the general on June 23. Petraeus was chosen to replace McChrystal and assumed command of ISAF in July.

In July 2010, an online watchdog group known as Wikileaks began releasing a large trove of documents related to the conflicts in Afghanistan and Iraq, the war on terror, and U.S. diplomacy. Wikileaks was launched in 2006 and nominally led by Australian Julian Assange. The group sought to gain access to classified documents and reports and release that information to the public. A U.S. Army enlisted intelligence specialist, Bradley Manning, was able to obtain a large number of classified files and then forward them to Wikileaks. Manning was subsequently arrested on more than 20 charges, including aiding the enemy. Wikileaks arranged to release the information along with a number of leading newspapers, including *The New York Times*, the *Guardian* (the United Kingdom), *Der Spiegel* (Germany), and *Le Monde* (France). The Obama administration sought to prevent or delay the release of the materials when U.S. intelligence sources became aware that Wikileaks and the various news media had possession of them. U.S. officials argued that the information and materials could harm ongoing operations or threaten the lives or safety of American agents or those working with, or for, the United States. Once pressure began to be exerted on Wikileaks, the organization posted a large "insurance" file online that contained a number of classified documents. Wikileaks threatened to release the information if governments or agencies attempted to censor the site or prosecute Wikileaks members.

The initial batch of more than 75,000 documents placed online dealt with Operation Enduring Freedom and included information on civilian deaths caused by coalition attacks. The documents indicated that civilian deaths and military losses caused by "friendly fire" (incidents when coalition forces accidently killed or injured their own troops) were more common than the Defense Department had reported. Some documents did reveal the names and information about Afghans who had worked with the coalition (Wikileaks claimed that it attempted to work with the United States and other coalition members to remove such identifying data, but that it received little or no cooperation—a charge denied by various officials). Some information was redacted or removed from the documents.

A subsequent release of 400,000 documents in October on the Iraq War was also condemned by the Obama administration. However, in many cases American military officials were able to relocate or remove Iraqis who would otherwise have been at risk once it was revealed that they had worked with the coalition. Among the more damaging revelations was proof that U.S. officials had received reports about the torture of Iraqis, but did little to investigate or stop the practices until the Abu Ghraib scandal. In November, another large release of documents took place with major newspapers publishing the data simultaneously with Wikileaks. The November release included U.S. diplomatic cables and revealed sensitive information about American interaction with foreign governments and leaders. For instance, some of the documents contained highly critical opinions of Karzai by U.S. diplomats and condemned the level of corruption in the Afghan government.

Pakistan

Relations between the United States and Afghanistan continued to be complicated by Pakistan. The Obama administration expanded the use of unmanned aerial drones to attack suspected al Qaeda and Taliban figures and facilities in Pakistan. The United States also increased the number and scope of cross-border incursions into Pakistan by U.S. special operations forces. These raids were vigorously condemned by Pakistani politicians, who charged that the attacks undermined public confidence in the government and turned people against the coalition. Some reports indicated that the nation's intelligence agencies were secretly cooperating with the United States to coordinate the strikes. In October 2009, Clinton traveled to Pakistan, where she attempted to address concerns by government officials. However, she also pressed Pakistani prime minister Yousuf Gilani to take stronger action against the insurgents.

Pakistani forces launched a major offensive in October 2009 against al Qaeda and Taliban fighters. More than 30,000 troops were deployed in the South Waziristan area. In response, the insurgents conducted a series of terrorist attacks throughout Pakistan. Approximately 600 militants were killed in the fighting, but at least 5,000 insurgents were able to escape to other areas of Pakistan. Meanwhile, more than 500 civilians were estimated to have been killed in the fighting, which also displaced more than 200,000 people. The viciousness of the combat led the United Nations and other international agencies to suspend humanitarian and economic development projects in the region. The Pakistani military was able to capture or destroy the main militant bases and seized a large volume of weapons and munitions. By the end of the year, more than 3,000 civilians had been killed in fighting in Pakistan, and more than 7,300 injured. In addition, approximately 3,000 soldiers and insurgents were killed, including those killed by U.S. aerial strikes. The number of dead and wounded increased more than 45 percent over the previous year. During 2009, there were over 2,500 terrorist attacks. Reports indicated that almost 10 percent of the country (4 million people) was under the effective control of the Taliban or its tribal allies.

Violence continued in 2010. Political infighting between Islamic parties in Karachi led the government to ban public gatherings in the region in June. Meanwhile, a massive car bombing in July killed more than 105 people, further undermining the authority and legitimacy of the government. Significantly, an increasing number of newspaper and media reports linked Pakistan's intelligence services and military with the Taliban and other anti-government groups. Speculation increased that hardliners in the intelligence and military were endeavoring to undermine the civilian government in order to undertake a coup. Torrential rains caused massive flooding in July 2010. As much as one-fifth of the country was flooded, leaving more than 1,750 people dead, 1.8 million homes destroyed, and 8 million people displaced or left homeless by the disaster. Insurgent groups took advantage of the disaster to increase their influence and spread into areas where the government was unable to provide relief supplies or humanitarian aid.

As violence and instability spread through Pakistan, the Obama administration continued to expand its raids and aerial attacks in the country, placing the Pakistani government in an increasingly untenable position. For instance, in September 2010 alone, the United States conducted 21 airstrikes, killing more than 100 Pakistanis, including civilians. That same month, the Pakistani government blocked a major NATO supply route that ran through its territory into Afghanistan after an aerial strike killed three Pakistani soldiers. The route was used by the coalition to move approximately 40 percent of its supplies into Afghanistan. The government further threatened to use military force to repeal future coalition attacks or raids. The Obama administration was forced to issue an apology to the Pakistanis. The route was reopened on October 10. However, the United States continued its attacks, with 18 strikes in October. When airstrikes killed 36 Pakistanis, mainly civilians, in March 2011, Pakistan canceled strategic talks with the United States over security cooperation on the future of Afghanistan.

On May 2, 2011, U.S. special operations forces killed bin Laden in a safe haven in Abbottabad, Pakistan. The demise of the al Qaeda leader led to increased calls for the United States to withdraw from Afghanistan. Meanwhile, the raid raised tensions with Pakistan following accusations by some U.S. officials and media outlets that bin Laden must have received some aid and assistance from Pakistani military or intelligence sources during his stay.

The Afghan Withdrawal Plan

After he entered office, Obama announced plans to begin withdrawing U.S. forces from Afghanistan in July 2011. However, after the troop surge began, McChrystal and other military commanders argued that 2011 was too early. By 2010, U.S. officials conceded that American troops would remain in Afghanistan past the initial withdrawal date.

Meanwhile, in 2010, U.S. surveys found that Afghanistan had vast, undiscovered mineral wealth. Estimates were that Afghanistan had more than $900 billion in cobalt, copper, gold, and iron reserves. In addition, the country had untapped reserves of oil and gas worth $225 billion. The discovery should have prompted massive foreign investment; however, the continuing insurgency prevented most outside firms from investing in the country. A Chinese firm did launch a five-year $3 billion project to develop what turned out to be the world's second largest copper reserve. Partially because of the Chinese venture and foreign aid, Afghanistan's economy grew by 22.5 percent in 2009. The dramatic growth did lead to higher inflation, which rose 20 percent in 2009. In January 2010, Afghanistan met the criteria to qualify for the IMF's Heavily Indebted Poor Countries (HIPC) program. As a result, 96 percent of the country's foreign debt, or $1.6 billion, was erased. With an expanding economy and some improvements in security as a result of the troop surge, Karzai and other Afghan leaders began to call for the withdrawal of foreign forces. In July 2010, the Afghan president ordered the disbandment of private militias in an effort to reduce the power of regional warlords. There was also a significant decrease in opium poppy production from 2009 to 2010. Opium production fell from 6,900 metric tons in 2009 to 3,600 metric tons in 2010, a 48 percent decrease.[10] The decrease was the result of enhanced counternarcotics operations and the emergence of an agricultural disease that affected the crops.

At a July 2010 international conference in Kabul, Karzai argued that improvements in the country meant that foreign forces should be withdrawn from Afghanistan by the end of 2014. The conference endorsed Karzai's proposal. When NATO officials met in Lisbon in November, they agreed on a plan to withdraw ISAF forces, including American troops, by the end of 2014. That date became the Obama administration's new timetable for withdrawal. On June 22, 2011, Obama announced that he would begin withdrawing troops committed to Afghanistan during the surge, with a goal of redeploying 33,000 troops back to the United States by the fall of 2012.

Guantanamo and Homeland Security

In one of his first acts as president, Obama banned torture and other forms of excessive interrogations. He signed executive order on January 22, 2009, which revoked previous measures enacted during the Bush administration, and instead required that all interrogations be conducted in accordance with the guidelines in the *Army Field Manual*, which conformed to the Geneva Conventions. Obama's executive order also created a committee, led by Attorney General Eric Holder, to examine U.S. interrogation methods and determine if further refinement was needed. The group was also tasked to review policies, such as rendition, and determine if they were constitutional and conformed with international law. Meanwhile, Obama allowed rendition to continue. In August, the administration announced that it would continue rendition, but that it would employ greater oversight to prevent abuses. Specifically, the United States declared that it would seek pledges from countries that received prisoners that those states would not use torture or other harsh interrogation techniques. Human rights groups and civil libertarians decried the decision and accused the Obama administration of hypocrisy for criticizing the Bush administration's use of the tactic but continuing to use it. They also condemned the plan to gain promises from other states that illicit interrogation tactics would not be used. The criticism centered on this question: why send detainees to a prison in another country if they are to be treated as they would in the United States? The answer, human rights groups claimed, was that the program would continue to be a cover to allow the CIA and other intelligence agencies to have prisoners tortured in other countries while U.S. personnel would be able to claim that they had not been directly involved in the interrogations.

Along with the order barring torture, Obama also issued an executive order to close the detention facility in Guantanamo Bay within one year (by the end of January 2010). The announcement of the closure was hailed by human rights groups and received praise from foreign governments, especially in the Islamic world. At the time, the Guantanamo facility held about 245 prisoners. In addition to pledging to close the site, Obama also suspended the ongoing military tribunals that were trying suspected terrorists. The president ordered the creation of a special commission which would seek to develop a system to transfer some of the detainees to other countries for trial or detention. The body would also examine what was the best way to try remaining detainees. The president's executive order also required that prisoner facilities and treatment conform to existing international law, including the Geneva Conventions.

The Obama administration planned to transfer as many prisoners as possible to foreign countries and transfer the remaining ones to maximum security prisons in the United States, where they would face trial in federal courts. However, a public outcry against moving the prisoners to the United States led members of Congress, including Democrats, to object to the administration's plans. In November 2009, Obama announced that the United States would not close the detention center at Guantanamo by his promised deadline. The administration had been unable to develop formal plans to close the center. However, the president reiterated his pledge to close the facility.

One trial was completed in New York on November 17, 2010, when Ahmed Khalfan Ghailani was convicted on 285 counts related to the 1998 Embassy Bombings in Africa. This prompted widespread opposition to future court hearings because the sentence was 20 years to life, a verdict many called lenient in light of the loss of life in the bombings and because some testimony was excluded because it was obtained through coercive interrogations techniques. In January 2011, Congress included language in a defense expenditure bill, which Obama signed, that denied funding to close the facility or transfer prisoners to the United States. The legislation effectively left Guantanamo in operation for the foreseeable future.

By the end of 2010, there were approximately 170 detainees remaining at Guantanamo. In March 2011, Obama reversed his earlier ban on military tribunals and ordered the resumption of trials for Guantanamo detainees using the special military commissions. The U.S. military was ordered to begin proceedings against some 80 of the remaining prisoners. The government retained the option to try prisoners in federal courts.

Homeland Security

In what became known as the Christmas Day Bomb Plot, Umar Farouk Abdulmutallab, a Nigerian-born al Qaeda terrorist, tried unsuccessfully to detonate explosives packed in his underwear aboard a flight from Amsterdam to Detroit on December 25, 2009. Passengers detained the terrorist after the explosive failed to detonate. U.S. and foreign intelligence agencies had obtained information about Abdulmutallab's terrorist links after his father visited the U.S. embassy in Abuja, Nigeria, to warn about his son. Other intelligence also emerged about a potential al Qaeda plot to bomb airlines; however, U.S. officials provided Abdulmutallab a student visa, enabling him to travel to the United States. The episode highlighted continuing flaws in U.S. counterterrorism efforts, including problems with sharing intelligence. Homeland Security Secretary Janet Napolitano was widely criticized for her reaction to the event after she made a statement about homeland security that "the system worked." Napolitano was actually referring to the precautions that took effect after the terrorist was detained. Nonetheless, her reaction sparked a public outcry.

Partially in response to the Christmas Day bomb plot, Congress enacted legislation that extended various provisions of the Patriot Act for one year in February 2010. Controversial components of the act, including roving wiretaps and the seizure of records or property, were part of the legislation, even through liberal Democrats had initially opposed extending the provisions.

On May 1, 2010, in Times Square, New York, a vendor reported a smoking vehicle which police discovered contained a homemade explosive device with propane canisters, gasoline, fireworks, nails, and other potential shrapnel. The police evacuated thousands of people from the area and were to disable the device. Faisal Shahzad, a Pakistani-born U.S. citizen, was arrested for the plot, and intelligence officials discovered that he had ties to the Taliban and had traveled to Pakistan to undergo terrorist training.

On May 20, 2010, Obama asked Director of National Intelligence (DNI) Dennis Blair to resign as the result of a number of intelligence failures, including the failed 2009 Christmas Day bomb plot and the 2010 Times Square car bomb. There were also reported tensions between Blair and the president over the threat posed by Iran's nuclear program, with the DNI urging stronger action against Tehran. Blair left office on May 28 and was replaced by James Clapper, who became DNI on August 9.

Domestic Politics and the 2010 Midterm Elections

Obama came into office with very high expectations. He also faced historic challenges. Much of the first two years of his presidency was focused on domestic issues. Obama had two main priorities. First was the passage of a series of measures to improve the economy and better regulate financial markets to prevent the conditions that caused the Great Recession. Obama signed an $800 billion economic stimulus package in an effort to jumpstart the economy. The stimulus effort caused a record federal deficit of $1.3 trillion and caused the nation's budget deficit to rise to 9.91 percent of GDP in 2009 (the highest level since World War II). Meanwhile, the total national debt rose to 93.4 percent of GDP, or $13.5 trillion, by 2010. Despite federal efforts to prime the economy, economic growth and employment remained sluggish. Unemployment rose to 10 percent by the end of 2009 and was 9.4 percent in 2010, levels not seen since the Great Depression of the 1930s. The woeful state of the U.S. economy overshadowed the president's other initiatives and constrained his ability to focus on foreign and security policy. Meanwhile, Obama chose to seek approval of a broad health care reform package. The measure was ultimately passed along partisan lines with all 59 Democrats, and independent Joe Lieberman, voting for the measure in the Senate, while all Republicans voted against it. In the House, all 178 Republicans, plus 34 conservative Democrats, voted against the measure, while 219 Democrats voted in favor of it. The debate over health care distracted the Obama administration from efforts to revive the economy and address foreign and security issues. By the time health care reform was signed on March 23, Obama's public approval rating had fallen from 62 percent when he entered office to 46 percent. It remained below 50 percent through 2010 and into 2011. More significantly, by February 2011, only 40 percent of the American people approved of Obama's handling of U.S. national security. Meanwhile, on April 20, the BP Deepwater Horizon oil rig exploded in the Gulf of Mexico. A resultant leak released the equivalent of more than 5,000 barrels of oil per day into the Gulf for almost three months before the leak was capped. The administration faced significant domestic criticism for its oversight of the worst environmental disaster in U.S. history.

One manifestation of voter discontent with the Obama administration occurred in the 2010 midterm elections. There were troubling signs for the Democrats when Republicans captured the governorships of Virginia and New Jersey. In addition, a Republican, Scott Brown, won a special election in Massachusetts to gain the Senate seat of Democrat Ted Kennedy, who died in office and who had held the seat for almost 50 years. This ended the Democrats' ability to stop filibusters in the Senate. In the 2006 and 2008 congressional balloting, Democrats had captured a number of moderate or even traditionally conservative districts. However, the party lost the majority of those seats in the 2010 balloting. In that election, Democrats lost six seats in the Senate, leaving the balance at 53 Democrats (including Lieberman) and 47 Republicans. In the House, Democrats lost their majority in the largest defeat since 1948. Democrats lost 63 seats, reducing their number to 193, while Republicans gained a majority with 242 seats (its largest number of seats in the house since the 1946 elections). With Republicans in control of the House and able to filibuster legislation in the Senate, Obama's broad political power and influence were greatly curtailed.

Beginning in December 2010, a series of popular demonstrations and revolts swept across the Middle East and North Africa. The uprisings were dubbed the

"Arab Spring." Regimes in Egypt and Tunisia were deposed, while armed insurrections emerged in Libya and Yemen. The popular movements threatened pro-U.S. governments in Bahrain, Jordan, and Morocco and created a dilemma for the Obama administration, which tried to balance support for traditional allies and for the pro-democracy movements. Meanwhile, a coalition of nations, including the United States, launched military attacks against Libya in support of anti-government forces. The intervention followed passage of a UN Security Council resolution that established a no-fly zone over Libya to protect civilians. Critics condemned U.S. participation in the intervention by the Obama administration since a congressional resolution to use force was not obtained.

Conclusion

Obama was elected on a platform that opposed many of the main tenets of Bush's security policy. Once in office, he did refine many policies and shift focus in a number of areas. However, he also continued many of the policies of his predecessor. This was not unusual or unheard of in American foreign and security policy. For instance, rendition began under President Bill Clinton, although Bush expanded its use. Successive American presidents since the 1970s had endeavored to develop effective counterterrorism strategies. Most endeavored to build on the tactics and strategies of their predecessors.

Bush began his tenure as a controversial figure, and the war on terror at first elevated his popularity and political power, but then the war in Iraq undermined his public approval ratings and led to the Democrats taking control of Congress in 2006. Obama came in with a popular mandate, but within two years, his party lost control of Congress and his personal popularity declined precipitously. Nonetheless, he oversaw the effective end of the Iraq War and was president as a series of revolts and uprisings swept through the Middle East and threatened to reshape the regional order. Political changes affected longstanding U.S. allies, such as Egypt, as well as foes such as Libya.

The 9/11 attacks were the most devastating and bloody terrorist attacks in history. Yet, the U.S. struggle against terrorism did not begin under George W. Bush. As noted earlier, there were large-scale terrorist attacks under Presidents Reagan and later Clinton. However, no other president attempted to wage an inclusive, global struggle to suppress terrorism. After the 9/11 attacks, Bush and his closest advisors endeavored to launch a global campaign that would permanently eliminate terrorism as a major security threat. However, Bush's strategy emphasized military power, combined with a variety of intelligence and law enforcement operations. Although the United States did support efforts to spread democracy, critics charged that the U.S. counterterrorism strategies failed to address the underlying causes of terrorism, including economic underdevelopment, a lack of political opportunity, and the ongoing Arab-Israeli conflict.

Had Bush limited the war on terror to Afghanistan, his presidency would have been a very different one. Operation Iraqi Freedom strained relations between the United States and many of its closest allies. The war in Iraq also drew militants from around the world to join a broad anti-U.S. campaign. Those militants were essentially defeated in Iraq by a combination of military force and political integration. However, as it was in 2001, Afghanistan has again become the central front in the war on terror. The challenge for Obama and future U.S. presidents is to prevent the rise of terrorist states as Afghanistan was in 2001, and develop effective counterterrorism strategies at home and abroad. These policies have to be able to contain terrorism without irreversibly changing the nature of the U.S. political system, with its extensive civil liberties and individual freedoms, while maintaining the United States' place in the world as a leader in the effort to democratize and expand economic opportunities around the globe.

Notes

1. Barack Obama, "Cairo Speech," Cairo, June 4, 2009.

2. White House, "Notice on Continuation of the National Emergency with Respect to the Actions of the Government of Syria," May 9, 2010.

3. Barack Obama, "The Way Forward in Afghanistan and Iraq," West Point, N.Y., December 1, 2009.

4. Barack Obama, "Iraq Speech," Washington, D.C., August 31, 2010.

5. White House, *National Security Strategy*, May (Washington, D.C.: White House, 2010), 22.

6. Obama, "The Way Forward."

7. Ibid.

8 NATO, "NATO Afghan First Policy," Brussels, April 23, 2010.

9. NATO, "NATO Afghan First Policy."

10. UNODOC, "Afghanistan Opium Survey Findings, 2010," (New York: UNODOC, 2010), 12.

Chronology

1970s

1970

July 17   New Orleans International Airport institutes first Federal Aviation Administration (FAA) passenger screening protocol.

September 6–9   "Dawson's Field Hijacking" by the Popular Front for the Liberation of Palestine. The hijackers seize control of two American and one Swiss commercial aircraft.

September 9   UN Security Council adopts Resolution 286 condemning the hijacking of aircraft and the resulting threat to innocent civilians.

September 11   President Nixon announces expansion of Kennedy-era Sky Marshal program and the development of increased surveillance techniques in airports. He also declares a new policy whereby the United States will hold states responsible for actions against U.S. citizens during hijackings.

September 15   The Jordanian military attacks Palestinian positions and expels Palestinian Liberation Organization (PLO) officials in response to the "Dawson's Field Hijacking."

1971

February 2   Convention to Prevent and Punish the Acts of Terrorism Taking the Forms of Crimes Against Persons and Related Extortion That are of International Significance adopted by the Organization of American States.

May 14   The Supreme Court case *United States v. Lopez* finds the FAA's passenger profiling system is constitutional.

November 28   Wash Tel, the prime minister of Jordan, is assassinated in Cairo, Egypt, by the Palestinian terrorist group Black September.

1972

February 2   FAA issues rules to air carriers for screening passengers and baggage.

March 9   President Nixon orders air carriers to submit written security protocols.

September 5   "The Munich Massacre," in which Black September terrorists take 11 Israeli athletes hostage at the Munich Olympics. The hostages and a German police officer are killed in the attack.

December 5   FAA orders commercial airlines to screen all passengers and carry-on bags for weapons.

December 28   Israeli Embassy is seized in Thailand by Black September.

1973

January 5   Airports in the United States are equipped with metal detectors and X-ray machines to screen passengers and baggage.

March 2   Black September terrorists assassinate the U.S. ambassador to Sudan.

October 6–26   Arab nations, led by Egypt and Syria, fight Israel in the Yom Kippur War (also known as the Ramadan War).

December 17   Five Arab terrorists attack multiple planes in Rome, Italy. The terrorists surrender in Kuwait.

1974

February 22   Attempted hijacking of a commercial airline with the intent to crash into the White House.

August 5   U.S. Anti-hijacking or Air Transportation Security Act of 1974 (Pub. L. 93-366) enters into law.

August 9   Gerald Ford becomes president of the United States upon the resignation of Richard Nixon.

September 8   Trans World Airline flight 841 from Tel Aviv to New York City crashes killing 88. Believed to be Abu Nidal Organization suicide bomber.

November 22   UN General Assembly Resolution 3236 recognizes the PLO and the right of Palestinian people to independence.

1975

January 3	Transportation Safety Act of 1974 is signed into law.
April 1	National Transportation Safety Board becomes independent agency.

1976

March 21	FAA requires foreign air carriers entering the United States to have written security systems in place.
June 27	Air France Flight 139 hijacked by members of Revolutionary Cells and Popular Front for the Liberation of Palestine—External Operations. Plane recaptured by Israeli commandos.

1977

October 13	Lufthansa flight 181 hijacked by members of the Popular Front for the Liberation of Palestine.
November 2	James "Jimmy" Carter is elected president of the United States over incumbent Gerald Ford.
November 20	Specially trained dog units are placed strategically across the United States in airports to detect bombs and narcotics.

1978

April 8	European Convention on the Suppression of Terrorism enters into force.
April 28	The president of Afghanistan is assassinated during a coup, which installs a communist government in the country.
September 17	Israel and Egypt sign the Camp David Accords.
October 25	The Foreign Intelligence Surveillance Act (FISA) is enacted. Among other restrictions, the law requires U.S. intelligence agencies to obtain a warrant from a special court, the Foreign Intelligence Surveillance Court, before eavesdropping or conducting surveillance within the United States.

1979

February 14	U.S. ambassador to Afghanistan is kidnapped and later killed in Kabul.
November 4	Iranian militants storm the U.S. Embassy in Tehran and take more than 50 Americans hostage.
November 20	The "Grand Mosque Seizure" in Saudi Arabia in which radical Islamists take over the Al-Masjid al-Haram Mosque. More than

100 are killed and wounded when Saudi security forces recapture the site.

November 22   Islamic militants attack the U.S. Embassy in Islamabad, Pakistan, while anti-American riots sweep the country after false reports from Iran indicate an American connection to the "Grand Mosque Seizure."

December 24   The Soviet Union invades and conquers Afghanistan.

December 26   Osama bin Laden leaves for Afghanistan to join the Mujahedeen and fight against the Soviet occupation.

1980s

1980

April 30   Members of the Democratic Revolutionary Movement for the Liberation of Arabistan capture the Iranian Embassy in London.

September 22   Iraq invades Iran initiating an eight-year war.

May   The FBI creates the nation's first counterterrorism task force in New York City.

November 4   Ronald Reagan is elected president of the United States over incumbent James Carter. Reagan wins on a campaign that highlighted the poor U.S. economy and security problems highlighted by the Iran hostage crisis and the Soviet invasion of Afghanistan.

1981

January 20   Last American Embassy hostages in Iran are released.

June 7   Israel conducts a preemptive air strike, which destroys an Iraqi nuclear plant that was part of a weapons of mass destruction (WMD) program to develop nuclear weapons.

October 6   Anwar al-Sadat, president of Egypt, is assassinated by Islamist militants.

December 4   U.S. president Ronald Reagan issues Executive Order 12333 which expands the abilities of the Central Intelligence Agency to gather domestic intelligence in cases of suspected espionage or terrorism. The order also strengthens prohibitions against U.S. personnel taking part in plans or efforts to assassinate individuals.

1982

August 11   Pan Am Flight 830 is bombed by Mohammed Rashed, killing one.

1983

April 18	Hezbollah carries out a suicide attack on the U.S. Embassy in Beirut Lebanon, killing 63.
July 19	David S. Dodge of American University of Beirut is kidnapped and held hostage by Hezbollah for 12 months.
October 23	Truck bombings by Islamic Jihad in West Beirut, Lebanon, kills 241 U.S. Marines and 58 French soldiers.
December 12	American and French embassies in Kuwait are bombed by Islamic militants.

1984

March 16	William Buckley, CIA station chief to Lebanon, is kidnapped and eventually killed.
September 20	Bombing of American Embassy in Lebanon by Islamic Jihad kills 24.
November 6	Ronald Reagan wins reelection as president of the United States over Democrat Walter Mondale. Mondale's running mate, Geraldine Ferraro, becomes the first woman vice presidential candidate.
December 3	Kuwait Airways Flight 221 is hijacked by Islamic Jihad and taken to Tehran, Iran. Two Americans are killed.

1985

March 16	Terry Anderson kidnapped in Beirut, Lebanon, and held hostage for more than six years by Hezbollah.
June 9	Thomas Sutherland kidnapped in Beirut, Lebanon, and held hostage for five years by Hezbollah.
June 14	Transworld Airlines (TWA) Flight 847 is hijacked by Islamic Jihad. One American killed.
August 8	President Reagan signs the International Security and Development Cooperation Act of 1985 into law.
October 7	The Italian passenger liner *Achille Lauro* is hijacked by terrorists linked to the PLO and Libya. One American is killed.
November 23	Egypt Air Flight 648 is hijacked by the Abu Nidal Organization, resulting in 60 killed and 30 injured.
December 17	Airports in Rome and Vienna are bombed, killing 20. The attacks are linked to Libya and are in response to the United States sending forces into Gulf of Sidra.

December 27	Members of Abu Nidal Organization launch simultaneous attacks on El Al Israel Airline ticket counters in Rome and Vienna, killing 18 and wounding 110.

1986

April 5	Libyan terrorists bomb a nightclub in Berlin frequented by U.S. military personnel.
April 15	U.S. forces bomb Tripoli and Benghazi in retaliation for April 5 bombing.
April 17	Three American University of Beirut employees are shot by pro-Libyan organization.
September 6	Abu Nidal Organization attacks a synagogue in Istanbul and Pan Am Flight 73, killing 44.
September 9	Frank Reed of the American University in Beirut is kidnapped and held hostage for 44 months.

1987

January 20	Terry Waite kidnapped and held hostage by Hezbollah for five years.
November 4	South Asian Association for Regional Cooperation (SARC) Regional Convention on Suppression of Terrorism is adopted.
December 8	The first Palestinian Intifada against Israel begins in Israeli-controlled areas of the West Bank and Gaza.
December 14	The Palestinian group Hamas is formed.

1988

February 17	U.S. Marine lt. colonel William Higgins is killed by Hezbollah.
February 24	Protocol for the Suppression of Unlawful Acts of Violence at Airports Serving International Civil Aviation enters into force.
March 16	Iraqi security forces use chemical weapons against Kurds. The following month, chemical weapons are used against Iranian soldiers in the Iran-Iraq War.
April 5	Kuwait Airline Flight 422 is hijacked by Hezbollah. Two passengers are killed.
April 14	USO club in Naples, Italy, is attacked by car bomb, killing one. Organization of Jihad Brigades claims responsibility.

August	The al Qaeda ("the base" or "the foundation" in Arabic) terrorist organization is believed to have formed in Afghanistan by Osama bin Laden and other Mujahedeen.
August 20	A UN-sponsored ceasefire ends the Iran-Iraq War.
November 8	George H.W. Bush is elected president of the United States over Michael Dukakis. Bush wins largely on the Reagan legacy.
December 21	Pan Am Flight 103 is destroyed by a terrorist bomb over Lockerbie, Scotland, killing 270. Libya later accepts responsibility for the attack.

1989

February 15	After a bloody occupation, the Soviet Union withdraws from Afghanistan as a result of the 1988 Geneva Accords.
June 3	Ayatollah Khomeini dies in Iran.
September 19	UTA Flight 772 explodes over Niger. Libya is believed responsible.

1990s

1990

March-April	Afghan refugees who fled their country during the Soviet Union begin to return in large numbers under a program overseen by the United Nations.
May 15	President's Commission on Aviation Security and Terrorism issues final report. The commission was set up in response to Lockerbie bombing.
May 22	U.S. Biological Weapons Anti-Terrorism Act of 1989 (Pub. L. 101-298) enters into force.
July 25	U.S. ambassador to Iraq sends signals indicating lack of U.S. interest in "Arab-Arab conflicts."
August 2	Iraq invades Kuwait.
August 6	UN Security Council Resolution 661 is adopted, imposing sanction on Iraq.
November 16	President Bush signs Aviation Security Improvement Act of 1990 (Pub. L. 101-604) into law.

1991

January 17	Operation Desert Storm, the U.S.-led liberation of Kuwait, commences.

January 18–19	Iraqi agents attempt bombing of U.S. ambassador to Indonesia and U.S. library in Manila.
February	The United States ends military aid to groups in Afghanistan.
February 28	Ceasefire in Operation Desert Storm declared by President Bush.
March 10	U.S. ground forces begin redeployment out of Persian Gulf.
April 3	UN Security Council Resolution 687 is adopted, establishing the United Nations Special Commission (UNSCOM) to oversee Iraq terms for ceasefire.
June 9	The United Nations begins inspections to dismantle Iraq's WMD programs.
October 11	UN Security Council Resolution 715 is adopted, demanding Iraqi compliance with weapons inspections.

1992

January 21	UN Security Council Resolution 731 is adopted, condemning Libya over Pan Am Flight 103 over Lockerbie.
March 1	International Convention for the Suppression of Unlawful Acts of Violence Against the Safety of Maritime Navigation enters into force.
March 31	UN Security Council Resolution 748 is adopted, placing sanctions on Libya and expelling Libyan nationals involved in terrorism activities in other states related to Lockerbie Bombing.
June 24	Burhanuddin Rabbani becomes president of Afghanistan after the removal of Soviet-backed government by mujahedeen forces.
August	No-fly zones in Northern and Southern Iraq are established. These remain in force until 2003.
November 3	Bill Clinton is elected president of the United States, defeating George H. W. Bush and H. Ross Perot. Clinton's campaign focuses on domestic issues at a time when the United States was in the midst of an economic recession.
March 17	The Israeli Embassy in Buenos Aires, Argentina, is car bombed by Hezbollah, killing 29 and injuring 242.
July	The United Nations begins the destruction of Iraq's WMD stockpiles.
December 29	Al Qaeda bomb two targets in Aden, Yemen, in a failed attempt to kill American soldiers.

1993

January 25	Mir Amal Kansi kills two CIA employees at CIA headquarters with a rifle in response to U.S. policies in the Middle East.
February 26	Terrorists attempt to destroy the World Trade Center in New York City with a truck bomb, killing six and injuring more than 1,000.
April 14	Iraqi agents unsuccessfully attempt to assassinate former U.S. president George H.W. Bush.
June 23	FBI spoils al Qaeda plot to destroy targets in New York and New Jersey, including the UN Headquarters and the Statue of Liberty.
October 3–4	The Battle of Mogadishu prompts a withdrawal of U.S. forces from Somalia.
November 11	UN Security Council Resolution 883 adopted expressing determination to eliminate international terrorism and imposing stricter sanctions on Libya over Lockerbie bombing.
September 13	PLO and Israel sign Oslo Accords.

1994

February 25	The "Hebron Massacre" in which Israeli-American right-wing extremist Dr. Baruch Goldstein opens fire on Muslim worshippers in Hebron, Israel, killing 29 and wounding more than 150.
June 20	Ramzi Yousef, the mastermind behind the 1993 World Trade Center attack, bombs Imam Reza shrine in Iran, killing 26 and injuring hundreds.
September 12	A stolen Cessna aircraft purposefully crashes near White House.
October 26	Jordan and Israel sign peace treaty.
November 5	The Taliban capture Kandahar, Afghanistan, marking the beginning of Taliban consolidation of control of the country.
December 11	Ramzi Yousef bombs Philippine Airlines flight PAL434 as a trial run for the Bojinka Plot—an attempt to assassinate Pope John Paul II and bomb 12 commercial airliners simultaneously.
December 25	French security forces disrupt a hijacking plot by Algerian Islamic terrorists that are tied to al Qaeda to seize an airliner and fly it into the Eiffel Tower in Paris.

1995

February 7	Ramzi Yousef is captured in Islamabad, Pakistan, and subsequently extradited to the United States.
March 8	Two U.S. diplomats are killed and one is injured in gunman attack in Karachi, Pakistan.
April 14	The UN Security Council through Resolution 986 creates the "Oil for Food" program.
April 19	Right-wing extremists detonate a truck at a federal building in Oklahoma City, killing 168 in the worst domestic terrorist attack to date in U.S. history (known as the "Oklahoma City Bombing").
June 21	President Clinton signs presidential directive (PDD-39) authorizing "rendition" and other counterterrorism measures.
August 25	Hamas bus bombing in Jerusalem kills six and injures over 100.
October 26	Palestinian Islamic Jihad founder Fathi al-Shaqaqi is assassinated.
November 4	Yitzhak Rabin, Israeli prime minister, is assassinated in Tel Aviv by Israeli extremists.
November 13	Bomb detonated at U.S. operated Saudi military training facility in Riyadh, Saudi Arabia. Islamic Movement of Change claims responsibility.
November 19	Egyptian Embassy in Pakistan bombed by Islamic Jihad.

1996

April 14	President Clinton signs into law the Antiterrorism and Effective Death Penalty Act in response to the Oklahoma City Bombing.
April 30	Israel and the United States sign a new accord to increase bilateral counterterrorism efforts.
June 12	UN Security Council Resolution 1060 adopted demanding Iraqi compliance with weapons inspections.
June 25	Islamic terrorists detonate a truck bomb at the Khobar Towers military barracks in Saudi Arabia, killing 19 and injuring more than 500.
August 25	Osama bin Laden declares war against the United States.
September 27	The Taliban captures Kabul, Afghanistan, and is effectively in control of Afghanistan as a whole.

November 1	The Arab news network Al Jazeera begins broadcasting.
November 5	Clinton is reelected president of the United States, defeating Bob Dole and H. Ross Perot.

1997

February 12	Final report of the White House Commission on Aviation Safety and Security is released.
February 23	Palestinian gunman opens fire on Empire State Building in New York.
May 24	Pakistan, Saudi Arabia, and the United Arab Emirates recognize the Taliban as the legitimate government of Afghanistan.
June 21	UN Security Council Resolution 1115 is adopted, demanding Iraqi compliance with weapons inspections.
October	The U.S. Department of State creates a foreign terrorist organizations list that designates 30 groups as terrorist entities.
October 23	UN Security Council Resolution 1134 is adopted, demanding Iraqi compliance with weapons inspections.
November 12	UN Security Council Resolution 1137 is adopted, demanding Iraqi compliance with weapons inspections.

1998

	U.S. military spending falls to $296.7 billion, or 3.1 percent of the country's GDP. This is the lowest dollar figure since 1979 and the lowest percentage of GDP since before World War II.
February 23	Osama bin Laden issues a fatwa, or religious decree, calling upon all Muslims to kill Americans and their allies.
March 2	UN Security Council Resolution 1154 adopted demanding Iraqi compliance with weapons inspections.
April 22	Arab Convention on the Suppression of Terrorism adopted by League of Arab States.
July 18	The European Union suspends aid to Afghanistan.
August 7	Al Qaeda conducts simultaneous truck bombings against the U.S. embassies in Nairobi, Kenya, and Dar-es-Salaam, Tanzania, killing 224 and wounding more than 4,000.
August 20	U.S. forces launch cruise missile strike of al Qaeda training camps in Afghanistan in response to the August 7 Embassy Bombings.

August 26	New York Grand Jury indicts Osama bin Laden for embassy bombings.
October 31	The Iraq Liberation Act becomes law in the United States, committing the government to regime change in Iraq.
September 9	UN Security Council Resolution 1194 adopted demanding Iraqi compliance with weapons inspections.
September 22	Taliban delegation expelled from Saudi Arabia.
November 5	UN Security Council Resolution 1205 adopted demanding Iraqi compliance with weapons inspections.
December 16–19	Operation Desert Fox, a four-day aerial bombardment, authorized by President Clinton after Iraq refuses to allow continued weapons inspections.

1999

January 16	U.S Department of Justice indicts Osama bin Laden.
February 2	U.S. demands extradition of Osama bin Laden from Taliban. The Taliban refuse.
February 7	King Hussein of Jordan dies. His son, Abdullah II, succeeds him.
March	Taliban and Northern Alliance reach peace agreement, but it collapses in July.
May 14	U.S. warns Pakistan to limit assistance of Taliban.
June 8	U.S. places Osama bin Laden as FBI most wanted fugitive.
July 6	The United States imposes economic sanctions on the Taliban because of their refusal to extradite bin Laden.
October 12	General Pervez Musharraf leads a military coup in Pakistan and takes control from the civilian government of Prime Minister Nawaz Sharif.
October 15	The UN Security Council adopts Resolution 1267 which lists al Qaeda and the Taliban as terrorist organizations and places economic and military sanctions on both groups.
December 14	Al Qaeda affiliated plot to bomb Los Angeles International Airport foiled.
December 17	UN Security Council Resolution 1284 adopted establishing the United Nations Monitoring, Verification and Inspection Commission (UNMOVIC) which replaces UNSCOM.

2000s

2000

January 3	Attempt to bomb USS *The Sullivans* foiled after militant's overloaded boat sinks.
February 11	Iraq announces that UN weapons inspectors will not be allowed to continue.
March 1	Hans Blix of Sweden is appointed head of UNMOVIC.
June 10	The president of Syria, Hafez al-Assad, dies. His son, Bashar al-Assad, becomes president of the country.
July 12	The Pakistani Embassy in Kabul is bombed causing minimal damage.
October 12	U.S. Navy destroyer the USS *Cole* bombed in Aden, Yemen, killing 17 and wounding 39.
November 7	In a disputed presidential election, Texas Republican governor George W. Bush, the son of former president George H. W. Bush, defeats Democratic vice president Al Gore, after a lengthy vote recount that proceeds into December.
December 12	U.S. Supreme Court halts the Florida state recounts, allowing an electoral victory for Bush in the presidential election.

2001

January 20	Bush is inaugurated as the 43rd president of the United States. In his inaugural address, Bush endeavors to heal the divisions caused by the divisive 2000 presidential balloting and presents an agenda that concentrates on domestic issues.
May 26	The UN Security Council issues a report that accuses the Taliban of cultivating and exporting heroin to finance the regime.
August 16	Zacarias Moussaoui, the "twentieth hijacker," is arrested for immigration violations.
September 9	Ahmad Shah Massoud, the leader of the Northern Alliance, is assassinated by al Qaeda.
September 11	Al Qaeda–sponsored, coordinated terrorists attacks on the World Trade Center and the U.S. Pentagon result in almost 3,000 deaths in the worst terrorist strike in history and the most damaging attack on the United States since the bombing of Pearl Harbor by Japan on December 7, 1941.

September 11	Israel and the Palestinians agree to a temporary cease-fire under pressure from the United States.
September 12	NATO invokes Article V of the North Atlantic Treaty.
September 12	UN Security Council unanimously passes Resolution 1368 denouncing the 9/11 attacks.
September 14	Congress passes a joint resolution granting President Bush the authority to use military force against the perpetrators of the 9/11 attacks.
September 18	Anthrax spores are mailed to five media outlets and two U.S. senators. Five people are killed and 17 others sickened.
September 20	U.S. and UK aircraft attack surface-to-air missile sites in Iraq. The following day, U.S. officials assert there is evidence of contacts between the Saddam regime and al Qaeda.
September 20	President Bush proposes the creation of the Office of Homeland Security to joint session of Congress.
September 23	President Bush signs Executive Order 13224 targeting the ability of terrorists to conduct financial transactions.
September 25	Saudi Arabia and United Arab Emirate end diplomatic and political relations with the Taliban.
September 28	UN Security Council Resolution 1373 adopted establishing UN Security Council Counter-Terrorism Committee.
September 29	In Washington, D.C., the group ANSWER organizes first large anti-war demonstration against military action against Afghanistan.
October 4	Operation Active Endeavour begins NATO patrols of the Mediterranean Sea to prevent the movement of terrorists and WMDs.
October 7	The invasion of Afghanistan, Operation Enduring Freedom, begins.
October 8	NATO deploys Airborne Warning and Control System (AWACS) aircraft to the United States as part of Operation Eagle Assist.
October 8	The Office of Homeland Security is created through Executive Order 13228. Pennsylvania governor Tom Ridge is appointed director.
October 17	Rehavam Zeevi, the Israeli tourism minister, is assassinated by a Palestinian terrorist group.

October 26	USA PATRIOT Act becomes law.
November 9	Mazar-e-Sharif, Afghanistan, is captured by coalition forces in a rout. The Taliban Regime begins to quickly collapse.
November 10	President Bush embraces, in a speech to the United Nations, a two-state solution for Arab-Israeli conflict.
November 11	Taloqan and Barniyan, Afghanistan, fall to the Northern Alliance.
November 13	Taliban forces abandon Kabul.
	NATO begins to develop contingency plans to provide humanitarian assistance to the Afghan people once the Taliban are defeated. President Bush issues military order outlining rules for the detention of non-citizens in the war on terror, establishing the precedent for "enemy combatants."
November 14	Jalalabad, Afghanistan, falls to the Northern Alliance.
	UN Security Council Resolution 1378 is adopted, demanding central role for the United Nations in Afghanistan.
November 16	Mohammed Atef, a leading al Qaeda military strategist, is killed by coalition forces in Afghanistan.
November 19	The Aviation and Transportation Security Act becomes law. The legislation establishes the Transportation Safety Administration (TSA).
November 25	John Walker Lindh, known as the "American Taliban," is captured by Northern Alliance forces in Afghanistan.
November 26	President Bush demands Iraq allow UN weapons inspections.
December 5	"Bonn Agreement" is reached between the United Nations, the Northern Alliance, and other anti-Taliban Afghan factions.
December 9	Kandahar, Afghanistan, falls to coalition forces, marking the end of the Taliban regime.
December 12	Coalition forces attack al Qaeda's main headquarters at Tora Bora, Afghanistan.
December 20	UN Security Council Resolution 1386 is adopted, forming the International Security Assistance Force (ISAF).
December 22	Hamid Karzai becomes the interim leader of Afghanistan.
December 22	Richard Reid, the "Shoe Bomber," attempts unsuccessfully to destroy a flight from Paris to Miami.
December 23	FAA adds random shoe inspection to airline security checks.

December 28	Justice Department attorneys issue a memo that asserts U.S. courts do not have jurisdiction over foreign prisoners captured during the invasion of Afghanistan and held at Guantanamo Bay.

2002

January 4	First U.S. soldier dies in combat in Afghanistan.
January 15	Operation Enduring Freedom in the Philippines begins.
January 16	UN Security Council adopts Resolution 1390, imposing sanctions against al Qaeda, Osama bin Laden, and the Taliban.
January 23	The Victims of Terrorism Relief Act of 2001 is signed into law.
January 23	Terrorists in Karachi, Pakistan, kidnap U.S. journalist Daniel Pearl and eventually murder him.
January 29	Bush delivers a State of the Union address listing Iran, Iraq, and North Korea as part of an "axis of evil" and first promulgating the Bush Doctrine of preemption.
March 1	Operation Anaconda, a major U.S.-led anti-Taliban campaign, begins in Afghanistan.
March 12	The UN Security Council adopts Resolution 1397 reaffirming commitment to a two-state solution in the Arab-Israeli Conflict.
March 28	The Arab League issues the Beirut Declaration rejecting military action against Iraq.
March 29	The UN Security Council adopts Resolution 1402 calling for Israel to withdraw from Palestinian areas and for the Palestinians to cease terrorist attacks against Israel.
April 10	International Convention for the Suppression of the Financing of Terrorism enters into force.
April 17	In a speech at the Virginia Military Institute, President Bush calls for an international effort to rebuild post-Taliban Afghanistan.
May	NATO and Russia agree to create the NATO-Russia Council, which serves as a means to coordinate security efforts and reduce tensions.
May	Debris removal from Ground Zero is completed, although examiners continue attempting to identify human remains at the site until 2005.
May 8	Jose Padilla is arrested in Chicago on suspicion of terrorism. Padilla was initially accused of attempting to use a "dirty

	bomb" (an explosive with radioactive material) in a terrorist attack.
June	A Loya Jirga ("Grand Council") begins meeting in Afghanistan to develop a new government and permanent constitution.
June 3	The Inter-American Convention Against Terrorism is adopted by the Organization of American States.
June 14	Al Qaeda terrorists detonate a bomb outside the U.S. consulate in Karachi. Eleven people are killed.
July 6	Afghan vice president Haji Abdul Qadir is killed by gunmen believed to be affiliated with al Qaeda.
September	The United States pre-deploys tanks and other mechanized vehicles in Kuwait for potential military action against Iraq.
	A group of Muslim extremists, the Buffalo Six, is arrested.
September 12	Bush addresses a special session of the United Nations, where he calls for an international effort to force Iraq to accept new WMD inspections.
September 16	Iraq agrees to allow UNSCOM inspectors to return to the country. Meanwhile, British prime minister Blair makes public an intelligence dossier that reports that the Saddam regime continues an active WMD program.
September 17	The Bush administration publishes the 2002 *National Security Strategy of the United States* codifying the Bush Doctrine.
September 22	Secretary of Defense Rumsfeld characterizes the divide between the European states on military action in Iraq as a split between "old Europe" and "new Europe."
October 2–24	The D.C. sniper attacks by John Allen Muhammad and Lee Boyd Malvo kill 10 and wound three.
October 4	Six suspected al Qaeda terrorists are captured in Buffalo, N.Y.
October 6	An explosives-laden ship is rammed into the side of the French oil tanker, the *Limburg*, off of the coast of Yemen by al Qaeda operatives, killing one and wounding four.
October 7	Operation Enduring Freedom—Horn of Africa begins.
October 10–11	U.S. Congress passes joint resolution authorizing use of force against Iraq.
October 12	Indonesian Islamic terrorist group, Jemaah Islamiyah detonates two bombs outside of a tourist location on the island of Bali

	killing 202 and injuring more than 200 others. A third bomb detonates outside of the U.S. consulate, causing little damage.
October 23–26	Chechen terrorists seize a theater in Moscow, leading to the deaths of at least 170.
November 3	Elections in Turkey bring the religious Islamic Justice and Development Party to power.
November 8	UN Security Council adopts Resolution 1441. The measure gives Iraq a final opportunity to comply with disarmament obligations, but threatens unidentified serious consequences if Iraq fails to comply with past UN resolutions.
November 9	In congressional midterm elections, Republicans gain two seats in the Senate (thereby regaining their majority in the Senate). They also add eight seats to their majority in the House.
November 15	Congress enacts legislation to provide $2.3 billion in funds for reconstruction efforts in Afghanistan. In addition, $1 billion is approved to support the NATO-led security force in the country.
November 25	U.S. Congress passes the Homeland Security Act establishing the Department of Homeland Security.
November 27	The National Commission on Terrorist Attacks Upon the United States, also known as the 9/11 Commission, is chartered.
December 6	Organization of African Union Convention on the Prevention and Combating of Terrorism enters into force.
December 7	Iraq provides UNSCOM with a 12,000-page disclosure report on its WMD program as required by UN Resolution 1441.
December 9	Coalition naval units near the Horn of Africa stop a North Korean ship. The ship is carrying Scud missiles and warheads.
December 31	In 2002, the U.S. federal budget deficit rises to 1.48 percent of GDP after several years of surpluses.

2003

January 7	The Select Committee on Homeland Security is created by U.S. Congress to coordinate oversight of DHS.
January 9	Hans Blix states there is "no smoking gun" in Iraq, alluding to the lack of any significant evidence of an ongoing Iraqi WMD program.

January 20	UN Security Council Resolution 1456 is adopted, calling on states to prevent and suppress support for terrorism.
January 24	The DHS officially begins operations. Tom Ridge is appointed the first secretary of DHS.
January 27	IAEA issues report noting no evidence of Iraqi WMD development. Mohamed El-Baradei and Hans Blix ask for more time for inspections.
January 28	President Bush delivers a State of the Union Address detailing his arguments for war against Iraq.
January 30	The NATO Eight (Czech Republic, Hungary, Italy, the Netherlands, Poland, Portugal, Spain, and the United Kingdom) express support for the U.S.-led war against Iraq.
February 5	U.S. secretary of state Powell presents the U.S. case for armed action against Iraq to the United Nations.
February 10	Belgium, France, and Germany veto a request by Turkey to invoke Article IV of the NATO charter.
February 11	France, Germany, and Russia issue a statement calling for additional time for UNMOVIC to continue its inspections. France and Russia, permanent members of the UN Security Council, also threaten to veto any resolution calling for the use of force against Iraq.
February 15	As part of a series of global protests, demonstrations occur throughout the United States and Europe.
March 1	Turkey's parliament denies permission for the United States to utilize Turkish territory for an invasion.
	A summit of Arab leaders calls for the Saddam regime to end its WMD programs and to disarm.
	Khalid Sheikh Mohammed, one of the planners of the 9/11 and Bali attacks, is captured in Pakistan and extradited to the United States.
	Iraq begins destruction of the missiles identified by UNMOVIC as violating UN Security Council Resolution 687.
March 7	The United States, Spain, and the United Kingdom introduce a resolution that would authorize the use of force unless Iraq takes enough steps so that the UN Security Council would certify by March 17 that Iraq had met all of the requirements of UN Security Council Resolution 1441.

March 15	UN Security Council members France, Russia, and China issue a statement asserting that inspections should continue and that there is no need to resort to force at this point.
	More than 60,000 people attend an anti-war rally in Washington, D.C.
March 16	The leaders of the United States, Spain, Portugal, and the United Kingdom again present their case for war at a summit in the Azores islands. They also accept that diplomatic efforts to end the crisis have failed and concede that war is imminent.
March 17	President Bush issues ultimatum to Iraq demanding that Saddam and his sons Uday and Qusay Hussein leave Iraq within 48 hours or face military action by the United States and its allies.
	Hans Blix issues a follow-up report which describes general improvements in cooperation from the Iraqis, but also cites some instances of continuing intransigence.
	Canadian Prime Minister Jean Chrétien issues a public statement that Canada will not join the coalition in any military action against Iraq.
	Department of Homeland Security commences Operation Liberty Shield to enhance homeland security in the event of war with Iraq.
	United Nations orders staff and weapons inspectors out of Iraq because of the threat of war.
March 18	U.S. releases statement declaring it has formed a "Coalition of the Willing" to undertake military action against Iraq.
March 19	President Bush approves Operation Iraqi Freedom. In an address to the nation, Bush announces military action against Iraq.
March 20	U.S. begins military strikes against Iraq.
March 23	A U.S. supply column is ambushed and 12 soldiers killed. Army private first class Jessica Lynch is captured along with five other soldiers.
	An estimated 200,000 people participate in an anti-war protest in New York.
March 28	The coalition begins landing ships and supplies at the port of Umm Qasr. Coalition forces surround Basra, Iraq, but efforts to incite an anti-Saddam rebellion among the Shiites in the region fail.

March 29	The largest anti-war demonstration in Boston since the Vietnam War is held.
April	The first teams from the Iraq Survey Group (ISG) are sent to Iraq.
April 2	U.S. House passes $79 billion Wartime Supplemental Appropriations bill.
April 3	U.S. armored forces advance to Saddam Hussein International Airport on the outskirts of Baghdad.
April 9	Coalition forces establish control of Baghdad, Iraq. Iraqis and U.S. soldiers tear down a large statue of Saddam in Firdos Square in Baghdad.
April 10	In Afghanistan, Karzai appoints 33-member group to draft a new constitution. The group completes its work in November.
April 15	The last major fighting of the initial Iraq invasion occurs when coalition forces capture Tikrit, Saddam's hometown and the center of his power.
April 21	Retired U.S. general Jay Garner arrives in Iraq to oversee reconstruction efforts and the transition to Iraqi civilian rule under the Coalition Provisional Authority (CPA).
May 1	President Bush announces the end of major combat operations in Iraq. Secretary of Defense Rumsfeld announces the end of major combat in Afghanistan.
May 1	Terrorist Threat Integration Center begins operations under Executive Order 13354.
May 11	Former ambassador L. Paul Bremer is appointed to lead the CPA and takes over from Jay Garner.
May 13	Suicide bombers attack compounds for foreign workers in Saudi Arabia, killing 34 and injuring more than 190.
May 22	UN Security Council passes Resolution 1483 ending economic sanctions against Iraq.
May 23	Bremer officially disbands the Iraq security forces.
June	A Shiite cleric, Muqtada al-Sadr, establishes a paramilitary force in Baghdad in June, the Mahdi Army.
June 24	House approves $29.4 billion in initial Homeland Security appropriations.
July 22	Saddam's sons, Uday and Qusay Hussein, are killed during a battle with U.S. troops in Mosul, Iraq.

July 23	Interim Iraqi governing council meets for the first time to begin preparing for the transition from coalition control.
August 5	A car bomb is detonated at the Marriot Hotel in Jakarta, Indonesia. Thirteen are killed and 149 are injured.
August 11	NATO takes command of ISAF and peacekeeping operation in Afghanistan.
August 14	UN Security Council Resolution 1500 is adopted, establishing United Nations Assistance Mission for Iraq (UNAMI).
August 17	Ali Hassan al-Majid, or "Chemical Ali," is captured by coalition forces.
August 19	UN headquarters in Baghdad is bombed, killing 23, including the head of the UN mission in Iraq, Sergio Viera DeMello. Over 100 are wounded.
	Taha Yasin Ramadan Al-Jizraqi, former Iraqi vice president, is captured.
August 29	Car bomb destroys the Imam Ali Mosque in Iraq, killing 124 including the Ayatollah Mohammad Baqir al-Hakim.
October 27	Suicide bomber attacks International Red Cross headquarters in Baghdad; this and other suicide attacks kill more than 200 on this day.
December 13	Saddam is captured by U.S. forces near Tikrit, Iraq, in a covert operation dubbed "Red Dawn."
December 14	Loya Jirga begins deliberations over the proposed new constitution in Afghanistan.
December 19	Muammar Gaddafi announces an end to Libya's chemical and nuclear weapons programs and invites UN weapons inspectors to oversee the destruction of WMDs and equipment.
December 31	By the end of the year, the U.S. federal budget deficit doubles to 3.48 percent of GDP.

2004

January	Forty-two of the 55 most wanted figures from the Saddam regime have been killed or captured by coalition forces.
January 4	A constitutional Loya Jirga approves a new constitution in Afghanistan
January 17	U.S. causalities reach 500 in Iraq.

January 22	The CIA issues a report that Iraq is on the verge of a civil war between the Shiites, Sunnis, and Kurds.
January 26	President Karzai signs into law a new Afghanistan Constitution.
February 4	Suicide bombers carry out attacks in the Kurdish regions of Iraq, killing more than 109.
March 2	Suicide attacks in Baghdad and Karbala kill more than 200 worshippers during a Shiite holy day.
March 5	Former UNMOVIC chief, Hans Blix, asserts that the Iraq War was illegal since the coalition did not allow the United Nations to conduct a full round of weapons inspections in Iraq.
March 8	The interim Iraqi government approves a temporary constitution for the country.
March 11	Al Qaeda terrorists detonate bombs on three commuter trains in Madrid, Spain. The attacks kill 201 and wound more than 1,400. The conservative government's handling of the strikes leads to its defeat in national elections by the opposition socialists.
March 26	UN Security Council Resolution 1535 is adopted, revitalizing and restructuring the UN Counter-Terrorism Committee.
March 31	Four U.S. military contractors are captured, tortured, and executed in Fallujah. Two of the bodies are hung from a bridge, which makes international media.
April	Fighting between the Mahdi Army and coalition forces begins as the militia group asserts control over a number of areas in Iraq. Combat lasts into June.
April 3	An international conference of donor states pledges $8.2 billion in reconstruction assistance for Afghanistan.
April 4	The United States launches Operation Vigilant Resolve to suppress insurgents in Fallujah.
April 18	Jose Zapatero, the newly elected socialist prime minster of Spain, orders Spanish troops out of Iraq, partially in response to the Madrid bombing in March.
April 21	Al Qaeda suicide attacks kill 73 in Basra and Zubeir.
April 28	The UN Security Council passes Resolution 1540, which calls on all member states to make the proliferation of WMDs a

crime and to enhance border and transportation security to prevent proliferation.

Graphic images of prisoner abuse at the U.S.-run Abu Ghraib are first reported in the media.

The last Spanish troops withdraw from Iraq.

May 5	Bush delivers an apology over the abuse scandal on Al Hurra, a U.S.-financed Arab language media outlet.
May 11	Nicholas Berg, an American businessman, is kidnapped by al Qaeda and beheaded in retaliation for the Abu Ghraib scandal.
May 17	Izzedin Salim, a moderate Shiite leader and the chair of the Iraqi interim government, is assassinated by al Qaeda in a car bombing.
May 19	U.S forces mistakenly target a wedding party, killing 42 civilians in the Mukaradeeb Wedding Massacre.
June	The United States completes a redeployment of American forces that reduces their number from 135,000 to 115,000. Meanwhile, terrorist attacks across Iraq kill more than 250.
June 6	After being defeated by coalition forces, Sadr orders the Mahdi Army to stop fighting and announces he will transition his militia into a political grouping.
June 7	The United Nations adopts Resolution 1546, which affirms the authority and legitimacy of Iraq's interim government.
June 24	Muqtada al-Sadr declares cease-fire.
June 28	The United States officially transfers control of the Iraq to the coutnry's interim government. Iyad Allawi is sworn in as prime minister of the interim government, while Ghazi Mashal Ajil al-Yawer assumes the largely symbolic post of president.
July 1	The trial of Saddam Hussein begins in Bagdad.
July 26	9/11 Commission issues *The 9/11 Commission Report*.
July 21	Project Bioshield Act is signed into law.
July 29	In his acceptance speech at the Democratic National Convention, presidential candidate John Kerry declares, "I'm reporting for duty."
August 13	Militia fighters retreat to the Iman Ali Shrine in Najaf, Iraq. Standoff is ended through the intervention of the Grand Ayatollah Sistani.

August 20	A yearlong, nationwide voter registration drive is completed in Afghanistan. More than 10.6 million are registered to vote amid Taliban and al Qaeda attacks.
September 8	U.S. causalities reach 1,000 in Iraq.
September 16	UN Secretary General Annan notes that he believes the Iraq War was not in line with international law and therefore illegal.
September 30	The ISG issues its main report finding no evidence that Iraq had stockpiles of WMDs or an active and ongoing WMD program at the time of the invasion.
October 4	UN Security Council Resolution 1566 is adopted, condemning terrorism and strengthening anti-terror legislation.
October 9	Hamid Karzai is elected president of Afghanistan with 55.4 percent of the vote against more than a dozen other candidates.
October 29	Osama bin Laden releases a video taking responsibility for 9/11 terrorist attacks.
November 2	U.S. president Bush is reelected, defeating his Democratic opponent U.S. senator John F. Kerry in a campaign that focused primarily on the wars in Afghanistan and Iraq and the war on terror. The Republicans increase their majorities in the House and Senate.
November 8	Operation Phantom Fury begins to secure Fallujah, Iraq.
November 11	Longtime Palestinian leader Yasser Arafat dies.
November 15	Secretary of State Colin Powell retires; National Security Advisor Condoleezza Rice replaces him. Her assistant, Stephen Haldey, becomes national security advisor.
December 7	Karzai is inaugurated as Afghanistan's first freely elected president.
December 17	The Intelligence Reform and Terrorism Prevention Act is signed into law, creating the National Counterterrorism Center and the office of the Director of National Intelligence (DNI).
December 31	By the end of the year, there are 18,300 U.S. troops in Afghanistan.

2005

January 20	In his inauguration speech, Bush argues that it is the "policy" of the United States to support democratization around the world.

January 30	Iraqis vote for a 275-member transitional assembly. The body is tasked to create a constitution for the country.
February 10	NATO announces it will expand its role in Afghanistan.
February 14	Former Lebanese prime minister Rafik Hariri is assassinated.
February 15	Michael Chertoff appointed secretary of the U.S. Department of Homeland Security.
February 28	In what becomes known as the Cedar Revolution, the pro-Syrian government resigns in Lebanon.
March 23	U.S. and new Afghani government enter into "strategic partnership."
March 31	U.S. bans lighters from passengers and carry-on luggage.
April 6	The transitional assembly elects Jalal Talabani, a Kurd, as president of Iraq.
April 11	Mass peaceful protest in Baghdad is held by supporters of Muqtada al-Sadr.
April 21	Ambassador to Iraq John Negroponte is appointed first U.S. director of national intelligence.
April 27	Syria withdraws its forces from Lebanon under international pressure.
May	Allegations surface of prisoner abuse by U.S. troops and intelligence officials in Afghanistan.
May 11	Bush approves a supplemental appropriations bill that provides $76 billion for the ongoing conflicts in Afghanistan and Iraq. This is in addition to the $496.3 billion defense budget.
May 29	Operation Lightening begins in an effort to quell Baghdad insurgents.
June 14	Massoud Barzani is elected to regional presidency of Iraqi Kurdistan region.
July 7	London bombings, often referred to as "7/7"; Islamic militants detonated four bombs, killing 56 and injuring over 700.
	Insurgents kidnap Angelo de la Cruz, a Philippine citizen. The Philippine government agrees to end its small 51-member military mission in Iraq early. Cruz is released on July 20.
August 27	Bush issues Executive Order 13355, which affirms the powers of the newly created director of national intelligence and improves coordination and cooperation among U.S. intelligence agencies.

September 14	UN Security Council Resolution 1624 is adopted, calling on states to prohibit incentive for terrorist acts and to deny safe haven for terrorists.
September 18	Afghanistan conducts parliamentary and regional elections after repeated delays. Women win 28 percent of the seats in the parliament.
October 7	The IAEI and its chief, El Baradei, are awarded the Nobel Prize for Peace for their efforts to stop the proliferation of nuclear weapons.
October 15	Iraqi Transitional Assembly completes a draft constitution which is approved in a referendum by a vote of 78.6 in favor and 21.4 percent opposed.
October 19	The trial of Saddam Hussein begins.
October 26	U.S. casualties in Iraq reach 2,000.
November	Sunni tribal leaders in Anbar province decide to reject sectarian violence and ally themselves with the Iraqi government and the U.S.-led coalition. Other Sunni leaders join in what becomes known as the Sunni Awakening (also known as the "Sons of Iraq" movement). The Sunni Awakening is instrumental in reducing violence in Iraq.
November 14–18	There are five separate suicide attacks in Kabul over a five-day-period.
December	U.S. troop strength in Iraq rises to 156,000.
December 15	Elections are conducted in Iraq for the new permanent national assembly, the Council of Representatives.
December 18	Bush admits that much of the intelligence that was used to justify military action against Iraq proved to be false.
December 23	Karzai appoints a new cabinet as a result of ongoing tensions with conservative lawmakers in the Afghan parliament.
December 30	Bush signs the Detainee Treatment Act which mandated that both lawful and unlawful enemy combatants detained by the United States could not be subject to cruel or unusual interrogations in accordance with international law and customs. The Act also denied detainees the power to challenge their status in U.S. courts.

2006

	The U.S. Drug Enforcement Agency becomes the lead organization in efforts to suppress the illicit drug trade in Afghanistan.

February 5	Twenty-three al Qaeda prisoners escape from a Yemini prison, including 13 figures that were convicted for participating in the 2000 attack on the USS *Cole*.
February 22	Sunni insurgents bomb a Shiite holy site in Samarra. The attack unleashes a wave of Sunni-Shiite sectarian violence across Iraq.
March 10	Congress reauthorizes the Patriot Act with changes and revisions to the more controversial aspects of the measure.
March 15	Congress forms the Iraq Study Group. The bipartisan group consists of 10 senior and well-known foreign policy and political officials, including former secretaries of state James A. Baker III, Lawrence Eagleburger, and former defense secretary William J. Perry.
March 16	Former Afghan president Mojaddedi survives an assassination attempt. Mojaddedi was a vocal critic of Pakistan, and many Afghans blame Pakistani intelligence officials for the attack.
June	The Iraqi government asks the United States to develop a timeline for the withdrawal of coalition forces from Iraq.
June 7	Abu Musab al-Zarqawi is killed by U.S. forces in Baghdad, Iraq.
July 27	International Compact With Iraq is launched between Iraq and the United Nations.
July 31	NATO takes command of the southern region of Afghanistan and takes command of military operations to displace the Taliban.
August 10	After a failed attempt to bomb a UK-U.S. flight, the Transportation Security Administration bans all liquids, gels, and aerosols. All footwear requires mandatory inspection.
September 21	NATO leaders agree to take command of all security operations in Afghanistan.
September 25	TSA enacts 3-1-1 rule for travel-sized toiletries in carry-on bags.
October 17	Military Commissions Act of 2006 passes authorizing trial by military commission for violations of the law of war.
November	The Automatic Targeting System, designed to assess the risk factors of across U.S. border travelers, is implemented, raising concern among civil liberties activists.

November 5	Former Iraqi leader Saddam Hussein is convicted of his role in the execution of 149 Shiites who took part in an assassination plot.
November 7	In U.S. midterm congressional elections, Democrats regain control of Congress, securing majorities in both the House of Representatives and the Senate. The balloting was perceived as a referendum on the Bush presidency. Anti-war Democratic leader Nancy Pelosi (California) would become the first female speaker of the House.
November 8	Donald Rumsfeld resigns as secretary of defense; former CIA director and national security advisor Robert Gates replaces him.
November 21	Iraq and Syria restore diplomatic ties after a 24-year hiatus.
December 6	Iraq Study Group issues "The Way Forward: A New Approach," which argues for a diplomatic solution to the Iraq War, including engaging Iran and Syria in crafting a end to the conflict.
December 19	Mullah Akhtar Osmani, the fourth senior ranking Taliban leader, is killed in a U.S. airstrike.
December 30	Saddam Hussein is executed by hanging by the Iraqi government.
December 31	More than 18,000 Iraqi civilians die in 2006 as a result of the insurgency and sectarian violence.
	By year's end, Afghanistan is the source of 92 percent of the world's heroin. Opium poppy production in Afghanistan peaks that year at 8,500 metric tons. The illicit drug trade in Afghan is worth $2.7 billion, at a time when legal exports account for only $600 million.

2007

January	The National Intelligence Estimate report is released. *Prospects for Iraq's Stability: A Challenging Road Ahead* indicates continuing deterioration of the security situation in Iraq. It uses the analogy "Civil War" to describe Iraq.
January 8	U.S. aircraft fire on suspected al Qaeda positions in Somalia.
January 10	In an effort to quell the continuing insurgency, Bush announces plans to deploy a "surge" of an additional 20,000 combat troops to Iraq.

January 13	The Association of Southeast Asian Nations (ASEAN) Convention on Counter Terrorism is adopted.
January 26	Army lt. general David Petraeus is given operational command of U.S. forces in Iraq.
February 6	Operation Enduring Freedom-Trans Sahara begins operations.
February 13	Negropointe resigns as DNI in order to become deputy secretary of state. Retired admiral John McConnell replaces him as DNI.
February 16	The House passes a non-binding resolution opposing President Bush's proposed troop surge, on a vote of 246 to 182. A filibuster blocks a concurrent measure in the Senate. Bush continues the surge in spite of congressional opposition.
February 26	Iraq government approves measures to manage Iraqi oil resources.
April	Coalition forces intercept a large shipment of Iranian weapons destined for the Taliban.
April 11	International Red Cross issues a report on deteriorating humanitarian conditions in Iraq.
May 1	President Bush vetoes legislation that establishes a withdrawal timetable and exit date for the U.S. occupation of Iraq.
May 12	Mullah Dadullah, senior military commander for the Taliban, is killed by U.S. and UK forces.
May 13	Beginning of a continuing series of minor border skirmishes between the Afghan National Army and Pakistani Armed Forces.
June 16	U.S.-led forces launch Operation Phantom Thunder, the largest military campaign in Iraq since the initial invasion. The operation is designed to suppress the insurgency and reduce sectarian violence.
July 7	International Convention for the Suppression of Acts of Nuclear Terrorism enters into force.
August 3	Congress enacts the Protect America Act of 2007 which amends the 1978 Federal Intelligence Surveillance Act to expand the powers of U.S. intelligence agencies to conduct electronic espionage within the United States.
August 14	Operation Phantom Thunder ends. There are 140 U.S. soldiers killed, along with 240 Iraqi security forces. Estimates are that 1,190 insurgents are killed, and more than 6,700 captured.

August 29	Moqtada al-Sadr orders ceasefire for the Mahdi Army after violence between Shiite factions escalates.
September 29	Karzai offers to allow the Taliban to be part of the government if it renounces violence. The Taliban rejects the initiative and declare they will not negotiate as long as foreign troops are in Afghanistan.
October	Turkish security forces conduct a series of raids into Iraq in an attempt to suppress anti-Turkish Kurdish rebels, based in northern Iraq.
December 17	The United Kingdom turns control of the Basra Province over to Iraq government.
December 31	During 2007, the number of civilian casualties in Iraq is dramatically reduced, falling to 8,000, less than half the number of the previous year.

2008

January 5	Council of Europe Convention on Laundering, Search, Seizure, and Confiscation of the Proceeds from Crime and on the Financing of Terrorism enters into force.
January 8	U.S. and Iraqi forces initiate a large offensive in Mosul, Iraq, against al Qaeda-led insurgents.
January 12	Iraq approves "reconciliation" measure allowing former Ba'ath Party members into civil service and military.
March 24	U.S. casualties in Iraq reach 4,000.
April 27	President Karzai survives an assassination attempt when insurgents attack a military parade in Kabul, Afghanistan.
June 12	Although participants criticize the government for widespread waste and fraud, the Afghan Support Conference pledges $15–20 billion for economic development.
July 7	The Indian embassy is bombed in Kabul, killing 58.
July 10	General David Petraeus takes over U.S. Central Command; General Ray Odiemo takes over Multinational Force in Iraq.
July 14	Iraq calls for timetable for U.S. withdrawal.
July 16	End of U.S. troop "surge" in Iraq that began in 2007.
July 29	U.S. and pro-government Sunni militias attack the remaining al Qaeda stronghold in Iraq. By mid-August, coalition forces have captured or killed more than 4,000 al Qaeda fighters and other insurgents, including 24 senior leaders.

July 30	Executive Order 13470 further enhances the role of the Director of National Intelligence.
October 1	U.S. Africa Command (AFRICOM) begins operations.
September	Bush deploys an additional 4,500 troops to Afghanistan in what was described alternatively as a "mini-surge" or "quiet surge."
September 3	The United States acknowledges for the first time that U.S. special operations forces conducted raids into Pakistan against al Qaeda and Taliban facilities.
November 4	Democrat Barack Obama is elected president of the United States defeating Republican Senator John McCain in a campaign that focused on the deteriorating domestic economy and the war on terror. The Democrats increase their majorities in the House and Senate. In the Senate, the Democrats secure a filibuster-proof majority. Obama retains Gates as secretary of defense to ensure continuity in the military operations in Afghanistan and Iraq.
November 27	Status of Forces Agreements is signed between the United States and Iraq, stipulating a withdrawal of U.S. military forces from Iraq by December 31, 2011.
December 31	By year's end, there are 48,250 U.S. combat troops in Afghanistan. The number of Afghan children enrolled in school has increased from 900,000 in 2001 to 5 million.

2009

January 1	U.S. hands control of Green Zone in Baghdad to Iraq government.
January 5	U.S. Embassy in Baghdad opens.
January 20	Obama is inaugurated as the 44th president of the United States.
January 22	Obama signs executive orders that forbid the torture of prisoners and orders the closure of the detention facility at Guantanamo Bay within one year. The president also suspends the ongoing military tribunals of unlawful enemy combatants.
	Former Senate Majority Leader George Mitchell (Maine) is appointed special envoy for Middle East peace.
February 17	President Obama approves an additional 17,000 troops for Afghanistan.
February 27	Obama announces timeline for withdrawal from Iraq.

March	The Department of Defense is directed by the Obama administration to stop using the phrase "war on terror" and instead use "overseas contingency operations."
March 27	Obama issues a new strategy for Operation Enduring Freedom which calls for U.S. military officials to treat the Afghan and Pakistani insurgencies as a single, integrated conflict.
April	Following a series of meetings between U.S. officials and their NATO counterparts, the alliance agrees to deploy and additional 5,000 troops to Afghanistan.
May 1	The United Kingdom ends combat mission in Iraq.
May 11	General Stanley McChrystal is given command of U.S. forces in Afghanistan in order to implement a new counterinsurgency strategy.
June 4	Obama delivers a major address in Cairo, Egypt, in an effort to reduce anti-American sentiment and reach-out to the Muslim world.
June 30	U.S. turns Iraqi security over to Iraq forces.
July 31	All other remaining coalition troops are withdrawn from Iraq leaving the United States as the remaining foreign force.
August 20	In Afghan presidential elections, Karzai leads the initial balloting, but he fails to gain more than 50 percent of the vote necessitating a run-off election under Afghan law.
November	The Obama administration admits it will not close the Guantanamo Bay detention center by year's end.
November 7	After a run-off is scheduled, Karzai's opponent, former Foreign Minister Abdullah Abdullah, withdraws from the election claiming that the potential for fraud will make any additional balloting illegitimate.
November 19	President Karzai is declared the winner of the contested August balloting and inaugurated for a second term.
December 1	The United States announces that it will deploy an additional 30,000 troops to Afghanistan in a troop surge, bringing the U.S. total in the country to 100,000, out of the 140,000 coalition soldiers.
December 25	Abdul Farouk Abdulmutallab, a Nigerian, is arrested after he unsuccessfully attempts to detonate an underwear bomb onboard Norwest Flight 253 in an incident that came to be known as the "Christmas Day Bombing."

December 31	Unemployment in the United States reaches 10 percent, while the federal budget deficit climbs to 9.91 percent of GDP (the highest level since World War II).

2010s

2010

February 27	Obama signs legislation which extends several controversial provisions of the Patriot Act for an additional year.
March 7	National legislative elections are conducted in Iraq. No single party or coalition gains a majority in the parliament, prompting months of negotiations to form a new government.
April	NATO initiates the "Afghan First" program which calls on the alliance to use local suppliers and contractors in Afghanistan in an effort to improve the Afghan economy and bolster relations between coalition forces and localities.
April 20	An explosion destroys the BP Deepwater Horizon Oil rig in the Gulf of Mexico, causing a massive oil spill in the worst environmental disaster in U.S. history. The Obama administration is criticized for its response to the event which undermines public confidence in the Obama presidency.
May	The Obama administration publishes a new national security strategy.
May 1	Attempted terrorist bombing occurs in Times Square, New York City.
May 10	Obama orders DNI Dennis Blair to resign because of the intelligence failures related to the Christmas Day Bombing and the Times Square Bombing.
May 24	The number of U.S. troops in Afghanistan surpasses the number in Iraq for the first time (94,000 in Afghanistan versus 92,000 in Iraq).
June 2–4	A Loya Jirga appointed by Karzai, and consisting of tribal and clan leaders, meets in Kabul to develop plans to bring peace to Afghanistan. The summit calls for negotiations with moderate Taliban leaders.
June 23	President Obama accepts the resignation of the U.S. military commander in Afghanistan, General Stanley McChrystal, after the general and his staff make disparaging comments about the president and other U.S. political officials.

July	The online watchdog group Wikileaks begins publishing a large cache of classified U.S. documents online. The information had been obtained from an Army intelligence specialist, Bradley Manning. The initial postings were related to Operation Enduring Freedom. Wikileaks releases a second batch of 400,000 documents in October on the Iraq War, and a massive number of diplomatic cables and documents the following month.
August 9	James Clapper becomes DNI.
August 24	U.S. completes withdrawal of more than 90,000 combat troops from Iraq. 49,700 remaining.
August 31	Official end of U.S. combat operations in Iraq.
September 1	Operation New Dawn begins, marking the end of Operation Iraqi Freedom.
November 1	Secure Flight, a TSA-mandated federal program designed to screen all domestic and international passengers aboard commercial flights against "no-fly" lists and other measures, is fully implemented.
November 2	In congressional midterm elections, Republicans gain six seats in the Senate, and regain control of the House of Representatives, by gaining 63 additional seats in balloting that many perceived as a referendum on the Obama presidency.
November 6	Former President Bush praises Obama's troop surge in Afghanistan in his memoirs.
November 11	Prime Minister Maliki is reappointed following months of negotiations over the formation of a new government in Iraq.
November 17	The first federal trial of a Guantanamo Bay detainee is completed in New York.
November 19–20	At the alliance's 2010 Lisbon summit, NATO and Karzai agree to the gradual withdrawal of NATO forces with a target date of 2014 for the removal of all foreign troops.
December 18	Protests in Tunisia against the dictatorial regime of Zine El Abidine Ben Ali mark the beginning of the Arab Spring, a series of popular uprisings against governments in the Middle East. Ali resigns and flees into exile in January 2011.
December 31	By year's end, there are 98,000 U.S. troops, and more than 32,000 soldiers from other countries, in Afghanistan as part of the NATO-led coalition.

2011

January	Congress passes legislation that denies funds to transfer prisoners from Guantanamo Bay to the United States or to try them in federal courts.
February 11	Egyptian president Hosni Mubarak resigns following a series of protests against his regime.
March	As U.S. forces continue to be withdrawn from Iraq, by March, 4,440 American service members had been killed in the Iraq conflict. In Afghanistan, 1,504 U.S. service members had been killed between 2001 and March 2011.
	Obama reverses his earlier decision and orders military tribunals to resume trying court cases for unlawful combatants held at Guantanamo Bay.
March 19	U.S. and allied forces launch attacks against the regime of Libyan leader Muammar Gaddafi in support of anti-government rebels.
May 2	Osama bin Laden is killed in Abbottabad, Pakistan, by U.S. special operations forces.

Biographies

Allawi, Ayad (1945–). Ayad Allawi was a moderate Iraqi Shiite political leader. Born into a wealthy Shiite family, Allawi was an early opponent of the Saddam regime. He spent most of his life in exile and earned a medical degree from the University of London. He helped form one of the largest opposition groups, the Iraqi National Accord (INA). The INA recruited members from the Iraqi military and civil service. It also formed links with the United States and received funding and support from U.S. intelligence agencies. The INA attempted a failed coup against Saddam in 1996 and Allawi's extended family in Iraq suffered various forms of repression because of his involvement. Meanwhile, Allawi would survive three assassination attempts throughout his career. After the invasion of Iraq, Allawi returned to his native country and emerged as a leading political figure among secular Shiites. He was appointed to the interim governing council and later elected to the rotating presidency of the body in October 2003. Meanwhile, the INA transitioned into a formal Iraqi political party. In May 2004, Allawi was appointed Iraq's interim prime minister. He formed a close working relationship with U.S. officials and was instrumental in convincing the Americans to turn political power over to the interim Iraqi government. On June 28, Allawi accepted the transfer of sovereignty from the U.S.-led coalition. His tenure as prime minister was challenged by the rising insurgency, but Allawi endeavored to overcome sectarian divisions and reach out to Sunni, Shiite, and Kurdish groups. The INA placed third in the January 2005 legislative balloting in Iraq. Ibrahim al-Jaafari replaced Allawi as prime minister after the elections. Allawi remained active in politics and formed a new electoral coalition ahead of the 2010 parliamentary elections, the Iraqi National List. The new grouping included a range of secular parties. It narrowly won the balloting and secured 91 seats, but did not capture an absolute majority in the assembly. Negotiations over a new government dragged on for months before incumbent Prime Minister Nouri al-Maliki was able to form a new coalition government. Allawi emerged as the head of the parliamentary opposition and the de facto leader of Iraq's secular parties.

Bin Laden, Osama (1957–2011). Osama Muhammad Awad bin Laden was one of the founders and the leader of the al Qaeda terrorist group. Born to a wealthy Saudi family, bin Laden studied economics before being drawn to fundamentalist Islam. When the Soviets invaded Afghanistan in 1979, bin Laden raised money for the anti-Soviet rebel Mujahedeen and then traveled to Pakistan to train with other insurgents. Bin Laden fought against the Soviets and then formed the Maktab al-Khidimat (MAK). He recruited fighters for the MAK and used his personal fortune to buy weapons. Bin Laden later split with the other MAK leaders because he wanted the group to undertake more combat activities. In 1988, bin Laden founded al Qaeda ("the base" or "foundation"). He sought to create an organization that emphasized the importance of jihad or holy war to liberate Muslim countries from foreign domination and Western culture. The al Qaeda leader asserted that any means were justified in the defense of Islam, including attacks against civilians.

When Iraq invaded Kuwait in 1990, bin Laden offered to raise troops to defend Saudi Arabia in case Iraq took military action against the kingdom. The royal government rejected the offer. Meanwhile, U.S. troops were deployed to Saudi Arabia. Bin Laden became increasingly critical of the Saudi government and the royal family because of his opposition to foreign forces on Saudi soil (which he considered to be a sacrilege). He also began to plan terrorist attacks overseas in countries, including the United States. Saudi authorities expelled bin Laden in 1991, and he returned to Afghanistan, before going into exile in the Sudan. Al Qaeda began to funnel money to, and provide support for, Islamic terrorist groups around the world. Bin Laden and al Qaeda were linked to attacks such as the 1993 World Trade Center bombing. Because of his activities, the Saudis revoked his citizenship in 1994. He was expelled from the Sudan in 1996 and returned to Afghanistan where he established a network of terrorist training camps. He also worked closely with the Taliban and worked with the group to fight the Northern Alliance. In 1998, bin Laden issued a religious decree or fatwa that called on Muslims to attack Americans and their allies. He began to plan for ever larger attacks on the United States and its interests and was responsible for financing the 1998 Embassy Bombings in Kenya and Tanzania.

President William J. Clinton responded to the embassy bombings with missile strikes on suspected al Qaeda camps in Afghanistan and Sudan. Meanwhile, bin Laden and his al Qaeda leadership continued to plan and fund additional attacks. By 2001, al Qaeda had become a series of loosely affiliated terrorist groups around the world. Bin Laden essentially functioned as a figure head for the organization, and worked to provide funding and support for terrorist operations. These included, most notably, the failed 1999 Millennium Bombing Plots, the 2000 USS *Cole* Bombing, and the 9/11 terrorist attacks. After the terrorist attacks of 9/11, the Bush administration indicted bin Laden on charges related to the terrorist attacks. During Operation Enduring Freedom the U.S.-led coalition overthrew the Taliban, but failed to capture bin Laden and the senior leadership of al Qaeda.

Bin Laden subsequently operated from a series of clandestine bases in Pakistan and remained al Qaeda's spiritual leader. He continued to promote radical, extremist Islam through videos and communiqués until his death on May 1, 2011, during an operation by U.S. special operations forces.

Blair, Tony (1953–). Tony Blair served as prime minister of the United Kingdom from 1997 to 2007. During his tenure Blair was a close ally of the United States and expanded the special relationship between the United States and Great Britain. Blair won his first parliamentary seat as a member of the Labour Party in 1983 and became leader of the party in 1994. He endeavored to move the Labour Party to the political center and rejected many of the more left-wing policy stances that had been hallmarks of the party. In 1997, Labour won a majority in the parliamentary elections, for the first time in nearly two decades. Blair, at 44 years old, subsequently became the youngest British prime minister of the twentieth century. As prime minister, Blair focused his foreign policy around improving relations with the European Union while maintaining the strong relationship with the U.S. Blair endorsed the continuation of sanctions on Iraq following the first Gulf War and continued to support the Gulf War–era no-fly zones over Iraq. In 1998, Blair was instrumental in securing NATO approval for a humanitarian intervention in the Kosovo conflict.

Blair responded to the 9/11 terrorist attacks by offering the United States a range of military and diplomatic support. The British government provided forces for Operation Enduring Freedom in Afghanistan and increased intelligence and law enforcement cooperation with the United States. Blair and U.S. president George W. Bush formed a close working relationship that characterized Anglo-American relations for the remainder of Blair's tenure.

The prime minister worked with Bush and other allies in an unsuccessful effort to gain a United Nations resolution specifically authorizing the use of force in Iraq after the adoption of Security Council Resolution 1441. Blair subsequently supported the U.S.-led invasion of Iraq and the United Kingdom provided the second largest-troop commitment throughout Operation Iraqi Freedom. Domestic opposition to the Iraq War undermined Blair's popularity, but he gained reelection in 2005, albeit with a reduced majority in Parliament. Opposition to the war continued to grow, especially after revelations that the Blair government relied on faulty intelligence in making its public case for war to the British people.

Blair resigned as prime minister in 2007. His ten-year tenure made him the longest-serving Labour prime minister in British history. Blair subsequently became an international diplomat. He represented the United Nations, EU, United States, and Russia as a special envoy to the Middle East.

Bush, George W. (1946–). Republican George Walker Bush served as the 43rd president of the United States from 2000 until 2008. Bush is the son of the 41st president of the United States, George H. W. Bush, and was raised in Midland,

Texas. The future president completed his undergraduate degree at his father's alma mater, Yale, and then received a master's of business administration (MBA) from Harvard in 1975 (Bush became the first president with an MBA). Bush married Laura Welch in 1977; the couple had two children. After college and service in the Air National Guard, Bush worked in the oil industry in Texas for over a decade. In 1989 he became part owner of the baseball team the Texas Rangers.

Bush's first foray into politics resulted in failure. He unsuccessfully ran for Congress as a Republican in 1978. His first successful political campaign was the 1994 gubernatorial race in Texas, where his popularity as owner of the Rangers and son of the former president. He served as governor of Texas from 1995 to 2001.

In 2000, Bush was elected president in contested balloting in which he won the majority of the Electoral College votes, but lost the popular to his Democratic opponent, Vice President Al Gore (the election was decided after a series of court cases and a controversial ballot recount). Upon entering office Bush focused on domestic issues, including the enactment of $1.3 trillion in tax cuts and educational reform, the No Child Left Behind initiative. The tax cut initiative prompted Republican senator Jim Jeffords (Vermont) to resign from the GOP, thereby giving Democrats control of the Senate.

Bush initially pursued a controversial foreign policy. His administration did not support the Kyoto Protocol, a UN-backed climate control initiative, arguing that the measure would undermine the U.S. economy since developing nations such as China and India would be exempted from some provisions of the Protocol. Bush was also criticized for his decision to pursue a ballistic missile defense system and his later withdrawal from the 1972 Anti-Ballistic Missile Treaty between the United States and Russia.

The 9/11 al Qaeda terrorist attacks defined the Bush presidency and transformed his government into a wartime administration. Bush enjoyed tremendous popular and political support in the aftermath of the attacks, and the United States regained a significant amount of international goodwill. A range of individual countries and international organizations, including the UN, NATO, and the EU, provided various forms of military, intelligence, law-enforcement and diplomatic cooperation. The broad, anti-terrorism effort was dubbed the war on terror.

Bush secured a congressional authorization to use military force against the Taliban and al Qaeda. The United States subsequently led an invasion of Afghanistan (Operation Enduring Freedom) on October 7, 2001. U.S. and coalition special operations forces worked with anti-Taliban factions, including the Northern Alliance, to combat the Taliban and al Qaeda. Coalition forces and their anti-Taliban allies quickly overran enemy positions through a combination of aerial and missile strikes. By the end of November, the Taliban and its al Qaeda allies had been overthrown. Afghan opposition figure Hamid Karzai was subsequently appointed president of Afghanistan. The United States initiated an effort to secure international aid and undertake economic reconstruction. Following the defeat of the Taliban, the United States maintained about 20,000 troops in the country to provide security. A UN-authorized international security force was also deployed to Afghanistan, and in 2006 NATO took command of coalition security operations in the country.

The Bush administration sought to promote democracy and free trade as part of its foreign policy, concurrent with the war on terror. Bush supported the expansion of NATO to countries in Central and Eastern Europe, including states that had been satellites of the former Soviet Union. During Bush's tenure, NATO added seven new members, and approved the ascension of an additional two (who formally joined the alliance in 2009). The Bush administration supported democracy movements in various countries, including Lebanon and Ukraine. The Bush administration undertook several efforts to resolve the Arab-Israeli conflict. The central initiative was the "roadmap for peace" which called for Israel to withdraw from Palestinian land, with the ultimate goal of the creation of a Palestinian state. In exchange, the plan called on the Palestinian government to recognize the state of Israel and conduct democratic elections.

Bush's public approval ratings soared to record levels in the aftermath of 9/11. He had the highest approval numbers ever recorded for a U.S. president. Bush used his domestic popularity and increased political clout to enact a number of initiatives in the war on terror. His administration oversaw the greatest reorganization of the federal bureaucracy since World War II when it consolidated 22 agencies and bureaus and 180,000 federal employees into the newly created Department of Homeland Security (DHS) in 2002 (the DHS became the third largest federal agency). In addition, Congress enacted the Patriot Act in 2001. The measure dramatically increased the surveillance and detention powers of the federal government and expanded the scope of what was defined as terrorism. The act was the centerpiece of Bush's domestic counterterrorism efforts. However, civil libertarians criticized the measures for infringing on the individual and group freedoms of Americans. Bush and his administration were also criticized for America's detention and treatment of captured fighters in the war on terror. These fighters were designated unlawful enemy combatants and held at a detention facility in Guantanamo Bay, Cuba. Civil libertarians argued that the detainees should be tried in federal courts, while the Bush administration instead ordered the use of military tribunals to try the terrorists and insurgents. Meanwhile, revelations that the Bush administrations used rendition, torture, and black sites undermined the image and prestige of Bush and his officials.

In his 2002 State of the Union address, Bush labeled Iran, Iraq, and North Korea as members of an "axis of evil," and pledged to undertake preemptive military action to prevent a WMD attack on the United States. Bush's pledge was codified in the 2002 *National Security Strategy of the United States*. The document called for the preemptive use of force to protect the United States from imminent threats and pledged U.S. support for democratization and was the basis for the Bush Doctrine. Bush and members of his administration subsequently began to argue for the use of force against Iraq if the regime of Saddam Hussein did not allow international WMD inspections and comply with past UN Security Council Resolutions. Bush secured a congressional authorization to use force against Iraq in October 2002 and a UN Security Council resolution which threatened "serious consequences" if Iraq did not allow WMD inspections. Bush faced domestic and international criticism for not allowing UN inspections more time before a U.S.-led coalition began military action against Iraq in March 2003. Coalition forces quickly toppled the Saddam regime and had captured Baghdad in April. However, the conflict created serious diplomatic cleavages with traditional U.S. allies such as France, Germany, and Turkey. A post-invasion insurgency spread throughout Iraq and created more U.S. casualties than had the initial combat. By the time Bush left office, more than 4,000 U.S. troops had been killed in Iraq. A troop surge of more than 30,000 soldiers in 2007 helped significantly reduce violence in Iraq and Bush subsequently approved a plan to withdraw U.S. forces from Iraq by the end of 2011.

The continuing insurgency in Iraq undermined Bush's domestic popularity, as did his administration's response to Hurricane Katrina in 2005 (the largest natural disaster in U.S. history). The administration was criticized for the slow and inadequate delivery of aid in the immediate aftermath of the storm. By 2006, Bush's approval ratings had dropped below 50 percent. Partially as a result of this decline, Democrats regained control of both houses of Congress in the 2006 midterm elections.

Among his other foreign policy initiatives was a $15 billion aid package to African states to combat the spread of HIV/AIDS. Bush also attempted with some success to initiate international action to address the humanitarian crisis in Darfur. The Bush administration endeavored to use diplomacy and sanctions to resolve a crisis over North Korea's nuclear program following nuclear tests by that country in 2006.

When Bush left office in 2009, his public approval rating was the lowest ever recorded, making Bush the chief executive with both the highest and lowest approval ratings.

Cheney, Richard B. "Dick" (1941–). In the aftermath of the 9/11 terrorist attacks, Richard "Dick" Bruce Cheney emerged as one of the most influential and public vice presidents in American history. Cheney had a long public career which began in 1969 as an assistant to Donald Rumsfeld in the administration of President Richard M. Nixon. Cheney went on to be appointed the youngest White House chief of staff in 1975, and then serve in the House of Representatives (1979–1989). He was secretary of defense under President George W. Bush, where he oversaw the 1989 invasion of Panama and the 1991 Persian Gulf War. In that post, he worked closely with General Colin Powell, the chairman of the Joint Chiefs of Staff. After Bush left office in 1993, Cheney had a successful business career.

George W. Bush chose Cheney to be his running mate in the 2000 election. Unlike other vice presidents who assumed a mainly ceremonial role, Cheney distinguished himself early in the Bush presidency as a strategist and policy entrepreneur. He was responsible for convincing the new president to appoint Powell as secretary of state and Rumsfeld as secretary of defense. Many described Cheney's role as that of a chief operating officer, one that managed many of the day-to-day operations of the White House. Significantly, the vice president's staff worked more closely with the White House staff than had ever been the case. Consequently, even Cheney's aides exerted an unprecedented degree of influence in the administration.

When the Bush administration first took office, the Senate was evenly divided between Republicans and Democrats. Since the vice president was constitutionally the president of the Senate, Cheney cast the deciding vote on measures in which there was a tie. This gave the Republicans a de facto majority in the chamber until Vermont senator Jim Jeffords resigned from the Republican Party over a disagreement with Bush over the president's 2001 tax cuts. In addition to his role in the Senate, Cheney also maintained a high degree of influence in the House. He had retained relationships with many senior House members from his own time in the chamber. Cheney also arranged to have an office in the House office building in order to regularly meet with members of the chamber.

Following the 9/11 terrorist attacks, Cheney's influence in the administration increased. The president came to rely on his vice president's advice and counsel. Cheney was a staunch proponent of increasing counterterrorism measures to protect U.S. infrastructure, including power plants, transportation networks and ports and airports. He played a role in the creation of the Office, and later Department, of Homeland Security and the formulation of the Patriot Act. Cheney also successfully argued for an expansion of the war on terrorism beyond Afghanistan. He believed that the United States should provide military and economic assistance to countries around the world that were fighting terrorist insurgencies.

Cheney exerted significant influence among the National Security Council. The vice president was a leading neoconservative who contended that the United States should use its power and influence to promote democracy and freedom around the world, even if it meant the use of the military, or the threat of the use of force. Cheney's influence was magnified because of the presence of like-minded allies in the administration, including Rumsfeld and Deputy Secretary of Defense Paul Wolfowitz. The vice president emerged as the leader of the hawkish wing of the administration, as opposed to the moderate faction, led by Powell. Cheney and his allies played an instrumental role in the development of the Bush Doctrine and its assertion that the United States would undertake preemptive military action to ameliorate prevent significant threats to America, including the threat posed by WMDs.

Cheney argued strongly for military action against Iraq. He emerged as the administration's leading public proponent for the use of force against the regime of Saddam Hussein. After the fall of Saddam, Cheney remained the staunchest defender of the invasion, even as the insurgency in Iraq grew and the war became increasingly unpopular domestically. Cheney's hawkish approach to foreign and security policy made him unpopular with moderates and liberals in Congress. In addition, the vice president faced a number of ethical issues, including concerns over his management of a 2002 energy task force, because of Cheney's resistance to having records of the body's meeting made public. Questions also arose over the vice president's connections with the Halliburton Corporation, where Cheney had previously served as chief executive officer, and the company's ability to secure contracts for Iraqi security and reconstruction contracts. Declining public popularity, combined with concerns over Cheney's health (he had four heart attacks before he entered office), led to speculation that, first, Bush would replace him prior to the 2004 balloting, and later that Cheney would resign after the 2006 elections. However, he remained in office until 2009.

Chirac, Jacques (1932–). Jacques Rene Chirac was president of France from 1995 to 2007. In 1932, Chirac was born in Paris and received a prestigious education, before entering a career in politics in 1962. He served under various French prime ministers and was elected to the National Assembly in 1967. In 1974, President Giscard d'Estaing appointed Chirac prime minister, a post he held for two years. Chirac became the leader of the main French conservative party, and in 1977, he was elected mayor of Paris, France's capital and largest city. From 1977 to 1995, Chirac remained mayor of Paris and was a deputy in the National Assembly.

In 1995, Chirac was elected president of France. He had spent time in the United States as a youth and was initially the most pro-American French president to that time. Chirac worked to repair tensions between the two countries on a number of issues, including French participation in NATO (France had withdrawn from NATO's integrated military command structure in 1966) and international efforts to end ongoing conflicts in the Balkans. Tensions between the two countries did emerge after Chirac insisted on the continuation of French nuclear tests in the South Pacific. In addition, Chirac sought to end international sanctions on the Iraq regime of Saddam Hussein.

Chirac responded to the 9/11 terrorist attacks with full diplomatic, military, intelligence, and law enforcement support and cooperation. France volunteered forces for Operation Enduring Freedom and collaborated with the administration of President George W. Bush in efforts to combat terrorism in Africa and Asia. However, Chirac vehemently opposed the invasion of Iraq. Instead he argued for expanded UN WMD inspections in Iraq. During the diplomatic wrangling over a possible UN resolution specifically authorizing the use of force, France consistently threatened to veto any measure permitting military action (along with fellow permanent Security Council member Russia). Opposition to the Iraq War bolstered Chirac's popularity domestically on the eve of national elections in France in 2002. He won reelection after far-right-wing candidate Jean-Marie Le Pen placed second in the balloting and forced a run-off election (most liberals and socialists voted for Chirac rather than Le Pen).

Chirac faced a range of domestic problems during his second term, including allegations of corruption and urban riots. However, he endeavored to repair relations with the United States. France increased its troop strength in Afghanistan and cooperated with the Bush administration on other international security issues, including efforts to prevent Iran from developing nuclear weapons. Chirac left office on May 16, 2007. In May 2011, a corruption trial began for Chirac and nine other officials accused of abusing their offices by providing jobs for friends and supporters.

Clinton, Hillary R. (1947–). Hillary Rodham Clinton was first lady of the United States during her husband President Bill Clinton's two terms in office, before being elected a U.S. senator and then appointed secretary of state in the administration of President Barack Obama. She was the first first lady to hold elected office. Clinton was born in Chicago in 1947. While in law school at Yale University, Clinton worked for several political campaigns, including George McGovern's 1972 presidential bid. In 1973, after graduation from Yale, Clinton worked for the Judiciary Committee of the House of Representatives during Richard M. Nixon's 1973 impeachment. She later took a faculty position at the University of Arkansas Law School and married Bill Clinton on 1975. She continued in private practice after her husband was elected governor in 1978. She was the first lady of Arkansas for 12 of the next 14 years. During this period, Clinton concentrated on her legal career.

In 1992, Bill Clinton was elected president and Hillary became first lady of the United States. She sought an expanded role as first lady with some policy influence. In 1993, she was appointed to chair the Task Force on National Health Care Reform. The resultant recommendations of the body were perceived as too liberal and provoked a backlash that allowed the Republicans to recapture control of both houses of Congress in the 1994 midterm elections. Clinton shifted her focus to broader issues such as the global movement for women's rights and domestic children's healthcare. Her role in domestic issues was muted throughout the remainder of the Clinton presidency, although she helped initiate the 1997 Children's Health Insurance Program which provided federal funds to states to insure otherwise uninsured minors. She also authorized two successful children's book. Throughout her marriage, Clinton faced a series of marital infidelities and stood by her husband during his impeachment in 1998–1999.

In the waning days of her husband's presidency, party leaders urged Clinton to use her fame to seek an open Senate seat in New York. She was not a resident of the New York, but the first family purchased a home in the state and she declared her candidacy. Clinton initially faced a difficult opponent in New York mayor Rudy Giuliani. Clinton ran a centrist campaign which emphasized job creation and targeted incentives for higher education and healthcare. Giuliani withdrew after he was diagnosed with prostate cancer. Clinton defeated the GOP replacement candidate, Rick Lazio, by a margin of 55 percent to 43 percent.

Once in office, Clinton became an advocate for homeland security. She voted in favor of the 2001 Patriot Act and the 2001 Authorization to Use Force in Afghanistan. In 2002, she voted to approve military action against Iraq. Clinton voted for the 2002 Homeland Security Act and to confirm Homeland Security Secretary Tom Ridge. Clinton also supported increases in the defense budget and an expansion of the size of the U.S. military. By 2005, she became increasingly critical of the Bush administration's management of the Iraq conflict. She subsequently called for the resignation of Defense Secretary Donald Rumsfeld, but refused to call for a set timetable for withdrawal from Iraq, a stance that put her at odds with the anti-war wing of the Democratic Party.

On domestic and social issues, Clinton established a more liberal record. She voted in favor of Bush's educational initiative, the 2001 No Child Left Behind Act, but opposed the administration's tax cut proposals. She voted against the 2003 Partial Birth Abortion Ban. Clinton opposed Bush's more conservative judicial nominees and voted against the nominations of future Supreme Court justices John Roberts and Samuel Alito. She also voted against the 2004 and 2006 proposed constitutional amendments to ban same-sex marriage, as well as the 2006 proposed amendment to ban on flag desecration. She was highly critical of the Bush administration's management of the relief effort following Hurricane Katrina in 2005. She proposed the creation of an independent investigative body, similar to the 9/11 Commission, but her legislation was defeated in the Senate. In 2003, she was given a record advance of $8 million for her autobiography, *Living History.*

Clinton was reelected in 2006. She unsuccessfully campaigned for the Democratic presidential nomination in 2008, but lost to Obama, who went on to win the general election. Clinton was subsequently appointed secretary of state. She formed a close working relationship with Secretary of Defense Robert Gates, but publicly declared her intention to resign rather than serve a second term if Obama was reelected.

Gaddafi, Muammar (1942–). Muammar Abu Minyar al-Gaddafi has been the dictator of Libya since 1969. Gaddafi was born in the desert outside of Sirt, Libya, in 1942. After graduating from Libya's national military academy, Gaddafi was commissioned in the Libyan Army in 1966. Three years later, he participated in a military coup that deposed the country's monarchy. A military government was put in power and Gaddafi emerged as the leader of the country, despite his relative youth (he was 27 years old). The new leader embarked on a program that he terms "Islamic Socialism" in which he attempted to integrate Arab nationalism with a socialist economy. Major industries, including the energy sector, were nationalized under government control. Meanwhile, the Libyan leader endeavored to convince other Arab leaders to create a grand federation of states in the Middle East as a means to counter the global influence of the United States and Western Europe. Gaddafi was also a major supporter of the PLO, providing financial and military assistance to the group in their armed struggle against Israel. Under Gaddafi, Libya also supported a number of Islamic terrorist groups. Terrorist training facilities were established in several locations in Libya, and even non-Islamic groups such as the Irish Republican Army received funding and training from the Gaddafi regime.

Although his dictatorial regime did not tolerate political dissent, Gaddafi did use proceeds from the country's oil and gas exports to significantly improve and expand social programs for Libyans. Housing, education, and health care programs were dramatically expanded throughout Libya during his tenure. However, political opponents were routinely jailed, tortured, and even executed. In 1993, disaffected military officers attempted unsuccessfully to assassinate Gaddafi and overthrow his government.

Through the 1980s and 1990s, relations were increasingly strained between the United States and Libya. In 1982, the administration of President Ronald W. Reagan placed economic sanctions on Libya because of the regime's support of international terrorism. The action angered Gaddafi, who increasingly supported anti-U.S. terrorism. Libya was behind the 1986 Berlin Disco Bombing in which terrorists targeted a nightclub in Berlin that was frequented by U.S. service personnel. The attack killed three and injured over 200. In response, Reagan ordered airstrikes on Libya and deployed naval forces in waters claimed by the Gaddafi regime.

In 1988, Pan Am Flight 103 exploded over Lockerbie, Scotland killing 189. Up to that point it was the worst terrorist strike against American civilians. Intelligence revealed that Libya had been behind the attack. In response, the international community, led by the United Nations, imposed economic and military sanctions on the Gaddafi regime. After intense negotiations Gaddafi agreed to turn over two suspects in the Lockerbie bombing. Libya formally accepted responsibility for the bombing in 2003 and agreed to pay $270 million to the families of the victims of the attack. The United Nations and most European states subsequently repealed sanctions against Libya.

Gaddafi perceived al Qaeda as a threat to his regime and waged a lengthy campaign against al Qaeda-backed terrorists in Libya. He condemned the 9/11 attacks and offered limited intelligence cooperation to the United States and European nations. Following the overthrow of the Iraqi regime of Saddam Hussein, Gaddafi pledged to dismantle his WMD programs and offered to allow international monitors to verify the destruction of existing WMD stockpiles. In response to continued cooperation the administration of President George W. Bush ended economic sanctions against Libya in 2003. Three years later, the Bush administration restored full diplomatic relations with the Gaddafi regime. Libya was also removed from the State Department's list of state-sponsors of terrorism. U.S. energy companies began to invest in Libya's oil and gas industry.

In 2009, Gaddafi successfully negotiated a deal with the British government to allow convicted Lockerbie bomber Abdelbaset Megrahi to return to Libya after being released from a Scottish prison on humanitarian grounds. The release was condemned by several world leaders. In 2007 and 2008, Gaddafi signed new economic agreements with a range of countries, including France and Italy. In the first official visit from a U.S. secretary of state since 1953, Condoleezza Rice traveled to Libya in September 2008. In 2011, President Barack Obama ordered air and missile strikes against Libya after a UN resolution authorized a no-fly zone over the country following a rebellion against the Gaddafi regime.

Gates, Robert M. (1943–). Robert Michael Gates had a long and distinguished career as a public servant and served as secretary of defense under presidents Bush and Obama. Gates was born in Wichita, Kansas, and earned a PhD in history from Georgetown University in 1974. Meanwhile, Gates served in the Air Force and in the CIA. In 1974, he was appointed to the staff of the National Security Council. He subsequently served in a variety of posts in the CIA before being appointed director of the agency in 1991. He resigned from the CIA two years later and became an academic, eventually becoming president of Texas A&M University in 2002.

After Donald Rumsfeld resigned as secretary of defense in 2006, Bush appointed Gates to replace him. Gates had a reputation for honesty and directness with Congress, which helped reduce tensions between the executive and legislative branches on defense issues during the final years of the Bush presidency. He subsequently oversaw the troop surge in Iraq and coordinated the strategy that led to reduced violence in the country. After Obama was elected in 2008, the new president asked Gates to remain in office in order to provide continuity in the military campaigns in Afghanistan and Iraq. He became the first secretary of defense to remain in office following the election of a new president. Gates managed the withdrawal of combat troops from Iraq in 2010 and the Afghan troop surge.

Giuliani, Rudolph W. L. "Rudy" (1944–). A moderate Republican, Rudolph "Rudy" Giuliani served two terms as the mayor of New York and led the city's response to the 9/11 terrorist attacks. The son of Italian immigrants, Giuliani became a lawyer and then joined the Office of the U.S. Attorney in 1970. In

1981, he was appointed associate attorney general in the Reagan administration and then U.S. attorney for southern New York. Giuliani prosecuted a number of high profile cases and sought to use his fame to become New York's mayor in 1989; however, he narrowly lost the race to Democrat David Dinkins. In 1993, Giuliani launched a pro-business campaign, anti-crime campaign and became the first Republican elected mayor of New York since 1969.

During his first term, Giuliani initiated a series of programs that significantly reduced crime (a decrease of 57 percent during his tenure). The mayor also launched several urban renewal programs, including a renovation of Times Square, and oversaw reforms to the city administration. Giuliani reduced taxes in the city by $2.5 billion, but still managed to turn a $2.3 billion deficit into a surplus. He was reelected by a landslide in 1997. In 1999, Giuliani announced his intent to seek an open Senate seat for New York (his Democratic opponent was Hillary Rodham Clinton). Giuliani's moderate social policies alienated the state's conservatives and constrained his fundraising efforts. He withdrew from the race in 2000 after he was diagnosed with prostate cancer and amid a public divorce.

Although he had already had a long and distinguished career, the defining moment of Giuliani's career was the 2001 terrorist attacks on New York's World Trade Center. Giuliani oversaw the rescue efforts and coordinated the combined local, state and federal initiatives in the aftermath of the attacks in New York. He also emerged as the defiant public face of the city during the crisis. Giuliani was wide praised for his leadership and named *Time*'s man of the year in 2001. The mayor lent his support to an effort that would have extended his term under emergency legislation; however, the state majority of the legislature opposed the extension and Giuliani left office on December 31, 2001.

After he left office, Giuliani engaged in private practice and became a consultant, including service as a homeland security advisor to the Mexican government. He campaigned for George W. Bush in the 2004 election and was offered the position of secretary of the Department of Homeland Security following the election. He declined. In 2006, Giuliani also rejected calls for him to run against Clinton in that year's senatorial race or to campaign for the governorship of New York. Giuliani conducted an unsuccessful bid to capture the Republican presidential nomination in 2008.

Hastert, John Dennis (1942–). Dennis Hastert was elected speaker of the House in 1999 following the resignation of Newt Gingrich. Hastert's low-key style contrasted with that of his predecessor and he was initially seen as a speaker who could build bipartisan consensus on most issues. On January 6, 1999, Hastert was the first speaker of the House to deliver his acceptance speech from the floor of the House as opposed to the speaker's podium. In addition, Hastert allowed Minority Leader Richard Gephardt to preside over the House for a short period as a signal of his bipartisanship. Also, unlike Gingrich, Hastert made it clear that he did not have aspirations for higher office.

Hastert and the senior Republican leadership in the House were able to maintain party discipline to a great degree and regularly enact legislation, despite a limited majority of less than twelve seats in the 106th and 107th Congresses. Under Hastert, the House regularly passed conservative bills only to have them blocked in the more moderate Senate. For instance, the House passed the Bush administration's energy bill, which included provisions to allow drilling in the Alaska National Wildlife Refuge, only to have the measure defeated in successive sessions of the Senate. Among Hastert's legislative priorities were tax reductions, Social Security reform and strengthening national security. Hastert has repeatedly announced support for various plans to replace the income tax with a national sales tax.

In the 107th Congress, Hastert led the effort to enact the Bush administration's No Child Left Behind educational program (2002) and tax reductions. The speaker also oversaw the passage of a range of national security programs, including the Patriot Act (2001), the creation of the Office, and later Department, of Homeland Security (2002), and the authorization to use force against Iraq (2002). An initiative to reform campaign laws, created divisions within the GOP, but Hastert was able to secure bipartisan support to pass the measure. Commonly known as the McCain-Feingold Law (named after its cosponsors, Republican John McCain of Arizona and Democrat Russ Feingold of Wisconsin), the measure became law in 2002. Hastert campaigned vigorously for fellow Republicans in the 2002 midterm elections and the GOP increased its majority in the House by eight seats.

In the 108th Congress, Hastert implemented a conservative agenda that included passage of additional tax cuts and the Ban on Partial Birth Abortions (2004). Other significant measures from the session were the Medicare Prescription Drug Benefit (2003) which was the most significant reform to the program since its inception. In the 2004 elections, the Republicans further increased their majority in the House by three seats. Hastert's leadership team was by beset by ethical problems in the 109th Congress. House Majority Leader, Tom Delay of Texas, resigned his post in 2005 after being indicted for violations of campaign finance laws. Hastert faced questions over campaign contributions to his 2004 reelection bid and turned $70,000 in questionable donations over to charitable organizations. Additional tax cuts were enacted in the 109th Congress, as was emergency funding in the aftermath of Hurricane Katrina in 2005. Meanwhile, both parties sought to gain political advantage ahead of the 2006 midterm elections which constrained Hastert's legislative agenda and put Republican control of the House in jeopardy. Hastert did not seek a leadership position in the House after the Republican defeat in 2006, and resigned from Congress the following year.

Hekmatyar, Gulbuddin (1947–). Gulbuddin Hekmatyar was a former Mujahedeen and Afghan warlord. Hekmatyar formed an Afghan opposition group, Hezb-i-Islami ("The Islamic Party") in 1977. Following the Soviet invasion of

Afghanistan in 1979, Hekmatyar emerged as an important Mujahedeen leader. By the mid-1980s, his group had developed ties with both Libya and Iran, who supplied funding and munitions. Hekmatyar also received significant backing from Pakistan. Following the Soviet withdrawal, Hekmatyar was appointed prime minister of Afghanistan in 1993. However, he lost his position in 1994 and joined the opposing side in the ongoing Afghan civil war. Hekmatyar again served as prime minister in 1996, but was forced from office when the Taliban captured Kabul. The former Mujahedeen leader and his Islamic Party fought the Taliban over the next several years. During Operation Enduring Freedom, Hekmatyar resolved his differences with the Taliban and opposed the U.S.-led invasion. By 2002, the Islamic Party had joined the growing Taliban-led insurgency in Afghanistan. Pressure from the United States and Afghanistan forced Iran and Pakistan to close offices of the Islamic party in their countries. On May 6, 2002, Hekmatyar survived a U.S. airstrike on a convoy he was traveling with, and the former Mujahedeen subsequently urged his followers to undertake a jihad against the United States and the international coalition. By 2003, Hekmatyar was the most significant, non-Taliban Afghan warlord who was fighting the government of Hamid Karzai and the U.S.-led coalition. Hekmatyar and his supporters became increasingly involved in opium production, using funds from the illicit drug trade to finance military operations. Although the Afghan warlord denied any formal alliance with the Taliban or al Qaeda, his forces increasingly cooperated with other insurgency groups to fight international troops. Meanwhile, moderates within the Islamic Party sought reconciliation with the central government and in 2010, the group split into rival factions.

Hussein, Saddam (1937–2006). Saddam Hussein Abd al-Majidida al-Tikriti served as president of Iraq from 1979 until 2003. Saddam was born in 1937 near Tikrit, Iraq. He joined the Ba'ath Party in 1957. The group was an opposition party dedicated to the overthrow of the Iraqi monarchy. After the king was deposed, Saddam participated in an unsuccessful U.S.-backed coup attempt to overthrow the anti-Western government of Abd al Karim Qasim. The Ba'ath succeeded in deposing Qasim in 1963. Thereafter, Saddam rose quickly through the ranks of the party. In 1969, he was appointed a deputy to the Iraqi president and promoted to general in the Army in 1976. Three years later he forced President Ahmad Hassan al Bakr to retire and appointed himself leader of Iraq.

Saddam initially enjoyed diplomatic, financial and military support from the United States and other Western powers. He emerged as a fervent anti-communist and took steps to combat Islamic fundamentalism. After the Iranian Revolution, he appeared to be the Arab leader best able to balance the increasingly fundamentalist Iranian government. Domestically, Saddam introduced a number of reforms that led to increasing economic prosperity. He also increased social services, including education and healthcare. Iraq was divided along ethnic and religious lines, and Saddam utilized brutal suppression to end sectional strife. His regime also brutally repressed opposition figures and political groupings. Campaigns against the Kurds in Northern Iraq in the late 1980s and against the Shiites in the South, killed more than 300,000.

In 1980, Saddam launched an eight-year war against Iran. The conflict was marked by intense combat that left almost a million soldiers and civilians dead on both sides. The United States and other Western powers, principally France, backed Iraq in the war and provided the Saddam regime with weapons and munitions. During the war, Saddam authorized the use of chemical weapons at a point when the Iranians appeared to be gaining the upper hand. His regime also used chemical weapons to suppress Iraqi civilians. The war ended in a stalemate in 1988, but left Iraq with a massive $75 billion foreign debt. Meanwhile, an Iraqi program to develop nuclear weapons was forestalled in 1981, when Israeli aircraft bombed the nation's main nuclear reactor and nuclear research facility.

Tensions between Iraq and Kuwait escalated rapidly after the end of the Iran-Iraq War. Saddam was convinced that the Kuwaitis were exceeding their oil production quotas established by the Organization of Petroleum Exporting Countries (OPEC), and therefore causing fuel prices to decline. He also believed that the Kuwaitis were illegally taping into Iraqi oil reserves. In August 1990, Iraq invaded and quickly overran Kuwait. Reports at the time indicated that Saddam did not believe that the United States or other countries would take military action to defend Kuwait. However, the administration of President George H. W. Bush secured a series of UN Security Council resolutions that condemned the invasion and threatened strong action if Iraq did not withdraw. The United States assembled a massive coalition of countries opposed to the occupation of Kuwait and launched a military offensive against Iraq in January 1991. Coalition force quickly defeated the Iraqi forces and recaptured Kuwait. Saddam was forced to accept a ceasefire in March. Under the agreement that ended the war, Saddam agreed to abide by a series of UN resolutions that called for Iraq to dismantle its WMD programs under international monitoring. In addition, no fly zones were established over Northern and Southern Iraq in an effort to prevent the suppression of the Kurds and Shiites. Economic and military sanctions were also levied against Iraq.

During the 1990s, Saddam resisted compliance with the UN resolutions and repeatedly challenged the no fly zones and avoided cooperation with the WMD inspections. In 1993, Iraqi intelligence agents attempted to assassinate former President Bush, prompting airstrikes by the United States. After Iraq expelled UN WMD inspectors in 1998, the U.S. and the UK responded with airstrikes and cruise missile attacks. Meanwhile, on October 31, 1998, President Bill Clinton signed the Iraq Liberation Act which called for an end to the Saddam regime and committed the United States to provide aid to anti-Saddam groups.

After the 9/11 attacks, U.S. intelligence officials accused the Saddam regime of supporting anti-American terrorist groups. In January 2002, President George W.

Bush labeled Iraq as a part of an "axis of evil" that included Iran and North Korea. The Bush administration subsequently launched an international effort to force Iraq to again permit WMD inspections. UN Security Council Resolution 1441 ordered Iraq to resume inspections or face "serious consequences" and in October 2002, the U.S. Congress authorized the use of force against Iraq. The Saddam regime initially endeavored to obstruct the inspections, but became increasingly cooperative in the spring of 2003. However, the Bush administration charged that the Iraqis remained non-compliant and the U.S. president gave Saddam a 48-hour ultimatum to leave Iraq in March 2003. Saddam refused and instead resolved to fight the U.S.-led coalition. At the onset of the war, the Iraqi leader remained more concerned with the prospects for an internal revolt than the danger of the American-led forces. Coalition troops quickly overwhelmed the Iraqis and captured Baghdad on April 9. Saddam and his family and closest advisors went into hiding. He was captured by U.S. forces on December 13 in northern Iraq.

The United States turned Saddam over to Iraqi authorities who charged the former dictator with a range of offensives. On November 5, 2006, after a lengthy trial, Saddam was convicted of ordering the execution of more than 100 Shiites in the 1980s and was sentenced to be executed. He was hanged on December 30, 2006.

Karzai, Hamid (1957–). Hamid Karzai was the first post-Taliban leader of Afghanistan and the first freely elected president in the country's history. In 1957, Karzai was born in Kandahar to a prominent Pashtun family. He was educated in India, and moved to Pakistan in 1983, where he joined became a member of an Afghan opposition group working to force the Soviets to end their occupation of Afghanistan. Karzai emerged as a leading political figure and became a deputy foreign minister in 1992 after the Soviets withdrew and a new Afghan government was formed. He initially backed the Taliban which he perceived to be a force that would end the ongoing civil war in Afghanistan and reduce the power of regional warlords. However, once the Taliban took control of the government, Karzai broke with the group over its efforts to impose sharia law throughout the country and its repression of political and religious minorities. Karzai's father was murdered by the Taliban in 1999. The future president subsequently began to work with the Northern Alliance.

Karzai supported the U.S.-led coalition in its effort to topple the Taliban following the 9/11 terrorist attacks on the United States. After the regime was overthrown, Karzai emerged as a leading consensus candidate to lead Afghanistan. Following a meeting of anti-Taliban groups in December 2001, he was appointed as the leader of the interim Afghan government. His position was confirmed by a Loya Jirga in 2002. The new leader was forced to make a number of compromises as he formed a coalition government. He had to carefully balance the interests of competing clans and tribes and ensure representation across all ethnic groups. Karzai's efforts to develop a moderate Islamic government were opposed by religious conservatives, creating rifts in the new government. Attempts to secure foreign aid and investment were undermined by a growing insurgency, led by the Taliban and al Qaeda. Meanwhile, regional warlords often ignored Karzai's government. Nonetheless, he was elected president in 2004 in the freest and fairest elections in the country's history.

After 2004, corruption and inefficiency increasingly undermined the popularity and authority of Karzai and his government. Foreign donors also became increasingly reluctant to provide aid and assistance. Domestic unease with the government led to riots in Kabul in 2006. By the end of his second term in office, Karzai had survived four assassination attempts. Although he generally enjoyed good relations with the United States, Karzai did oppose U.S.-led efforts to isolate Iran. The president also endeavored to have the United States exert greater pressure on Pakistan to suppress insurgents who launched raids into Afghanistan from bases on Pakistani territory. Meanwhile, the administrations of both presidents George W. Bush and Barack Obama pressured Karzai to reduce corruption and to take greater action to curb the drug trade.

In the 2009 presidential elections, charges of voter fraud and intimidation undermined the credibility of the balloting. Karzai was initially proclaimed the winner, but a recount revealed that he had not secured the necessary 50 percent majority needed to become president. This should have prompted a run-off election under Afghan law, however, Karzai's main challenger, former Foreign Minister Abdullah Abdullah withdrew from the elections. The challenger argued that corruption would prevent a credible run-off. Karzai was subsequently proclaimed the winner and inaugurated for a second term on November 19, 2009.

In an effort to stem the rising violence in Afghanistan Karzai offered to negotiate with moderate Taliban leaders. Although his efforts were initially rebuffed, a peace Loya Jirga endorsed talks in June 2010. Meanwhile, in November 2009, NATO agreed to withdraw foreign troops from Afghanistan by the end of 2014.

Kerry, John F. (1943–). John Forbes Kerry was the 2004 Democratic presidential candidate. Kerry earned a degree in political science from Yale in 1966. That year he was commissioned in the U.S. Navy and served in Vietnam from 1968 to 1969, where he received the Silver Star for bravery and three Purple Hearts for wounds suffered in combat. In spite of his awards, Kerry became convinced that the American effort in Vietnam was doomed to failure. After his return from Vietnam, Kerry became prominent in the anti-war movement. He cofounded the Vietnam Veterans of America and was the leader of the protest group Vietnam Veterans against the War. Kerry was arrested in 1971 for protesting the conflict. Kerry ran unsuccessfully for Congress in 1972, and then entered law school. Kerry received a law degree in 1976 and served as a prosecuting attorney until 1979 when he entered private practice. In 1982, he was elected lieutenant governor of Massachusetts. He launched a campaign to coordinate efforts among state governments to reduce acid rain. In 1984, he decided to run for the Senate after the incumbent decided to retire. Kerry won a close primary victory, but was easily elected in the general balloting.

Kerry established a record as one of the more liberal members of the Senate, though he was a member of the Democratic Leadership Council, comprised of centrist members of the Party. He was a staunch supporter of abortion rights and marriage rights for same-sex couples. Kerry opposed plans to privatize Social Security and repeated voiced opposition to capital punishment. He did support various free trade measures, including the North American Free Trade Agreement (NAFTA) and expanded trade with China, although he later opposed trade liberalization accords with Latin America. Kerry has been a strong advocate for national service and supported the Clinton's administration's Americorps program. He has also proposed an expansion of the Peace Corps and a national service program for teenagers after they graduated high school.

Kerry was an early and vocal critic of the Reagan administration's policies toward Nicaragua and helped initiate the investigation that resulted in the Iran-Contra Scandal. After launching investigations into the ties between U.S. intelligence operations and Panamanian dictator Manual Noriega, Kerry voted to support the 1989 U.S. invasion of Panama. However, he opposed the 1991 U.S. military action against Iraq after the invasion of Kuwait. The senator argued that sanctions should be expanded before military strikes were undertaken.

From 1987 to 1989, Kerry chaired the Democratic Senatorial Campaign Committee and helped coordinate the strategy that led to a gain of one seat for the Democrats in the Senate in the 1988 elections. In 1996, Kerry faced a difficult reelection campaign against popular Massachusetts governor William Weld. The two candidates negotiated campaign spending caps of $6.9 million each. When polls showed Kerry and Weld tied in the weeks before the election, Kerry authorized his staff to exceed the spending limitations. He was reelected. In 2000, Kerry was one of a number of Democrats considered to be Al Gore's running mate. Although he was not selected, Kerry raised funds and campaigned for Gore. Kerry was married to Julia Thorne from 1970 to 1988, and subsequently, in 1995, to Teresa Heinz, the multimillionaire widow of former Republican senator John Heinz.

Kerry voted for the 2001 Patriot Act and the authorization to use force against the Taliban regime in Afghanistan. He also voted to grant Bush the power to undertake military action against Iraq in 2002, although he argued that the administration should exhaust all diplomatic avenues before it resorted to force. Kerry was easily reelected to the Senate in 2002. He opposed the Bush administration's tax reductions and helped coordinate opposition to the plan to open the Alaska National Wildlife Refuge (ANWR) to oil exploration.

Kerry decided to run for the presidency in 2004. He faced a tough primary fight in a crowded field of candidates. Vermont governor Howard Dean took an early lead in the primary contest by emphasizing his opposition to the Iraq War. Kerry adopted a nuanced policy about the conflict, one with broader appeal to moderate voters. Kerry argued that since the invasion had occurred, the commitment in Iraq became a strategic interest. He criticized the Bush administration's management of the post-invasion insurgency. After the Midwest Caucuses, Kerry gained a lead in the nomination process and became the Party's candidate. He chose Senator John Edwards of North Carolina as his running mate in an effort to secure votes in the South.

Kerry's record in Vietnam became a campaign issue when questions were raised about Bush's service in the Air National Guard, thereby launching investigations into the records of both candidates. A group of Vietnam veterans raised questions about Kerry's awards and his subsequent anti-war actions. Kerry was also criticized by Bush for perceived inconsistencies on Iraq and the broader war on terror. Kerry's campaign suffered from a lack of focus. Midway through his electoral effort, Kerry replaced his campaign manager. Bush won the election 51 percent to 48 percent.

After the election, Kerry increased his criticism of the Bush administration, especially its foreign and national security policies. In 2006, Kerry worked with fellow senators such as John McCain to force the administration to compromise on its policies on detainee treatment. He also supported compromise legislation on immigration in 2006.

Al-Maliki, Nouri (1950–). Nouri Kamil Mohammed Hasan al-Maliki was prime minister of Iraq and a leading Shiite political figure. Maliki joined the outlawed Islamic Dawa Party as a youth and went into exile after he was given a 24-year prison sentence for his membership in the party and his opposition to the Saddam regime. Maliki lived in exile in Iran until 1990, where he developed ties with Iranian political figures, although he would later distance himself from Iranian influence. He was in Syria through the 1990s, working to support Iraqi opposition groups (he was briefly a member of the Iraqi National Congress). Following the U.S.-led invasion of Iraq, Maliki returned to Iraq where he helped oversee coalition efforts to remove former regime members from the military and civil service. He was elected as a representative to the transitional parliament in 2005 and was a member of the group that drafted Iraq's new, permanent constitution. In May 2006, he was appointed prime minister. During his tenure, Maliki pursued aggressive policies to suppress the growing insurgency in Iraq. He was an ardent proponent of transferring security control from coalition troops to Iraq security forces. Maliki was also a vocal critic of civilian casualties in the conflict, arguing that the coalition needed to do a better job of minimizing civilian losses during its operations. Maliki was instrumental in negotiating a ceasefire deal with the Mahdi Army and spreading the Sunni Awakening. He also negotiated an end to a Sunni boycott of the national legislature in 2008. By 2007, Maliki had begun to work for a quick withdrawal of U.S. and coalition forces from Iraq. His efforts culminated in a 2008 agreement with the Bush administration that set December 31, 2011 as the date for the withdrawal of the last U.S. troops. Meanwhile, Maliki was elected secretary general of the Dawa Party. In legislative elections in 2010, Maliki's party placed second with 89 seats in the assembly. However, no single party had an absolute majority in the parliament. Maliki was able to gain the support of smaller parties and groups and form a coalition government in December 2010. He was subsequently became prime minister for a second term.

McCain, John S. (1936–). John Sidney McCain was a longtime senator from Arizona and Republican presidential candidate. McCain was born in the U.S. Panama Canal Zone in 1936 and went on to graduate from the Naval Academy and become a naval pilot. He served in Vietnam, where he was shot down and captured. McCain was a prisoner of war for six years and was tortured during his captivity. After retiring from the Navy, McCain was elected as a Republican to represent Arizona in the U.S. House of Representatives in 1982. Four years later, he was elected to the Senate.

McCain campaigned for the Republican presidential nomination in 2000. He was defeated by George W. Bush, who went on to win the balloting. McCain became identified as a leader of the moderate wing of the Grand Old Party. He was generally conservative on foreign and security policy, but moderate on most social issues. McCain developed a reputation in his early career as a politician who voted according to principle, not the party line. He famously broke with his Republican colleagues on several major pieces of tax legislation. He voted against tax cuts in 2003 and has joined with Democrats in opposition to the elimination of the inheritance tax. In the 107th Congress, McCain compiled one of the most liberal voting records of all the Senate Republicans (ranking sixth out of 49). However, in the 108th and 109th Congresses, his record was much more conservative.

McCain helped form the "Gang of 14," a group of seven Republican and seven Democratic senators who joined together to negotiate a compromise over judicial appointments by the Bush administration. The group agreed that the seven Democrats would not support filibusters, except under extraordinary circumstances, while the Republicans would refuse to support the planned "nuclear option" of Senate Majority Leader Bill Frist which would have prohibited filibusters of judicial nominees. The agreement was criticized by the Senate leadership and partisans in both parties, but it allowed several nominees to proceed, including future Supreme Court Justice Samuel Alito in 2006, despite filibuster attempts by Senate Democrats.

McCain's experiences as a prisoner of war during the Vietnam War prompted him to oppose the Bush administration's use of extrajudicial interrogation methods against enemy combatants. The administration opposed limitations on the detention and interrogation of unlawful combatants and threatened to veto any legislation that constrained its treatment of detainees. In 2005, McCain offered an amendment which would protect U.S. personnel from prosecution for past participation in interrogations, but also prohibited cruel or degrading treatment of detainees in the future. The White House eventually accepted the compromise in December 2005. The 2005 accord was followed by another compromise in 2006 over detainee rights and the role of military tribunals in prosecuting unlawful combatants. Once again, McCain and moderate Republicans led the effort to resolve differences between the White House and the Senate. McCain also embraced moderate positions on a variety of other issues. The senator also adopted a pro-environmental stance on issues such as global warming and expanded energy production. For instance, in 2005, he voted against administration proposals to open the Alaska National Wildlife Refuge to oil exploration. McCain's position on stem cell research has shifted. Initially opposed on moral grounds, by 2004, the senator began issuing statements in support of stem cell research. Furthermore, in 2004 and 2006, McCain voted against the Federal Marriage Amendment to the Constitution, which would have defined marriage as a union between a man and a woman. McCain launched investigations into professional baseball and warned in 2006 that the sport might need new legislation to prevent steroid use and end other unethical practices.

Although McCain's moderate stance on a variety of issues often placed him at odds with Bush and conservatives within the Republican Party, the senator generally supported the majority of the administration's policies. McCain endorsed Bush's No Child Left Behind educational initiative and did vote in favor of most of the administration's proposed tax reductions. McCain has also repeatedly proclaimed his pro-life stance on abortion issues. On immigration, McCain supported Bush's initiative to expand the number of guest workers permitted in the United States. In 2005, he co-sponsored, along with Democratic senator Ted Kennedy, a bill to expand the guest worker visa program, a measure that was broadly opposed by conservatives.

McCain was also a staunch supporter of Bush's national security policies. Throughout his career, he was a strong supporter of the military and increased benefits for military personnel and their families. Following the September 2001 terrorist attacks, McCain voted in favor of the 2001 Patriot Act and successive measures to create and strengthen the Department of Homeland Security. He also backed the 2003 invasion of Iraq and voted for subsequent legislation to fund operations and reconstruction in Iraq and Afghanistan. In 2004, McCain did call for the deployment of more U.S. troops in Iraq and for more concentrated efforts to bolster Iraqi security forces so that they could assume the burden of national defense. McCain was chosen to deliver a speech at the Republican National Convention in 2004 on national security.

During the 2004 election, McCain campaigned for Bush. He broadly praised the president and administration for its conduct of the war on terror and national security policies. McCain quickly dismissed speculation in 2004 that he would join Democrat John Kerry's campaign as the vice presidential candidate. However, McCain condemned political advertisements that were critical of Kerry's war service in Vietnam.

McCain won the 2008 Republican presidential nomination. He chose Alaska governor Sarah Palin was his running mate, the first woman to be a Republican vice presidential candidate. During the general campaign, McCain emphasized his military service and capabilities as commander-in-chief. He lost the balloting to Democrat Barack Obama. McCain subsequently emerged as one of the leading critics of Obama's budgetary policies.

McConnell, Addison Mitchell "Mitch" (1942–). Addison Mitchell "Mitch" McConnell was the Republican minority leader in the Senate. First elected in 1984, McConnell compiled a record that made him one of the leaders of the conservative wing of the Republican Party. In 2002, McConnell was reelected to the Senate with 65 percent of the vote, the largest margin of victory for a Republican in Kentucky's history. That same year, McConnell was elected majority whip (he was unanimously reelected to the position in 2004). As majority whip, he quickly developed a reputation for using the arcane rules of the Senate to either pass or block legislation. For instance, in 2005, McConnell was able to block an amendment to raise the minimum wage that had been attached to budget legislation that most members of the Senate favored. He was less successful in maintaining party discipline as a moderate group of Republican senators emerged which repeatedly challenged the leadership on legislative issues such as immigration and the treatment of detainees in the war on terror.

McConnell opposed bipartisan efforts to reform campaign finance laws. He was personally one of the most prodigious fundraisers for the Republican Party and believed that most reforms would put the GOP at a disadvantage in campaign contributions. He tried unsuccessfully to block passage of the 2002 Bipartisan Campaign Finance Reform Act (commonly known as the McCain-Feingold Act after its sponsors, Senators John McCain and Russ Feingold). McConnell argued that the legislation violated the spirit of the Constitution's free speech and free association rights and that the Act would unfairly benefit organizations, such as unions, which traditionally backed Democratic candidates. After the McCain-Feingold Act was signed into law, McConnell challenged the law in court. In 2003, in *McConnell v. Federal Elections Commission*, the Supreme Court upheld the main components of the Act although it did strike down some provisions. McConnell's belief in the importance of free speech also led him to vote against the constitutional amendments to prevent the desecration of the American flag.

McConnell's personal political philosophy has been described as libertarian in light of his opposition to government interference in the economy. He was also strongly pro-business and was given a 100 percent rating by the U.S. Chamber of

Commerce for his voting record. McConnell has been a strong supporter of George W. Bush and worked closely with the White House to enact the president's agenda. McConnell's wife, Elaine Chao, was appointed secretary of labor in 2001, further tying the senator to the administration. McConnell helped guide through the main priorities of Bush's security program, including the 2001 Patriot Act (and its subsequent renewals), the 2002 Homeland Security, and the 2002 congressional authorization to use force against Iraq. After several failures, in 2003, McConnell and Senate Republicans successfully enacted a ban on partial birth abortions.

McConnell exercised considerable influence over politics in Kentucky. He campaigned heavily for Ernie Fletcher who, in 2003, became the first Republican governor of Kentucky in 30 years. After Senate Majority Leader Bill Frist announced his retirement at the end of his term in 2006, McConnell became the leader of the Senate Republicans.

Mohammad, Khalid Sheikh (1964–). Khalid Sheikh Mohammad was a leading member of al Qaeda and responsible for a series of terrorist strikes, including the 9/11 attacks. Mohammad was born in Kuwait to Pakistani parents. As a youth he was drawn to fundamentalist Islam, and joined the Muslim Brotherhood at age 16. He later went to the United States and attended North Carolina Agricultural and Technical State University and earned a degree in mechanical engineering in 1986. Mohammad then traveled to Afghanistan to fight the Soviet occupation. During this period, he met Osama bin Laden and the two began a long-term working relationship.

After the Soviet withdrawal from Afghanistan, Mohammad spent time in Bosnia raising money for Bosnian Muslims in their fight against the Serbs. He subsequently emerged as a significant fundraiser for a variety of Muslim extremist groups. Mohammad helped finance the 1993 World Trade Center bombings and was involved in the planning of Operation Bojinka, an abortive attempt to simultaneously destroy twelve commercial aircraft. The plot was led by Mohammad's nephew Ramzi Yousef, but discovered in 1995, before it could be implemented. Yousef was apprehended in Pakistan and Mohammad was indicted by the United States for his role in the failed plot. Mohammad fled Qatar after authorities agreed to extradite him to the United States.

In late 1996, Mohammad was back in Afghanistan and working with bin Laden. Mohammad emerged as a leading planner for al Qaeda terrorist operations. He used the basic strategy that had been developed for Operation Bojinka as the template to plan the 9/11 attacks. Sometime in late 1999 or early 2000, Mohammad presented the plot to bin Laden, who approved the attack. Mohammad subsequently helped with the logistics of the attack. He went on to plan other strikes, including the abortive effort by Richard Reid, the Shoe Bomber, to destroy a commercial flight with a bomb in his shoe. Mohammad also worked to finance the 2002 Bali Bombings.

U.S. and Pakistani intelligence services worked together to capture Mohammad in Pakistan in 2003. He was subsequently turned over to U.S. officials and transferred to the detention facility at Guantanamo Bay in 2006. It was later revealed that Mohammad had been waterboarded while in captivity. In March 2007, Mohammad confessed to planning the attacks on the WTC and other attacks. In February 2008, Department of Defense prosecutors charged Mohammad and others with the 9/11 attacks.

Musharraf, Pervez (1943–). Seyd Pervez Musharraf served as president of Pakistan from 2001 until 2008. Musharraf was born in Delhi, India, but moved Pakistan when he was four. He became a military officer and served in the Indo-Pakistani War of 1965, and in several border conflicts in the contested region of Kashmir. Musharraf became army chief of staff in 1998 and lead the Pakistani forces served during the 1999 Kargil War with India. On October 12, 1999, he took part in a military coup that displaced the prime minister, Nawaz Sharif. Sharif had attempted to replace Musharraf after the military defeat of the Kargil War. After serving as interim leader of Pakistan, Musharraf became president in June 2001.

In the aftermath of 9/11, Musharraf became a close ally of the United States. He supported Operation Enduring Freedom and the broader war on terror. Musharraf endeavored to use the relationship with the United States to counter perceived threats from India. In return for his support, the Bush administration provided Pakistan with military and economic assistance. The fall of the Taliban in Afghanistan resulted in a large number of insurgents crossing the border into Pakistan where they became allied with anti-government tribes and clans. Consequently, the Taliban were able to launch an insurgency in Pakistan while they used bases in that country to undertake cross-border raids into Afghanistan. By 2005, the Taliban and al Qaeda were in the midst of a major terrorist campaign against the Musharraf regime. Efforts to suppress the insurgents were only marginally successful and undermined Musharraf's popularity because of his inability to contain the violence. Friction between the United States and Pakistan also increased as the Bush administration pressured Musharraf to suppress the insurgents. The United States also began to fire unmanned aerial drones at Taliban and al Qaeda targets in Pakistan and conduct cross-border incursions. These actions were widely opposed by the Pakistani people and political elite. Domestic pressure increased for Musharraf to resign and allow open elections. Musharraf resigned from his position as chief of army staff in November of 2007 and then won the 2007 Pakistani presidential election in controversial balloting. However, under threat of impeachment by the National Assembly of Pakistan, Musharraf resigned from office and left the country in August 2008.

Obama, Barack H. (1961–). Barack Hussein Obama was the 44th president of the United States and the first African American elected as the country's chief executive. Obama was born in Hawaii. He received a law degree from Harvard in 1991 and then joined a civil rights law firm. Obama was active in Democratic politics from a young age and worked on campaigns and voter registration drives while still a college student. He was elected to the state senate in Illinois in 1996 where he supported a range of social legislation, including a state earned income tax credit and increased funding for early education. Obama developed a reputation as a consensus-builder in the state senate for his effectiveness in reaching out to Republicans to build bipartisan support for initiatives. In 1999, he made an unsuccessful primary bid in a contest for the U.S. House of Representatives.

In 2004, Obama decided to run for an open seat from Illinois in the U.S. Senate. Although relatively unknown outside of Chicago, Obama's campaign benefited from a scandal-plagued Republican opponent who was eventually replaced by Alan Keyes. His keynote address at the Democratic convention also brought Obama significant national attention. Far ahead of Keyes in pre-election polls, Obama traveled outside of Illinois to campaign for other Democratic candidates on the weeks before the election. He won the balloting with 70 percent of the vote and became only the third African American popularly elected to the Senate.

While the Democratic Party wanted to prominently feature Obama in the national spotlight as a reflection of the party's commitment to diversity, he chose to adopt a low profile in the Senate and concentrate on policy issues. He embraced centrist policies on most issues and continued to demonstrate the bipartisan tendencies that had marked his career in state politics. He joined with Republicans in calling for stronger action toward the humanitarian crisis in Darfur and offered a moderate energy plan which called for incentives for U.S. automakers in exchange for improvements in fuel efficiency. Liberal members of the party criticized Obama for supporting Condoleezza Rice in her Senate confirmation hearings to be secretary of state, while conservatives were unhappy with his support for an increase in the minimum wage. In 2005, in the wake of a series of congressional scandals, the Democratic leadership appointed Obama as their leading spokesperson on ethics reforms. Obama developed a series of reforms; however, most were opposed by senior senators of both parties. One of Obama's proposals, the creation of an independent office to investigate Congress, was opposed by a majority of both Republicans and Democrats and was defeated on a vote of 67–30. Obama also emerged a vocal critic of the Bush administration's management of the relief effort following Hurricane Katrina in 2005 and of the Iraq War.

Obama secured the Democratic presidential nomination in 2008. He went on to defeat Republican senator John McCain (Arizona), with 52.9 percent of the vote to McCain's 45.7 percent. The campaign centered on Obama's opposition to the Iraq War and calls for economic reforms. Obama contrasted himself and his policies with those of the Bush administration in a campaign whose slogan was "Hope and Change." In concurrent congressional balloting, Democrats increased their majorities in both houses of Congress, including gaining a filibuster-proof majority in the Senate. Once in office, Obama focused on domestic issues, including efforts to revive the U.S. economy and enact reform health care. The Obama administration's $780 billion stimulus failed to significantly improve the U.S. economy and caused the federal budget deficit to swell to over $1.3 trillion in 2009. Combined with controversy over the enactment of healthcare reform, the lagging economy and deficit undermined Obama's public approval ratings. Meanwhile, Obama accelerated the withdrawal of troops from Iraq and undertook a troop surge in Afghanistan in 2010 in an effort to contain the growing insurgency there. The president also endeavored to improve perceptions of the United States, particularly in the Muslim world. In congressional midterm elections in 2010, the Democrats lost control of the House of Representatives and lost seats in the Senate in balloting that was seen as a referendum on Obama's presidency.

Pearl, Daniel (1963–2002). Daniel Pearl was an American journalist investigating al Qaeda in Pakistan who was kidnapped and murdered in 2002. Pearl was born in Princeton, New Jersey, but grew up in California, where he graduated from Stanford University. Pearl had a distinguished career as a journalist and became the bureau chief for the *Wall Street Journalist* in Southwest Asia. Although he was based in India, Pearl was in Pakistan researching a story on Richard Reid, the Shoe Bomber. He was kidnapped on January 23, 2002. A group calling itself the National Movement for the Restoration of Pakistani Sovereignty claimed responsibility and made various demands, including the release of jailed terrorists in Pakistan. The group also asserted that Pearl was a U.S. spy and published videos and photos of Pearl in captivity. On February 21, the kidnappers released a video of Pearl being killed and then decapitated. Pearl's body was discovered three months near Karachi. It had been cut into several pieces. The FBI and Pakistani law enforcement officials worked together to investigate the murder. Four suspects were arrested and later convicted of the crime on July 15, 2002. The accused leader of the group, Ahmed Omar Saeed Sheikh, was sentenced to be executed.

Pelosi, Nancy (1940–). Nancy Patricia D'Alesandro Pelosi was the first female speaker of the House of Representatives. Pelosi was born in Baltimore, Maryland, but moved to San Francisco, California, where she was elected to the House of Representatives in 1987. One of her most famous early achievements was the 1989 Pelosi Amendment. This measure made it a requirement for international financial organizations such as the World Bank to conduct environmental studies to investigate how their programs or activities impacted the local ecology. Organizations that failed to complete these surveys risked losing U.S. funding. Pelosi opposed U.S. participation in the 1991 Gulf War and voted against the authorization to use force in that conflict. Following the 9/11 attacks Pelosi supported the invasion of Afghanistan and voted in favor of the Patriot Act.

Pelosi rose through the ranks of Congress and was elected minority whip in 2001 and then minority leader in 2002. After initial cooperating with the administration of George W. Bush following 9/11 Pelosi sought to distance herself and her party from the domestic politics and war in Iraq. Pelosi argued that the reason the Democrats suffered losses in the 2002 congressional midterm elections was that they were unable to distinguish themselves from Republicans. She opposed the 2003 Iraq War and voted against the authorization to use force prior to that conflict. After Democrats gained control of the House of Representatives in the 2006 midterm congressional elections Pelosi was elected speaker. She attempted unsuccessfully to deny funding for the ongoing conflict in Iraq in an effort to force President Bush to develop a timetable to withdraw troops from that country. She also opposed the troop surge in Iraq in 2007. In 2008, Pelosi was reelected speaker. Following the 2010 congressional balloting in which Republicans regained control of the House, Pelosi was reelected minority leader.

Powell, Colin (1937–). Colin Powell was the secretary of state during the first term of George W. Bush and the first African American to lead the State Department. A native of New York, Powell graduated from the City College of New York in 1958, was commissioned in the Army and served in the Vietnam War, where he was decorated for bravery. Powell had a distinguished career in the military, rising to become a four-star general. He was chairman of the Joint Chiefs of Staff, the nation's highest ranking military position, during the Persian Gulf War. He had a major influence on U.S. military strategy through the development of the Powell Doctrine, which called for the establishment of clear objectives and the deployment of overwhelming force before the nation used military force.

Powell also held a variety of political posts during his career. He was appointed national security advisor in 1987, a post he held until 1989. He also served as a special representative of the president to Haiti in 1994. Powell was a foreign and security policy advisor to George W. Bush during the latter's 2000 presidential campaign and was subsequently appointed secretary of state. Powell was a key figure in the Bush administration but was at times marginalized for his moderate political views, often clashing with Vice President Richard Cheney and Secretary of Defense Donald Rumsfeld. Prior to the invasion of Afghanistan following the 9/11 attacks, Powell worked to garner support for Operation Enduring Freedom and secured significant multilateral assistance. He helped convince NATO to invoke its collective defense clause for the first time in the organization's history in response to the 9/11 attacks.

Powell argued that military force should only be used as a last resort, nonetheless, he became the administration's main public advocate among the global community for military action against Iraq in 2002. He was unable to form an international coalition of the size and depth that had backed Operation Enduring Freedom and divisions emerged between the United States and many of its key allies prior to the invasion of Iraq. Powell did convince Bush to attempt to gain UN support for military action against Iraq, even though the effort was unsuccessful. Powell's influence in the administration waned following the invasion of Iraq in 2003 and he resigned in 2004.

Rice, Condoleezza (1954–). Condoleezza Rice was the nation's first female national security advisor during the first term of President George W. Bush and served as secretary of state during his second term. Rice was born in Birmingham, Alabama. She worked for the State Department before earning a PhD in political science from the University of Denver. Rice became a specialist on the Soviet Union and taught at Stanford University. From 1989 to 1991, Rice was a staff member of on the National Security Council. She was a foreign policy advisor to George W. Bush during his 2000 presidential campaign. Bush subsequently appointed Rice as the first American female national security advisor.

Rice formed a close relationship with Bush and the president relied on Rice for advice and counsel in the aftermath of the 9/11 attacks. She worked with Secretary of State Colin Powell on the efforts to form a diplomatic coalition to support the U.S. response to the terrorist attacks. She also worked with Secretary of Defense Donald Rumsfeld on the military response. Rice was instrumental in the development of the "Bush Doctrine" of preemption and helped craft the 2002 *National Security Strategy of the United States*. She was also one of the main proponents of the invasion of Iraq in 2003.

After Powell resigned in 2004, Rice was appointed secretary of state, becoming the second woman and second African American to hold the post. Once in office, Rice undertook a major diplomatic effort to repair strained relations with allies such as France and Germany that had opposed the Iraq War. Concurrently Rice also endeavored to garner support for the coalition in Iraq, including new troop contributions. Her tenure as secretary saw the influence and status of the State Department elevated in comparison with other departments, including the Defense Department.

Rice left office on January 20, 2009, and returned to academia. She became a professor at the Stanford Graduate School of Business and a faculty member in Stanford's Global Center for Business and the Economy.

Ridge, Thomas J. (1945–). Thomas "Tom" Joseph Ridge was the first secretary of homeland security. Born in Munhall, Pennsylvania, Ridge earned a law degree from Dickinson University in 1972. He was decorated for bravery while in the Army during the Vietnam War. He was elected as a Republican member of the House of Representatives in 1982. Ridge later became governor of Pennsylvania in 1994.

President Bush appointed Ridge the first director of the Office of Homeland Security and the former governor became the first secretary of the Department of Homeland Security (DHS) in 2003. He had the monumental task of leading the consolidation of 22 federal agencies encompassing 180,000 employees, into a single department. This was the most comprehensive reorganization of the federal bureaucracy in over 50 years. Because of a good working relationship with both the executive and legislative branches Ridge was able to accomplish many of the administration's post 9/11domestic security goals. During his tenure Ridge was criticized over a range of issues, including border control and civil liberties. Ridge was also criticized for recommending a national amnesty for illegal immigrants currently within the United States. Meanwhile, the DHS color-coded threat alert system, the Homeland Security Advisory System continued to be criticized until plans for its replacement were announced in 2010. Ridge resigned in 2004 for personal problems, but remained active in the political arena. He was subsequently appointed as a security advisor by the government of Albania in 2006 and endorsed John McCain in the 2008 elections.

Rumsfeld, Donald H. (1932–). Donald Henry Rumsfeld served as secretary of defense under President George W. Bush. Rumsfeld was born in Chicago, Illinois, and graduated from Princeton University in 1954. After serving in the Navy, Rumsfeld began a political career. He became a congressional aide in 1957 and was elected to the United States House of Representatives in 1962. Rumsfeld was a moderate Republican who served three terms before he joined the administration of Richard M. Nixon as the director of the Office of Economic Opportunity (future vice president Richard Cheney served as Rumsfeld's deputy during Rumsfeld's tenure in the post). Rumsfeld was appointed as the U.S. ambassador to NATO in 1974, then White House chief of staff, and, finally, secretary of defense the next year.

Rumsfeld left office in 1977 and launched a successful business career. After George W. Bush was elected in 2000, Cheney convinced the new president to appoint Rumsfeld as secretary of defense. Rumsfeld thus became both the youngest and oldest person to serve as secretary of defense. He initially worked to transition the military from its Cold War posture to a leaner and more adaptable force.

The new secretary played a pivotal role in the military response to the 9/11 attacks. Rumsfeld convinced Bush to utilize special operations forces and air power, along with the Northern Alliance to combat the Taliban and al Qaeda. The secretary was widely credited for the speedy defeat of the Taliban and al Qaeda, but he was also criticized since bin Laden and so many of the senior al Qaeda and Taliban leadership escaped. The use of small special operations groups hand-in-hand with high-technology air power became known as the "Rumsfeld Doctrine."

Rumsfeld emerged as one of the strongest advocates for the Bush Doctrine of preemption, including military action against Iraq. He approved a plan to invade Iraq that originally envisioned a two-front invasion from Turkey in the north and Kuwait in the south, involving 230,000 troops. However, domestic opposition in

Turkey prevented the northern front and the United States instead invaded from the south, along with an airborne drop in the north, with 140,000 men. Despite the new plans, the invasion proceeded quickly and the U.S.-led coalition overran Baghdad within a month. However, after the fall of the regime, a widespread insurgency emerged that caused more casualties than the initial invasion. Rumsfeld was blamed for the lack of post-war planning and for not having enough troops to prevent the insurgency. Rumsfeld resigned in 2006 following heavy losses in the 2006 midterm congressional elections.

Schröder, Gerhard F. (1944–). Gerhard Fritz Kurt Schröder served as chancellor of Germany from 1998 to 2005. Schröder joined the Social Democratic Party (Sozialdemokratische Partei Deutschlands, SPD), eventually becoming the leader of the SPD's youth organization. In 1986, Schröder was elected to the lower house of parliament, the Bundestag. Four years later, he became the leader of the state legislature of Lower Saxony. Schröder became leader of the SPD in 1998 and was the party's candidate for chancellor in national elections. The SPD won the elections and formed a coalition government with the Green Party.

After he entered office, Schröder initially concentrated on domestic issues, including economic reforms. His foreign policy priorities included deeper EU integration. Schröder was in office when the EU adopted the euro as its common currency. The chancellor also supported NATO intervention in Kosovo. Following the 9/11 attacks, Schröder offered his full support to the United States. Germany provided intelligence and law enforcement cooperation, and subsequently deployed troops as part of the NATO-led mission in Afghanistan. Schröder opposed the Guantanamo Bay detainment facility and later used opposition to the proposed U.S. military action against Iraq as a pillar for his reelection campaign in 2002. This began a period of tension between the United States and Germany, and Schröder emerged as one of the leading international opponents to the use of force against Iraq. Schröder won reelection, albeit with a smaller majority.

In early elections in 2005, Schröder's coalition lost its majority in the legislature. The conservative Christian Democratic Party (Christlich Demokratische Union, or CDU), led by party Angela Merkel, won the largest number of votes and formed a coalition government. Following these elections, Schröder resigned his seat in the Bundestag on November 23, 2005.

Tenet, George J. (1953–). From 1997 to 2005 George John Tenet was the director of the Central Intelligence Agency (CIA). A native of New York City, Tenet earned a bachelor's degree from Georgetown University in 1976 and a master's degree from Columbia University. Tenet worked on the Senate staffs of both Republicans and Democrats. President Clinton appointed Tenet to the National Security Council in 1993. Two years later, he became deputy director of the CIA. Tenet became acting director of the agency following the resignation of CIA head John Deutch in 1996. He became permanent head of the CIA the next year.

During Tenet's tenure, terrorism emerged as a major security threat to the United States. In the aftermath of the 1998 Embassy Bombings in Africa, Tenet directed the CIA increase its counterterrorism operations. In 2001, Tenet became the first CIA director in 28 years to remain in office through a new presidential election when George W. Bush asked Tenet to remain in office. Tenet endeavored to impress upon the new president the growing danger of international terrorism and Bush directed his administration to undertake a complete reexamination of U.S. national security threats in August 2001.

Past attempts to penetrate these global terrorist networks with U.S.-backed agents had been stifled because of a 1995 measure that put restrictions on the use of human intelligence. The legislation was put in place to prevent the CIA or other intelligence agencies from supporting or paying foreign individuals that were believed to be involved in human rights violations. The restrictions constrained the ability of intelligence units to recruit members of terrorist groups or develop information networks in countries such as Afghanistan or Pakistan. The inability to properly use human intelligence was compounded by a lack of cooperation between the nation's two primary intelligence services, the CIA and the FBI. Restrictions had been put in place to restrict cooperation between the nation's main domestic intelligence agency, the FBI, and its foreign intelligence agency, the CIA. The lack of intelligence sharing between the two agencies caused a large amount of intelligence relating to the 9/11 terrorists to go unnoticed. Tenet had worked through the 1990s to have these constraints removed. These impediments were directly addressed following the 9/11 attacks. Restrictions on human intelligence were lifted and new directives on intelligence sharing were enacted. One of the reforms that resulted from the attacks that Tenet did not support was the creation of the director of national intelligence to oversee the entire intelligence community. The CIA director argued that the new post would undermine the ability his agency to provide information directly to the president.

Tenet oversaw the collection and preparation of intelligence that was used to justify the invasion of Iraq in 2003. Later evidence, including work by the Iraq Survey Group, found that some of the information collected by the CIA was false or misleading, especially intelligence on Iraq's WMD programs. Tenet faced growing congressional criticism in the aftermath of the Iraq invasion. He issued his resignation on June 3, 2004, and left office in 2005.

Wolfowitz, Paul D. (1943–). Paul Dundes Wolfowitz was a leading neoconservative in the administration of President George W. Bush, and played a major role in the development of the controversial Bush Doctrine. Wolfowitz was born in New York, New York, in 1943. In 1972, he earned a PhD in political science from the University of Chicago. He went on to work for a variety of government agencies. In 1980, he left government and began teach political science at Johns Hopkins University. A year later, he returned to the government as the chief of the State

Department's Policy Planning Staff under President Ronald W. Reagan. Wolfowitz served in a variety of posts, including ambassador to Indonesia. From 1989 to 1993, he was an undersecretary in the Defense Department, where he worked for then–Secretary of Defense Dick Cheney. Wolfowitz helped develop strategies for the 1989 invasion of Panama and the 1991 Persian Gulf War. He also worked on efforts to reform the U.S. military in the aftermath of the Cold War and refocus the armed forces to better address new international threats. Wolfowitz subsequently returned to academia and eventually became dean of the School of Advanced and International Studies at Johns Hopkins University.

George W. Bush asked Wolfowitz to serve as a foreign and security policy advisor during his 2000 presidential campaign, and subsequently appointed him deputy secretary of defense. Wolfowitz helped craft the military response to the 9/11 attacks. Secretary of Defense Donald Rumsfeld and Wolfowitz both argued that the Taliban regime in Afghanistan could be overthrown using a combination of special operations forces and local, anti-Taliban militias, such as the Northern Alliance, supported by U.S. airpower and missile strikes. Their strategy proved highly effective in defeating the Taliban and their al Qaeda allies, but the lack of troops also allowed many enemy fighters, including Osama bin Laden, to flee across the border to Pakistan. Wolfowitz subsequently was instrumental in the creation of the Bush Doctrine which called for the preemptive use of military force to forestall potential security threats to the United States. He was also influential in the codification of the Bush Doctrine through the 2002 *National Security Strategy of the United States*.

Wolfowitz was one of the foremost advocates for military action against Iraq in 2002 and 2003. He argued that Iraq's WMD programs posed a substantial risk to the United States. Wolfowitz helped develop the strategy used to invade Iraq. He maintained that the Iraqi regime of Saddam Hussein could be overthrown using a minimal number of U.S. troops, even though most senior military commanders argued that the United States needed a far more substantial number of forces for the attack (eventually, 140,000 American troops were involved in the initial invasion). Wolfowitz faced increasing criticism as the insurgency in Iraq grew. Nonetheless, he retained the favor and support of Bush who nominated him in 2004 to become director of the World Bank. In 2007, a corruption scandal involving a pay raise for a female employee of the World Bank who was romantically linked to Wolfowitz led to the latter's resignation. Wolfowitz became a visiting fellow at the American Enterprise Institute and chairman of the U.S.-Taiwan Business Council.

Al Zarqawi, Abu Musab (1966–2006). Born Ahmad Fadeel al Nazal al Khalayleh, Abu Musab al-Zarqawi was originally from Amman, Jordan, but spent his formative years in Zarqa, Jordan. Zarqawi became an extremist in his youth. He traveled to Afghanistan in 1989, where he established links with Osama bin Laden. In the

1990s, Zarqawi founded a terrorist group that sought to establish an Islamic regime in Jordan. In 1992, Zarqawi was arrested in Jordan for conspiracy to overthrow the monarchy. He was released from prison in 1999, and soon thereafter he was involved an attempt to destroy the Radisson Hotel in Amman, Jordan. Zarqawi fled Jordan to avoid arrest and went first to Pakistan, and then to Afghanistan. Once back in Afghanistan, he reestablished contacts with bin Laden. Zarqawi established a militant training camp with the support of bin Laden and al Qaeda, and launched another Islamist terrorist organization, Jund al-Sham ("Soldiers of the Levant"). Zarqawi fought against coalition forces during Operation Enduring Freedom and then fled to Northern Iraq where we fought the Kurds as part of the Islamic terrorist group, Ansar al Islam ("Partisans of Islam").

After the U.S.-led invasion of Iraq, Zarqawi emerged as the leader of al Qaeda in Iraq. He was even granted the title "Emir of Al Qaeda in the Country of Two Rivers." Zarqawi played a major role in the transition of the insurgency from guerilla attacks on coalition forces to suicide bombings and roadside bombings. He released a number of video and audio tapes in a public relations campaign intended to undermine Iraqi confidence in the country's interim government and the coalition. Zarqawi also used al Qaeda networks and financing to draw foreign recruits to Iraq to fight the coalition. In September 2005, Zarqawi declared an aggressive offensive on the Shiite population of Iraq in an effort to start a civil war between Sunnis and Shiites. Although violence escalated significantly, Zarqawi's tactics ultimately backfired and alienated many Sunnis in Iraq and even some al Qaeda leaders who criticized his attacks on fellow Muslims.

Zarqawi was killed in a coalition air strike on June 7, 2006.

Primary Documents

1. The Invasion of Kuwait and UN Security Council Resolutions 660 and 678 (1990)

Following the invasion of Kuwait by Iraq on August 2, 1990, the UN Security Council "condemned" the act of aggression in Resolution 660 on the same day. The vote was 14–0, with Yemen abstaining. The measure also called for talks between the two nations to end the conflict. The Council:

1). *Condemns* [all italics in the original] the Iraqi invasion of Kuwait;
2). *Demands* that Iraq with draw immediately and unconditionally all its forces to the positions in which they were located on 1 August 1990;
3). *Calls upon* Iraq and Kuwait to being immediately intensive negotiations for the resolution of their differences and supports all efforts in this regard, and especially those of the Arab League;

Source: UN Security Council, "Resolution 660," August 2 (New York: United Nations Department of Public Information, 1990).

When Iraq refused to withdraw from Iraq, in spite of international pressure and negotiations, including the enactment of economic and military sanctions and the deployment of a military coalition in the region, the United Nations Security Council passed Resolution 678 on November 29, 1990. The resolution provided authorization to use military force against Iraq in order to expel the country's forces from Kuwait, but gave the Iraqi regime of Saddam Hussein a last chance to comply with Resolution 660. The Security Council stated that it:

1). *Demands* [all italics in the original] that Iraq comply fully with Resolution 660 (1990) and all subsequent relevant resolutions, and decides, while maintaining all its decisions to allow Iraq one final opportunity, as a pause of goodwill, to do so;
2). *Authorizes* Member States co-operating with the Government of Kuwait, unless Iraq on or before 15 January 1991 fully implements, as set forth in

paragraph 1 above, the above-mentioned resolutions, to use all necessary means to uphold and implement Resolution 660 (1990) and all subsequent relevant resolutions and to restore international peace and security in the area;

Source: UN Security Council, "Resolution 678," November 29 (New York: United Nations Department of Public Information, 1990).

2. President Clinton's Speech on Iraq and WMD Inspections (1998)

Throughout the 1990s, strife between the United States and Iraq continued over Iraq's willingness to allow United Nations weapons inspectors to examine, monitor, and destroy, if found, the country's weapons of mass destruction programs. In early 1998, tensions escalated over Iraq's threats to expel UN inspectors. In an address on February 17, 1998, President Bill Clinton outlined the problems the international community had faced from the Iraqi regime of Saddam Hussein. In his address, Clinton mentioned presented a detailed overview of Iraq past transgressions. The president also makes it clear that he would use military force if Iraq continued to obstruct UN inspectors (Clinton would later authorize missile strikes against Iraq). The president begins this section of his address by arguing that Saddam represented one of the most significant threats to the United States and to international security:

There is no more clear example of this threat than Saddam Hussein's Iraq. His regime threatens the safety of his people, the stability of his region and the security of all the rest of us.

I want the American people to understand first the past how did this crisis come about and I want them to understand what we must do to protect the national interest, and indeed the interest of all freedom loving people in the world.

Remember, as a condition of the ceasefire after the Gulf War, the United Nations demanded not the United States the United Nations demanded, and Saddam Hussein agreed to declare within 15 days this is way back in 1991 within 15 days his nuclear, chemical and biological weapons and the missiles to deliver them, to make a total declaration. That's what he promised to do.

The United Nations set up a special commission of highly trained international experts called UNSCOM, to make sure that Iraq made good on that commitment. We had every good reason to insist that Iraq disarm. Saddam had built up a terrible arsenal, and he had used it not once, but many times, in a decade long war with Iran, he used chemical weapons, against combatants, against civilians, against a foreign adversary, and even against his own people.

And during the Gulf War, Saddam launched Scuds against Saudi Arabia, Israel and Bahrain.

Now, instead of playing by the very rules he agreed to at the end of the Gulf War, Saddam has spent the better part of the past decade trying to cheat on this solemn commitment. Consider just some of the facts

Iraq repeatedly made false declarations about the weapons that it had left in its possession after the Gulf War. When UNSCOM would then uncover evidence that gave lie to those declarations, Iraq would simply amend the reports.

For example, Iraq revised its nuclear declarations four times within just 14 months and it has submitted six different biological warfare declarations, each of which has been rejected by UNSCOM. . . .

Despite Iraq's deceptions, UNSCOM has nevertheless done a remarkable job. Its inspectors the eyes and ears of the civilized world have uncovered and destroyed more weapons of mass destruction capacity than was destroyed during the Gulf War.

This includes nearly 40,000 chemical weapons, more than 100,000 gallons of chemical weapons agents, 48 operational missiles, 30 warheads specifically fitted for chemical and biological weapons, and a massive biological weapons facility at Al Hakam equipped to produce anthrax and other deadly agents. . . .

If Saddam rejects peace and we have to use force, our purpose is clear. We want to seriously diminish the threat posed by Iraq's weapons of mass destruction program. We want to seriously reduce his capacity to threaten his neighbors. . . .

Dealing with Saddam Hussein requires constant vigilance. We have seen that constant vigilance pays off. But it requires constant vigilance. Since the Gulf War, we have pushed back every time Saddam has posed a threat.

Source: Bill Clinton, "Pentagon Address," speech, Arlington, Virginia, February 17, 1998; transcript by CNN Politics.

3. Regime in Iraq as U.S. Policy: The Iraq Liberation Act (1998)

Partially because of Iraq's continued resistance to UN weapons inspections and because of its history of threats to international peace, including the 1990 invasion of Kuwait, in October 1998, Congress enacted a law whereby it became the official policy of the United States to support regime change in Iraq. The legislation began by listing the major abuses or offenses of the Saddam regime. The list included actions taken by the regime against regional peace and stability and repressive acts taken against its own citizens. Section 3 of the law then officially declared that the United States supported regime change in Iraq. Section 4 of the measure then listed a number of measures that the president could undertake to undermine the regime, including support for Iraqi groups opposed to the Saddam government. The law begins:

The Congress makes the following findings:

(1) On September 22, 1980, Iraq invaded Iran, starting an 8 year war in which Iraq employed chemical weapons against Iranian troops and ballistic missiles against Iranian cities.

(2) In February 1988, Iraq forcibly relocated Kurdish civilians from their home villages in the Anfal campaign, killing an estimated 50,000 to 180,000 Kurds.

(3) On March 16, 1988, Iraq used chemical weapons against Iraqi Kurdish civilian opponents in the town of Halabja, killing an estimated 5,000 Kurds and causing numerous birth defects that affect the town today.

(4) On August 2, 1990, Iraq invaded and began a 7 month occupation of Kuwait, killing and committing numerous abuses against Kuwaiti civilians, and setting Kuwait's oil wells ablaze upon retreat.

(5) Hostilities in Operation Desert Storm ended on February 28, 1991, and Iraq subsequently accepted the ceasefire conditions specified in United Nations Security Council Resolution 687 (April 3, 1991) requiring Iraq, among other things, to disclose fully and permit the dismantlement of its weapons of mass destruction programs and submit to long-term monitoring and verification of such dismantlement.

(6) In April 1993, Iraq orchestrated a failed plot to assassinate former President George Bush during his April 14–16, 1993, visit to Kuwait.

(7) In October 1994, Iraq moved 80,000 troops to areas near the border with Kuwait, posing an imminent threat of a renewed invasion of or attack against Kuwait.

(8) On August 31, 1996, Iraq suppressed many of its opponents by helping one Kurdish faction capture Irbil, the seat of the Kurdish regional government.

(9) Since March 1996, Iraq has systematically sought to deny weapons inspectors from the United Nations Special Commission on Iraq (UNSCOM) access to key facilities and documents, has on several occasions endangered the safe operation of UNSCOM helicopters transporting UNSCOM personnel in Iraq, and has persisted in a pattern of deception and concealment regarding the history of its weapons of mass destruction programs.

(10) On August 5, 1998, Iraq ceased all cooperation with UNSCOM, and subsequently threatened to end long-term monitoring activities by the International Atomic Energy Agency and UNSCOM.

(11) On August 14, 1998, President Clinton signed Public Law 105–235, which declared that "the Government of Iraq is in material and unacceptable breach of its international obligations" and urged the President "to take appropriate

action, in accordance with the Constitution and relevant laws of the United States, to bring Iraq into compliance with its international obligations."

(12) On May 1, 1998, President Clinton signed Public Law 105–174, which made $5,000,000 available for assistance to the Iraqi democratic opposition for such activities as organization, training, communication and dissemination of information, developing and implementing agreements among opposition groups, compiling information to support the indictment of Iraqi officials for war crimes, and for related purposes. . . .

SECTION 3. SENSE OF THE CONGRESS REGARDING UNITED STATES POLICY TOWARD IRAQ. [all bold in original]

It should be the policy of the United States to support efforts to remove the regime headed by Saddam Hussein from power in Iraq and to promote the emergence of a democratic government to replace that regime.

SECTION 4. ASSISTANCE TO SUPPORT A TRANSITION TO DEMOCRACY IN IRAQ.

(a) AUTHORITY TO PROVIDE ASSISTANCE [all capitalization in original].—The President may provide to the Iraqi democratic opposition organizations . . . the following assistance:

(1) BROADCASTING ASSISTANCE.—(A) Grant assistance to such organizations for radio and television broadcasting by such organizations to Iraq.

(B) There is authorized to be appropriated to the United States Information Agency $2,000,000 for fiscal year 1999 to carry out this paragraph.

(2) MILITARY ASSISTANCE.—(A) The President is authorized to direct the drawdown of defense articles from the stocks of the Department of Defense, defense services of the Department of Defense, and military education and training for such organizations.

(B) The aggregate value (as defined in section 644(m) of the Foreign Assistance Act of 1961) of assistance provided under this paragraph may not exceed $97,000,000.

(b) HUMANITARIAN ASSISTANCE.—The Congress urges the President to use existing authorities under the Foreign Assistance Act of 1961 to provide humanitarian assistance to individuals living in areas of Iraq controlled by organizations designated in accordance with section 5, with emphasis on addressing the needs of individuals who have fled to such areas from areas under the control of the Saddam Hussein regime.

(c) RESTRICTION ON ASSISTANCE.—No assistance under this section shall be provided to any group within an organization designated in accordance with . . . which group is, at the time the assistance is to be provided, engaged in military cooperation with the Saddam Hussein regime.

Source: U.S. Congress, Iraq Liberation Act, Public Law 105-338, October 31, 1998.

4. Osama bin Laden's Fatwa Urging Jihad against the United States (1998)

In a call for jihad (holy war) against the United States, its allies, and Israel, al Qaeda leader argues that it is the duty of all Muslims to attack the West because of the continuing presence of American troops on the Arabian Peninsula, U.S.-led economic and military sanctions against Iraq and what he describes as an effort to undermine Muslim countries in the Middle East. Bin Laden also contends that religious dogma and tradition make it every Muslim's duty to attack civilians and military targets in the West in order to defend Islam:

> Praise be to Allah, who revealed the Book, controls the clouds, defeats factionalism, and says in His Book [the Koran]: "But when the forbidden months are past, then fight and slay the pagans wherever ye find them, seize them, beleaguer them, and lie in wait for them in every stratagem (of war);" and peace be upon our Prophet, Muhammad Bin-'Abdallah, who said: I have been sent with the sword between my hands to ensure that no one but Allah is worshipped, Allah who put my livelihood under the shadow of my spear and who inflicts humiliation and scorn on those who disobey my orders.

> The Arabian Peninsula has never—since Allah made it flat, created its desert, and encircled it with seas—been stormed by any forces like the crusader armies spreading in it like locusts, eating its riches and wiping out its plantations. All this is happening at a time in which nations are attacking Muslims like people fighting over a plate of food. In the light of the grave situation and the lack of support, we and you are obliged to discuss current events, and we should all agree on how to settle the matter.

> No one argues today about three facts that are known to everyone; we will list them, in order to remind everyone:

> First, for over seven years the United States has been occupying the lands of Islam in the holiest of places, the Arabian Peninsula, plundering its riches, dictating to its rulers, humiliating its people, terrorizing its neighbors, and turning its bases in the Peninsula into a spearhead through which to fight the neighboring Muslim peoples.

> If some people have in the past argued about the fact of the occupation, all the people of the Peninsula have now acknowledged it. The best proof of this is the Americans' continuing aggression against the Iraqi people using the Peninsula as a staging post, even though all its rulers are against their territories being used to that end, but they are helpless.

> Second, despite the great devastation inflicted on the Iraqi people by the crusader-Zionist alliance, and despite the huge number of those killed, which has exceeded 1 million despite all this, the Americans are once again trying to

repeat the horrific massacres, as though they are not content with the protracted blockade imposed after the ferocious war or the fragmentation and devastation.

So here they come to annihilate what is left of this people and to humiliate their Muslim neighbors.

Third, if the Americans' aims behind these wars are religious and economic, the aim is also to serve the Jews' petty state and divert attention from its occupation of Jerusalem and murder of Muslims there. The best proof of this is their eagerness to destroy Iraq, the strongest neighboring Arab state, and their endeavor to fragment all the states of the region such as Iraq, Saudi Arabia, Egypt, and Sudan into paper statelets and through their disunion and weakness to guarantee Israel's survival and the continuation of the brutal crusade occupation of the Peninsula.

All these crimes and sins committed by the Americans are a clear declaration of war on Allah, his messenger, and Muslims. And ulema [Muslim scholars] have throughout Islamic history unanimously agreed that the jihad is an individual duty if the enemy destroys the Muslim countries . . .

On that basis, and in compliance with Allah's order, we issue the following fatwa to all Muslims:

The ruling to kill the Americans and their allies—civilians and military— is an individual duty for every Muslim who can do it in any country in which it is possible to do it, in order to liberate the al-Aqsa Mosque and the holy mosque [Mecca] from their grip, and in order for their armies to move out of all the lands of Islam, defeated and unable to threaten any Muslim. This is in accordance with the words of Almighty Allah, "and fight the pagans all together as they fight you all together," and "fight them until there is no more tumult or oppression, and there prevails justice and faith in Allah."

Source: *Jim Lehrer Newshour*, "Bin Laden's Fatwa Transcript," PBS (February 23, 1998).

5. *The 9/11 Commission Report*, "Counterterrorism Evolves" (2004)

The bipartisan 9/11 Commission was created to examine what happened during the terrorist attacks and to develop recommendations to prevent future strikes. The commission conducted numerous hearings, studied documents and other evidence, and explored what went wrong and those things that went right during the attacks. One area that drew significant criticism from the group was the U.S. intelligence community. The commissioners asserted that many of the U.S. intelligence agencies had not evolved, or reorganized, to address the new threats posed by global terrorism. The Central Intelligence Agency (CIA) was the subject of significant disparagement over its ability to adjust its culture and operations to protect the nation against terrorism:

> The CIA's Directorate of Intelligence retained some of its original character of a university gone to war. Its men and women tended to judge one another by the quantity and quality of their publications (in this case, classified publications). Apart from their own peers, they looked for approval and guidance to policymakers. During the 1990s and today, particular value is attached to having a contribution included in one of the classified daily "newspapers"—the Senior Executive Intelligence Brief—or, better still, selected for inclusion in the President's Daily Brief [intelligence reports delivered to the president].
>
> The CIA had been created to wage the Cold War. Its steady focus on one or two primary adversaries, decade after decade, had at least one positive effect: it created an environment in which managers and analysts could safely invest time and resources in basic research, detailed and reflective. Payoffs might not be immediate. But when they wrote their estimates, even in brief papers, they could draw on a deep base of knowledge.
>
> When the Cold War ended, those investments could not easily be reallocated to new enemies. The cultural effects ran even deeper. In a more fluid international environment with uncertain, changing goals and interests, intelligence managers no longer felt they could afford such a patient, strategic approach to long-term accumulation of intellectual capital. A university culture with its versions of books and articles was giving way to the culture of the newsroom.
>
> During the 1990s, the rise of round-the-clock news shows and the Internet reinforced pressure on analysts to pass along fresh reports to policymakers at an ever-faster pace, trying to add context or supplement what their customers were receiving from the media. Weaknesses in all-source and strategic analysis were highlighted by a panel, chaired by Admiral David Jeremiah, that critiqued the intelligence community's failure to foresee the nuclear weapons tests by India and Pakistan in 1998, as well as by a 1999 panel, chaired by Donald Rumsfeld, that discussed the community's limited ability to assess the ballistic missile threat to the United States. Both reports called attention to the dispersal of effort on too many priorities, the declining attention to the craft of strategic analysis, and security rules that prevented adequate sharing of information. Another Cold War craft had been an elaborate set of methods for warning against surprise attack, but that too had faded in analyzing new dangers like terrorism.

Source: U.S. National Commission on Terrorist Attacks Upon the United States, *9/11 Commission Report: Final Report of the National Commission on Terrorist Attacks Upon the United States*, July (Washington, D.C.: GPO, 2004), 90–1.

6. George W. Bush, Address to the Nation, September 20, 2001 (2001)

On September 20, 2001, U.S. President George W. Bush addressed a joint session of Congress and the American people. In the somber address, the president endeavored to rally Americans and explain his administration's response. Bush also identifies al Qaeda as the perpetrators of the attacks and issues an ultimatum to the Taliban and other regimes that support terrorism. Bush thanked both Americans and people around the world for their sacrifices and efforts in the aftermath of the 9/11 terrorist attacks, and for their support for the United States. Bush also thanked British prime minister Tony Blair, who was in the United States in attendance at the address.

Tonight we are a country awakened to danger and called to defend freedom. Our grief has turned to anger, and anger to resolution. Whether we bring our enemies to justice, or bring justice to our enemies, justice will be done.

I thank the Congress for its leadership at such an important time. All of America was touched on the evening of the tragedy to see Republicans and Democrats joined together on the steps of this Capitol, singing "God Bless America." And you did more than sing; you acted, by delivering $40 billion to rebuild our communities and meet the needs of our military. . . .

And on behalf of the American people, I thank the world for its outpouring of support. America will never forget the sounds of our National Anthem playing at Buckingham Palace, on the streets of Paris, and at Berlin's Brandenburg Gate.

We will not forget South Korean children gathering to pray outside our embassy in Seoul, or the prayers of sympathy offered at a mosque in Cairo. We will not forget moments of silence and days of mourning in Australia and Africa and Latin America.

Nor will we forget the citizens of 80 other nations who died with our own: dozens of Pakistanis; more than 130 Israelis; more than 250 citizens of India; men and women from El Salvador, Iran, Mexico and Japan; and hundreds of British citizens. America has no truer friend than Great Britain. Once again, we are joined together in a great cause—so honored the British Prime Minister has crossed an ocean to show his unity of purpose with America. Thank you for coming, friend. [At this point, Bush acknowledges the presence of Blair]

On September the 11th, enemies of freedom committed an act of war against our country. Americans have known wars—but for the past 136 years, they have been wars on foreign soil, except for one Sunday in 1941. Americans have known the casualties of war—but not at the center of a great city on a peaceful morning. Americans have known surprise attacks—but never before on thousands of civilians. All of this was brought upon us in a single day—and night fell on a different world, a world where freedom itself is under attack.

Americans have many questions tonight. Americans are asking: Who attacked our country? The evidence we have gathered all points to a collection of loosely affiliated terrorist organizations known as al Qaeda. They are the same murderers indicted for bombing American embassies in Tanzania and Kenya, and responsible for bombing the USS Cole.

Al Qaeda is to terror what the mafia is to crime. But its goal is not making money; its goal is remaking the world—and imposing its radical beliefs on people everywhere.

The terrorists practice a fringe form of Islamic extremism that has been rejected by Muslim scholars and the vast majority of Muslim clerics—a fringe movement that perverts the peaceful teachings of Islam. The terrorists' directive commands them to kill Christians and Jews, to kill all Americans, and make no distinction among military and civilians, including women and children.

This group and its leader—a person named Osama bin Laden—are linked to many other organizations in different countries, including the Egyptian Islamic Jihad and the Islamic Movement of Uzbekistan. There are thousands of these terrorists in more than 60 countries. They are recruited from their own nations and neighborhoods and brought to camps in places like Afghanistan, where they are trained in the tactics of terror. They are sent back to their homes or sent to hide in countries around the world to plot evil and destruction.

The leadership of al Qaeda has great influence in Afghanistan and supports the Taliban regime in controlling most of that country. In Afghanistan, we see al Qaeda's vision for the world.

Afghanistan's people have been brutalized—many are starving and many have fled. Women are not allowed to attend school. You can be jailed for owning a television. Religion can be practiced only as their leaders dictate. A man can be jailed in Afghanistan if his beard is not long enough.

The United States respects the people of Afghanistan—after all, we are currently its largest source of humanitarian aid—but we condemn the Taliban regime. It is not only repressing its own people, it is threatening people everywhere by sponsoring and sheltering and supplying terrorists. By aiding and abetting murder, the Taliban regime is committing murder.

And tonight, the United States of America makes the following demands on the Taliban: Deliver to United States authorities all the leaders of al Qaeda who hide in your land. Release all foreign nationals, including American citizens, you have unjustly imprisoned. Protect foreign journalists, diplomats and aid workers in your country. Close immediately and permanently every terrorist training camp in Afghanistan, and hand over every terrorist, and every person in their support structure, to appropriate authorities. Give the

United States full access to terrorist training camps, so we can make sure they are no longer operating.

These demands are not open to negotiation or discussion. The Taliban must act, and act immediately. They will hand over the terrorists, or they will share in their fate.

Source: George W. Bush, "Address to the Nation," speech, Washington, D.C., September 20, 2001.

7. UN Security Council Resolution 1373 (2001)

In response to the 9/11 terrorist attacks, the UN Security Council adopted Resolution 1373 on September 28, 2001. The measure called for all states to work together to deny financing and other support to terrorist groups. The world body also urged states to share intelligence and enhance law enforcement cooperation to investigate terrorist groups and their supporters. The document also denounced terrorism as a threat to world peace and stability and called on member states to join and ratify international anti-terrorism conventions. Finally, the resolution recognized the right of states to self-defense, and therefore the right of the United States to take military action against the perpetrators of the attacks. The Security Council declared that

its unequivocal condemnation of the terrorist attacks which took place in New York, Washington, D.C., and Pennsylvania on 11 September 2001, and expressing its determination to prevent all such acts,

Reaffirming further [all italics in original] that such acts, like any act of international terrorism, constitute a threat to international peace and security,

Reaffirming the inherent right of individual or collective self-defense as recognized by the Charter of the United Nations as reiterated in resolution 1368 (2001),

Reaffirming the need to combat by all means, in accordance with the Charter of the United Nations, threats to international peace and security caused by terrorist acts,

Deeply concerned by the increase, in various regions of the world, of acts of terrorism motivated by intolerance or extremism,

Calling on States to work together urgently to prevent and suppress terrorist acts, including through increased cooperation and full implementation of the relevant international conventions relating to terrorism,

Recognizing the need for States to complement international cooperation by taking additional measures to prevent and suppress, in their territories through all lawful means, the financing and preparation of any acts of terrorism,

Reaffirming the principle established by the General Assembly in its declaration of October 1970 (resolution 2625 (XXV)) and reiterated by the

Security Council in its resolution 1189 (1998) of 13 August 1998, namely that every State has the duty to refrain from organizing, instigating, assisting or participating in terrorist acts in another State or acquiescing in organized activities within its territory directed towards the commission of such acts,

Acting under Chapter VII of the Charter of the United Nations,

1. *Decides* that all States shall:

(a) Prevent and suppress the financing of terrorist acts;

(b) Criminalize the willful provision or collection, by any means, directly or indirectly, of funds by their nationals or in their territories with the intention that the funds should be used, or in the knowledge that they are to be used, in order to carry out terrorist acts;

(c) Freeze without delay funds and other financial assets or economic resources of persons who commit, or attempt to commit, terrorist acts or participate in or facilitate the commission of terrorist acts; of entities owned or controlled directly or indirectly by such persons; and of persons and entities acting on behalf of, or at the direction of such persons and entities, including funds derived or generated from property owned or controlled directly or indirectly by such persons and associated persons and entities;

(d) Prohibit their nationals or any persons and entities within their territories from making any funds, financial assets or economic resources or financial or other related services available, directly or indirectly, for the benefit of persons who commit or attempt to commit or facilitate or participate in the commission of terrorist acts, of entities owned or controlled, directly or indirectly, by such persons and of persons and entities acting on behalf of or at the direction of such persons;

2. *Decides also* that all States shall:

(a) Refrain from providing any form of support, active or passive, to entities or persons involved in terrorist acts, including by suppressing recruitment of members of terrorist groups and eliminating the supply of weapons to terrorists;

(b) Take the necessary steps to prevent the commission of terrorist acts, including by provision of early warning to other States by exchange of information;

(c) Deny safe haven to those who finance, plan, support, or commit terrorist acts, or provide safe havens;

(d) Prevent those who finance, plan, facilitate or commit terrorist acts from using their respective territories for those purposes against other States or their citizens;

(e) Ensure that any person who participates in the financing, planning, preparation or perpetration of terrorist acts or in supporting terrorist acts is brought to justice and ensure that, in addition to any other measures against them, such terrorist acts are established as serious criminal offences in domestic laws and regulations and that the punishment duly reflects the seriousness of such terrorist acts;

(f) Afford one another the greatest measure of assistance in connection with criminal investigations or criminal proceedings relating to the financing or support of terrorist acts, including assistance in obtaining evidence in their possession necessary for the proceedings;

(g) Prevent the movement of terrorists or terrorist groups by effective border controls and controls on issuance of identity papers and travel documents, and through measures for preventing counterfeiting, forgery or fraudulent use of identity papers and travel documents;

3. *Calls upon* all States to:

(a) Find ways of intensifying and accelerating the exchange of operational information, especially regarding actions or movements of terrorist persons or networks; forged or falsified travel documents; traffic in arms, explosives or sensitive materials; use of communications technologies by terrorist groups; and the threat posed by the possession of weapons of mass destruction by terrorist groups;

(b) Exchange information in accordance with international and domestic law and cooperate on administrative and judicial matters to prevent the commission of terrorist acts;

(c) Cooperate, particularly through bilateral and multilateral arrangements and agreements, to prevent and suppress terrorist attacks and take action against perpetrators of such acts;

(d) Become parties as soon as possible to the relevant international conventions and protocols relating to terrorism, including the International Convention for the Suppression of the Financing of Terrorism of 9 December 1999;

(e) Increase cooperation and fully implement the relevant international conventions and protocols relating to terrorism and Security Council resolutions 1269 (1999) and 1368 (2001);

(f) Take appropriate measures in conformity with the relevant provisions of national and international law, including international standards of human rights, before granting refugee status, for the purpose of ensuring that the asylum seeker has not planned, facilitated or participated in the commission of terrorist acts;

(g) Ensure, in conformity with international law, that refugee status is not abused by the perpetrators, organizers or facilitators of terrorist acts, and that claims of political motivation are not recognized as grounds for refusing requests for the extradition of alleged terrorists;

4. *Notes* with concern the close connection between international terrorism and transnational organized crime, illicit drugs, money-laundering, illegal arms-trafficking, and illegal movement of nuclear, chemical, biological and other potentially deadly materials, and in this regard *emphasizes* the need to enhance coordination of efforts on national, subregional, regional and international levels in order to strengthen a global response to this serious challenge and threat to international security;

5. *Declares* that acts, methods, and practices of terrorism are contrary to the purposes and principles of the United Nations and that knowingly financing, planning and inciting terrorist acts are also contrary to the purposes and principles of the United Nations.

Source: UN Security Council, "Resolution 1373," September 28 (New York: United Nations Department of Public Information, 2001).

8. The USA PATRIOT ACT (2001)

The 2001 Uniting and Strengthening America by Providing Appropriate Tools Required to Intercept and Obstruct Terrorism Act (USA PATRIOT Act) expanded the powers of the federal government to conduct electronic surveillance and detain and prosecute suspected terrorists. Many civil libertarians condemned the legislation as an unwarranted expansion of the government's powers. However, the act also included language that condemned racial profiling and discrimination against Arab and Muslim Americans.

SECTION 102. SENSE OF CONGRESS CONDEMNING DISCRIMINATION AGAINST ARAB AND MUSLIM AMERICANS [all capitalization in the original].

(a) FINDINGS.—Congress makes the following findings:

(1) Arab Americans, Muslim Americans, and Americans from South Asia play a vital role in our Nation and are entitled to nothing less than the full rights of every American.

(2) The acts of violence that have been taken against Arab and Muslim Americans since the September 11, 2001, attacks against the United States should be and are condemned by all Americans who value freedom.

(3) The concept of individual responsibility for wrongdoing is sacrosanct in American society, and applies equally to all religious, racial, and ethnic groups.

(4) When American citizens commit acts of violence against those who are, or are perceived to be, of Arab or Muslim descent, they should be punished to the full extent of the law.

(5) Muslim Americans have become so fearful of harassment that many Muslim women are changing the way they dress to avoid becoming targets.

(6) Many Arab Americans and Muslim Americans have acted heroically during the attacks on the United States, including Mohammed Salman Hamdani, a 23-year-old New Yorker of Pakistani descent, who is believed to have gone to the World Trade Center to offer rescue assistance and is now missing.

(b) SENSE OF CONGRESS.—It is the sense of Congress that—(1) the civil rights and civil liberties of all Americans, including Arab Americans, Muslim Americans, and Americans from South Asia, must be protected, and that every effort must be taken to preserve their safety;

(2) any acts of violence or discrimination against any Americans be condemned; and

(3) the Nation is called upon to recognize the patriotism of fellow citizens from all ethnic, racial, and religious backgrounds.

Source: U.S. Congress, United and Strengthening American by Providing Appropriate Tools Required to Intercept and Obstruct Terrorism (USA PATRIOT Act), Public Law 107-56, October 26, 2001.

9. George W. Bush, State of the Union Address, January 29, 2002 (2002)

In his 2002 State of the Union Address, U.S. president George W. Bush outlined the broad strategy, objectives, and goals of the U.S.-led war on terrorism. Bush declared that one goal was to destroy the existing terrorist networks and prevent them from launching attacks such as the 9/11 strikes again. The second objective was to keep regimes that sponsored terrorism from gaining weapons of mass destruction. The president specifically discussed the invasion of Afghanistan as part of Operation Enduring Freedom, and cited other U.S. counterterrorism efforts in countries such as the Philippines and Bosnia. He then cited Iran, Iraq, and North Korea as rogue regimes that were part of an "axis of evil" which threatened international peace and security. The address was one of the first major addresses to discuss preemption, the use of force to prevent an attack on the United States. It was also the beginning of the administration's effort to build a case for military action against Iraq.

Our nation will continue to be steadfast and patient and persistent in the pursuit of two great objectives. First, we will shut down terrorist camps, disrupt terrorist plans, and bring terrorists to justice. And, second, we must prevent the terrorists and regimes who seek chemical, biological or nuclear weapons from threatening the United States and the world.

Our military has put the terror training camps of Afghanistan out of business, yet camps still exist in at least a dozen countries. A terrorist underworld—including groups like Hamas, Hezbollah, Islamic Jihad, Jaish-i-Mohammed—operates in remote jungles and deserts, and hides in the centers of large cities.

While the most visible military action is in Afghanistan, America is acting elsewhere. We now have troops in the Philippines, helping to train that country's armed forces to go after terrorist cells that have executed an American, and still hold hostages. Our soldiers, working with the Bosnian government, seized terrorists who were plotting to bomb our embassy. Our Navy is patrolling the coast of Africa to block the shipment of weapons and the establishment of terrorist camps in Somalia.

My hope is that all nations will heed our call, and eliminate the terrorist parasites who threaten their countries and our own. Many nations are acting forcefully. Pakistan is now cracking down on terror, and I admire the strong leadership of President Musharraf.

But some governments will be timid in the face of terror. And make no mistake about it: If they do not act, America will.

Our second goal is to prevent regimes that sponsor terror from threatening America or our friends and allies with weapons of mass destruction. Some of these regimes have been pretty quiet since September the 11th. But we know their true nature. North Korea is a regime arming with missiles and weapons of mass destruction, while starving its citizens.

Iran aggressively pursues these weapons and exports terror, while an unelected few repress the Iranian people's hope for freedom.

Iraq continues to flaunt its hostility toward America and to support terror. The Iraqi regime has plotted to develop anthrax, and nerve gas, and nuclear weapons for over a decade. This is a regime that has already used poison gas to murder thousands of its own citizens—leaving the bodies of mothers huddled over their dead children. This is a regime that agreed to international inspections—then kicked out the inspectors. This is a regime that has something to hide from the civilized world.

States like these, and their terrorist allies, constitute an axis of evil, arming to threaten the peace of the world. By seeking weapons of mass destruction, these regimes pose a grave and growing danger. They could provide these arms to terrorists, giving them the means to match their hatred. They could attack our allies or attempt to blackmail the United States. In any of these cases, the price of indifference would be catastrophic.

We will work closely with our coalition to deny terrorists and their state sponsors the materials, technology, and expertise to make and deliver weapons of mass destruction. We will develop and deploy effective missile defenses to protect America and our allies from sudden attack. And all nations should know: America will do what is necessary to ensure our nation's security.

We'll be deliberate, yet time is not on our side. I will not wait on events, while dangers gather. I will not stand by, as peril draws closer and closer. The United States of America will not permit the world's most dangerous regimes to threaten us with the world's most destructive weapons.

Our war on terror is well begun, but it is only begun. This campaign may not be finished on our watch—yet it must be and it will be waged on our watch.

We can't stop short. If we stop now—leaving terror camps intact and terror states unchecked—our sense of security would be false and temporary. History has called America and our allies to action, and it is both our responsibility and our privilege to fight freedom's fight.

Source: George W. Bush, "State of the Union Address to the Nation," speech, Washington, D.C., White House Press Release (January 29, 2002).

10. Preemption and the National Security Strategy of the United States (2002)

Bush introduced the concept of preemptive military action to the American people in his January 2002 state of the union address. His administration codified preemption as a security policy in the 2002 *National Security Strategy of the United States*. All presidents are required to prepare a national security strategy to inform Congress, the American people and the rest of the world of the security priorities and policies of the United States. The 2002 strategy proved to be highly controversial since it was used to justify the invasion of Iraq. The summary argued that the United States had always reserved the right to act preemptively to prevent a threat from harming America. It also argued that changes in the type and nature of the threats facing the United States since the end of the Cold War required recalculations of the nation's security policy. Global terrorism had emerged as the most significant threat to U.S. national security and the United States need to aggressively suppress the terrorists. The strategy document contended,

The United States of America is fighting a war against terrorists of global reach. The enemy is not a single political regime or person or religion or ideology. The enemy is terrorism—premeditated, politically motivated violence perpetrated against innocents.

In many regions, legitimate grievances prevent the emergence of a lasting peace. Such grievances deserve to be, and must be, addressed within a political process. But no cause justifies terror. The United States will make no concessions to terrorist demands and strike no deals with them. We make no distinction between terrorists and those who knowingly harbor or provide aid to them.

The struggle against global terrorism is different from any other war in our history. It will be fought on many fronts against a particularly elusive enemy over an extended period of time. Progress will come through the persistent accumulation of successes—some seen, some unseen.

Today our enemies have seen the results of what civilized nations can, and will, do against regimes that harbor, support, and use terrorism to achieve their political goals. Afghanistan has been liberated; coalition forces continue to hunt down the Taliban and al-Qaida. But it is not only this battlefield on which we will engage terrorists. Thousands of trained terrorists remain at large with cells in North America, South America, Europe, Africa, the Middle East, and across Asia.

Our priority will be first to disrupt and destroy terrorist organizations of global reach and attack their leadership; command, control, and communications; material support; and finances. This will have a disabling effect upon the terrorists' ability to plan and operate.

We will continue to encourage our regional partners to take up a coordinated effort that isolates the terrorists. Once the regional campaign localizes the threat to a particular state, we will help ensure the state has the military, law enforcement, political, and financial tools necessary to finish the task.

The United States will continue to work with our allies to disrupt the financing of terrorism. We will identify and block the sources of funding for terrorism, freeze the assets of terrorists and those who support them, deny terrorists access to the international financial system, protect legitimate charities from being abused by terrorists, and prevent the movement of terrorists' assets through alternative financial networks.

However, this campaign need not be sequential to be effective, the cumulative effect across all regions will help achieve the results we seek. . . .

It has taken almost a decade for us to comprehend the true nature of this new threat. Given the goals of rogue states and terrorists, the United States can no longer solely rely on a reactive posture as we have in the past. The inability to deter a potential attacker, the immediacy of today's threats, and the magnitude of potential harm that could be caused by our adversaries' choice of weapons, do not permit that option. We cannot let our enemies strike first.

- In the Cold War, especially following the Cuban missile crisis, we faced a generally status quo, risk-averse adversary. Deterrence was an effective defense. But deterrence based only upon the threat of retaliation is less likely to work against leaders of rogue states more willing to take risks, gambling with the lives of their people, and the wealth of their nations.

- In the Cold War, weapons of mass destruction were considered weapons of last resort whose use risked the destruction of those who used them. Today, our enemies see weapons of mass destruction as weapons of choice. For rogue states these weapons are tools of intimidation and military aggression against their neighbors. These weapons may also allow these states to attempt to blackmail the United States and our allies to prevent us from deterring or repelling the aggressive behavior of rogue states. Such states also see these weapons as their best means of overcoming the conventional superiority of the United States.

- Traditional concepts of deterrence will not work against a terrorist enemy whose avowed tactics are wanton destruction and the targeting of innocents; whose so-called soldiers seek martyrdom in death and whose most potent protection is statelessness. The overlap between states that sponsor terror and those that pursue WMD compels us to action.

For centuries, international law recognized that nations need not suffer an attack before they can lawfully take action to defend themselves against forces that present an imminent danger of attack. Legal scholars and international jurists often conditioned the legitimacy of preemption on the existence of an imminent threat—most often a visible mobilization of armies, navies, and air forces preparing to attack.

We must adapt the concept of imminent threat to the capabilities and objectives of today's adversaries. Rogue states and terrorists do not seek to attack us using conventional means. They know such attacks would fail. Instead, they rely on acts of terror and, potentially, the use of weapons of mass destruction—weapons that can be easily concealed, delivered covertly, and used without warning.

The targets of these attacks are our military forces and our civilian population, in direct violation of one of the principal norms of the law of warfare. As was demonstrated by the losses on September 11, 2001, mass civilian casualties is the specific objective of terrorists and these losses would be exponentially more severe if terrorists acquired and used weapons of mass destruction.

The United States has long maintained the option of preemptive actions to counter a sufficient threat to our national security. The greater the threat, the greater is the risk of inaction— and the more compelling the case for taking anticipatory action to defend ourselves, even if uncertainty remains as to the time and place of the enemy's attack. To forestall or prevent such hostile acts by our adversaries, the United States will, if necessary, act preemptively.

The United States will not use force in all cases to preempt emerging threats, nor should nations use preemption as a pretext for aggression. Yet in an age where the enemies of civilization openly and actively seek the world's most destructive technologies, the United States cannot remain idle while dangers gather. We will always proceed deliberately, weighing the consequences of our actions. To support preemptive options, we will:

- build better, more integrated intelligence capabilities to provide timely, accurate information on threats, wherever they may emerge;
- coordinate closely with allies to form a common assessment of the most dangerous threats; and

- continue to transform our military forces to ensure our ability to conduct rapid and precise operations to achieve decisive results.

The purpose of our actions will always be to eliminate a specific threat to the United States or our allies and friends. The reasons for our actions will be clear, the force measured, and the cause just.

Source: White House, *National Security Strategy of the United States* (Washington, D.C.: GPO, 2002).

11. The Congressional Authorization to Use Force against Iraq (2002)

On October 11, 2002, Congress passed the Iraq War Resolution and Bush signed the measure into law on October 16. The resolution granted the president the power to use military force against Iraq. The measure was instrumental in the Iraq War, since the 1973 War Powers Act forbade the president from deploying the military in a combat situation for more than 60 days without the approval of Congress. In the resolution, Congress detailed the past provocations committed by Iraq, including the invasion of Kuwait and noncompliance with UN resolutions requiring the Saddam regime to submit to international WMD inspections. The Iraq War Resolution also noted that regime change was U.S. policy as a result of the 1998 Iraq Liberation Act. In line with assertions from the Bush administration, the resolution linked possible military action against Iraq with the boarder war on terror:

Whereas the Iraq Liberation Act of 1998 (Public Law 105-338) expressed the sense of Congress that it should be the policy of the United States to support efforts to remove from power the current Iraqi regime and promote the emergence of a democratic government to replace that regime;

Whereas on September 12, 2002, President Bush committed the United States to "work with the United Nations Security Council to meet our common challenge" posed by Iraq and to "work for the necessary resolutions," while also making clear that "the Security Council resolutions will be enforced, and the just demands of peace and security will be met, or action will be unavoidable";

Whereas the United States is determined to prosecute the war on terrorism and Iraq's ongoing support for international terrorist groups combined with its development of weapons of mass destruction in direct violation of its obligations under the 1991 cease-fire and other United Nations Security Council resolutions make clear that it is in the national security interests of the United States and in furtherance of the war on terrorism that all relevant United Nations Security Council resolutions be enforced, including through the use of force if necessary. . . .

Whereas the President and Congress are determined to continue to take all appropriate actions against international terrorists and terrorist organizations, including those nations, organizations, or persons who planned, authorized, committed, or aided the terrorist attacks that occurred on September 11, 2001, or harbored such persons or organizations;

Whereas the President has authority under the Constitution to take action in order to deter and prevent acts of international terrorism against the United States, as Congress recognized in the joint resolution on Authorization for Use of Military Force (Public Law 107-40); and

Whereas it is in the national security interests of the United States to restore international peace and security to the Persian Gulf region. . . .

The core of the resolution was Section 3, which expressly granted the president the authority to use force in order to protect the United States and to force Iraq to comply with existing UN Security Council resolutions. However, military action was only supposed to be undertaken is the president determined that all other options had been tried or were not likely to succeed:

SEC. 3. AUTHORIZATION FOR USE OF UNITED STATES ARMED FORCES.

(a) AUTHORIZATION [all capitalizations in original]- The President is authorized to use the Armed Forces of the United States as he determines to be necessary and appropriate in order to—

(1) defend the national security of the United States against the continuing threat posed by Iraq; and

(2) enforce all relevant United Nations Security Council resolutions regarding Iraq.

(b) PRESIDENTIAL DETERMINATION—In connection with the exercise of the authority granted in subsection (a) to use force the President shall, prior to such exercise or as soon thereafter as may be feasible, but no later than 48 hours after exercising such authority, make available to the Speaker of the House of Representatives and the President pro tempore of the Senate his determination that—

(1) reliance by the United States on further diplomatic or other peaceful means alone either (A) will not adequately protect the national security of the United States against the continuing threat posed by Iraq or (B) is not likely to lead to enforcement of all relevant United Nations Security Council resolutions regarding Iraq; and

(2) acting pursuant to this joint resolution is consistent with the United States and other countries continuing to take the necessary actions against international terrorist and terrorist organizations, including those nations, organizations, or persons who planned, authorized, committed or aided the terrorist attacks that occurred on September 11, 2001.

Source: U.S. Congress, Authorization for Use of Military Force against Iraq Resolution of 2002, Public Law 107-243, October 16, 2001.

12. UN Security Council Resolution 1441: Iraq and WMDs (2002)

After more than a decade of efforts to force Iraq to fully comply with UN resolutions to allow international verification that the Saddam regime had dismantled its WMD programs, the Security Council unanimously adopted Resolution 1441 on November 2, 2002. The measure called on Iraq to fully comply with past resolutions or "face serious consequences" which the United States and other later interpreted to mean military action. Passed after the U.S. Congress had already granted Bush the authorization to use force against Iraq, most countries perceived Resolution 1441 as the last chance for Saddam to fulfill the obligations of past UN measures (there was a short timetable given to Saddam in which he had to begin compliance). The result of the resolution was that UN WMD inspections were resumed in Iraq, but the Saddam regime did initially continued to obstruct the work of the international observers. The resolution declared that the Security Council:

has repeatedly warned Iraq that it will face serious consequences as a result of its continued violations of its obligations. . . .

1. *Decides* [all italics are in original] that Iraq has been and remains in material breach of its obligations under relevant resolutions, including resolution 687 (1991), in particular through Iraq's failure to cooperate with United Nations inspectors and the IAEA, and to complete the actions required under paragraphs 8 to 13 of resolution 687 (1991);

2. *Decides*, while acknowledging paragraph 1 above, to afford Iraq, by this resolution, a final opportunity to comply with its disarmament obligations under relevant resolutions of the Council; and accordingly *decides* to set up an enhanced inspection regime with the aim of bringing to full and verified completion the disarmament process established by resolution 687 (1991) and subsequent resolutions of the Council;

3. *Decides* that, in order to begin to comply with its disarmament obligations, in addition to submitting the required biannual declarations, the Government of Iraq shall provide to UNMOVIC [UN Monitoring, Verification,

and Inspection Commission], the IAEA [International Atomic Energy Agency], and the Council, not later than 30 days from the date of this resolution, a currently accurate, full, and complete declaration of all aspects of its programmes to develop chemical, biological, and nuclear weapons, ballistic missiles, and other delivery systems such as unmanned aerial vehicles and dispersal systems designed for use on aircraft, including any holdings and precise locations of such weapons, components, sub-components, stocks of agents, and related material and equipment, the locations and work of its research, development and production facilities, as well as all other chemical, biological, and nuclear programmes, including any which it claims are for purposes not related to weapon production or material;

4. *Decides* that false statements or omissions in the declarations submitted by Iraq pursuant to this resolution and failure by Iraq at any time to comply with, and cooperate fully in the implementation of, this resolution shall constitute a further material breach of Iraq's obligations and will be reported to the Council for assessment in accordance with paragraphs . . . below;

5. *Decides* that Iraq shall provide UNMOVIC and the IAEA immediate, unimpeded, unconditional, and unrestricted access to any and all, including underground, areas, facilities, buildings, equipment, records, and means of transport which they wish to inspect, as well as immediate, unimpeded, unrestricted, and private access to all officials and other persons whom UNMOVIC or the IAEA wish to interview in the mode or location of UNMOVIC's or the IAEA's choice pursuant to any aspect of their mandates; further *decides* that UNMOVIC and the IAEA may at their discretion conduct interviews inside or outside of Iraq, may facilitate the travel of those interviewed and family members outside of Iraq, and that, at the sole discretion of UNMOVIC and the IAEA, such interviews may occur without the presence of observers from the Iraqi Government; and *instructs* UNMOVIC and *requests* the IAEA to resume inspections no later than 45 days following adoption of this resolution and to update the Council 60 days thereafter.

Source: UN Security Council, "Resolution 1441," November 2 (New York: United Nations Department of Public Information, 2002).

13. Hans Blix's Report on Iraqi Compliance with UN Security Council Resolution 1441 (2002)

After the adoption of UN Security Council Resolution 1441 (see above), Hans Blix, the head of UNMOVIC provided a series of reports and updates on Iraqi cooperation with UN WMD inspections. Blix's reports tended to portray a very complicated relationship between the Iraqi regime and the UN inspectors. On the one hand, the Saddam regime was increasingly more cooperative than it had been in the past. On the other hand, the Iraqis continued to obstruct the UN in a variety of ways. For instance, when required to produce a comprehensive report on the nation's WMD programs, the Iraqis prepared a 12,000-page tome that was not updated, contained little new information, and seemed designed to slow the inspections. In his March report, Blix reported on some minor discoveries by the UN inspections, and asked for more time for inspections to continue. Blix orally reported his findings to the Security Council on March 7, 2003.

Inspections in Iraq resumed on 27 November 2002. In matters relating to process, notably prompt access to sites, we have faced relatively few difficulties and certainly much less than those that were faced by UNSCOM in the period 1991 to 1998. This may well be due to the strong outside pressure.

Some practical matters, which were not settled by the talks, Dr. ElBaradei and I had with the Iraqi side in Vienna prior to inspections or in resolution 1441 (2002), have been resolved at meetings, which we have had in Baghdad. Initial difficulties raised by the Iraqi side about helicopters and aerial surveillance planes operating in the no-fly zones were overcome. This is not to say that the operation of inspections is free from frictions, but at this juncture we are able to perform professional no-notice inspections all over Iraq and to increase aerial surveillance. . . .

Documents and interviews [bold in original]

Iraq, with a highly developed administrative system, should be able to provide more documentary evidence about its proscribed weapons programmes. Only a few new such documents have come to light so far and been handed over since we began inspections. It was a disappointment that Iraq's Declaration of 7 December did not bring new documentary evidence. I hope that efforts in this respect, including the appointment of a governmental commission, will give significant results. When proscribed items are deemed unaccounted for it is above all credible accounts that is needed – or the proscribed items, if they exist.

Where authentic documents do not become available, interviews with persons, who may have relevant knowledge and experience, may be another way of obtaining evidence. UNMOVIC has names of such persons in its records and they are among the people whom we seek to interview. In the last month, Iraq has provided us with the names of many persons, who may be relevant sources of information, in particular, persons who took part in various phases of the unilateral destruction of biological and chemical weapons, and proscribed missiles in 1991. The provision of names prompts two reflections:

The first is that with such detailed information existing regarding those who took part in the unilateral destruction, surely there must also remain records regarding the quantities and other data concerning the various items destroyed.

The second reflection is that with relevant witnesses available it becomes even more important to be able to conduct interviews in modes and locations, which allow us to be confident that the testimony is given without outside influence. While the Iraqi side seems to have encouraged interviewees not to request the presence of Iraqi officials (so-called minders) or the taping of the interviews, conditions ensuring the absence of undue influences are difficult to attain inside Iraq. Interviews outside the country might provide such assurance. It is our intention to request such interviews shortly. Nevertheless, despite remaining shortcomings, interviews are useful. Since we started requesting interviews, 38 individuals were asked for private interviews, of which 10 accepted under our terms, 7 of these during the last week.

As I noted on 14 February, intelligence authorities have claimed that weapons of mass destruction are moved around Iraq by trucks and, in particular, that there are mobile production units for biological weapons. The Iraqi side states that such activities do not exist. Several inspections have taken place at declared and undeclared sites in relation to mobile production facilities. Food testing mobile laboratories and mobile workshops have been seen, as well as large containers with seed processing equipment. No evidence of proscribed activities have so far been found. Iraq is expected to assist in the development of credible ways to conduct random checks of ground transportation.

Inspectors are also engaged in examining Iraq's programme for Remotely Piloted Vehicles (RPVs). A number of sites have been inspected with data being collected to assess the range and other capabilities of the various models found. Inspections are continuing in this area.

There have been reports, denied from the Iraqi side, that proscribed activities are conducted underground. Iraq should provide information on any underground structure suitable for the production or storage of WMD. During inspections of declared or undeclared facilities, inspection teams have examined building structures for any possible underground facilities. In addition, ground penetrating radar equipment was used in several specific locations. No underground facilities for chemical or biological production or storage were found so far.

I should add that, both for the monitoring of ground transportation and for the inspection of underground facilities, we would need to increase our staff in Iraq. I am not talking about a doubling of the staff. I would rather have twice the amount of high quality information about sites to inspect than twice the number of expert inspectors to send.

Recent developments

On 14 February, I reported to the Council that the Iraqi side had become more active in taking and proposing steps, which potentially might shed new light on unresolved disarmament issues. Even a week ago, when the current quarterly report was finalized, there was still relatively little tangible progress to note. Hence, the cautious formulations in the report before you.

As of today, there is more. While during our meetings in Baghdad, the Iraqi side tried to persuade us that the Al Samoud 2 missiles they have declared fall within the permissible range set by the Security Council, the calculations of an international panel of experts led us to the opposite conclusion. Iraq has since accepted that these missiles and associated items be destroyed and has started the process of destruction under our supervision. The destruction undertaken constitutes a substantial measure of disarmament – indeed, the first since the middle of the 1990s. We are not watching the breaking of toothpicks. Lethal weapons are being destroyed. However, I must add that no destruction has happened today. I hope it's a temporary break.

To date, 34 Al Samoud 2 missiles, including 4 training missiles, 2 combat warheads, 1 launcher and 5 engines have been destroyed under UNMOVIC supervision. Work is continuing to identify and inventory the parts and equipment associated with the Al Samoud 2 programme.

Two 'reconstituted' casting chambers used in the production of solid propellant missiles have been destroyed and the remnants melted or encased in concrete.

The legality of the Al Fatah missile is still under review, pending further investigation and measurement of various parameters of that missile.

More papers on anthrax, VX and missiles have recently been provided. Many have been found to restate what Iraq had already declared, some will require further study and discussion.

There is a significant Iraqi effort underway to clarify a major source of uncertainty as to the quantities of biological and chemical weapons, which were unilaterally destroyed in 1991. A part of this effort concerns a disposal site, which was deemed too dangerous for full investigation in the past. It is now being re-excavated. To date, Iraq has unearthed eight complete bombs comprising two liquid-filled intact R-400 bombs and six other complete bombs. Bomb fragments were also found. Samples have been taken. The investigation of the destruction site could, in the best case, allow the determination of the number of bombs destroyed at that site. It should be followed by a serious and credible effort to determine the separate issue of how many

R-400 type bombs were produced. In this, as in other matters, inspection work is moving on and may yield results.

Iraq proposed an investigation using advanced technology to quantify the amount of unilaterally destroyed anthrax dumped at a site. However, even if the use of advanced technology could quantify the amount of anthrax, said to be dumped at the site, the results would still be open to interpretation. Defining the quantity of anthrax destroyed must, of course, be followed by efforts to establish what quantity was actually produced.

With respect to VX, Iraq has recently suggested a similar method to quantify a VX precursor stated to have been unilaterally destroyed in the summer of 1991.

Iraq has also recently informed us that, following the adoption of the presidential decree prohibiting private individuals and mixed companies from engaging in work related to WMD, further legislation on the subject is to be enacted. This appears to be in response to a letter from UNMOVIC requesting clarification of the issue.

What are we to make of these activities? One can hardly avoid the impression that, after a period of somewhat reluctant cooperation, there has been an acceleration of initiatives from the Iraqi side since the end of January.

This is welcome, but the value of these measures must be soberly judged by how many question marks they actually succeed in straightening out. This is not yet clear.

Against this background, the question is now asked whether Iraq has cooperated "immediately, unconditionally and actively" with UNMOVIC, as required under paragraph 9 of resolution 1441 (2002). The answers can be seen from the factual descriptions I have provided. However, if more direct answers are desired, I would say the following:

The Iraqi side has tried on occasion to attach conditions, as it did regarding helicopters and U-2 planes. Iraq has not, however, so far persisted in these or other conditions for the exercise of any of our inspection rights. If it did, we would report it.

It is obvious that, while the numerous initiatives, which are now taken by the Iraqi side with a view to resolving some long-standing open disarmament issues, can be seen as "active," or even "proactive," these initiatives 3-4 months into the new resolution cannot be said to constitute "immediate" cooperation. Nor do they necessarily cover all areas of relevance. They are nevertheless welcome and UNMOVIC is responding to them in the hope of solving presently unresolved disarmament issues.

Source: UN Security Council, "Oral Introduction of the 12th Quarterly Report by UNMOVIC President Dr. Hans Blix," UN Security Council Transcript, New York, March 7, 2003.

14. Tony Blair's Iraq War Speech (2003)

British prime minister Tony Blair was one of the closest allies of U.S. president George W. Bush in the aftermath of the 9/11 terrorist attacks. Besides Bush, Blair emerged as the world leader who was the foremost proponent of military action against Iraq. On the eve of the invasion of Iraq on March 5, 2004, Blair explained to the British people his reasons for supporting the use of force against Iraq. For the prime minister, the necessity of war with Iraq was part of a broader realignment of international relations that had been prompted by the 9/11 attacks and existing trends in global affairs. Terrorism had changed the nature of security threats. Blair argued that state sovereignty had also been significantly eroded in the past decades. States now had to be held accountable for the actions that occurred within their borders. Therefore, military action against Afghanistan was justified because the country allowed terrorists to operate from its soil. Blair also cited instances such as Kosovo and Sierra Leone when the international community undertook action in response to humanitarian concerns. He further argued that action had to be taken to prevent the proliferation of WMD materials. Blair noted,

> The threat we face is not conventional. It is a challenge of a different nature from anything the world has faced before. It is to the world's security, what globalisation is to the world's economy.
>
> It was defined not by Iraq but by September 11th. September 11th did not create the threat Saddam posed. But it altered crucially the balance of risk as to whether to deal with it or simply carry on, however imperfectly, trying to contain it.
>
> Let me attempt an explanation of how my own thinking, as a political leader, has evolved during these past few years. Already, before September 11th the world's view of the justification of military action had been changing. The only clear case in international relations for armed intervention had been self-defence, response to aggression. But the notion of intervening on humanitarian grounds had been gaining currency. I set this out, following the Kosovo war, in a speech in Chicago in 1999, where I called for a doctrine of international community, where in certain clear circumstances, we do intervene, even though we are not directly threatened. I said this was not just to correct injustice, but also because in an increasingly inter-dependent world, our self-interest was allied to the interests of others; and seldom did conflict in one region of the world not contaminate another. We acted in Sierra Leone for similar reasons, though frankly even if that country had become run by gangsters and murderers and its democracy crushed, it would have been a long time before it impacted on us. But we were able to act to help them and we did.

So, for me, before September 11th, I was already reaching for a different philosophy in international relations from a traditional one that has held sway since the treaty of Westphalia in 1648; namely that a country's internal affairs are for it and you don't interfere unless it threatens you, or breaches a treaty, or triggers an obligation of alliance. I did not consider Iraq fitted into this philosophy, though I could see the horrible injustice done to its people by Saddam.

However, I had started to become concerned about two other phenomena.

The first was the increasing amount of information about Islamic extremism and terrorism that was crossing my desk. Chechnya was blighted by it. So was Kashmir. Afghanistan was its training ground. Some 300 people had been killed in the attacks on the USS Cole and US embassies in East Africa. The extremism seemed remarkably well financed. It was very active. And it was driven not by a set of negotiable political demands, but by religious fanaticism.

The second was the attempts by states—some of them highly unstable and repressive—to develop nuclear weapons programmes, CW and BW materiel, and long-range missiles. What is more, it was obvious that there was a considerable network of individuals and companies with expertise in this area, prepared to sell it.

Source: Tony Blair, "Speech on Iraq," Sedgefield, United Kingdom, March 4, 2004; reprinted as "Speech Given by the Prime Minister in Sedgefield, Justifying Military Action in Iraq and Warning of the Continued Threat of Terrorism," *Guardian*, March 5, 2004.

15. Bush's Ultimatum to Saddam (2003)

On March 18, 2003, Bush delivered a televised speech in which he issued an ultimatum to Saddam Hussein. The president declared that the Iraqi leader and his two sons had 48 hours to leave Iraq or the United States and its allies would commence military action against Iraq. Bush advised all foreigners to leave Iraq and warned Iraqi military and political officials to avoid sabotage or war crimes during the coming conflict. The president also pledged that the war was with the regime and not against the Iraqi people to whom he promised a better future. Bush framed his ultimatum by insisting that the decision on whether or not there would be war lay with Saddam. If he departed voluntarily, the Iraqi leader could avoid bloodshed. Bush argued,

All the decades of deceit and cruelty have now reached an end. Saddam Hussein and his sons must leave Iraq within 48 hours. Their refusal to do so will result in military conflict, commenced at a time of our choosing. For their own safety, all foreign nationals—including journalists and inspectors—should leave Iraq immediately.

Many Iraqis can hear me tonight in a translated radio broadcast, and I have a message for them. If we must begin a military campaign, it will be directed against the lawless men who rule your country and not against you. As our coalition takes away their power, we will deliver the food and medicine you need. We will tear down the apparatus of terror and we will help you to build a new Iraq that is prosperous and free. In a free Iraq, there will be no more wars of aggression against your neighbors, no more poison factories, no more executions of dissidents, no more torture chambers and rape rooms. The tyrant will soon be gone. The day of your liberation is near.

It is too late for Saddam Hussein to remain in power. It is not too late for the Iraqi military to act with honor and protect your country by permitting the peaceful entry of coalition forces to eliminate weapons of mass destruction. Our forces will give Iraqi military units clear instructions on actions they can take to avoid being attacked and destroyed. I urge every member of the Iraqi military and intelligence services, if war comes, do not fight for a dying regime that is not worth your own life.

And all Iraqi military and civilian personnel should listen carefully to this warning. In any conflict, your fate will depend on your action. Do not destroy oil wells, a source of wealth that belongs to the Iraqi people. Do not obey any command to use weapons of mass destruction against anyone, including the Iraqi people. War crimes will be prosecuted. War criminals will be punished. And it will be no defense to say, "I was just following orders."

Should Saddam Hussein choose confrontation, the American people can know that every measure has been taken to avoid war, and every measure will be taken to win it. Americans understand the costs of conflict because we have paid them in the past. War has no certainty, except the certainty of sacrifice.

Yet, the only way to reduce the harm and duration of war is to apply the full force and might of our military, and we are prepared to do so. If Saddam Hussein attempts to cling to power, he will remain a deadly foe until the end. In desperation, he and terrorists groups might try to conduct terrorist operations against the American people and our friends. These attacks are not inevitable. They are, however, possible. And this very fact underscores the reason we cannot live under the threat of blackmail. The terrorist threat to America and the world will be diminished the moment that Saddam Hussein is disarmed.

Source: George W. Bush, "Iraq War Ultimatum," speech, Washington, D.C., March 18, 2003.

16. The Iraq Survey Group's Interim Report on Iraq's WMD Programs (2004)

The Iraq Survey Group was formed to collect and analyze evidence about Iraq's WMD programs. Members of the group were deployed to Iraq after the U.S.-led invasion and travelled the country examining potential WMD sites, analyzing documents and other evidence and interviewing regime officials. Despite a geographically widespread effort, the team was unable to discover any significant evidence of ongoing WMD programs in Iraq. The Survey Group did report that evidence indicated that Saddam planned to reconstitute his WMD programs, mainly his chemical weapons capabilities, once international sanctions were removed. The team also determined that Iraq viewed its main threat to be Iran as a result of the legacy of the Iran-Iraq War. Despite these plans, Iraq did not possess a WMD programs that would have constituted a clear and present danger to the United States or other Western or regional powers at the time of the invasion of Iraq. The Iraq Study Group divided its report into several sections, including areas on ballistic missiles, nuclear weapons, chemical weapons, and biological weapons. Among the key findings of the group:

Saddam [all italics and bold in the original] *wanted to recreate Iraq's WMD capability—which was essentially destroyed in 1991—after sanctions were removed and Iraq's economy stabilized, but probably with a different mix of capabilities to that which previously existed. Saddam aspired to develop a nuclear capability—in an incremental fashion, irrespective of international pressure and the resulting economic risks—but he intended to focus on ballistic missile and tactical chemical warfare (CW) capabilities.*

• *Iran was the pre-eminent motivator of this policy.* All senior level Iraqi officials considered Iran to be Iraq's principal enemy in the region. The wish to balance Israel and acquire status and influence in the Arab world were also considerations, but secondary.

• *Iraq Survey Group (ISG) judges that events in the 1980s and early 1990s shaped Saddam's belief in the value of WMD.* In Saddam's view, WMD helped to save the Regime multiple times. He believed that during the Iran-Iraq war chemical weapons had halted Iranian ground offensives and that ballistic missile attacks on Tehran had broken its political will. Similarly, during Desert Storm, Saddam believed WMD had deterred Coalition Forces from pressing their attack beyond the goal of freeing Kuwait. WMD had even played a role in crushing the Shi'a revolt in the south following the 1991 cease-fire.

• *The former Regime had no formal written strategy or plan for the revival of WMD after sanctions.* Neither was there an identifiable group of

WMD policy makers or planners separate from Saddam. Instead, his lieutenants understood WMD revival was his goal from their long association with Saddam and his infrequent, but firm, verbal comments and directions to them.

The Survey Group found that Iraq retained some intellectual capabilities to revive a nuclear weapons program, but that the regime had otherwise not undertaken significant steps to develop nuclear weapons. In terms of chemical and biological weapons, the teams found that

Saddam [all italics and bold in original] *never abandoned his intentions to resume a CW effort when sanctions were lifted and conditions were judged favorable:*
• Saddam and many Iraqis regarded CW as a proven weapon against an enemy's superior numerical strength, a weapon that had saved the nation at least once already—during the Iran-Iraq war—and contributed to deterring the Coalition in 1991 from advancing to Baghdad.

While a small number of old, abandoned chemical munitions have been discovered, ISG judges that Iraq unilaterally destroyed its undeclared chemical weapons stockpile in 1991. There are no credible indications that Baghdad resumed production of chemical munitions thereafter, a policy ISG attributes to Baghdad's desire to see sanctions lifted, or rendered ineffectual, or its fear of force against it should WMD be discovered.
• The scale of the Iraqi conventional munitions stockpile, among other factors, precluded an examination of the entire stockpile; however, ISG inspected sites judged most likely associated with possible storage or deployment of chemical weapons.

Iraq's CW program was crippled by the Gulf war and the legitimate chemical industry, which suffered under sanctions, only began to recover in the mid-1990s. Subsequent changes in the management of key military and civilian organizations, followed by an influx of funding and resources, provided Iraq with the ability to reinvigorate its industrial base.
• Poor policies and management in the early 1990s left the Military Industrial Commission (MIC) financially unsound and in a state of almost complete disarray.
• Saddam implemented a number of changes to the Regime's organizational and programmatic structures after the departure of Husayn Kamil [his son-in-law who defected and informed the West about Saddam's WMD programs].
• Iraq's acceptance of the Oil-for-Food (OFF) program was the foundation of Iraq's economic recovery and sparked a flow of illicitly diverted funds that could be applied to projects for Iraq's chemical industry.

The way Iraq organized its chemical industry after the mid-1990s allowed it to conserve the knowledge-base needed to restart a CW program, conduct a modest amount of dual-use research, and partially recover from the decline of its production capability caused by the effects of the Gulf war and UN-sponsored destruction and sanctions. Iraq implemented a rigorous and formalized system of nationwide research and production of chemicals, but ISG will not be able to resolve whether Iraq intended the system to underpin any CW related efforts. . . .

Iraq would have faced great difficulty in re-establishing an effective BW agent production capability. Nevertheless, after 1996 Iraq still had a significant dual-use capability—some declared—readily useful for BW if the Regime chose to use it to pursue a BW program. Moreover, Iraq still possessed its most important BW asset, the scientific know-how of its BW cadre.

• Any attempt to create a new BW program after 1996 would have encountered a range of major hurdles. The years following Desert Storm wrought a steady degradation of Iraq's industrial base: new equipment and spare parts for existing machinery became difficult and expensive to obtain, standards of maintenance declined, staff could not receive training abroad, and foreign technical assistance was almost impossible to get. Additionally, Iraq's infrastructure and public utilities were crumbling. New large projects, particularly if they required special foreign equipment and expertise, would attract international attention. UN monitoring of dual-use facilities up to the end of 1998, made their use for clandestine purpose complicated and risk laden.

Depending on its scale, Iraq could have re-established an elementary BW program within a few weeks to a few months of a decision to do so, but ISG discovered no indications that the Regime was pursuing such a course.

Source: Iraq Survey Group, "Comprehensive Report of the Special Advisor to the Director of Central Intelligence on Iraq's WMD," September (Washington, D.C.: CIA, 2004).

17. Declaration by NATO and the Islamic Republic of Afghanistan (2006)

As the war in Iraq waged, the United States sought to have NATO play a greater role in Afghanistan. On September 6, 2006, NATO and the government of Afghanistan signed a framework agreement on a long-term security partnership. Goals of the declaration included a broad agreement to increase security assistance from NATO members to Afghanistan and to formalize NATO's role in the country. NATO officials were insistent that the Afghan government recognize the importance of improving relations with neighboring countries, mainly Pakistan, in order to reduce support for the insurgency in Afghanistan. The Afghan government also pledged to improve both the number of quality of its own security forces, a task for which NATO promised to provide support. The declaration marked the growing involvement of NATO in Afghanistan and followed the decision by NATO to take command of coalition forces fighting the insurgency in the country. The accord began,

1. Building on the success of the National Assembly elections in 2005, the completion of the Bonn process and the results of the London Conference, in particular the Afghanistan Compact, NATO remains committed to working together with the Government of Afghanistan and other international organisations to help build a peaceful, stable and democratic Afghanistan. NATO acknowledges the importance of stability and security in Afghanistan to Central and South Asia and the wider international community, and the challenging nature of the security threats facing the Afghan Government. The Afghan Government's ultimate aim is to take full responsibility for its own security. To achieve this goal, strong and visible international commitment continues to be important to promote stability in Afghanistan, both through the deployment of international military forces and through support for the development of effective Afghan national security and defence institutions. Reaffirming NATO's determination in this regard, and in response to President Karzai's request for a broad and long-term relationship with NATO, Allied Foreign Ministers agreed in December 2005 to develop a programme of cooperation with Afghanistan. This programme builds on NATO's unique relationship with Afghanistan and reflects the Alliance's support for Afghanistan's national sovereignty, independence and territorial integrity. The relationship between NATO and Afghanistan is not limited to the provisions of this programme.

2. The Government of Afghanistan and Allies recognise that security cannot be provided by military means alone. Security requires good governance, justice and the rule of law, reinforced by reconstruction and development, as well as international, and particularly regional co-operation. In this context, the Declaration on Good-neighbourly Relations signed in Kabul on 22 December 2002 between Afghanistan and its neighbours plays an important role. Afghanistan also considers terrorism, extremism and drug trafficking as major challenges to security, and is committed to taking full advantage of international support and assistance, and to cooperating with the international community to build capacity to eliminate these threats.

3. Afghanistan recognises that at present it is unable to fully meet its own security needs and highly appreciates NATO's contribution to providing security and stability in Afghanistan, Afghanistan is determined to develop rapidly the capabilities of its national security and defence institutions to

meet national requirements, operate more effectively alongside ISAF and international military forces, and improve their capacity for independent action. Afghanistan stands ready to further broaden cooperation with the Alliance aimed at promoting interoperability with NATO member states' forces, as well as activities supporting defence reform, defence institution building and military aspects of security sector reform as well as other areas mutually agreed. Longer term, Afghanistan aspires to contribute to security and stability by taking part in NATO-led peacekeeping operations.

Source: NATO, "Declaration by the North Atlantic Treaty Organization and the Islamic Republic of Afghanistan," Brussels, September 6, 2006.

18. The Iraq Study Group Reports on the Rise in Violence in Iraq (2006)

The bipartisan Iraq Study Group was formed by Congress and tasked to develop solutions to end the Iraq conflict. The group was co-chaired by former secretary of state James A. Baker, III, and former congressman Lee H. Hamilton (Indiana) (Hamilton had also served as vice chairman of the 9/11 Commission) and included a range of leading American foreign and security policy experts and ex-officials. The group concluded that violence in Iraq was escalating rapidly and threatened to plunge the country into a full-scale civil war. The group made a number of recommendations, including urging the Bush administration to engage regional powers such as Syria and Iran in a diplomatic solution to the insurgency. The report began by summarizing the security conditions in Iraq at the time. The group highlighted the rise in violence and detailed how an increasingly different range of groups had become involved:

Attacks against U.S., Coalition, and Iraqi security forces are persistent and growing. October 2006 was the deadliest month for U.S. forces since January 2005, with 102 Americans killed. Total attacks in October 2006 averaged 180 per day, up from 70 per day in January 2006. Daily attacks against Iraqi security forces in October were more than double the level in January. Attacks against civilians in October were four times higher than in January. Some 3,000 Iraqi civilians are killed every month.

Sources of Violence

Violence is increasing in scope, complexity, and lethality. There are multiple sources of violence in Iraq: the Sunni Arab insurgency, al Qaeda and affiliated jihadist groups, Shiite militias and death squads, and organized criminality. Sectarian violence—particularly in and around Baghdad—has become the principal challenge to stability.

Most attacks on Americans still come from the Sunni Arab insurgency. The insurgency comprises former elements of the Saddam Hussein regime, disaffected Sunni Arab Iraqis, and common criminals. It has significant support within the Sunni Arab community. The insurgency has no single leadership but is a network of networks. It benefits from participants' detailed knowledge of Iraq's infrastructure, and arms and financing are supplied primarily from within Iraq. The insurgents have different goals, although nearly all oppose the presence of U.S. forces in Iraq. Most wish to restore Sunni Arab rule in the country. Some aim at winning local power and control.

Al Qaeda is responsible for a small portion of the violence in Iraq, but that includes some of the more spectacular acts: suicide attacks, large truck bombs, and attacks on significant religious or political targets. Al Qaeda in Iraq is now largely Iraqi-run and composed of Sunni Arabs. Foreign fighters—numbering an estimated 1,300—play a supporting role or carry out suicide operations. Al Qaeda's goals include instigating a wider sectarian war between Iraq's Sunni and Shia, and driving the United States out of Iraq.

Sectarian violence causes the largest number of Iraqi civilian casualties. Iraq is in the grip of a deadly cycle: Sunni insurgent attacks spark large-scale Shia reprisals, and vice versa. Groups of Iraqis are often found bound and executed, their bodies dumped in rivers or fields. The perception of unchecked violence emboldens militias, shakes confidence in the government, and leads Iraqis to flee to places where their sect is the majority and where they feel they are in less danger. In some parts of Iraq—notably in Baghdad—sectarian cleansing is taking place. The United Nations estimates that 1.6 million are displaced within Iraq, and up to 1.8 million Iraqis have fled the country.

Shiite militias engaging in sectarian violence pose a substantial threat to immediate and long-term stability. These militias are diverse. Some are affiliated with the government, some are highly localized, and some are wholly outside the law. They are fragmenting, with an increasing breakdown in command structure. The militias target Sunni Arab civilians, and some struggle for power in clashes with one another. Some even target government ministries. They undermine the authority of the Iraqi government and security forces, as well as the ability of Sunnis to join a peaceful political process. The prevalence of militias sends a powerful message: political leaders can preserve and expand their power only if backed by armed force.

The Mahdi Army, led by Moqtada al-Sadr, may number as many as 60,000 fighters. It has directly challenged U.S. and Iraqi government forces, and it is widely believed to engage in regular violence against Sunni Arab civilians. Mahdi fighters patrol certain Shia enclaves, notably northeast Baghdad's teeming neighborhood of 2.5 million known as "Sadr City." As the Mahdi Army has grown in size and influence, some elements have moved beyond Sadr's control.

The Badr Brigade is affiliated with the Supreme Council for the Islamic Revolution in Iraq (SCIRI), which is led by Abdul Aziz al-Hakim. The Badr Brigade has long-standing ties with the Iranian Revolutionary Guard Corps. Many Badr members have become integrated into the Iraqi police, and others play policing roles in southern Iraqi cities. While wearing the uniform of the security services, Badr fighters have targeted Sunni Arab civilians. Badr fighters have also clashed with the Mahdi Army, particularly in southern Iraq.

Criminality also makes daily life unbearable for many Iraqis. Robberies, kidnappings, and murder are commonplace in much of the country. Organized criminal rackets thrive, particularly in unstable areas like Anbar province. Some criminal gangs cooperate with, finance, or purport to be part of the Sunni insurgency or a Shiite militia in order to gain legitimacy. As one knowledgeable American official put it, "If there were foreign forces in New Jersey, Tony Soprano would be an insurgent leader."

Source: Iraq Study Group, "The Iraq Study Group Report," December 6, 2006, 10–11.

19. Obama's Cairo Speech and U.S.-Muslim Relations (2009)

In an effort to reach out to the Islamic world, Obama delivered his first major foreign policy speech in Cairo, Egypt. Obama was attempting to repair relations between the United States and Muslims which had deteriorated during the Bush presidency because of the war on terror and the invasion of Iraq in particular. Obama began his speech by discussing the broad tensions that existed between Islam and the West, and then went on to speak about the sources of contemporary strains, including the 9/11 Attacks. Obama began by declaring,

We meet at a time of great tension between the United States and Muslims around the world—tension rooted in historical forces that go beyond any current policy debate. The relationship between Islam and the West includes centuries of coexistence and cooperation, but also conflict and religious wars. More recently, tension has been fed by colonialism that denied rights and opportunities to many Muslims, and a Cold War in which Muslim-majority countries were too often treated as proxies without regard to their own aspirations. Moreover, the sweeping change brought by modernity and globalization led many Muslims to view the West as hostile to the traditions of Islam.

Violent extremists have exploited these tensions in a small but potent minority of Muslims. The attacks of September 11, 2001 and the continued efforts of these extremists to engage in violence against civilians has led some in my country to view Islam as inevitably hostile not only to America and Western countries, but also to human rights. All this has bred more fear and more mistrust.

So long as our relationship is defined by our differences, we will empower those who sow hatred rather than peace, those who promote conflict rather than the cooperation that can help all of our people achieve justice and prosperity. And this cycle of suspicion and discord must end.

I've come here to Cairo to seek a new beginning between the United States and Muslims around the world, one based on mutual interest and mutual respect, and one based upon the truth that America and Islam are not exclusive and need not be in competition. Instead, they overlap, and share common principles—principles of justice and progress; tolerance and the dignity of all human beings.

The president also spoke of the long historic ties between Islam and the United States and the need for all cultures to respect each other's beliefs and traditions:

I also know that Islam has always been a part of America's story. The first nation to recognize my country was Morocco. In signing the Treaty of Tripoli in 1796, our second President, John Adams, wrote, "The United States has in itself no character of enmity against the laws, religion or tranquility of Muslims." And since our founding, American Muslims have enriched the United States. They have fought in our wars, they have served in our government, they have stood for civil rights, they have started businesses, they have taught at our universities, they've excelled in our sports arenas, they've won Nobel Prizes, built our tallest building, and lit the Olympic Torch. And when the first Muslim American was recently elected to Congress, he took the oath to defend our Constitution using the same Holy Koran that one of our Founding Fathers—Thomas Jefferson—kept in his personal library. . . .

So I have known Islam on three continents before coming to the region where it was first revealed. That experience guides my conviction that partnership between America and Islam must be based on what Islam is, not what it isn't. And I consider it part of my responsibility as President of the United States to fight against negative stereotypes of Islam wherever they appear.

But that same principle must apply to Muslim perceptions of America. Just as Muslims do not fit a crude stereotype, America is not the crude stereotype of a self-interested empire. The United States has been one of the greatest sources of progress that the world has ever known. We were born out of revolution against an empire. We were founded upon the ideal that all are created equal, and we have shed blood and struggled for centuries to give meaning to those words—within our borders, and around the world. We are shaped by every culture, drawn from every end of the Earth, and dedicated to a simple concept: E pluribus unum–"Out of many, one."

Finally, Obama called on the United States and the international community, including Muslim nations, to confront the sources of conflict between them and work to develop solutions to ease tensions. However, he also made it clear that the United States would take action to protect its citizens.

> And this is a difficult responsibility to embrace. For human history has often been a record of nations and tribes—and, yes, religions—subjugating one another in pursuit of their own interests. Yet in this new age, such attitudes are self-defeating. Given our interdependence, any world order that elevates one nation or group of people over another will inevitably fail. So whatever we think of the past, we must not be prisoners to it. Our problems must be dealt with through partnership; our progress must be shared.
>
> Now, that does not mean we should ignore sources of tension. Indeed, it suggests the opposite: We must face these tensions squarely. And so in that spirit, let me speak as clearly and as plainly as I can about some specific issues that I believe we must finally confront together.
>
> The first issue that we have to confront is violent extremism in all of its forms. . . . I made clear that America is not—and never will be—at war with Islam. We will, however, relentlessly confront violent extremists who pose a grave threat to our security—because we reject the same thing that people of all faiths reject: the killing of innocent men, women, and children. And it is my first duty as President to protect the American people.

Source: Barack Obama, "Remarks by the President on a New Beginning," speech, Cairo, Egypt, June 4, 2009.

20. Obama: The Way Forward in Afghanistan (2009)

After months of deliberations and study, Obama outlined his administration's approaches to the ongoing conflict in Afghanistan in a speech to the cadets at the U.S. Military Academy at West Point, New York, on December 1, 2009. In the address, Obama announced his plan to undertake a troop surge and deploy an additional 30,000 troops to Afghanistan in order to suppress the al Qaeda and Taliban insurgency. The president also promised to expand the nation's diplomatic efforts to better engage countries in the region in developing a comprehensive settlement in Afghanistan. He further noted that he viewed the insurgency in Pakistan, along with the Afghan conflict, as one central issue. At the end of his address, Obama explained why he was increasing the U.S. commitment to Afghanistan at the same time that the nation was ending its participation in the conflict in Iraq. Obama maintained that his administration would carefully link U.S. capabilities and resources with the nation's interests in a veiled reference to the Bush administration's overextension of American power during the Iraq War. He also tied U.S. involvement in Afghanistan to the broader missions of U.S. foreign policy, including past efforts to spread democracy and ensure international peace and stability.

As President, I refuse to set goals that go beyond our responsibility, our means, or our interests. And I must weigh all of the challenges that our nation faces. I don't have the luxury of committing to just one. Indeed, I'm mindful of the words of President Eisenhower, who—in discussing our national security—said, "Each proposal must be weighed in the light of a broader consideration: the need to maintain balance in and among national programs."

Over the past several years, we have lost that balance. We've failed to appreciate the connection between our national security and our economy. In the wake of an economic crisis, too many of our neighbors and friends are out of work and struggle to pay the bills. Too many Americans are worried about the future facing our children. Meanwhile, competition within the global economy has grown more fierce. So we can't simply afford to ignore the price of these wars.

All told, by the time I took office the cost of the wars in Iraq and Afghanistan approached a trillion dollars. Going forward, I am committed to addressing these costs openly and honestly. Our new approach in Afghanistan is likely to cost us roughly $30 billion for the military this year, and I'll work closely with Congress to address these costs as we work to bring down our deficit.

But as we end the war in Iraq and transition to Afghan responsibility, we must rebuild our strength here at home. Our prosperity provides a foundation for our power. It pays for our military. It underwrites our diplomacy. It taps the potential of our people, and allows investment in new industry. And it will allow us to compete in this century as successfully as we did in the last. That's why our troop commitment in Afghanistan cannot be open-ended—because the nation that I'm most interested in building is our own.

Now, let me be clear: None of this will be easy. The struggle against violent extremism will not be finished quickly, and it extends well beyond Afghanistan and Pakistan. It will be an enduring test of our free society, and our leadership in the world. And unlike the great power conflicts and clear lines of division that defined the 20th century, our effort will involve disorderly regions, failed states, diffuse enemies.

So as a result, America will have to show our strength in the way that we end wars and prevent conflict—not just how we wage wars. We'll have to be nimble and precise in our use of military power. Where al Qaeda and its allies attempt to establish a foothold—whether in Somalia or Yemen or elsewhere—they must be confronted by growing pressure and strong partnerships.

And we can't count on military might alone. We have to invest in our homeland security, because we can't capture or kill every violent extremist abroad. We have to improve and better coordinate our intelligence, so that we stay one step ahead of shadowy networks.

We will have to take away the tools of mass destruction. And that's why I've made it a central pillar of my foreign policy to secure loose nuclear materials from terrorists, to stop the spread of nuclear weapons, and to pursue the goal of a world without them—because every nation must understand that true security will never come from an endless race for ever more destructive weapons; true security will come for those who reject them.

We'll have to use diplomacy, because no one nation can meet the challenges of an interconnected world acting alone. I've spent this year renewing our alliances and forging new partnerships. And we have forged a new beginning between America and the Muslim world—one that recognizes our mutual interest in breaking a cycle of conflict, and that promises a future in which those who kill innocents are isolated by those who stand up for peace and prosperity and human dignity.

And finally, we must draw on the strength of our values—for the challenges that we face may have changed, but the things that we believe in must not. That's why we must promote our values by living them at home—which is why I have prohibited torture and will close the prison at Guantanamo Bay. And we must make it clear to every man, woman and child around the world who lives under the dark cloud of tyranny that America will speak out on behalf of their human rights, and tend to the light of freedom and justice and opportunity and respect for the dignity of all peoples. That is who we are. That is the source, the moral source, of America's authority.

Since the days of Franklin Roosevelt, and the service and sacrifice of our grandparents and great-grandparents, our country has borne a special burden in global affairs. We have spilled American blood in many countries on multiple continents. We have spent our revenue to help others rebuild from rubble and develop their own economies. We have joined with others to develop an architecture of institutions—from the United Nations to NATO to the World Bank—that provide for the common security and prosperity of human beings.

We have not always been thanked for these efforts, and we have at times made mistakes. But more than any other nation, the United States of America has underwritten global security for over six decades—a time that, for all its problems, has seen walls come down, and markets open, and billions lifted from poverty, unparalleled scientific progress and advancing frontiers of human liberty.

For unlike the great powers of old, we have not sought world domination. Our union was founded in resistance to oppression. We do not seek to occupy other nations. We will not claim another nation's resources or target other peoples because their faith or ethnicity is different from ours. What we have fought for—what we continue to fight for—is a better future for our children and grandchildren. And we believe that their lives will be better if other peoples' children and grandchildren can live in freedom and access opportunity.

As a country, we're not as young—and perhaps not as innocent—as we were when Roosevelt was President. Yet we are still heirs to a noble struggle for freedom. And now we must summon all of our might and moral suasion to meet the challenges of a new age.

Source: Barack Obama, "Remarks by the President in Address to the Nation on the Way Forward in Afghanistan and Pakistan," speech, West Point, N.Y., December 1, 2009.

21. Obama's National Security Strategy (2010)

In 2010, the Obama administration released a new national security strategy for the United States. The strategy was much broader than Bush's and encompassed such wide-ranging issues as food security and education. One area of focus was the legal aspects of the war on terror, including both domestic and international issues. The president stressed the need for the United States to lead by example and pledged that his administration would ban torture and enhance civil liberties within the United States. Obama declared,

More than any other action that we have taken, the power of America's example has helped spread freedom and democracy abroad. That is why we must always seek to uphold these values not just when it is easy, but when it is hard. Advancing our interests may involve new arrangements to confront threats like terrorism, but these practices and structures must always be in line with our Constitution, preserve our people's privacy and civil liberties, and withstand the checks and balances that have served us so well. To sustain our fidelity to our values—and our credibility to promote them around the world—we will continue to:

Prohibit Torture without Exception or Equivocation: Brutal methods of interrogation are inconsistent with our values, undermine the rule of law, and are not effective means of obtaining information. They alienate the United States from the world. They serve as a recruitment and propaganda tool for terrorists. They increase the will of our enemies to fight against us, and endanger our troops when they are captured. The United States will not use or support these methods.

Legal Aspects of Countering Terrorism: The increased risk of terrorism necessitates a capacity to detain and interrogate suspected violent extremists, but that framework must align with our laws to be effective and sustainable. When we are able, we will prosecute terrorists in Federal courts or in reformed military commissions that are fair, legitimate, and effective. For detainees who cannot be prosecuted—but pose a danger to the American people—we must have clear, defensible, and lawful standards. We must have fair procedures and a thorough process of periodic review, so that any prolonged detention is carefully evaluated and justified. And keeping with our Constitutional system, it will be subject to checks and balances. The goal is an approach that can be sustained by future Administrations, with support from both political parties and all three branches of government.

Balance the Imperatives of Secrecy and Transparency: For the sake of our security, some information must be protected from public disclosure—for instance, to protect our troops, our sources and methods of intelligence-gathering or confidential actions that keep the American people safe. Yet our democracy depends upon transparency, and whenever possible, we are making information available to the American people so that they can make informed judgments and hold their leaders accountable. For instance, when we invoke the State Secrets privilege, we will follow clear procedures so as to provide greater accountability and to ensure the privilege is invoked only when necessary and in the narrowest way possible. We will never invoke the privilege to hide a violation of law or to avoid embarrassment to the government.

Protect Civil Liberties, Privacy, and Oversight: Protecting civil liberties and privacy are integral to the vibrancy of our democracy and the exercise of freedom. We are balancing our solemn commitments to these virtues with the mandate to provide security for the American people. Vigorous oversight of national security activities by our three branches of government and vigilant compliance with the rule of law allow us to maintain this balance, affirm to our friends and allies the constitutional ideals we uphold.

Uphold the Rule of Law: The rule of law—and our capacity to enforce it—advances our national security and strengthens our leadership. At home, fidelity to our laws and support for our law enforcement community safeguards American citizens and interests, while protecting and advancing our values. Around the globe, it allows us to hold actors accountable, while supporting both international security and the stability of the global economy. America's commitment to the rule of law is fundamental to our efforts to build an international order that is capable of confronting the emerging challenges of the 21st century.

Draw Strength from Diversity: The United States has benefited throughout our history when we have drawn strength from our diversity. While those who advocate on behalf of extremist ideologies seek to sow discord among ethnic and religious groups, America stands as an example of how people from different backgrounds can be united through their commitment to shared values. Within our own communities, those who seek to recruit and radicalize individuals will often try to prey upon isolation and alienation. Our own commitment to extending the promise of America will both draw a contrast with those who try to drive people apart, while countering attempts to enlist individuals in ideological, religious, or ethnic extremism.

Source: United States, White House, *National Security Strategy of the United States* (Washington, D.C.: GPO, 2010).

Glossary

Abu Sayyaf: "Bearer of the sword" in Arabic, Abu Sayyaf is a Filipino Islamic terrorist group with ties to al Qaeda.

Air Force One: A converted Boeing 747 aircraft that is the official airplane of the president of the United States.

Al Jazeera: A news service, based in Qatar. Al Jazeera is generally regarded as an Arab-centric alternative to Western media outlets such as the Cable News Network or the British Broadcasting Corporation.

Al Qaeda: An Islamic terrorist group led by Osama bin Laden which undertook a global campaign against the United States, Europe and pro-Western regimes in the Middle East. Al Qaeda was responsible for the 9/11 attacks on the United States.

Al Qaeda in Iraq: A faction of al Qaeda that carried out an insurgency against U.S.-led coalition forces in Iraq.

Anthrax: A disease caused by bacteria. Anthrax is highly lethal to humans and its spores can be used as a biological weapon.

Arab Spring: A series of popular uprisings against autocratic governments in the Middle East and North Africa that began in December 2010.

AWACS: Airborne Warning and Control System, an advanced aerial radar system used to detect other aircraft or missiles.

Ayatollah: A Shiite Muslim spiritual leader.

Bali Bombing: A series of terrorist attacks on the Indonesian island of Bali that killed more than 200 on October 12, 2002, and were carried out by an Islamic terrorist group.

Black Site: A secret prison outside of the United States, used by U.S. intelligence officials to conduct interrogations or detentions that would not be legal on American territory.

Blowback: Unanticipated consequences. The term is often used in association with military, intelligence or political actions that have unexpected negative consequences for a government.

Brigade: A military unit with about 4,000 troops.

Bush Doctrine: A controversial U.S. foreign and security policy, enacted under President George W. Bush, which declared that the United States would preemptively use force to prevent attacks on America (*see* Preemption).

Car Bomb: A vehicle packed with explosives and used as a weapon by terrorist groups. Car bombs can be denoted by a fuse, remote control or a suicide driver.

Cheat and Retreat: A phrase used to describe Iraqi leader Saddam Hussein's approach to UN weapons inspections in the 1990s. Iraqis would not comply with UN mandates ("cheat"), but would seek to avoid punishment through limited compliance when caught ("retreat").

Civil Liberties: Rights and freedoms that protect individuals and groups from unconstitutional government action.

Coalition Provisional Authority (CPA): A transitional government created by the United States and its allies after the fall of the regime of Saddam Hussein. The CPA was tasked to govern the country until an Iraqi government could be formed.

Collateral Damage: A term for the unintended casualties or destruction that results from a military campaign or terrorist act.

Covert Operations: Secret, often undercover, military or intelligence missions.

Cruise Missile: A self-propelled, highly accurate guided missile that has an extensive range and travels at high speeds. Cruise missiles may be launched from ships, mobile ground launchers, or airplanes.

Delta Force: An elite U.S. covert military unit.

Dirty Bomb: An explosive device that contains both conventional and radioactive materials. The detonation of a dirty bomb would cause immediate damage from its explosion and spread radioactive materials to contaminate the surrounding area.

Drones: Unmanned aerial vehicles used for military and intelligence operations, including reconnaissance and aerial attacks. Drones are smaller and less expensive than conventional aircraft and allow aerial missions without exposing pilots to risk. In the war on terror, the United States increasingly used an attack drone, the Predator, to undertake targeted attacks against individuals and small groups.

Dual-Use Technology: Equipment or materials that have legitimate use in commerce or agriculture or manufacturing, but may also be used to produce weapons or WMDs.

Embedded Reporters: Journalists who were allowed to operate within military units to report on the wars in Afghanistan and Iraq.

Enemy Combatant: A fighter or other enemy agent that could can be detained for the duration of an armed conflict. Enemy combatants are typically civilians, and distinct from prisoners of war who are captured while serving in uniform. Unlawful enemy combatants are individuals who are fighting illicitly in a conflict and usually not subject to the protections of international law.

Executive Order: A presidential decree that creates a new law. Executive orders do not need to be approved by Congress.

Extradition: Domestic or international agreements whereby states or countries agree to turn accused criminals over to the entity that seeks to prosecute them.

Fatah: "Victory" or "conquest" in Arabic, the Fatah Party is one of the largest political parties among the Palestinians, along with Hamas. It was founded in 1957 by Yasser Arafat.

Fatwah: An Islamic religious decree or declaration.

Geneva Conventions: A series of international agreements which govern the humane treatment of civilians and prisoners during armed conflicts.

Gross Domestic Product: The sum total of a country's economic output. GDP is the most commonly used measure to determine whether a nation's economy is growing or contracting.

Ground Zero: A commonly used name for the areas of the WTC in New York that were destroyed by the 9/11 attacks.

Habeas Corpus: A court order or writ to force officials to bring a person before the court to determine whether or not that person is being held lawfully. Courts, individuals, or other parties may file writs of habeas corpus to challenge whether someone is being lawfully detained.

Hamas: A Palestinian political and military organization which is the chief rival to Fatah. Hamas engaged in a lengthy terrorist campaign against Israel.

Hamburg Cell: A group of radical Islamist terrorists that were based at the Al Quds Mosque in Hamburg, Germany. Several members of the cell participated in the 9/11 attacks.

Hawala: An informal banking system, common in the Islamic world that permits loans, payments, and the transfer of monies with little oversight or record. Terrorist groups have used the system to raise funds without attracting official notice.

Hezbollah: The "Party of God" in Arabic, a Shiite Islamic terrorist group based in Lebanon that is responsible for a series of attacks against Western targets and Israel.

Improvised Explosive Device (IED): Also commonly known as a "roadside bomb," IEDs are homemade explosive devices used in attacks against vehicles or troop columns by terrorists or guerillas. Insurgents widely used IEDs to attack U.S.-coalition forces in Afghanistan and Iraq.

Intifada: In Arabic meaning "shaking off," a popular uprising by Palestinians against Israeli rule.

Islamic Jihad: An Islamic terrorist group that has conducted a series of attacks against American and Western targets.

Jihad: In Arabic, "holy war" or "struggle," an armed effort to defend Islam from attackers.

Khobar Towers: A U.S. military housing complex in Dhahran, Saudi Arabia that was struck by an al Qaeda-affiliated terrorist attack on June 25, 1996, killing 19 Americans and injuring more than 370.

Koran: The Muslim holy book.

Kurds: An ethnic group of about 35 million in Iran, Iraq, Syria, and Turkey. The overwhelming majority of Kurds are Muslim and have a distinct language. Kurds faced a history of repression throughout the Middle East and initiated autonomy movements in Turkey and Iraq.

Lockerbie Bombing: A Libyan terrorist bombing that destroyed Pan Am Flight 103 on December 21, 1988, over Lockerbie, Scotland, killing 270.

Loya Jirga: A Pashtun term meaning "grand Assembly." In Afghanistan, Loya Jirgas are called to decide matters of national importance and include representatives from all groups. For instance, after the fall of the Taliban, a Loya Jirga met to develop a new constitution for Afghanistan.

Mujahedeen: Muslim fighters who carried out a guerilla campaign against the Soviet occupation of Afghanistan from 1979 to 1989.

Mullah: An Islamic religious leader.

Mustard Gas: A blister agent that is used as a chemical weapon. Mustard gas causes severe burns and can also cause blindness.

Neoconservatives: A conservative political movement in the United States which emphasized the importance of U.S. global leadership and military power to promote democratization and free trade.

NATO 8: Eight members of the North Atlantic Treaty Organization (see below) that supported the U.S.-led invasion of Iraq, including the Czech Republic, Hungary, Italy, the Netherlands, Poland, Portugal, Spain, and the United Kingdom.

North Atlantic Treaty Organization (NATO): Formed in 1949, NATO was initially an anti-Soviet alliance and a collective security organization for Western Europe, the United States, and Canada. However, with the end of the Cold War, NATO broadened its focus and took on missions in the Balkans, Africa, Afghanistan, and Iraq. The alliance originally had 12 members, but several rounds of expansion increased its size to 28 by 2010, including Albania, Belgium, Bulgaria, Canada, Croatia, Czech Republic, Denmark, Estonia, France, Germany, Greece, Hungary Iceland, Italy, Latvia, Lithuania, Luxembourg, the Netherlands, Norway,

Poland, Portugal, Romania, Slovenia, Slovakia, Spain, Turkey, the United Kingdom, and the United States.

Northern Alliance: An anti-Taliban Afghan coalition that was comprised mainly of ethnic Tajiks, Uzbeks and Turkmen.

Palestinian National Authority: The government of the autonomous Palestinian territories in the West Bank and Gaza.

Pashtun: An ethnic group in Afghanistan and Northwestern Pakistan, numbering approximately 40 million. Pashtuns are the largest ethnic group in Afghanistan. Most Pashtuns are Sunni Muslims.

Patriot Act: A 2001 U.S. law formally known as the Uniting and Strengthening America by Providing Appropriate Tools Required to Intercept and Obstruct Terrorism Act (USA PATRIOT Act) which increased the surveillance and arrest powers of domestic law enforcement in an effort to improve American homeland security.

Peshmerga: Armed Kurdish fighters. Peshmerga militias fought alongside the U.S.-led coalition against regime forces in the Iraq War.

Posse Comitatus Act: A U.S. law enacted in 1878 that constrains the government's ability to use military forces in domestic law enforcement.

Precision-Guided Munitions: Highly accurate missiles or bombs that are guided to their target through the use of GPS or lasers.

Preemption: A tactic whereby one country will attack another that is on the verge of launching an attack of its own.

Provincial Reconstruction Teams (PRTs): Regional civil-military units that were deployed in Afghanistan and Iraq after the U.S.-led invasions of those countries to promote economic development and political integration with the central government.

Racial Profiling: A practice whereby law enforcement officials target individuals because of their race or ethnicity.

Racketeer Influenced and Corrupt Organization (RICO): A federal stature that allows law enforcement to prosecute individuals that belong to criminal organizations.

Recession: An economic slowdown that includes at least two quarters of negative GDP growth.

Rendition: The extrajudicial transfer of terrorists or suspected terrorists from one country to another. Rendition is typically undertaken in an effort to hide news about the capture of an individual or to subject a captive to interrogation techniques that would be considered illegal or immoral in the country that captured the suspect.

Republican Guard: Elite, well-armed and trained Iraq military units.

Ricin: A protein from the castor bean that is toxic to humans if exposed in high dosages. Ricin can be used as a biological weapon.

Saddam Fedayeen: "Saddam's Martyrs" or "Men of Saddam," an irregular, but well-armed and well-trained Iraqi paramilitary force that led the initial insurgency during Operation Enduring Freedom.

Sarin: A highly toxic nerve gas.

Sharia: Islamic holy law.

Sharga: An extremely hot, dry windstorm in Iraq.

Shia Islam: One of the two main branches of Islam. Shiites believe that only Ali, the fourth caliph, was the legitimate successor to Mohammad as the leader of Islam.

Shock and Awe: The phrase used to describe a military attack that relies on overwhelming force to disorient and disrupt the enemy.

Signing Statements: Presidential interpretations of recently enacted legislation that explain to federal agencies how the law will be implemented. Signing statements have sometimes been used to subtly alter the meaning of provisions from their original intent.

Sleeper Cell: A group of terrorists or enemy agents who remain dormant for long periods of time and integrate into their surrounding community before they take action against their host country.

Smith Act: Formerly known as the Alien Registration Act, the 1940 Smith Act forbade anyone in the United States form advocating the overthrow of the American government. The act was ruled unconstitutional in 1969.

Special Air Service (SAS): An elite British covert military unit.

State Sponsor of Terrorism: A country that provides financial or material support to terrorist groups.

Suicide Bombers: Terrorists who knowingly undertake attacks that result in their deaths.

Sunni Islam: One of the two main branches of Islam. Sunnis comprise the majority of Muslims and believe that Mohammad's first four successors, the caliphs, were his legitimate heirs and their heirs remain the leaders of Islam.

Sunset Provisions: Time limitations for legislation; a mandate to end a law, or specific features of a law, after a certain period.

Terrorism: Deliberate and illicit acts of violence, usually directed against civilians and nonmilitary targets by non-state actors as part of a campaign of intimidation and force to prompt policy changes.

Taliban: An extremist Sunni Muslim group that was formed in Afghanistan and is now also active in Pakistan. The Taliban ruled Afghanistan from 1996 to 2001 when they were overthrow by a U.S.-led military coalition because of their support for terrorism. The group subsequently launched an insurgency against both the Afghan and Pakistani governments.

Twin Towers: Two largely identical skyscrapers that were part of the World Trade Center and which were destroyed by the 9/11 terrorist attacks.

Ulema: Muslim scholars.

Unlawful Enemy Combatant: (*see* Enemy Combatant).

UNMOVIC: The United Nations Monitoring, Verification, and Inspection Commission, an international body created to oversee efforts to prevent the proliferation of weapons of mass destruction.

Vilnius Group: Ten central and Eastern European countries that supported the U.S.-led invasion of Iraq, including Albania, Bulgaria, Croatia, Estonia, Latvia, Lithuania, Macedonia, Romania, Slovakia, and Slovenia.

VX: A highly toxic chemical weapon banned by the 1993 Chemical Weapons Convention.

Weapons of Mass Destruction (WMD): Nuclear, biological or chemical weapons. These weapons are capable of causing massive casualties and most are now forbidden by a series of international agreements, including the Nuclear Non-Proliferation Treaty (1968), the Biological Weapons Convention (1972), and the Chemical Weapons Convention (1993).

Waterboarding: An interrogation technique that involves submerging a prisoner under water for for lengthy periods, almost to the point of drowning, in an attempt to compel them to reveal information. Waterboarding is generally considered a form of torture.

Yom Kippur War: Also known as the Ramadan War, a military conflict between Israel and an Arab coalition in 1973.

Selected Bibliography

Agresto, John. *Mugged by Reality: The Liberation of Iraq and the Failure of Good Intentions*. New York: Encounter Books, 2007.

Albright, Madeleine, with Bob Woodward. *Madame Secretary: A Memoir*. New York: Miramax Books, 2003.

Alexander, Yonah. *Palestinian Religious Terrorism: Hamas and Islamic Jihad*. Ardsley, NY: Transnational Publishers, 2002.

Alfonsi, Christian. *Circle in the Sand: Why We Went Back to Iraq*. New York: Doubleday, 2006.

Allawi, Ali A. *The Occupation of Iraq: Winning the War, Losing the Peace*. 2nd ed. New Haven: Yale University Press, 2008.

Anderson, Sean K., and Stephen Sloan. *Historical Dictionary of Terrorism*. 2nd ed. Lanham, MD: Rowman and Littlefield, 2002.

Arreguin-Toft, Ivan. *How the Weak Win Wars: A Theory of Asymmetric Conflict*. New York: Cambridge University Press, 2005.

Atkinson, Rick. *Crusade: The Untold Story of the Persian Gulf War*. Boston: Houghton Mifflin, 1993.

Apaza, Carmen. *Integrity and Accountability in Government: Homeland Security and the Inspector General*. Aldershot: Ashgate, 2011.

Baker, James A., III, with Thomas M. DeFrank. *The Politics of Diplomacy: Revolution, War, and Peace, 1989–1992*. New York: Putnam, 1995.

Barber, Benjamin R. *Fear's Empire: War, Terrorism, and Democracy*. New York: Norton, 2003.

Barnett, Thomas P. M. *The Pentagon's New Map: War and Peace in the Twenty-First Century*. New York: Putnam, 2004.

Beckman, James. *Comparative Legal Approaches to Homeland Security*. Aldershot: Ashgate Publishing, 2007.

Belasco, Amy. *The Cost of Iraq, Afghanistan and Other Global War on Terror Operations since 9/11*. Washington, DC: CRS, 2010.

Benjamin, Daniel, and Steven Simon. *The Age of Sacred Terror: Radical Islam's War against America*. New York: Random House, 2002.

Benjamin, Daniel, and Steven Simon. *The Next Attack: The Failure of the War on Terror and a Strategy for Getting It Right*. New York: Henry Holt, 2005.

Bergen, Peter L. *Holy War, Inc.: Inside the Secret World of Osama Bin Laden*. New York: The Free Press, 2001.

Benjamin, Daniel, and Steven Simon. *The Osama bin Laden I Know*. New York: Free Press, 2006.

Blix, Hans. *Disarming Iraq*. New York: Pantheon Books, 2004.

Bloom, Mia. *Dying to Kill: The Allure of Suicide Terror*. New York: Columbia University Press, 2005.

Boot, Max. *The Savage Wars of Peace: Small Wars and the Rise of American Power*. New York: Basic Books, 2002.

Bouillon, Markus E., David M. Malone, and Ben Roswell. *Iraq: Preventing a New Generation of Conflict*. Boulder, CO: Lynne Rienner, 2007.

Braude, Joseph. *The New Iraq: Rebuilding the Country, Its People, the Middle East and the World*. New York: Basic Books, 2003.

Bremmer, L. Paul, and Malcolm McConnell. *My Year in Iraq: The Struggle to Build a Future of Hope*. New York: Simon & Schuster, 2006.

Brill, Steven. *After: How America Confronted the September 12 Era*. New York: Simon & Schuster, 2003.

Brown, Cynthia. *Lost Liberties: Ashcroft and the Assault on Personal Freedom*. New York: New Press, 2003.

Brzezinski, Matthew. *On the Front Lines of Homeland Security: An Inside Look at the Coming Surveillance State*. New York: Bantam, 2004.

Buckley, Mary, and Robert Singh, eds. *The Bush Doctrine and the War on Terrorism: Global Responses, Global Consequences*. New York: Routledge, 2006.

Burke, Jason. *Al-Qaeda: The True Story of Radical Islam*. New York: Penguin Books, 2004.

Byman, Daniel L., and Kenneth M. Pollack. *Things Fall Apart: Containing the Spillover From an Iraqi Civil War*. Washington, DC: Brookings Institute Press, 2007.

Byman, Daniel L., and Matthew Waxman. *Confronting Iraq: U.S. Policy and the use of Force Since the Gulf War*. Santa Monica: Rand, 2000.

Campbell, Colin, and Bert A. Rockman. *The Clinton Legacy*. New York: Chatham House, 2000.

Carafano, James Jay, and Paul Rosenzweig. *Winning the Long War: Lessons from the Cold War for Defeating Terrorism and Preserving Freedom*. Washington, DC: Heritage Foundation, 2005.

Caram, Peter. *The 1993 World Trade Center Bombing: Foresight and Warning*. London: Janus Publishing, 2002.

Carr, Caleb. *The Lessons of Terror*. New York, Random House, 2003.

Chomsky, Noam. *9/11*. New York: Seven Stories Press, 2001.

Cigler, Alan J., ed. *Perspectives on Terrorism: How 9/11 Changed U.S. Politics.* New York: Houghton Mifflin Company, 2002.

Clarke, Richard. *Against All Enemies: Inside America's War on Terror.* New York: The Free Press, 2004.

Clinton, Bill. *My Life.* New York: Alfred A. Knopf, 2004.

Cole, Leonard A. *The Anthrax Letters: A Medical Detective Story.* Washington, DC: Joseph Henry Press, 2003.

Combs, Cindy. *Terrorism in the Twenty-First Century.* Upper Saddle River, NJ: Prentice-Hall, 2003.

Coppieters, Bruno, and Nick Fotion. *Moral Constraints on War: Principles and Cases.* Washington, DC: Brookings Institution Press, 2002.

Cordesman, Anthony S., and Ahmed S. Hashim. *Iraq: Sanctions and Beyond.* Boulder, CO: Westview Press, 1997.

Cronin, Audrey Kurth, and James M. Ludes, eds. *Attacking Terrorism: Elements of aa Grand Strategy.* Washington, DC: Georgetown University Press, 2004.

Daalder, Ivo H., and James M. Lindsey. *America Unbound: The Bush Revolution in Foreign Policy.* Washington, DC: Brookings Institute Press, 2003.

Daalder, Ivo H., Nicole Gnesotto, and Philip Gordon, eds. *Crescent of Crisis: U.S.-European Strategy for the Greater Middle East.* Washington, DC: Brookings Institute Press, 2006.

Danner, Mark. *Torture and Truth: America, Abu Ghraib, and the War on Terror.* New York: New York Review Books, 2004.

Davis, Paul K., and Brian Michael Jenkins. *Deterrence and Influence in Counterterrorism: A Component in the War on al Qaeda.* Santa Monica: RAND, 2002.

Diamond, Larry. *Squandered Victory: The American Occupation and the Bungled Effort to Bring Democracy to Iraq.* New York: Times Books, 2005.

Dolan, Chris J. *In War We Trust: The Bush Doctrine and the Pursuit of Just War.* Aldershot: Ashgate, 2005.

Dorrien, Gary. *Imperial Designs: Neoconservatism and the New Pax Americana.* New York: Routledge, 2004.

Duelfer, Charles A. *Hide and Seek: The Search for Truth in Iraq.* Washington, DC: PublicAffairs, 2009.

Elshtain, Jean Bethke. *Just War against Terror: The Burden of American Power in a Violent World.* New York: Basic Books, 2003.

Emerson, Steven. *American Jihad: The Terrorists Living Among Us.* New York: The Free Press, 2002.

Eksterowicz, Anthony J., and Glenn P. Hastedt, eds. *Presidents and War.* New York: Nova Science, 2010.

Evans, Anthony A. *The Gulf War: Desert Shield and Desert Storm, 1990–1991.* London: Greenhill, 2003.

Fallows, James. *Blind into Baghdad: America's War in Iraq.* New York: Vintage Books, 2006.

Fawn, Rick, and Raymond Hinnebusch, eds. *The Iraq War: Causes and Consequences*. Boulder, CO: Lynne Rienner, 2006.

Feith, Douglas J. *War and Decision: Inside the Pentagon at the Dawn of the War on Terrorism*. Reprint. New York: HarperCollins, 2009.

Ferguson, Niall. *Colossus: The Price of America's Empire*. New York: Penguin Press, 2004.

Flynn, Stephen. *American the Vulnerable: How Our Government Is Failing to Protect the US from Terrorism*. New York: HarperCollins, 2004.

Forest, James J. F., ed. *Countering Terrorism and Insurgency in the 21st Century: International Perspectives*. Vols. 1–3. Westport, CT: Praeger, 2007.

Forest, James J. F., ed. *The Making of a Terrorist*. Westport, CT: Praeger, 2005.

Franks, Tommy. *American Soldier*. New York: HarperCollins, 2004.

Freedman, Lawrence, ed. *Superterrorism: Policy Responses*. Malden, MA: Blackwell, 2002.

Freedman, Lawrence, and Efraim Karsh. *The Gulf Conflict, 1990–1991: Diplomacy and War in the New World Order*. Princeton: Princeton University Press, 1993.

Friedman, Thomas L. *Longitudes and Attitudes: Exploring the World After September 11*. New York: Farrar, Straus and Giroux, 2002.

Frum, David, and Richard Perle. *An End to Evil: How to Win the War on Terror*. New York: Random House, 2003.

Fukuyama, Francis. *State-Building: Governance and World Order in the 21st Century*. Ithaca, NY: Cornell University Press, 2004.

Gaddis, John Lewis. *Surprise, Security, and the American Experience*. Cambridge, MA: Harvard University Press, 2004.

Garrison, Jim. *America as Empire: Global Leader or Rogue Power?* San Francisco, CA: BErrett-Koehler, 2004.

Gephardt, Richard. "We Are All Tied Together in a Single Garment of Destiny." *Foreign Affairs*, February 21, 2003,

Gerges, Fawaz A. *The Far Enemy: Why Jihad Went Global*. Cambridge: Cambridge University Press, 2005.

Gertz, Bill. *Breakdown: How America's Intelligence Failures Led to September 11*. Washington, DC: Regnery, 2002.

Glad, Betty, and Chris J. Dolan, eds. *Striking First: The Preventive War Doctrine and the Reshaping of US Foreign Policy*, New York: Palgrave Macmillan, 2004.

Goodman, Melvin A. *Failure of Intelligence: The Decline and Fall of the CIA*. Lanham, MD: Rowman and Littlefield, 2008.

Gordon, Michael R., and Bernard E. Trainor. *The Generals' War: The Inside Story of the Conflict in the Gulf*. Boston: Little, Brown, 1995.

Gray, Colin S. *The Sheriff: America's Defense of the New World Order*. Lexington, KY: University Press of Kentucky, 2004.

Grillot, Suzette, Rebecca Cruise, with Valerie D'Erman. *Protecting Our Ports: Domestic and International Politics of Containerized Freight Security.* Aldershot: Ashgate, 2010.

Griset, Pamela L., and Sue Mahan. *Terrorism in Perspective.* Thousand Oaks: Sage, 2003.

Gunaratha, Rohan. *Inside Al-Qaida: Global Network of Terror.* New York: Columbia University Press, 2002.

Gurtov, Me. *Superpower on Crusade: The Bush Doctrine in US Foreign Policy.* Boulder, CO: Lynne Rienner, 2006.

Haass, Richard. *The Opportunity: America's Moment to Alter History's Course.* New York: Public Affairs, 2005.

Haass, Richard. *War of Necessity, War of Choice: A Memoir of Two Iraq Wars.* New York: Simon & Schuster, 2010.

Hadar, Leon. *Sandstorm: Policy Failure in the Middle East.* New York: Palgrave Macmillan, 2005.

Hanson, Victor Davis. *An Autumn of War: What America Learned From September 11 and the War on Terrorism.* New York: Anchor Books, 2002.

Hendrickson, Ryan C. *The Clinton Wars: The Constitution, Congress, and War Powers.* Nashville, TN: Vanderbilt University Press, 2002.

Hersh, Seymour. *Chain of Command.* New York: HarperCollins, 2004.

Herspring, Dale R. *Rumsfeld's Wars: The Arrogance of Power.* Lawrence, KS: University Press of Kansas, 2008.

Hillyard, Michael. *Homeland Security and the Need for Change.* San Diego, CA: Aventine Press, 2003.

Hirsh, Michael. *At War with Ourselves: Why America Is Squandering Its Chance to Build a Better World.* New York: Oxford University Press, 2003.

Hoffman, Bruce. *Inside Terrorism.* New York: Columbia University Press, 1998.

Hoge, James F., Jr., and Gideon Rose, eds., *How Did This Happen: Terrorism and the New World.* New York: Public Affairs, 2001.

Howard, Russell D., and Reid Sawyer, eds. *Terrorism and Counterterrorism: Understanding the New Security Environment.* Guilford, CT: McGraw Hill, 2002.

Hulnick, Arthur S. *Keeping Us Safe: Secret Intelligence and Homeland Security.* Westport, CT: Praeger, 2004.

Ignatieff, Michael. *The Lesser Evil.* Princeton, NJ: Princeton University Press, 2004.

Jacobson, Gary C. *A Divider, Not a Uniter: George W. Bush and the American People.* New York: Pearson Longman, 2007.

Jervis, Robert. *American Foreign Policy in a New Era.* New York: Routledge, 2005.

Kaplan, Robert D. *Imperial Grunts: The American Military on the Ground.* New York: Random House, 2005.

Kaplan, Lawrence, and William Kristol. *The War over Iraq: Saddam's Tyranny and America's Mission.* San Francisco, CA: Encounter Books, 2003.

Kaplan, Robert. *Imperial Grunts: The American Military on the Ground.* New York: Random House, 2005.

Kashmeri, Sarwar. *America and Europe After 9/11 and Iraq: The Great Divide.* Westport, CT: Praeger, 2007.

Kean, Thomas H., et al. *The 9/11 Commission Report: Final Report of the National Commission on Terrorist Attacks on the United States.* New York: W. W. Norton & Company, 2004.

Kegley, Charles W., ed. *The New Global Terrorism: Characteristics, Causes, Controls.* Upper Saddle River, NJ: Prentice Hall, 2003.

Kegley, Charles W., and Gregory A. Raymond. *After Iraq: The Imperiled American Imperium.* New York: Oxford University Press, 2007.

Kettl, Donald. *System Under Stress: Homeland Security and American Politics.* Washington, DC: CQ Press, 2004.

Kinzer, Stephen. *Overthrow: America's Century of Regime Change from Hawaii to Iraq.* New York: Henry Holt, 2006.

Kohut, Andrew, and Bruce Stokes. *America against the World: How We Are Different and Why We are Disliked.* New York: Times Books, 2006.

Korb, Lawrence, and Robert Boorstin. *Integrated Power: A National Security Strategy for the 21st Century.* New York: Center for American Progress, June 2005.

Kushner, Harvey, and Bart Davis. *Holy War on the Home Front: The Secret Islamic Terrorist Network in the United States.* New York: Sentinel, 2006.

Lansford, Tom. *All for One: Terrorism, NATO and the United States.* Aldershot: Ashgate, 2002.

Lansford, Tom, Robert J. Pauly, Jr., and Jack Covarrubias. *To Protect and Defend: US Homeland Security Policy.* Aldershot: Ashgate Publishing, 2006.

Lansford, Tom, Robert P. Watson, and Jack Covarrubias, eds. *America's War on Terror.* 2nd ed. Aldershot: Ashgate Publishing, 2009.

Laqueur, Walter. *The New Terrorism: Fanaticism and the Arms of Mass Destruction.* New York: Oxford University Press, 1999.

Laqueur, Walter. *No End to War: Terrorism in the Twenty-First Century.* New York: Continuum, 2003.

Lawyers Committee for Human Rights. *Assessing the New Normal: Liberty and Security for the Post-September 11 United States.* New York, 2003.

Levinson, Sanford, ed. *Torture: A Collection.* New York: Oxford University Press, 2004.

Lewis, Bernard. *The Crisis of Islam: Holy War and Unholy Terror.* New York: Modern Library, 2003.

Lowenthal, Mark M. *Intelligence: From Secrets to Policy.* Washington, DC: CQ Press, 2006.

Ludes, James M., and Audrey K. Cronin, ed. *Attacking Terrorism*. Washington, DC: Georgetown University Press, 2004.

Mackey, Chris and Gregg Miller. *The Interrogators: Inside the Secret War against Al Qaeda*. New York: Little, Brown, 2004.

Mann, James. *The Rise of the Vulcans: The History of Bush's War Cabinet*. New York: Viking Pengiun, 2004.

Maranto, Robert, Douglas M. Brattebo, and Tom Lansford, eds. *The Second Term of George W. Bush: Prospects and Perils*. New York: Palgrave Macmillan, 2006.

Martin, Gus., ed. *The New Era of Sacred Terrorism: Selected Readings*. Thousand Oaks, CA: Sage, 2004.

McDonald, Bryan, Richard Anthony Matthew, and Kenneth R. Rutherford. *Landmines and Human Security: International Politics and War's Hidden Legacy*. Albany: SUNY Press, 2004.

Mead, Walter Russell. *Power, Terror, Peace and War: America's Grand Strategy in a World at Risk*. New York: Knopf, 2004.

Melnick, Jeffrey. *9/11 Culture*. Somerset, NJ: Wiley Blackwell, 2009.

Merom, Gil. *How Democracies Lose Small Wars*. New York: Cambridge University press, 2003.

Meyer, Jeremy. *9-11: The Giant Awakens*. Belmont, CA: Wadsworth/Thompson Learning, 2003.

Miniter, Richard. *Losing Bin Laden: How Bill Clinton's Failures Unleashed Global Terror*. Washington, DC: Regnery Publishing, 2003.

Moore, Robin. *Hunting down Saddam: The Inside Story of the Search and Capture*. New York: St. Martin's Press, 2004.

Munoz, Heraldo. *A Solitary War: A Diplomat's Chronicle of the Iraq War and Its Lessons*. Golden, CO: Fulcrum Books, 2008.

Nacos, Brigitte L. *Terrorism and Counterterrorism: Understanding Threats and Responses in the Post-9/11 World*. New York: Longman, 2006.

New York Times. *Portraits, 9/11/2001: The Collected "Portraits of Grief."* New York: Times Books, 2002.

Nye, Joseph S. *The Paradox of American Power: Why the World's Only Superpower Can't Go It Alone*. New York: Oxford University Press, 2002.

O'Connell, Mary Ellen. *The Myth of Preventative Self-Defense*. Washington, DC: American Society of International Law, 2002.

O'Harrow, Robert. *No Place to Hide*. New York: Free Press, 2005.

Ochmanek, David. *Military Operations against Terrorist Groups Abroad*. Santa Monica, CA: Rand Corporation, 2003.

Packer, George. *The Assassin's Gate: America in Iraq*. New York: Farrar, Straus and Giroux, 2005.

Pape, Robert A. *Dying to Win: The Strategic Logic of Suicide Terrorism*. New York: Random House, 2005.

Pauly, Robert J., and Tom Lansford. *Strategic Preemption: US Foreign Policy and the Second Iraq War*. Aldershot: Ashgate, 2004.

Peleg, Ilan. *The Legacy of George W. Bush's Foreign Policy: Moving Beyond Neoconservatism*. Boulder: Westview Press, 2009.

Pelletiere, Stephen C. *Losing Iraq: Insurgency and Politics*. Westport, CT: Praeger, 2007.

Pemberton, Miriam, and William D. Hartung, eds. *Lessons from Iraq: Avoiding the Next War*. Boulder, CO: Paradigm Publishers, 2008.

Perl, Raphael. *U.S. Anti-Terror Strategy and the 9/11 Commission Report*. Washington, DC: Congressional Research Service, 2005.

Pious, Richard M. *The War on Terrorism and the Rule of Law*. Los Angeles: Roxbury Publishing, 2006.

Poland, James M. *Understanding Terrorism: Groups, Strategies, and Responses*. 3rd ed. Boston: Prentice Hall, 2010.

Posner, Richard. *Catastrophe*. New York: Oxford University Press, 2004.

Prados, John, ed. *America Confronts Terrorism*. Chicago: Ivan R. Dee, 2002.

Rabil, Robert G. *Syria, the United States, and the War on Terror in the Middle East*. Westport, CT: Praeger, 2006.

Rashid, Ahmed. *Taliban: Militant Islam, Oil and Fundamentalism in Central Asia*. New Haven, CT: Yale University Press, 2000.

Reeve, Simon. *The New Jackals: Ramzi Yousef, Osama bin Laden, and the Future of Terrorism*. Boston: Northeastern University Press, 1999.

Ricks, Thomas. *Fiasco: The American Military Adventure in Iraq, 2003–2005*. New York: Penguin, 2007.

Rose, David. *Guantanamo*. New York: New Press, 2004.

Rubin, Barry. *The Long War for Freedom: The Arab Struggle for Democracy in the Middle East*. Hoboken, NJ: John Wiley & Sons, 2006.

Rubin, Barry, and Judith Colp Rubin, eds. *Anti-American Terrorism and the Middle East: A Documentary Reader*. New York: Oxford University Press, 2002.

Ryan, David. *Frustrated Empire: US Foreign Policy 9/11 to Iraq*. Ann Arbor: Pluto Press, 2007.

Sabato, Larry J. *The Sixth Year Itch: The Rise and Fall of the George W. Bush Presidency*. New York: Pearson Longman, 2008.

Sageman, Marc. *Understanding Terror Networks*. Philadelphia: University of Pennsylvania, 2004.

Sammon, Bill. *Fighting Back: The War on Terrorism—from inside the Bush White House*. Washington, DC: Regnery Press, 2002.

Sarkesian, Sam C., John Allen Williams, and Stephen J. Cimbala. *U.S. National Security: Policymakers, Processes & Politics*. 4th ed. Boulder, CO: Lynne Rienner, 2008.

Schultz, Richard, and Andrew Dew. *Insurgents, Terrorists and Militias*. New York: Columbia University Press, 2006.

Shawcross, William. *Allies: The U.S., Britain, Europe and the War in Iraq*. New York: Public Affairs, 2004.

Shannon, Vaughn. *Balancing Act: US Foreign Policy and the Arb-Israeli Conflict*. Aldershot: Ashgate, 2003.

Sick, Gary S., and Lawrence G. Potter, eds. *The Persian Gulf at the Millennium: Essays in Politics, Economy, Security and Religion*. New York: St. Martin's 1997.

Snow, Donald. *What after Iraq?* New York: Pearson Longman, 2009.

Strasser, Steven. *The Abu Ghraib Investigations*. New York: PublicAffairs, 2004.

Sullivan, Mark P. *Latin America: Terrorism Issues*. Washington, DC: CRS, 2010.

Suskind, Ron, and Paul O'Neill. *The Price of Loyalty*. New York: Simon & Schuster, 2002.

Thompson, Marilyn W. *The Killer Strain, Anthrax and a Government Exposed*. New York: HarperCollins, 2003.

Tuman, Joseph S. *Communicating Terror: The Rhetorical Dimensions of Terrorism*. Thousand Oaks, CA: Sage, 2003.

United Nations, Office on Drugs and Crime, *Afghanistan Opium Survey: Summary Findings*, September. New York: United Nations, 2010.

United States. National Commission on Terrorist Attacks Upon the United States. *9/11 Commission Report: Final Report of the National Commission on Terrorist Attacks Upon the United States*. Washington, DC: GPO, July 2004.

United States. Office of Homeland Security. *National Strategy for Homeland Security*. Washington, DC: GPO, July 2002.

United States. White House. *National Security Strategy of the United States*. Washington, DC: GPO, May 2010.

United States. White House. *National Security Strategy of the United States*. Washington, DC: GPO, September 2002.

Verton, Dan. *Black Ice: The Invisible Threat of Cyber-Terrorism*. New York: McGraw-Hill, 2003.

Yetiv, Steve A. *Explaining Foreign Policy: U.S. Decision-Making and the Persian Gulf War*. Baltimore: Johns Hopkins University Press, 2004.

Yoo, John. *Fighting the New Terrorism*. Washington, DC: American Enterprise Institute, 2005.

Walt, Stephen M. *Taming American Power: The Global Response to U.S. Primacy*. New York: Norton, 2005.

Warshaw, Shirley Anne. *The Clinton Wars*. New York: Facts on File, 2004.

Watson, Robert P., ed. *The Roads to Congress 2008*. Lanham, MD: Lexington Books, 2010.

White, Jonathan R. *Terrorism: An Introduction*. 4th ed. Belmont, CA: Wadsworth-Thompson Learning, 2002.

Williams, Paul L. *The Al Qaeda Connection: International Terrorism, Organized Crime and the Coming Apocalypse*. Amherst, NY: Prometheus Books, 2005.

Woodward, Bob. *Bush at War*. New York: Simon & Schuster, 2002.

Woodward, Bob. *Plan of Attack*. New York: Simon & Schuster, 2004.

Woodward, Bob. *State of Denial*. New York: Simon & Schuster, 2006.

Worley, Robert D. *Waging Ancient War: Limits on Preemptive Force*. Carlisle, PA: Strategic Studies Institute, U.S. Army War College, 2003.

Wright, Lawrence. *The Looming Tower: Al-Qaeda and the Road to 9/11*. New York: Alfred A. Knopf, 2006.

Zinn, Howard. *Terrorism and War*. New York: Seven Stories Press, 2002.

Zunes, Stephen. *Tinderbox: U.S. Foreign Policy and the Roots of Terrorism*. Monroe, ME: Common Courage Press, 2003.

Index

About the Author

Tom Lansford is a professor of political science and the academic dean of the Gulf Coast at the University of Southern Mississippi. Dr. Lansford is a member of the governing board of the National Social Science Association and is coeditor for the journal *White House Studies*. He has published articles in journals such as *Defense Analysis*, *The Journal of Conflict Studies*, *European Security*, *International Studies, Security Dialogue*, and *Strategic Studies*. Dr. Lansford is the author, coauthor, editor, or coeditor of 31 books and the author of more than 100 essays, book chapters, encyclopedic entries, and reviews.